HISTORY OF RUSSIA

THE MACMILLAN COMPANY
NEW YORK · BOSTON · CHICAGO · DALLAS
ATLANTA · SAN FRANCISCO

MACMILLAN & CO., LIMITED
LONDON · BOMBAY · CALCUTTA
MELBOURNE

THE MACMILLAN COMPANY
OF CANADA, LIMITED
TORONTO

HISTORY OF RUSSIA

BY

S. F. PLATONOV

TRANSLATED BY E. ARONSBERG

EDITED BY F. A. GOLDER
STANFORD UNIVERSITY

New York
THE MACMILLAN COMPANY
1929

PREFACE

Professor Sergei Fedorovich Platonov, the grandson of a serf and the son of a city workman, was born in Chernigov in 1860. When he was quite small the family moved to the capital and Sergei had the opportunity to attend the public schools and the University of St. Petersburg. After graduating in 1881 the young man decided to become a teacher of history for he had been greatly influenced by the writings and lectures of Bestuzhev-Rumin, Kliuchevski, and Vasilevski. As he had no private means to pursue his graduate studies he was obliged to teach in public schools and give lessons in the homes of the rich. This kind of work took up much of his time and a great deal of his energy so that it was not before 1888 that he secured the degree of Master of Russian History. By this time the faculty of the University had formed such a high opinion of his ability that it appointed him privat-docent immediately after taking his degree and professor two years later. His fame as a scholar and teacher spread quickly and led to his selection as tutor to Grand Duke Michael and Grand Duchess Olga, brother and sister of Nicholas II. This position he held from 1895 to 1900 and the lessons in Russian history which this grandson of a serf taught the grandchildren of the Tsar Emancipator are embodied in this little book.

During the next fifteen years Professor Platonov divided his time between writing,[1] teaching, and directing students in their researches. In 1916 he retired on a pension and looked forward to devoting the rest of his life to study. He had barely planned out his new work when the Revolution broke out and swept away every bit of income that he had. Since then Sergei Fedorovich has acted as archivist, has lectured in numerous schools, has sat on various committees and commissions, and has done his best to keep the wolf from the door and the light of learning from going out.

Professor Platonov commenced his historical investigations without the preconceived ideas about Russian history prevailing in his day. He had nothing to prove or disprove. In his special field he took the Times of Troubles which in many respects comes nearer being the dividing line between Mediæval and Modern Russia than the Age of Peter. Sergei Fedorovich published, in 1888, his critical examination of the sources of this period, he edited them in 1891, and interpreted them in 1899. As an interpreter of the Russian people Professor Platonov stands above most of his contemporaries. He was born in a cottage, he gave lessons in mansions, and tutored in palaces. He understands Russian society, he knows its virtues and vices, and he appreciates its difficult problems. Unlike many of his colleagues he never had an "ism" to recommend for the salvation of Russia and was never heard on the political platform. He confined himself to teaching his students the social and cultural development of Russia and the way the

---

[1] Among his more recent publications are: Boris Godunov, Ivan the Terrible, Times of Troubles, and Colonization of Northern European Russia and Western Siberia.

lessons of the past could be applied to the present and to the future.

Realizing the need of a good college book on Russian history I recommended this volume to the Macmillans but I could not get the company to accept it unless I promised to edit the text and supervise the translation. In agreeing to do this I was influenced by the fact that Mr. Emanuel Aronsberg, who turned into very clear English Professor Presniakov's paper in the American Historical Review, consented to translate this work. He was ably assisted by Mr. M. M. Karpovich. Professor R. H. Lord of Harvard has been good enough to read over the manuscript and to make suggestions which have greatly helped me. It has been my duty as editor to revise parts of the translation and to abridge portions of the text and I assume full responsibility for the book as it stands. Nothing of importance has been left out; and though the English edition is less bulky, it has the substance and the spirit of the Russian.

In transliterating the Russian names into English we followed the system in use in the Library of Congress and Harvard University. The dates are those of the Russian old style and the maps are the same as those in the Russian text.

F. A. GOLDER.

Stanford University, Cal.
March, 1925.

CONTENTS

PART I

PART II

MAPS

HISTORY OF RUSSIA

HISTORY OF RUSSIA

PART ONE

INTRODUCTORY

1. THE SUBJECT OF A COURSE OF RUSSIAN HISTORY.
—The Russian State traces its beginnings to the ninth
century A.D.; but the Russian tribes who had founded
this state were in existence before that time. In the beginning of their historical career they occupied the territory
of the Dnieper River and its tributaries, the region
around Lake Ilmen and its river system, and the headwaters of the Western Dvina and the Volga.

The main object of a course of Russian history should
be to relate how a united Russian nation was gradually
formed out of these scattered tribes, and how it came
to occupy the enormous territory it now inhabits; also,
how a state was founded among the Russian Slavs, and
what changes have taken place in its political and social
organization before it took its present form of the
Russian Republic. Such a story naturally falls into three
separate parts: the first part tells the story of the Principality of Kiev, which united all the smaller tribes round
a common capital, the city of Kiev; the second deals
with Novgorod, Lithuania-Russia, and Moscow—states

which were founded on Russian soil after the collapse of the Principality of Kiev; and the third part gives an account of the Russian Empire, comprising all territories conquered and settled by the Russian people at various periods.

Before we commence the history of the Russian State, however, we have to study the conditions under which the various tribes of the Russian Slavs lived prior to the establishment of a political organization in their country. As these tribes were not the aboriginal and only inhabitants of that region, we must first learn *who had lived there before the Slavs and whom the latter found in the neighborhood* at the time they settled along the Dnieper and Lake Ilmen. And since the environment of these Russian Slavs influenced their economic and general condition, we shall have to learn something about the *character of the country* in which the Russian State came into existence, as well as about the *original conditions of life* among the Russian Slavs. After learning something about these things we will better understand the causes which led to the founding of a state among the Russian Slavs, and gain a clearer insight into the peculiar features of their social and political organization.

2. ABORIGINAL INHABITANTS OF EUROPEAN RUSSIA. —Throughout European Russia, but chiefly in the south, near the Black Sea, there have been discovered a large number of barrows or tumuli, cemeteries or burial mounds, ruins of cities and fortifications, as well as all kinds of household and personal articles, such as vessels, coins, precious ornaments, etc. Archæology has been able to determine to what particular people the various objects had belonged. The oldest and most remarkable among these antiquities are those left behind by the

Greeks and Scythians. We know, from the history of the ancient Hellas, that numerous Greek colonies had been planted upon the northern shores of the Black Sea, chiefly near the mouths of large rivers and convenient bays. The best known among these colonies were: Olbia, near the mouth of the Bug River, Chersonesus, in the vicinity of modern Sebastopol, Panticapea on the site of the city of Kerch, Phanagoria, on the Taman Peninsula, and Tanais, at the mouth of the Don River.

In colonizing the shore of the Black Sea the Greeks did not extend their dominions to the interior of the country, but succeeded none the less in subjecting the natives to their cultural influence and drawing them into a lively commercial intercourse. In exchange for Scythian grains and fish the Greeks gave textiles, wine, oil, and objects of luxury.

Trade had brought Greeks and natives into such close contact as to lead in the course of time to the formation of a number of so-called "Helleno-Scythian" mixed settlements; while Panticapea even became an important state, known as the Kingdom of the Bosphorus. Under the supremacy of the rulers of the Bosphorus were united several Greek cities along the coast, including the native tribes who dwelt near the sea in the region extending from the Crimea to the foothills of the Caucasus. The Kingdom of the Bosphorus and the cities of Chersonesus and Olbia attained a high level of prosperity and have left behind a number of remarkable relics of the past. Excavations made on the site of the ancient Panticapea and of Chersonesus and Olbia have bared the remains of fortifications and streets, of dwellings and temples, both pagan and Christian. In the tombs of these cities, as well as in the tumuli of the steppe, numerous objects of Greek art have been found, some of which are of a very high artistic value. Gold ornaments, and beautiful vases of most exquisite workmanship, brought to light by these excavations and assembled at the Hermitage Museum in Leningrad, form the finest collection of its kind in the world.

Side by side with typical products of Athenian workmanship, such as, for instance, painted vases showing scenes of Greek life, there are in this collection objects fashioned by Greek masters in the local style, evidently ordered by the native "barbarians" for themselves. Thus we find gold scabbards made for Scythian swords, which were unlike the Greek swords, decorated with purely Greek adornments, according to the taste of the Greek artisans. Metal or clay vases fashioned on Greek patterns were sometimes furnished with designs of Scythian, instead of Greek life, exhibiting figures of the native inhabitants and native scenes. Two such vases have become famous throughout the world. One, made of gold, was dug up in a tomb in the Kul-Oba mound near Kerch; the other, of silver, was found in the large mound in the vicinity of the small town of Nikopol, along the lower Dnieper, on the bank of Chertomlyka Creek. Both these vases show groups of Scythians in their native costumes and armed with their peculiar weapons. We thus see Greek art accommodating itself to the tastes of the local "barbarians."

To us, this fact is of importance for the reason that it enables us to become directly acquainted with the outward appearance of the Scythians with whom the Greeks had dealings on the shores of the Black Sea. In the figures of these Scythian warriors and horsemen skilfully engraved or drawn by the Greek masters we clearly see the typical features of the Aryan race, and, in all probability, its Iranian branch. The same conclusion is to be drawn from the descriptions of Scythian life which have come down to us from the ancient Greek writers, as well as from the evidence of Scythian burial grounds opened up by the archæologists. The Greek historian, Herodotus, who lived in the fifth century B.C. divides the Scythians into a great number of separate tribes, and distinguishes between agricultural and nomadic Scythians. The former he places in the steppe near the coast; the latter, farther north, along the middle course of the Dnieper. Agriculture was so highly developed by some of the Scythian tribes that they were in a position to export surplus grain to Greece. Herodotus was able to furnish interesting and reliable accounts of the Scythian tribes who were engaged in trade with the Greeks and the nomads who happened to live nearer to the sea. But the tribes that lived in the distant interior of the territory of present-day Russia were, of course, not so well known to the Greeks, and Herodotus tells fabulous stories about them.

About the time of the birth of Christ the Scythians are displaced by the Sarmatians, Alans, and Roxalans, who are spoken of as neighbors of the Greek settlements in southern Russia. Little is known of these peoples. It seems, however, that they all belonged to the same Iranian stock as their Scythian forerunners. Having retreated, in course of time, before the invasions of other tribes, these Iranians were finally able to maintain themselves only in the Caucasus Mountains, where their descendants are known today as Ossetins.

Germanic tribes known by the general name of Goths had, during the second and third centuries A.D., attempted to establish themselves on the northern shores of the Black Sea, in the place of the former inhabitants. About the middle of the fourth century a Goth chieftain, Hermanaric, united into one "kingdom" not only all the Goths but also the neighboring small tribes (probably Finns and Slavs). In his reign the Goths were destined to suffer the invasion of the Huns and to start, later on, upon their westward migration.

With the Hun invasion there begins a whole series of Asiatic raids on Russian territory, extending even into western Europe. The Huns, gradually approaching the Don River from the east, attacked the Goths in 375 A.D., overthrew their kingdom, and carried them along to the west. Hard pressed by the invaders, the Goths crossed the borders of the Roman Empire, while the Huns, now in possession of the Black Sea territory, roving back and forth between the Volga and the Danube, formed a vast state which included many of the tribes that had been reduced to submission. Later, in the fifth century, the Huns pushed on still farther to the west, establishing their rule in what is today Hungary, whence they made frequent raids on their neighbors, and sometimes even on Constantinople and into the territory of modern France. After the death of their famous chieftain, Attila, in the latter half of the fifth century, the Huns, weakened by internal dissensions and uprisings of the tributary tribes, were flung back east of the Dnieper and their state came to an end. In their place, however, there appeared out of Asia in the sixth century a new Mongolian tribe, the Avars, who maintained themselves in power along the Black Sea and in the plains of Hungary until the close of the eighth century, oppressing the conquered European tribes (the Russian Slavs among them) until the Germans and Slavs were strong enough to overcome them. So sudden and complete was the collapse of the Avar power that the Russian chronicler, who calls the Avars "Obry," after relating that not one of them survived, adds, "And there is a saying in Russia to this very day— 'To perish like the Obry!'" But, while it is true that the Avars thus perished, their place was soon taken by other invaders from the east, other hordes of the same Mongolian race, namely the Ugrians (Magyars) and Khazars.

The Ugrians, after some migrations within southern Russia, finally settled in the territory of modern Hungary, while the Khazars founded a vast empire stretching from the Caucasus to the Volga and middle Dnieper. Still, even the establishment of the Khazar State failed to halt the migrations of the peoples from the east. The Khazars were followed into the steppes of southern Russia by other Asiatics of Turko-Tartar stock—the Pecheniegs, Polovtsy, and, last of all (thirteenth century), the Tartars.

The southern steppes of present-day Russia thus served during a period of nearly a thousand years as a battle ground for the invading races. Goths were followed by Huns; Huns by Avars; Avars by Ugres and Khazars; Khazars by Pecheniegs; Pecheniegs by Polovtsy; and Polovtsy in turn gave way before the Tartars. Beginning with the Huns, wave after wave of Asiatic nomads poured into the northern sections of the Black Sea country through the passes of the Urals and Caucasus. These tribes kept near the seacoast, where the steppes were suitable to nomadic life; they did not go northward to the wooded belt of what is today central Russia. These forests afforded the local inhabitants, mostly Slavs and Finns, protection from utter ruin at the hands of the invaders.

3. The Russian Slavs and Their Neighbors.— The original home of the Slavs in Europe seems to have been on the northern slopes of the Carpathians, where the Slavs were known as "venedi" and "sclaveni" already in the time of the Goths and Huns. From this region they spread out in different directions: south (Balkan Slavs), west (Czechs, Moravians, Poles) and east (Russian Slavs). The eastern branch of the Slavs made its appearance on the Dnieper probably as early as the seventh century, pushing on until it reached Lake Ilmen, and the upper course of the Oka River. Of the Russian Slavs the Croatians and Volynians (Duliebs and Buzhans) remained near the Carpathian Mountains. The Poliane, Drevliane, and the Dregovichi established themselves on the right bank of the Dnieper and its tributaries. The Severiane, Radimichi, and Viatichi crossed the Dnieper and took up their abodes on the left bank tributaries of that river, the Viatichi pressing forward even to the Oka River. The Krivichi also left the Dnieper region for more northerly latitudes, settling along the headwaters of the Volga and Western Dvina, while a branch of the same tribe, the Slovenes, settled around Lake Ilmen. As they moved up the basin of the Dnieper, the Slavs were brought into direct touch, along the northern and northeastern borders of their new settlements, with *Finnish and Lithuanian tribes and Khazars.*

The least civilized of all the neighbors of the Slavs were the Finns, who formed, it seems, a branch of the Mongolian race. They had lived within the territory of present-day Russia from time immemorial, subject in

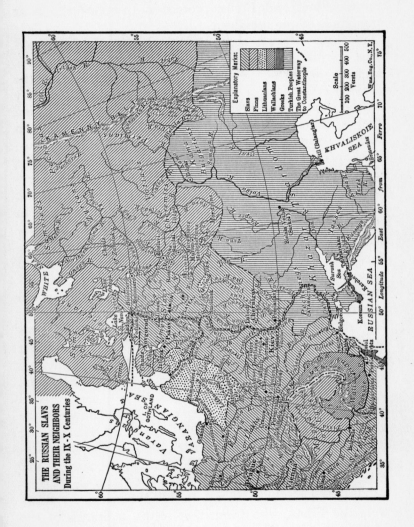

THE RUSSIAN SLAVS
AND THEIR NEIGHBORS
During the IX - X Centuries

Explanatory Marks:

Slavs
Finns
Lithuanians
Welkohians
Greeks
Turkish Peoples
The Great Waterway
to Constantinople

Scale
100 200 300 400 500
Versts

Wm. Eng. Co., N. Y.

KHVALISKOIE
SEA

RUSSIAN SEA

turn to the cultural influence of Scythians, Sarmatians, Goths, Lithuanians, and Slavs. They were divided into a great number of small tribes,[1] and lived in small settlements in the forest regions of northern Russia. Widely scattered and lacking all internal organization, these small Finnish hunting tribes long remained in a state of primitive barbarism, leading simple lives, and falling an easy prey to all invaders. They would either quickly submit to the more civilized newcomers, fusing with them, or else abandon their possessions to the intruders without any serious resistance, and move on farther into the north or east. In this way it happened that, as the Slavs gradually overspread central and northern Russia, large tracts of Finnish territory came into their possession and a Russianized Finnish element was peaceably assimilated by the Slav population. Only in rare instances, when the Finnish Shamanite priests (called "magicians" or "sorcerers" by the ancient Russians) incited their people to resistance, did the Finns attempt to oppose the Russian advance. These conflicts, however, invariably ended in the victory of the Slavs, and the Russification of the Finns, begun during the eighth and ninth centuries, went on uninterruptedly, and has continued down to our own day. Simultaneously with Slavonic influence, the Finns were also subjected to that of the Volga Bulgarians, (a Turkish people called Volga Bulgarians to distinguish them from the Danube Bulgarians). Reaching the mouth of the Kama, after they had left their former home along the lower Volga, these nomadic Bulgarians halted there and, finding nomadic life alone inadequate for their needs, they built some cities, especially Bulgar

[1] Chuds, Vesses, Emms, Esths, Merians, Mordvins, Cheremisses, Votiaks, Zyrians and many others.

on the Volga, which very quickly became lively commercial centers. Here Arabian and Khazar merchants, who came up the Volga, exchanged their merchandise (among other things, silver vessels, bowls, cups, etc.) for valuable furs which were brought down the Kama and upper Volga. This intercourse with Arabians and Khazars contributed to the spread of Mohammedanism and a certain degree of civilization among these Bulgarians and Finns.

The influence of the Bulgarian towns was felt also by the Russian Slavs who traded with the Bulgarians but later came into conflict with them. In a political sense, the Volga Bulgarians were not strong. Subject at first to the Khazars, they retained, however, a khan of their own, who in turn exercised authority over certain vassal rulers, or princes. After the collapse of the Khazar State the Bulgarians became independent, but they suffered a great deal from the Russians and were completely overthrown in the thirteenth century by the Tartars.[2]

The Lithuanian tribes,[3] who form a distinct branch of the Aryan race, lived already in remote antiquity (second century A.D.) in the country where the Slavs were to meet them at a later period. The home of the Lithuanians at that time was in the basins of the Niemen and Western Dvina Rivers, extending from the shores of the Baltic to the Pripiat River and the sources of the Dnieper and Volga. Gradually retreating before the advancing Slavs, the Lithuanians concentrated along the Niemen and Western Dvina, in the dense forests of the coastal region, where they preserved for a long time their original mode of existence. Their various tribes

[2] Their descendants, the Chuvashes, are a weak and poorly developed people.
[3] Lithuanians, Samogitians, Letts, Prussians, Iatviagians, and others.

were not united, but dwelt separately as independent clans, fighting one another. They had not as yet reached a high state of civilization. They deified the forces of nature, and had ancestor worship. Contrary to the old tales about the priests and sanctuaries of the Lithuanians, it has now been established that they had neither an influential caste of priests nor solemn religious ceremonies. Each family for itself would offer its sacrifices to greater and lesser deities, worship animals and sacred oaks, give special feasts for the souls of the departed, and practice divination. The rude and harsh customs of the Lithuanians, and their poverty and barbarism made them inferior to the Slavs to whom they abandoned their territories. In those places, however, where the Lithuanians came to be close neighbors of the Russians, they fell very noticeably under Russian cultural influence.

The Russian Slavs felt themselves to be superior to their Finnish and Lithuanian neighbors, and acted towards them in an aggressive manner. With the Khazars, on the other hand, it was a different matter. These people were firmly established in the Caucasus and the South Russian steppes, and had turned to agriculture, vine-growing, fishing, and commerce. They spent the winter in their cities, but moved for the summer into the steppe, to attend to their pastures, gardens, and fields. As the trade routes from Europe to Asia lay across Khazar territory, the towns along these routes gained vast commercial importance and influence. This was especially true of the Khazar capital, Itil, on the lower Volga, the city of Semender, in the Caucasus, and the fortress of Sarkel [4] on the Don, not far from the Volga. These towns were prominent as markets where Asiatic

[4] *Bielaia Viezha* in Russian, *i.e.,* "White Tower" or "White Tent."

merchants traded with Europeans, and where Moslems, Jews, pagans, and Christians mingled freely. Islamism and Judaism, especially, exercised a strong influence upon the Khazars. The Khan of the Khazars and his court professed the Jewish faith, while Mohammedanism predominated among the common people, although Christianity and paganism also had some foothold. This diversity of beliefs resulted in religious tolerance, attracting to the Khazar country immigrants from many lands. In the eighth century some Russian tribes [5] were conquered by the Khazars, but they were not oppressed. Indeed, this conquest made it easier for them to enter the markets of the Khazars and to engage in commercial dealings with the East. Numerous hoards of Arabian coins ("dirhems") found at various places in Russia bear witness to the progress of this eastern trade in the eighth, ninth and tenth centuries. During these centuries Russia was, at first, under the direct rule of the Khazars, and later under their influence. In the tenth century, however, after the Khazars had exhausted their strength in a desperate struggle against a new nomadic invasion— that of the Pecheniegs—the Russians themselves began to attack the Khazars and greatly contributed to their downfall.

Among the neighbors and fellow inhabitants of the Russian Slavs were the *Varangians*. It was said in Russia that these had lived "beyond the sea" whence they had come to the Slavs. The name Varangians was a general term applied to the Northmen who migrated from Scandinavia to other countries. They made their first appearance in the ninth century among the Slavonic tribes on the Volkhov and Dnieper Rivers, on the Black Sea and

[5] The Poliane, Severiane, Radimichi and Viatichi.

in Greece. They were organized into "druzhinas," (companies) ready to engage in trade or to enter the Russian and Greek military service, or to venture on any other profitable undertaking. It is difficult to establish precisely the causes that made it necessary for these Varangians to leave their native country and seek adventures in foreign lands—England, France, Spain, Italy. So many of them had come to Russia, since the middle of the ninth century, and so thoroughly had the Slavs become accustomed to their presence, that we may safely call them fellow inhabitants of the Russians. Both carried on a common trade with Greeks and Arabians, and fought shoulder to shoulder against common foes. At times they quarreled and fought: sometimes the Varangians downed the Slavs; at other times the Slavs got the upper hand and drove the Varangians "beyond the sea" to their own country.

With such close contact between Varangians and Slavs, it might have been expected that the former would greatly influence the latter, but there is little evidence of this, for the simple reason that the civilization of the Varangians was not superior to that of the Slavs.

4. CHARACTER OF THE COUNTRY SETTLED BY THE RUSSIAN SLAVS.—When they descended from the highlands of the Carpathians to the plains of central Russia, the Russian Slavs found themselves in many ways obliged to adapt their daily life to the geographical conditions they found in their new homes. The country occupied by them was a low, undulating plain, without mountains but diversified by an intricate network of rivers and streams. The absence of mountain barriers enabled the Slavs quickly and easily to extend their colonization. The rivers also, deep and wide and flowing

in all directions, greatly facilitated their expansion, serving as excellent means of communication.[6]   After they had ascended to the sources of the Dnieper, Volga, and Western Dvina, and had reached the Alaun Plateau, they pushed on to Lake Ilmen and the Volkhov River. They then had control of highly important lines of communication leading from the Baltic to the Black and Caspian Seas.   The most important of these waterways was what was known as "the great way from the Varangian land to the Greeks," which led from the Gulf of Finland through the Neva, Lake Ladoga, Volkhov, and Lake Ilmen to the Lovat River; thence by small, shallow streams and across some portages into the Western Dvina, and so to the Black Sea, to the "Greeks," *i.e.*, Byzantium. Slavs as well as Varangians used this great waterway. Another important route followed the course of the Volga, through the country of the Volga Bulgarians and Khazars, into the Caspian Sea.[7]   Still another route to the Khazar country was by way of the Dnieper, through the smaller streams to the Donets and the Don and thence either to the Azov or to the Caspian Sea.   These highways of commerce were used by the Slavs to reach the markets of the Greeks, Bulgarians and Khazars, and by foreign traders to come to the Russian cities.   As the Slavs came to know their river systems better, they pushed their colonization farther and deeper into the country of the Finns [8] and Khazars.[9]

The entire area of European Russia has been divided

[6] Each tribe settled along some river: Severiane on the Desna, Radimichi on the Sozh, Drevliane on the Pripiat, Polochane on the Polot.

[7] To reach the Volga, the Slavs descended its tributaries (Mologa and Sheksna) and the Msta River, which empties into Lake Ilmen.

[8] Rostov, Murom.

[9] Tmutarakan on the Sea of Azov.

into two zones, a northern and a southern. The boundary between the two may be approximated by drawing a line across the map from Kiev to the Volga, towards the mouth of the Kama River. To the south of this line we find, first, rich, black meadow land covered with thick grass and frequent patches of timber, but as we approach nearer and nearer the sea, we come to the *steppe*, *i.e.*, land without any timber, on parts of which there is a sparse growth of grass, and on other parts no vegetation at all. In occupying the basin of the Dnieper, the Slavs obviously avoided the steppe, and settled in the forest zone. The steppe was not safe, being constantly liable to attack by the nomadic tribes. The forest, on the other hand, was comparatively safe. There one could graze cattle, cultivate the ground, keep bees, hunt, fish, and cut timber for building and household needs. The forest thus shielded the Slavs from the fierce nomads, gave them their food, and supplied the merchandise for their markets. This explains why the Slavs shunned the steppe and were attracted by the forest, and why they expanded in the direction they did.

Conditions of life such as these in ancient Russia had their advantages as well as their disadvantages. The favorable topography of the country enabled the Slavs very quickly to settle vast areas, uninterruptedly pushing forward their settlements to the north and northeast.[10] The convenient waterways enabled the widely scattered tribes to maintain a lively intercourse with each other, and prevented a complete rupture of tribal relationships. This, in turn, facilitated the formation among the Slavs

[10] Throughout the course of Russian history, indeed, we observe an active, vigorous colonization by the Russian Slavs, first in European Russia and afterwards in Asia.

of a united state and a single church, gradually preparing the ground for the consolidation of all these tribes into a united Russian nation. The rivers, in their capacity of trade routes, fostered the growth of commerce, and contributed to the prosperity of the towns. It is clear, therefore, that the achievements of organized political and social life in ancient Russia were intimately bound up with geographical conditions.

It should be noted, however, that the same conditions also favored the enemies of the Russians. If the peaceful inhabitants could easily and conveniently move about the country, so could their enemies. Mountains did not bar their passage. Forests and swamps interposed no serious obstacles, for roads had already been laid down there, and the rivers carried friend and foe alike. Thus the nomadic hordes of the southern steppe constantly found their way into the interior of Russia, ravaged the settlements nearest the steppe, made captive the inhabitants, and drove off their cattle. The Russians had to be forever on the watch. They built fortified towns surrounded with ramparts and stockades in which they could take refuge. Sometimes they had to flee to the dense forests, burying whatever they could not take with them in their flight.[11] The constant menace of sudden attacks explains why the Slavs built no large and substantial houses, and did not burden themselves with cumbersome household goods. The Slav was ever ready to leave his home—either to move away temporarily or to abandon completely the threatened locality. This simplicity and mobility in the life of the ancient Slavs

[11] This explains the considerable number of hoards, or treasure-troves, discovered in Russian soil, containing sometimes coins and precious articles of very great value.

was noted by foreign travelers who had studied their customs.

5. ORIGINAL STATE OF SOCIETY AMONG THE RUSSIAN SLAVS.—During the first period of their existence on the Dnieper and Ilmen, the Russian Slavs preserved a patriarchal tribal organization. Each tribe was divided into clans, every man living "with his clan and in his place, and belonging to his own clan," as it used to be said in those days. The name "clan" designated a community of families related by blood, dwelling together, owning property in common, and ruled by one clan elder. These elders had a great deal of power over their clans; and when they met in common councils (*vieche*) they made decisions which affected the whole tribe. This, however, was true only on exceptional occasions, as, for instance, in moments of extreme danger threatening the whole tribe. But in course of time, after the various tribes and clans had spread over vast distances, the ties between the clans grew looser, and the clans began to break up into independent families. Each separate family became economically independent of the clan, and common clan property was replaced by family property. In the same way the authority of the clan chief also declined. He could not possibly rule all the households of his clan if these were scattered far and wide. His authority passed to the father of each separate family, the head of the household. With the break-up of the clan its members no longer felt themselves bound by a mutual relationship of blood, and in case of need they united for common action with their nearest neighbors instead of with their kinsmen. The *vieche* became an assembly of the householders of a given district, regardless of whether there was any blood relationship between them or not.

Brought together by some common interest, they formed a commune (*zadruga*, *verv*) and chose their elders to attend to the communal affairs. In this manner the original clan organization was gradually superseded by the commune, which was open to families having common interests, regardless of their clan and tribal affiliations. Such was the rule in localities where different tribes dwelt side by side, or in places which were being colonized simultaneously by more than one tribe.

The development of commerce on the Black Sea and the Caspian Sea led to the building of cities—Kiev, Chernigov, Liubech, Smolensk, Polotsk, Novgorod, and others. These served as the emporiums of traders and storage places for their merchandise. They were commercial centers for local and foreign merchants, and places for outfitting flotillas to the country of the Khazars and the Greeks. The necessity of protecting goods in storage and in transit led to the formation of armed *druzhinas*, or companies, recruited from among free and strong men, usually Varangians. These companies were commanded by Varangian leaders—*konungs* or princes—who were either themselves traders, or leaders of armed forces, ready to sell their services to guard cities or protect flotillas. Occasionally, some of these konungs seized the power and became the ruling princes of towns. As the surrounding country was generally subject to the authority of the city, there resulted the establishment of a regular principality, more or less extensive. According to tradition, such principalities were founded, among others, by Askold and Dir at Kiev, Rurik at Novgorod, and Rogvolod at Polotsk. But, side by side with the Varangians, the Russian Slavs set up principalities of their own; thus the Drevlians had a native prince named Mal.

The rise of cities, and the coming of foreign traders and military *druzhinas* still further undermined the ancient tribal order among the Russians, and led to the formation of associations based on economic interests. Some joined the military *druzhinas;* others, trading companies; still others, craft organizations. In place of the old patriarchal unions of blood relatives, social classes— warriors, traders, artisans—now began to form. They were no longer dependent upon the authority of their clan elders, but subject to the power of the city authorities— the princes and employers. The people who remained upon their fields and in their forest homes also felt the influence of the cities. In the patriarchal period, each clan and even family was, as a rule, self-sufficing. Commerce and cities created a demand for goods, chiefly honey, wax, and furs, and these came to be the leading articles of Russia's export. Under the stimulus of this demand from the cities, the rural population produced more than enough for its own needs, in order to have something to exchange for city merchandise or for money.

In this way the social conditions of the Russian Slavs gradually changed. From the patriarchal organization of clan and tribe they passed slowly to the communal system, combining, under the influence of the capital, or "elder" cities, in provinces (*volosts*) or principalities, where they were no longer held together by blood ties, but by civic and political bonds.

When the separate provinces and principalities of towns and tribes were assembled and consolidated under a single political authority, the foundation for the Russian State was laid.

CHAPTER ONE

FORMATION OF THE STATE OF KIEV

6. TRADITION OF THE CHRONICLES ON THE CALLING OF THE VARANGIAN PRINCES.—No distinct recollection has been preserved among the Russian Slavs as to how and when an organized state first appeared among them. Only after they had begun to take an interest in their own past did they commence to collect and write down the traditional accounts which were current among them with regard to the history of the Slavs in general and the Russians in particular, seeking references in the historical writings of the Greeks (the Byzantine "Chronicles") which had been translated into the Slav language. A collection of such popular traditions, combined with transcripts from the Greek chronicles, was made during the eleventh century at Kiev, giving a separate account of the beginnings of the Russian State and of the first princes of Kiev. In this account the narrative was arranged by years and brought down to 1074 A.D., the time in which the author of this "Original Chronicle" lived. According to tradition, this first chronicler was Nestor, a monk in the Pecherski Monastery of Kiev. This "Original Chronicle," however, was not to be the last. It was altered and amended several times, so as to combine in one single narrative various legends and historical records then existing at Kiev and other places. In this manner there came into being, at the beginning

of the twelfth century, the so-called "Collection of Chronicles," [1] compiled by Sylvester, Abbot of the Vydubitski Monastery of Kiev. This collection, known also as the "Story of Current Times," [2] was copied in various other cities and supplemented with historical entries made in Kiev, Novgorod, Pskov, Suzdal, and other towns. These collections of chronicles gradually increased in number. Every locality had a chronicler of its own, who began with the *"poviest"* and followed it up with an account of his own territory and city. This *"poviest"* is as follows:

In times past the Varangians, coming from "beyond the sea," had levied tribute on the Slavs of Novgorod, the Krivichi, and the neighboring tribes of the Finns. These tributary peoples finally rose in revolt against the Varangians, drove them back across the sea, and set out to govern themselves and to build cities. Soon, however, internal dissensions broke out among them, and there was no justice. They then decided to seek a prince to govern and establish justice among them. Accordingly, in 862 A.D., they sent across the sea, to the Russ Varangians [3] and said: "Our land is great and rich, but there is no order in it; come and rule and govern us." Three brothers, with their kinsmen and *druzhiny*, or military companies (the chronicler writes that they took with them the whole tribe of the *Russ*), accepted the call. The oldest of the three brothers, Rurik, settled in Novgorod; the second, Sineus, on Lake Bieloozero; and the third, Truvor, in Izborsk, near Pskov. Upon the

---

[1] *Lietopisny svod.*

[2] *Poviest vremennykh liet.*

[3] In the opinion of the chronicler this particular tribe of the Varangians was called Russ, just as other Varangian tribes were called Swedes, Normans, Angles, Goths.

death of Sineus and Truvor, Rurik became the sole reigning prince in the North; but his son, Igor, reigned both in Kiev and Novgorod. Thus was laid the foundation of the dynasty which united under its authority the tribes of the Russian Slavs.

In the traditional account of the chronicles not all is clear and reliable. In the first place, according to the chronicle, Rurik came to Novgorod with the Varangian tribe of the *Russ* in 862. But it is known that twenty years earlier the *Russ* had already fought against the Greeks on the Black Sea and that they had, for the first time, laid siege even to Tsargrad (Constantinople) in June, 860. Obviously *the chronology of these chronicles is inaccurate, and the date which they give for the founding of the principality of Novgorod is erroneous.* This happened because the years were marked in the text of the chronicles after the story of the beginnings of Russia had been written down, and because they were inserted by mere conjecture, from memory, and by a rough estimate. In the second place, the chronicles tell us that the *Russ* were supposed to be one of the Varangian tribes, that is to say, Scandinavians. But we know that the Greeks never identified the tribe of the *Russ*, whom they knew very well, with the Varangians. Likewise the Arabians, who were trading along the shores of the Caspian Sea, had been familiar with the tribe of the *Russ*, distinguishing them from the Varangians, whom they called "Varang." It thus appears that *there is some error or inaccuracy in the traditional story of the chronicles treating the Russ as a Varangian tribe.*[4]

[4] Since the eighteenth century historians have disagreed as to the Russ. The Academician Bayer held that they were Varangians or Normans. Lomonosov, on the other hand, claimed that the Russ were not Varangians, but Slavs from Prussia. The dispute about the origin

Let the fact be noted that in all those cases where the chronicles mention the *country*, the name of *Russ* is applied to the territory of Kiev and, in general, to territories subject to the princes of Kiev, that is to say, to a *Slavonic* country.   On the other hand, whenever the chronicles and Greek writers speak of the people, the name *Russ* is not applied to the Slavs but to the *Normans*, and by "Russian" language is meant not the Slavonic but the Norman speech.   The chronicles mention the names of envoys sent to Greece by the princes of Kiev, and these envoys are "of the tribe of the *Russ*," and their names are not Slavonic but Norman (nearly one hundred such names have been found).   The Greek Emperor, Constantine Porphyrogenetos, in his work on the "Administration of the Empire," cites the names of the cataracts of the Dnieper both "in Slavonic" and "in Russian," and here we find the "Slavonic" names closely resembling the Slavonic language, whereas the "Russian" names betray purely Scandinavian roots.   It seems certain, therefore, that the people who called themselves *Russ* spoke a Scandinavian dialect and belonged to the northern Germanic tribes,[4a] while the country known as Russia, or *Russ*, so called after this people, was a Slavonic country.

of the Russ was carried over into the nineteenth century, and both the Norman and Slav schools have many champions.

It would seem, however, that the name Russ was a general term used by the Slavs to designate the Varangians as a whole and not any particular tribe.   The Slavs called the principalities set up by the Varangians *Russian,* and their *druzhiny, Russ.*   As these *druzhiny* acted together with the Slavs, the term Russ came to be applied to the Slavs and their country.   The Greeks gave the name of Varangians to the Normans who entered the Greek service, but applied the term Russ to the Slavs and Normans who dwelt near the Black Sea.

[4a] "Gentis Sueonum," as a German chronicler of the ninth century has it.

The *Russ* first appeared among the Slavs on the Dnieper in the first half of the ninth century. Even before the descendants of Rurik had gone from Novgorod to Kiev, Varangian princes already reigned at Kiev, attacking Byzantium from this city (860). With the arrival of the Novgorodian princes, Kiev came to be the metropolis of all Russia.

7. THE REIGN OF THE VARANGIAN PRINCES.—There is almost no tradition preserved about the reign of the half-legendary Rurik at Novgorod. It is said that he did not at first live at Novgorod but at Ladoga, at the mouth of the Volkhov River, and that he transferred his capital to Novgorod only after the death of his brothers. His rule was supposed to have stirred up discontent and even open rebellion, under a certain Vadim the Brave; but Rurik suppressed the revolt and executed its leader. Some of the malcontents fled to Kiev, then ruled by Askold and Dir, two Varangian warriors who had left Rurik's *druzhina* and set up a principality of their own. It is, of course, hard to determine just how much truth there is in these legendary tales.

Upon the death of Rurik (879), his relative, Oleg, became Prince of Novgorod. He exercised the authority of a regent during the minority of Igor, the son of Rurik. Oleg, taking Igor with him, marched south, down the great way "from the Varangian land to the Greeks," captured Smolensk and Liubech on the Dnieper, and appeared in front of Kiev. By treachery he seized and put to death Askold and Dir, on the ground that they were "not princes and not of the princely blood," whereas he himself was a genuine prince, and Igor was the direct heir of Rurik himself. He established himself at Kiev, making it the capital of his principality and saying that Kiev was to be "the mother of Russian cities." In this way Oleg united under his sceptre all the principal tribes and important cities along the great waterway. Thus it was that Kiev became the rallying point for a vast empire, freeing the Russian tribes from their dependence upon the Khazars. After he had broken the Khazar yoke, Oleg tried to protect his country by erecting fortresses against the eastern nomads (Khazars and Pecheniegs) and building cities on the borders of the steppe.

Oleg did not, however, confine himself to the unification of the Slavs. He emulated the example of his predecessors in Kiev, Askold and Dir, and made a raid on Byzantium. "With horse and ship," he arrived under the walls of Constantinople (907), ravaged the surrounding country, and laid siege to the city. The Greeks were forced to open peace negotiations, to pay Oleg a "tribute," *i.e.*, to purchase immunity from further spoliation, and to conclude a treaty with him. Oleg's success made a profound impression in Russia, and his deeds are celebrated in song and story. They tell how Oleg put his boats on wheels and went sailing to Constantinople "across the fields"; and how he hung up his shield, "in token of victory," upon the gates of the city. Oleg was given the surname of *vieshchi*, *i.e.*, sage, or seer, because he was reputed to have superhuman wisdom. The work done by Oleg was, indeed, of extraordinary importance: *out of the isolated towns and tribes which he found he built up a powerful state, liberated the Slavs from Khazar dominion, and established, by his treaties, regular trade relations between Russia and Byzantium.* In a word, he was the founder of Russo-Slav independence and power.

Upon the death of Oleg (912), Igor, who seems to

have been deficient in military and administrative ability, came into power. He made two campaigns against the Greeks, one in Asia Minor and the other against Constantinople. The first time he suffered heavy defeat in a naval battle in which the Greeks employed special fireships, hurling "fire from tubes at the Russian boats." On the second occasion Igor did not even reach Constantinople, and made peace with the Greeks on the terms given in the treaty of 945, which was considered less favorable to the Russians than the treaties of Oleg. Igor's sad end in the country of the Drevliane, from whom he was attempting to collect a double tribute, the wooing of Olga, his widow, by the Drevlian prince, Mal, and her revenge on the Drevliane for the slaying of her husband, are related in great detail in the chronicles.

After Igor's death his widow Olga assumed the government of the principality. According to old Slavonic custom, a widow enjoyed civic independence and equal rights,[5] and there is, therefore, nothing unusual in the fact that Princess Olga became the head of the state. The chronicler treats her most sympathetically, calls her "the wisest of all people," and credits her with having made great efforts to organize her country properly, by traveling over her dominions and establishing order throughout. Her greatest claim to fame, however, was her conversion to Christianity and pious pilgrimage to Constantinople (957). According to the account given by the chronicles, Olga was baptized by "the emperor and the patriarch" at Constantinople, although it seems more likely that she was baptized in Russia before going

---

[5] Generally speaking, the condition of women among the Slavs seems to have been better than among other European races of the same period.

to Greece. Emperor Constantine Porphyrogenetos, who received Olga at his palace with great pomp, which he has described in his "Book of Ceremonies," speaks of her in an ordinary manner. But the tradition handed down in Russia has it that the emperor had been so much struck with the beauty and cleverness of Princess Olga that he desired her in marriage. She treated the patriarch with respect, but maintained an attitude of independence towards the emperor. The Russian chronicler says that she twice outwitted the emperor: first, when she rejected his proposal of marriage, and secondly, when she refused to pay tribute, or to give presents, which he is supposed to have expected. Such is the legend, which attributes to Olga extraordinary beauty and wisdom. After the triumph of Christianity in Russia, the memory of Princess Olga (under her baptismal name of Helen) began to be revered by the Orthodox Church, and she was canonized.

Igor and Olga's son, Sviatoslav, though he had a Slavonic name, seems to have been a typical Varangian warrior. He had scarcely reached manhood when he formed a large and valiant *druzhina* and set out to seek martial glory and spoils. He early freed himself from his mother's influence. When she wished him to be converted, he said: "How can I change my faith? The *druzhina* would laugh at me." He had come to be inseparable from the *druzhina*, sharing all the hardships of its campaigns, and moving with extraordinary swiftness, "stepping lightly, like a panther," in the words of the chronicler.

While his mother acted as regent, Sviatoslav warred with his neighbors. He marched against the Viatichi on the Oka and defeated them; then he turned on the Khazars and Bulgars and destroyed their power. In brief, he subjugated and ravaged the territories of all the eastern neighbors of Russia who had formed parts of the Khazar empire, and thus made Russia the principal power in the region of the Black Sea. But the fall of the Khazars opened the way for the advance of the nomadic Pecheniegs, who overran the South Russian steppes which had formerly been occupied by the Khazars.

On his return to Kiev after his eastern conquests, Sviatoslav was invited by the Greeks to help them in their struggle against the Danube Bulgarians. Assembling a vast army, he reduced Bulgaria to submission and established his residence in the city of Pereiaslavets on the Danube. "I want to live in Pereiaslavets," he said, "for here is the center of my dominions, and here are gathered together all kinds of merchandise. From the Greeks come gold, textiles, wines, and fruits; from the Czechs and Hungarians come silver and horses; and from Russia come furs, wax and honey, and slaves." While he was enjoying himself in his new capital, the Pecheniegs were laying siege to Kiev. The inhabitants, with Princess Olga and Sviatoslav's children, were barely able to hold out against the fierce enemy, and they sent messengers to Sviatoslav with reproaches and requests for help. He came and drove off the enemy, and was about to start south once more when the dying Olga begged him to stay in Russia at least till her death. But no sooner was she buried than he returned to Bulgaria, leaving his sons to act as the Princes of Russia. But the Greeks were not at all willing to see the Russians rule over the Bulgarians, and they insisted that Sviatoslav go back to Russia. When he refused, the Emperor John Zimisces besieged the Russian army in the fortress or Doristol (the modern Silistria), and forced Sviatoslav to make peace and evacuate Bulgaria. On his way home, Sviatoslav was surprised by the Pecheniegs near the cataracts of the Dnieper and killed, while his forces were scattered.

After the death of Sviatoslav, sanguinary conflicts broke out among his sons in Russia, in the course of which all of them, with the exception of Prince Vladimir, perished. Undermined by these conflicts, the Principality of Kiev began to show signs of disintegration, and Vladimir had to devote a great deal of energy to pacifying the Varangians in his service, to subduing the rebellious Slav tribes, and to protecting his provinces against the Volga Bulgarians and other neighbors. He was also drawn into war with the Greeks, the consequence of which was that he adopted the Christianity of the Greek Church. With this event of paramount importance there came to an end the first period of the reign of the Varangian dynasty in Russia.

8. THE MAIN SIGNIFICANCE OF THE RULE OF THE VARANGIAN PRINCES.—The principal events of this period, as we have seen, were the efforts of the Kiev princes: (1) to consolidate the scattered Russian tribes and form a united Russia; (2) to establish, as advantageously as possible, trade relations with their neighbors and insure the safety of commercial intercourse with foreign markets; (3) to defend Russia from her foreign enemies.

Having first taken possession of the entire route "from the Varangian land to the Greeks," from Ladoga to Kiev, the princes next tried to bring under their rule those Slav tribes (Drevliane and Viatichi) who lived at some distance from this trade route. The conquered provinces were governed either by the princes themselves or by their representatives or by the native leaders under the control of the princes. The main object of the government at that period was to collect *dan*, "tribute," and taxes of all kinds. During the winter the prince himself or his *posadniki* [5a] traveled through the provinces, dispensing justice and punishment, and gathering the *dan* in money or in kind. Later the *dan* thus collected was loaded on vessels, and brought to Kiev. In the hands of the princes of Kiev were thus concentrated large stocks of various goods in which the princes traded, sending them on their own account to Greece or the Khazars, or to the Danube.

In the spring this merchandise was loaded in large vessels, [6] holding several tons and carrying crews of forty or fifty men. In addition to the prince's boats, there were those of his *druzhina* and of the traders (*gosti*), and of the prince's guardsmen and the armed *druzhiny* of the traders. Contemporary descriptions indicate that, after being assembled for a final muster at Vitichevo, about 50 *versts* [7] below Kiev, the flotilla started on the "Greek road," proceeding down the Dnieper until it came to the cataracts. Here the cargo was unloaded and carried around the falls by the slaves who were being taken to the slave market, while the guardsmen stood watch. On coming out into the Black Sea, the Russians followed the Bulgarian coast to Constantinople.

The Greeks would not admit all the Russians into the city, but assigned them quarters in the suburb of St. Mama, where they remained about six months, until their business was finished. They were registered by the Greeks, and in accordance with the list thus obtained, were supplied with provisions. The Greeks permitted

[5a] Governors.
[6] Called *lodi*, boats with keels, hollowed out of a single tree stem.
[7] One verst = .66 miles.

not more than 50 Russians at a time, without arms and under a guide, to enter Constantinople proper. None were allowed to spend the winter in Greece. Outside of Constantinople the Russians held something like a fair, under Greek protection but also under Greek control, and surrounded with various precautions. The commercial and other relations of the Russians and Greeks were determined by treaties.

These trading expeditions to Constantinople, to the Khazars and to the Danube cost much planning and fighting. The campaigns of the princes of Kiev against Greece, and the campaigns of Sviatoslav on the Don and the Volga, had a close connection with the commercial affairs of Kiev. In this way the trade of Russia gave direction to the foreign policies of the princes of Kiev.

In addition to their commercial undertakings, the princes defended the country against external aggression. The tribes of the steppe threatened not only the Russian borderlands but the capital, Kiev itself, which was situated near the steppe. It was necessary to protect the capital with a chain of fortresses and similar means of defense. It was at times possible to establish friendly relations with the Pecheniegs, but as a rule the Russians were always at war with them.

From what has been said thus far concerning Russian trade, it is clear why Kiev was important, and why Oleg called her "Mother of Russian cities." Being the southernmost city on the Dnieper, and located at the edge of the steppe, she became the gathering place for all merchants engaged in foreign trade; the warehouse for goods to be exported and for goods imported; and, in short, the commercial metropolis of all Russia at that period; all other Russian trading towns being dependent upon her.

9. PAGANISM IN RUSSIA IN ANCIENT TIMES.—We have said before that Prince Vladimir Sviatoslavich of Kiev was converted to Christianity. Immediately following his conversion, the whole country adopted the Christian faith, and solemnly renounced heathenism.

Very little is known concerning the pagan beliefs of the Russian Slavs. They worshipped the forces of nature which were supposed to be personified in certain deities, such as *Dazhbog*, *Khors*, and *Veles*. *Dazhbog* was regarded as the giver of heat and light, the dispenser of all good; *Veles* was the patron of flocks, the "cattle-god"; the "Great *Khors*" was evidently the sun itself. *Perun* was the god of storm, of thunder and lightning. *Stribog* was the god of wind. *Svarog* was the heaven where *Dazhbog* had his dwelling; hence *Dazhbog* had the patronymic of *Svarozhich*, *i.e.*, "son of *Svarog*." The deity of the earth was "Dank Mother Earth"; and while she was regarded as the female ancestor, *Dazhbog* and *Veles* were considered the male progenitors of the human race. But none of these conceptions of godhood had attained the clearness found, for example, among the Greeks. Nor was religious ceremonial greatly developed. The Slavs had neither special temples nor special priests. Here and there, in open spaces, they erected crude images of their deities, and to these idols they offered sacrifice, sometimes even human. It is worth remarking that the Varangian mythology exercised no influence whatever upon this Slavonic mythology, probably because it was neither clearer nor more impressive than the latter. On the contrary, the Varangians who did not accept Christianity slipped easily into the Slavonic pagan practices.

Prince Igor (a Varangian by birth) and his Varangian *druzhina* swore by the Slav *Perun*, and worshipped his image.

Somewhat more highly developed than the cult of visible nature was ancestor worship. The long-dead ancestor of the clan was deified, and regarded as the living protector of his progeny. He was called the *rod* ("stem" or "progenitor") or the *shchur* ("great-great-grandfather"), and sacrifices were offered to him. The maternal ancestors were called *rozhanitsy* ("mothers of the clan") and were similarly venerated. With the disappearance of the clan, the place of the *shchur* was taken by the ancestor of the family, the *diedushka domovoi* ("granddaddy of the home"). He was the guardian of the household, who invisibly managed its affairs. Belief in a life after death, which underlay this cult of ancestor worship, was expressed in the belief that the souls of the departed wandered over the earth and dwelt in field, forest, and stream (as *rusalki*, *i.e.*, water-nymphs, etc.). Believing in the existence of invisible masters ruling men's homes, the Slav looked for similar masters outside the home; in the forest (*lieshie*, wood-sprites), and in the water (*vodianye*, water-sprites). To him all nature was animated with living spirits. He held communion with nature, he entered into its moods, he accompanied its changes with all kinds of special ceremonies. In this way there grew up a cycle of pagan holidays based upon the worship of nature and ancestors.

10. Christianity in Russia Prior to the Conversion of Prince Vladimir.—Christianity was introduced into Russia before the time of Prince Vladimir. In Igor's time there was already a Christian church at Kiev and, in the words of the chronicler, "there were many Varan-

gian Christians," even among Igor's own *druzhina* and family. But paganism lingered on, and was a force to reckon with. In 983 a pagan mob at Kiev killed two Varangian Christians, father and son, because the father refused to surrender his son as a sacrificial offering to the "gods." But the religion of Christ was making notable gains at Kiev when Prince Vladimir adopted it.

11. The Tradition of the Chronicles on the Conversion of Prince Vladimir.—Many traditions exist as to the baptism of Vladimir and the conversion of the Russians. According to different accounts the prince was baptized in Kiev, in the town of Vasilev,[8] or in the Greek town of Korsun [9] which he had captured from the Greeks. The following is the account given by a chronicler who wrote one hundred years after the conversion of Russia.

In 986 there came to Vladimir the Mohammedan Volga Bulgarians, then the Germans from the Pope of Rome; then the Khazar Jews, and finally a Greek philosopher of the Orthodox Church. All tried to convert Vladimir to their own faith. He listened, then sent them all away, detaining only the Greek. With him he conversed at length, and finally dismissed him with gifts and tokens of honor, without, however, committing himself. In the following year (987) Vladimir called together his advisers and told them about the visits of the missionaries and the impression made upon him by the Greek philosopher. His listeners suggested that he send men to the various countries to see "how each serves God." When, in the course of their wanderings, these

[8] About 35 *versts* from Kiev.
[9] Chersonesus, Crimea

men came to Constantinople, and saw the indescribable splendor of the Greek divine service, they were filled with wonder. On their return they made their report in favor of the Orthodox Church. Thereupon Vladimir asked his advisers: "Where shall we receive baptism?" and they answered, as one man: "Wherever it pleases you!" In the following year (988), Vladimir led his army against Korsun and laid siege to that city, which offered stubborn resistance. He vowed that he would adopt Christianity if he succeeded in taking the place. When he had captured the city, he sent word to the Emperors Basil and Constantine, the two brothers reigning at Constantinople, demanding their sister, Anna, in marriage. They declined to allow their sister to marry a pagan. Vladimir answered that he was prepared for baptism, whereupon the Greek Emperors sent their sister to Korsun, accompanied by clergymen, who baptized the Russian prince and married him to the princess. Just before his baptism Vladimir was taken ill and lost his eyesight; but he was miraculously cured during the administration of the sacrament of baptism. Having made peace with the Greeks and restored Korsun to them, he returned to Kiev with the Orthodox clergy, who baptized all the people of Russia.

Evidently we have here combined in one narrative several different legends: (1) that Vladimir had been urged by the Bulgarians, Khazars, Germans and Greeks settled in Kiev to adopt their respective religions; (2) that Vladimir, having lived in the darkness of paganism and physical blindness, was able miraculously to perceive at once both the spiritual and the physical light; (3) that Vladimir found it necessary, before accepting the Greek faith, to besiege the Greek city of Korsun, in order to conquer, as it were, the Greek faith as well as the city, taking it with the hand of a victor.

From the accounts of the Greeks and Arabs we learn something of Vladimir's campaigns against Korsun. One of the leaders of the Greek army, Bardas Phokas, revolted, and the Greek government, unable to suppress the revolt, called on Vladimir. He agreed (987) to aid Byzantium, in return for the hand of the Greek princess, Anna, and promised, in addition, to accept Christianity. Thanks to his help the revolt was crushed and Bardas Phokas perished; but the Greeks tried to evade the fulfillment of their promise. Vladimir then declared war on them, besieged and took Korsun, and forced them to keep their word. He then adopted Christianity and was given the princess in marriage (989). It is not known precisely where he was baptized or when, whether in 988 or in 989.

Returning to Kiev with his wife and Greek clergy, Vladimir set out to convert all his subjects to the new faith. The idols were cast down and flung into the river, and churches were erected where they had stood. The traditional account says that the new religion spread peaceably, except in a few places. In Novgorod, for instance, the use of force was necessary. In the more remote parts of the country paganism persisted for some centuries, and some of its ideas became interwoven with the new doctrine.

THE CONSEQUENCES OF THE ADOPTION OF CHRISTIANITY IN RUSSIA

12. ORGANIZATION OF THE CHURCH IN KIEV.—The conversion of the Russians must not be regarded as a

mere change of religion. Christianity, having become the dominant faith in Russia, expressed itself not alone in preaching and divine worship, but also in molding laws and institutions. From Greece there came into Russia the *hierarchy*. At the head of the Church was the Patriarch of Constantinople. Under him was the Metropolitan of Kiev, who was over the bishops, who in turn had charge over the lower clergy. In this way the clergy of the country was bound together. With Christianity came prayer books and sacred literature. Translations from the original Greek into popular Slavonic, easily understood by the Russians, had been made by the apostles of the Slavs, St. Cyril and St. Methodius, and their followers.

Soon after the adoption of Christianity, schools were opened, with clergymen as teachers, and the collecting and transcribing of books began. The metropolitan and the bishops with him governed and judged the people as was done by the clergy in Greece, on the basis of a special code of laws, the *Nomocanon*.[10] The Church owned land which was managed by the clergy and the monasteries in accordance with Byzantine customs and laws.

Thus there came into Russia, together with the new religion, new authorities, new education, new ideas of justice, new land owners, and new forms of land ownership. The Church became the channel through which Byzantine influence flowed into Russia. To appreciate this influence it is necessary to have some idea of the

[10] Known in Russia in its Bulgarian translation as the *Kormchaia Kniga, i.e.,* "Book of Rules," or "Administrative Code." In this book were laid down the Apostolic Church Rules, together with the rules of the ecumenical councils of the Church, besides the civil laws of the Orthodox Byzantine emperors.

political and social life of Russia before Christianity became the accepted religion.

13. CHARACTERISTICS OF THE PRE-CHRISTIAN LIFE OF THE RUSSIAN SLAVS.—The modern state has both the right and the duty to punish persons guilty of crime and misdemeanor and to prevent, as far as possible, every violation of law and order. At the present time a thief or an assassin is punished because he breaks the law of the land, and not because the victim or his friends desire to be avenged. In the days of Vladimir the crime committed was not against the state but against the individual. At that time the princes were not expected to maintain law and order unless requested to do so by the persons concerned. A man was protected, not by the prince, but by his own efforts and those of his kinsmen. So strong and widespread was "blood feud" or "vengeance" that it was sanctioned by the customs of that period.

It could not be otherwise in a society where the power of the prince was still weak, and where the prince himself was of alien race and surrounded by a *druzhina* of Varangians like himself. Society was divided into clans, *druzhinas*, communes, associations, each of which protected its own members. Any one expelled for any reason from his own group was defenseless, and could be "killed like a dog." Each clan lived by itself and in a state of hostility towards its neighbors. In order to secure wives, members of one clan captured or abducted the women of another. In the course of time it became customary to obtain the consent of the woman to be abducted, and to pay "bridal money" to the clan. Among some tribes the institution of marriage was almost what it is today, but in most of them it was very primitive, and polygamy was commonly practiced.

Society during the pagan period was divided into two classes—free and slave.[11] Slaves, who were very numerous, were harshly treated, and looked upon merely as work animals. They had no right to own property, or to testify in court. If they committed a crime, their master was held responsible, and he could punish them as he saw fit, even unto death.

In summing up we may say that the princes in pagan society had neither the authority nor the power of the modern state. Society was divided into independent corporate bodies, which protected their members as individuals and as a group. A person outside of this circle was an outlaw and an outcast. Polygamy, and the abduction and purchase of brides, were the rule. Slavery was very extensive. Might and not right ruled, and the individual counted for little.

14. INFLUENCE OF THE CHURCH UPON THE LIFE OF THE PEOPLE.—Christianity could not reconcile itself to these pagan practices. Along with the Christian doctrines, the Church introduced into Russia the elements of Byzantine civilization. Under its influence the Russians gradually changed. Some followed in the footsteps of the Master and offered inspiring examples of Christian life. They venerated the Church, loved books, and sometimes forsook the world altogether, and retired to monasteries and hermitages. Both by precept and example *the church showed the people how to live and act*, in private

---

[11] The freemen were called *muzhi,* or men, while the slaves were known as *cheliad,* or menials (in the singular: *kholop,* masculine, and *roba,* feminine).

as well as in public life, and thus molded public opinion and social institutions.

The Church held the princes responsible for law and order and impressed them with the idea that they were "ordained by God to punish evil doers and show mercy to the good." This Christian and Byzantine conception of the prince as a ruler by divine right, to be obeyed and honored "as a servant of the Lord," was opposed to the pagan view that the prince was a mere leader of a *druzhina*, and could be driven out and killed. In the course of time the Church succeeded in getting its ideas accepted, and thus helped to establish a stable political order.

The Church formed itself into a separate community, composed of the clergy and other persons employed in its service and dependent upon it. *It cared for and fed those who were unable to provide for themselves*, the poor, the sick, and the helpless, *and offered asylum to all izgoi, or outcasts*, who had lost the protection of their own secular associations or corporations. The Church ruled all her dependents as her own subjects, and judged them by her own laws [12] and customs. No matter how lowly his station, the ward of the Church was treated always in a Christian way, as a free man. In the eyes of the Church there was neither slave nor master: all were brethren in Christ. *Thus the Church offered to secular society the example of a new, more perfect and more humane order*, under which all the helpless and defenseless were able to find protection.

Furthermore the Church was instrumental in improving family life and the general standard of morality in Russian society. On the basis of the Greek ecclesiastical laws adopted and confirmed by the first Russian princes

[12] The *Book of Rules*.

in their "Church Statutes," all offenses against religion and morals came under the jurisdiction of the Church and not of the princes. These included all cases of sacrilege, heresy, witchcraft, heathenism, and family difficulties arising between husband and wife, parent and child. The Church vigorously opposed polygamy, abduction and purchase of wives, cruelty to wives and children. In dispensing justice in accordance with the laws of Byzantium, which were more advanced than the primitive juridical customs of pagan society, the clergy introduced better customs and fostered a better order in Russia.

In particular, the Church opposed the harsh forms of slavery existing in Russia. In their homilies, sermons, and discourses, the clergy continually exhorted masters to free their slaves, or at least to be kind to them, and to remember that the bondman is just as much a human being and a Christian as his master. And though these exhortations failed to do away with slavery altogether, they yet put the stamp of disapproval and sin on the institution.

The influence of the Church was felt not only in social but also in political life. At a time when the princes were weak and divided among themselves the Church stood undivided, with the metropolitan as its universally acknowledged head; and this church unity paved the way for political unity.

15. CHRISTIAN EDUCATION IN RUSSIA.—In addition to her social and political activities, the educational work of the Church was of the greatest importance. She educated the masses through the example of Christian living, through literature, and through Church art.

Examples of a Christian life were offered by the laity as well as by the clergy. The chronicler relates that

Prince Vladimir himself grew kind-hearted and charitable after his conversion, that he cared for the poor and helpless, and that he devoted attention to book-learning. This change of heart was true not only of the princes but also of the common people. Ilarion, for example, through his piety, erudition and remarkable gifts as a preacher, rose from the lower ranks of the priesthood to the seat of Metropolitan of Russia. St. Theodosius, Abbot of the Pecherski Monastery of Kiev, abandoned, when a young man, a wealthy home for a life of monastic poverty, and became celebrated as an ascetic, a writer, and a preacher. The influence of such persons upon Russian society was very great and beneficial. Often they collected about them a group of pious men who withdrew from the world into the depths of the wild forest, where they built churches and monasteries, cleared the land, worked, ministered, suffered, and died. Their austere mode of life, their loyalty to their order, the peculiar management of their establishment, based upon self-denial and unremitting toil for the common good, made a deep impression. By building churches and monasteries for them, by offering them land and slaves, gold and valuables, the people showed their eagerness to help these pious brethren. As a result, humble communities of monks grew into rich and well-organized monasteries which became religious and educational centers. The economic management of the monasteries was based on Byzantine methods. The Church tolerated no slavery. Its laborers, although bound to the lands of the Church, enjoyed civic rights. Church estates were better managed than those of the laity, and served as models for them.

The earliest Christian literature in Russia consisted of Bulgarian translations of the Bible, prayer books, homilies, historical works, the "Book of Rules," etc. Under the stimulus of these translations, a native Russian literature began to develop, in the form of chronicles, lives of the saints, homilies, and prayers. The authors were persons of little learning, and their efforts, with rare exceptions, were distinguished neither by erudition nor by literary craftsmanship. Their writings, nevertheless, exerted a notable influence upon the spiritual and cultural life of the country.

Lastly, the Christian religion initiated in Russia a new era in the domain of the arts. Pagan Russia had no temples, and only crude images of its deities. Christianity promoted the construction of stone buildings. The Church of the Assumption of the Holy Virgin, at Kiev,[13] was the first stone church in that city. It was followed by similar buildings at Kiev, Novgorod, and other important towns. These churches were built on Byzantine models and embellished with elaborate mosaics and frescoes. Under the impetus of church building, architecture and painting attained a high level in Kiev, and at the same time the other arts and crafts flourished, especially enamel and metal work. In every branch of art the Greek influence and Greek workers were of course paramount at the beginning, but the Russians very soon developed a national art, though one so deeply influenced by the Byzantine that it is known as Russo-Byzantine art.

[13] Called also the Church of the Desiatine, from the fact that Prince Vladimir allotted for its maintenance a *desiatine* (tithe) of his revenues.

THE STATE OF KIEV IN THE ELEVENTH AND TWELFTH
CENTURIES

16. Prince Iaroslav the Wise.—After the death of
St. Vladimir (1015), feuds broke out anew among the
princes. Vladimir's eldest son, Sviatopolk, upon his
accession to the throne of Kiev, set about getting rid of
his five brothers, and succeeded in putting three of them
to death. Of these, the Princes Boris and Glieb had had
no intention at all of opposing Sviatopolk's claims, and
their martyrdom and innocence aroused universal indignation against him, and caused their memory to be held
in pious veneration. They were canonized, and revered
as shining examples of brotherly love, while Sviatopolk
on the other hand was likened to Cain, and given the
appellation of "the Accursed." A fourth brother, Iaroslav of Novgorod, escaped, raised an army of Novgorodians and Varangians and marched against Sviatopolk.
Notwithstanding the support given the latter by Boleslaw
the Brave, King of Poland, Iaroslav drove him out and
established himself in Kiev.

Iaroslav's able government earned him great fame and
the title of "The Wise." He had a great collection of
books which he presented to the Cathedral of St. Sophia
of Divine Wisdom at Kiev. In the words of the chronicler he "sowed the hearts of faithful men with the wisdom of books." He opened schools, built churches, and
ordered the clergy to teach the people the Christian
religion.

Iaroslav was also a mighty warrior and defender of
his country against foreign aggression. In 1034 he inflicted a crushing blow on the Pecheniegs and drove them
from Kiev once for all. Most of them migrated soon

after this to the Balkan Peninsula, while those who remained became subjects of the Russian princes. The importance of this victory was not diminished even by the failure of Iaroslav's campaign against Byzantium (1043). The indecisive three years' war which resulted from this attack was Russia's last conflict with Byzantium.

Under Iaroslav, Kiev became a strong and flourishing state. He undertook extensive and magnificent building enterprises. He erected at Kiev many stone churches and monasteries, including the wonderful Cathedral of St. Sophia. At Novgorod, also, he began the building of a Cathedral of St. Sophia. For these enterprises he imported from Greece both artisans and materials, sparing no expense to achieve good results. For its own epoch, the Cathedral of St. Sophia at Kiev was one of the richest and most splendid structures in Europe. Under Iaroslav, commerce was carried on with nearly every country of southern and western Europe. He sent his traders and ambassadors to Germany, France, Hungary, Poland, and the Scandinavian countries. He contracted marriage alliances with friendly rulers, even at a great distance. He was himself married to a Swedish royal princess; his daughters married the kings of France, Hungary and Norway, respectively; three of his sons married the daughters of German princes, and the fourth son, a relative of Constantine Monamachus, Emperor of Byzantium. Thus under Iaroslav Russia became one of the European Powers, and the city of Kiev became a great commercial emporium for the trade flowing between Europe and Asia.

17. THE ORDER OF SUCCESSION AMONG THE PRINCES AFTER IAROSLAV THE WISE.—The unification of Russia

achieved by Iaroslav was undone by his sons and grand-sons. Under them the Principality of Kiev broke up into a number of separate provinces, united only by the church and the kinship of their rulers. Notwithstanding the fact that they were of the same dynasty, these princes were continually quarreling and fighting, and dragging their provinces and peoples down with them. Exhausted by the efforts expended to crush the Pecheniegs, Russia was not able to muster sufficient resources to defend itself against the Polovtsy, who appeared in the southern steppes about the middle of the eleventh century, and "tore asunder" the Russian territories, laid waste the country, and disrupted trade by occupying all the routes leading from Russia east and south. By the beginning of the thirteenth century Kiev Russia, exhausted and impoverished, declined; and the city of Kiev lost its importance.

One of the causes of this demoralization was the sys-tem of succession that prevailed after Iaroslav. The territory over which he reigned was regarded as the possession of the family as a whole. Before his death Iaroslav had set his oldest son, Iziaslav, to rule over Kiev and Novgorod; his second son, Sviatoslav, over Cher-nigov; and his third son, Vsevolod, over Pereiaslavl; giving the less desirable lands to the youngest sons. The oldest was called the "Grand Prince," and resided at Kiev; but he had no other authority over his brothers than his position as head of the family gave him. Each prince was independent in his own province, and each hoped to succeed his brothers above him until he secured Kiev, attained the title of "Grand Prince," and became the head of the family. According to the order of suc-cession, the grand prince was not succeeded by his son, but by his brother next in age, or, if no brothers were living, by his oldest nephew, *i.e.*, the son of his oldest brother. Hence, whenever a grand prince of Kiev died, his place should have been taken, rightfully, by his brother from Chernigov; the latter's place should have been taken by the third brother, who reigned at Pereiaslavl, and so on. With the death of the grand prince, his brothers "climbed up as on a ladder" towards the throne of the grand prince. If a prince died without reaching the headship, his children lost their right to succession in the princely family and were considered *izgoi*, or outcasts, for whom there was no "portion in the Russian land." The sons of the late grand prince were provided by the new grand prince with separate provinces, away from Kiev.

Such were the rules of succession recognized by all the members of the dynasty. In practice, however, it was exceedingly difficult to observe these rules and to recognize and harmonize the conflicting claims of the family. Prince Iziaslav Iaroslavich of Kiev was driven out by his subjects, and then, after he had succeeded in regaining his throne, by his own brothers, Sviatoslav and Vsevolod. He went to Germany, where he sought help from Emperor Henry IV and Pope Gregory VII, but in vain. Sviatoslav established himself at Kiev and reigned until his death. Then Vsevolod relinquished his claim in favor of Iziaslav who once more became Prince of Kiev and died a grand prince. After that Kiev came under the rule of Vsevolod. Thus we find that the sons of Iaroslav the Wise reigned at Kiev in the following order: Iziaslav, Sviatoslav, Iziaslav, Vsevolod. Had Sviatoslav abided by the custom of family seniority, he would never have become a grand prince, for he died before his elder brother, Iziaslav. Iziaslav and Vsevolod accordingly regarded Sviatoslav's sons, Oleg and Iaroslav, as *izgoi*, (outcasts), and refused to give them their "patrimony," Chernigov. This brought on a long and bloody war, in which brothers, nephews and cousins took part, for Oleg and Iaroslav were not the only *izgoi*. After many years of strife the princes decided to settle their differences at a general peace conference, which assembled at Liubech in 1097. It was here agreed that each prince should "possess his own patrimony," *i.e.*, that Sviatopolk should keep Kiev, where his father Iziaslav had reigned; that Sviatoslav's children should have Chernigov, which had once belonged to their father; and that Vladimir Monomakh should take Pereiaslavl, where his father, Vsevolod, had reigned. Thus the sons of Sviatoslav, formerly treated as outcasts, were recognized as full-fledged princes. The other outcast princes were provided with land on the southwestern frontiers of Russia.

But the turmoil did not cease even after this regulation of the succession. When Grand Prince Sviatopolk died at Kiev in 1113, the inhabitants passed over the sons of Sviatoslav of Chernigov, whom they held responsible for the civil war, and invited Vladimir Monomakh of Pereiaslavl to be their prince. He hesitated at first, but was finally prevailed upon to come to Kiev. In this case popular choice upset the regular order of family succession to the throne of the grand prince.

From all this it is easy to understand the political troubles of Kiev Russia. The order of princely succession established after Iaroslav was complex, unfair to the outcast princes, and encouraged violence. Of course it was the mass of the people who suffered the most, and after a time they refused to recognize the seniority rights of the princes, and took matters into their own hands. It is obvious that under conditions such as these a normal succession to the throne was impossible, and the clan system of succession was bound to fail.

18. VLADIMIR MONOMAKH AND THE DESTINIES OF THE THRONE OF THE GRAND PRINCIPALITY OF KIEV UP TO 1169.—The election of Vladimir Monomakh to the throne of Kiev was approved by the people, who admired him, and by the princes, who feared and respected him. At the time of his accession, Monomakh was 60 years of age, wealthy, powerful and experienced in government affairs. He put down lawlessness and civil war, and maintained order. He also proved himself the terror of the Polovtsy, who dared not molest the Russians during his lifetime. It is easy, therefore, to understand the feeling of loyalty and love Monomakh inspired in the Russian people, both in his lifetime and since. Of his character we may learn something from his written "Instruction" to his children and his "Epistle" to Prince Oleg Sviatoslavich. He urges his children to shun idleness, to depend upon themselves, to be hospitable and generous, to have faith in God, to show this faith in good deeds, to keep their oaths, to love peace, to be humble, and to protect the weak. In his epistle to Oleg, Monomakh gently reproaches him for beginning war against him without first seeking a peaceful solution.

The inauguration of Vladimir Monomakh as Grand Prince of Kiev over the heads of his elder relatives led to the dissolution of family unity among the princes of Kiev, and aggravated the enmity which already existed between the various branches of the dynasty. Upon the death of Monomakh, Kiev fell to the possession, not of his brothers, but of his sons, and remained in the family.

His eldest son, the capable Prince Mstislav (1125-1132), was succeeded by his brothers, one after another. As long as they lived in peace their power in Kiev remained unshaken; but when strife broke out among them they were attacked by the sons and grandsons of Oleg Sviatoslavich, princes of Chernigov.

Whenever the Monomakhians were not warring against the Olegs they were fighting among themselves, the younger sons of Monomakh (Iuri Dolgoruki and his heir, Andrei Bogoliubski) with the children of Monomakh's oldest son. This struggle went on until Kiev was in ruins; and when, towards the end of the twelfth century, Andrei Bogoliubski at last got control of the capital, he did not think it was worth holding. After looting it he left it to one of the younger princes, while he remained in his principality of Rostov-Suzdal.

Such was the sad fate of the principality and throne of Kiev. The princes found it easier to go to war than to work out a proper system of succession and a stable political administration. In the course of the struggle, the dynasty became split up into several distinct and naturally hostile branches, each with its "patrimony." The descendants of Oleg were in possession of Chernigov, the country of Sieversk, and the territory of Riazan; the older line of the Monomakhians held Smolensk, Pereiaslavl, and Volynian territories; and the younger Monomakhians claimed the territory of Rostov-Suzdal. At Polotsk, again, there had been in power, ever since the days of St. Vladimir, a separate branch of princes founded by Prince Iziaslav, son of Vladimir. As long as the title of "Grand Prince" was worth something, the princes fought for it, but when it had lost its importance nobody respected it or the holder of it. Each princely family had its own "Grand Prince," who recognized no superior. Russia crumbled to pieces, and in place of an undivided state there grew up a number of *volosts*, or provinces, eyeing each other with suspicion and hate.

Strangely enough, at the very time that the Kiev state was breaking up economically and politically, there developed a national consciousness. Even when fighting one another, the princes never lost sight of the fact that they were "grandsons of the same grandfather." The inhabitants of the various provinces regarded themselves as part of an indivisible "Russian Land," and were ever ready to die in its defense. This is brought out by the chroniclers and poets. One of the Kiev annalists explains at some length "whence came the Russian land." Kiev to him was the capital, not merely of a province, but of the whole great Russian land. The bard of the "Song of Igor's Campaign" refers to the Sieversk princes, who were defeated, as "Russians." The *druzhinas* he calls "Russian Hosts," and he has the whole of Russia lamenting the downfall of both, and weeping over the fact that the feuds among the princes brought on the great tragedy.

19. THE STRUGGLE AGAINST THE STEPPE.—Political chaos and attacks by wild nomads were the two calamities of Kiev Russia. Mention has already been made of the victory (1034) of Iaroslav over the Pecheniegs. Their place was taken by other nomads from Asia, the Polovtsy, even more powerful and turbulent. The Polovtsy first attacked Russia in 1061, and thenceforward they continued unceasingly to harass the Russians. They raided and burned villages and towns, and massacred or carried off the inhabitants into the Crimea, where they were sold for the slave markets of Europe and Asia. There were so many of these raids that it was hard to

keep track of them; fifty of the more important (between 1061 and 1210) have, however, been recorded. Naturally the regions bordering on the steppe—Kiev, Pereiaslavl, Chernigov—suffered the most, and these were the very places where the civil war was at its worst. So bitter was the feud between the Russian princes that they sometimes invited the Polovtsy to join them in their campaigns, or instigated them to attack the Russians on their own account. As a rule, however, the princes protected their people as best they could. Forts and walled towns were built, mounted guards and scouts were kept in the field.

Sometimes the Russians took the offensive and attacked the Polovtsy in their camps. Monomakh was particularly successful in this kind of warfare, and his success was due in large measure to his ability to unite the princes against the "pagans." But when he died, and the feuds broke out again, the raids of the Polovtsy became worse than ever. The few attempts made to carry the war into the enemy's country ended in failure. This was the case of the Princes of Sieversk, Igor and Vsevolod, sons of Sviatoslav, and grandsons of Oleg Sviatoslavich of Chernigov, whose expedition against the Polovtsy in 1185 ended in their defeat and capture. The details of this unfortunate campaign are given in the chronicles and in the famous epic known as "The Song of Igor's Campaign." [14] The rout of the Russian *druzhinas* in the distant steppe, the capture of several princes, and Igor's successful flight from captivity, profoundly impressed the Russians. The catastrophe was ascribed by the people to the lack of peace and solidarity among the princes of Russia. The author of the *Slovo* complains

[14] *Slovo o Polku Igorevie.*

bitterly of this calamity, and urges the princes to harmony and peace. But they persisted in their feuds, and the Polovtsy continued their steady encroachments on Russian soil. By the second half of the twelfth century they had almost completely overrun and partly settled Pereiaslavl. They had gained control of all the highways of commerce, and trade with the Caspian Sea, the Sea of Azov and the Black Sea gradually declined and finally died out altogether. Kiev lost her importance as an intermediary between the trade of the West and the East. The inhabitants of the South Russian principalities, deprived of security and employment owing to the ceaseless feuds and raids, abandoned their homes and moved northward and westward where they could have peace and security.

20. ORGANIZATION OF THE VARIOUS PROVINCES OR PRINCIPALITIES OF THE STATE OF KIEV.—As we have seen, the State of Kiev in the ninth century was composed of separate "provinces" or "principalities," over which the "Grand Prince" of Kiev ruled. He was represented in each province by an official called a *posadnik*, usually a son of the grand prince or a member of his *druzhina*. But when the undivided authority of the grand prince disappeared and the dynasty multiplied and split up into separate branches, every city of importance came to have its own prince. The most important of these city provinces were: Kiev, Chernigov-Sieversk, Volynia, and Galicia, in the south of Russia; Polotsk, Smolensk, Novgorod, Rostov-Suzdal and Murom-Riazan, in the north of Russia.

Each province or territory had one city as its capital, which was called the "great" city; and its other cities were known as *prigorody*, or "province towns." The institution of the *vieche* (sec. 5), which flourished in the pre-Varangian period and declined in the era of the strong grand princes, recovered some prestige with the break-up of the Principality of Kiev. Many of the *vieches* became so strong that they laid down the law to their rulers, invited in those they admired, drove out those who were objectionable, and called on others to cease their feuds. One of the recovered powers was the selection of town officials, especially the commander [15] of the town militia, [16] the governors of the provincial towns, and sometimes, as in the case of Novgorod, the governor of the capital itself.

No written documents of the work of the *vieche* have come down to us, and we know little of its procedure. Whenever the prince or the "city elders" had anything of importance to communicate, the *vieche* bell was rung and the free adult inhabitants assembled in an open place. If people from the country towns happened to be in the city, they also came. Usually the prince or the city elders opened the meeting by bringing before the assembly the business of the day and calling for a vote. There was no secret or individual ballot. The assembled multitude made known its will by a mighty shout, and if there was no strong opposition the vote was regarded as unanimous. If, however, the opposition was loud and persistent, and refused to accept the decision of the chairman, the question was finally settled by a free-for-all fight.

The prince was not altogether displaced by the *vieche*. He had his special functions and duties. In time of peace he shared with the *vieche* the administration of the

[15] *Tysiatski.*
[16] *Tysiacha* ("The Thousand").

province. He presided over the *vieche*, made reports to it, represented it in dealing with neighboring princes or foreign powers. He was the chief judge and passed judgment on all important cases, leaving the less important to his assistants, the *tiuny*.

In time of war the prince had much power. He was the head of his own *druzhina* and of the city militia. His *druzhina* was made up of two parts, the older and the younger. In the first group were the "boyars," the freemen of high rank, and in the second the *gridi*, the free and half-free, the younger officers and the rank and file. From the boyars the prince chose his *duma* or council, and his important officers. He seldom undertook anything of importance without first consulting the principal boyars, for if they disapproved of his action they would refuse to support him, and would even "ride away" with their *druzhinas* [17] to serve another prince. Such an act was not regarded as treason.

The size of the prince's *druzhina* was limited by his wealth derived from his estates, tribute (*dan* of the province) and court fees.

21. SOCIAL CLASSES.—Serving the prince and being a member of his *druzhina* was a great honor and carried high social standing. It was the door to the boyarship, the aristocracy of that day. With the development of economic life, there grew up social distinctions based on wealth and occupation; [18] distinctions between the inhabitant of the city and the dweller of the village. A person who lived in his own homestead and tilled his own soil was a *smerd*, or freeman; but when he worked another

---

[17] Every *boyar* had a *druzhina* of his own.
[18] The rich in the city were referred to as "better," and the poor as "younger" or "black."

man's land and was bound to him by certain obligations he was a *zakup*, or bondman. He remained in the state of bondage until he could free himself from his obligations and acquire a little place of his own and become once more a *smerd*. The *smerdy* lived in communes (*vervi* or *pogosti*) and paid "tribute" (taxes) to the prince.

Slavery continued to exist during this period, the slaves being recruited almost entirely from prisoners of war and bankrupt debtors. The children of slaves were classed as slaves. Though Christianity succeeded in doing away with the harsher side of slavery, the Church was not as yet strong enough to do away with slavery as an institution. In many of the boyar villages the entire working population consisted of slaves (*cheliad*).

22. LEGAL INSTITUTIONS.—St. Vladimir and his successors, under the influence of the Church, tried to do away with the harsh pagan customs and to establish order and justice on a Christian basis. Tradition has it that the first written code of laws, the *Russkaia Pravda*, appeared in the time of Iaroslav the Wise. It was amended by his immediate successors and served as a guide for the civil and church courts. This code limited legal self-help, personal vengeance, and put in their places a legal court procedure and payment for injuries. At first, payments were made in furs (*kuny*), but later in metal (*grivny*). The money value of a member of the prince's *druzhina* was 80 *grivny;* of a freeman, 40; of a woman, 20. Property theft, abduction and concealment of slaves were severely punished. Taking it as a whole, the *Russkaia Pravda* shows that Christian ideas of justice were slowly but surely supplanting pagan customs.

In summing up we may say that the Varangian princes

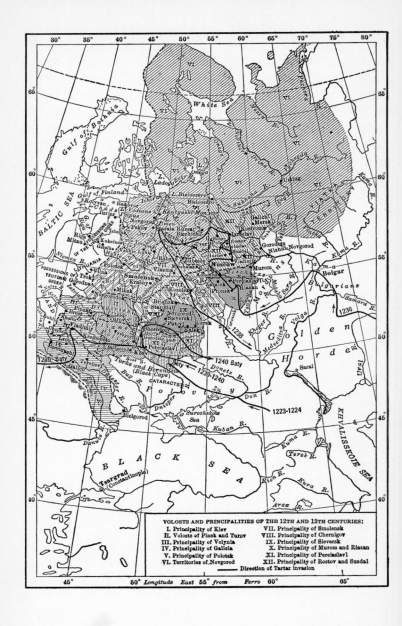

VOLOSTS AND PRINCIPALITIES OF THE 12TH AND 13TH CENTURIES:

I. Principality of Kiev
II. Volosts of Pinsk and Turov
III. Principality of Volynia
IV. Principality of Galicia
V. Principality of Polotsk
VI. Territories of Novgorod

VII. Principality of Smolensk
VIII. Principality of Chernigov
IX. Principality of Sieversk
X. Principality of Murom and Riazan
XI. Principality of Pereiaslavl
XII. Principality of Rostov and Suzdal

—— Direction of Tartar invasion

succeeded in uniting the scattered Russian tribes into a single political state. This union was, however, weak and mechanical, and fell to pieces when the princes began to fight among themselves. Real unity was brought about by Christianity and Byzantine culture. These influences, these spiritual ties, bound the Russians together into one strong state. Therein lies the principal historical significance of the Kiev period of Russian history.

CHAPTER TWO

NEW POLITICAL CENTERS

23. THE FORMATION OF NEW POLITICAL CENTERS AND THE FOREIGN INVASIONS OF THE THIRTEENTH CENTURY.—Towards the close of the twelfth century the city of Kiev, which had once aroused the admiration of foreign travelers by its splendor and riches, began to sink into poverty and desolation. The inhabitants of Kiev and the neighboring Dnieper provinces fled from the ravages of the Polovtsy and the feuds of the princes, seeking safety in the Carpathian Mountains and in the forest region of the Viatichi and beyond,[1] along the upper and middle Volga.

In the place and at the expense of the ancient capital there grew up, in the beginning of the thirteenth century, three new political centers: Lord Novgorod the Great, the city of Vladimir (in the Rostov-Suzdal region) and the city of Galich on the Dniester.

At Kiev, there was a struggle between the prince, the *vieche* and the boyars; while in each of the new centers one of these three political elements established itself in power at the expense of the other two. In Vladimir the prince controlled the government, in Novgorod the *vieche*, and in Galich the boyars. This accounts in part for the differences in their development.

Just as these new states were getting a good start,

[1] To the so-called Zaliesie (country beyond the forests).

Russia was invaded from all sides. The Tartars poured in from the southeast, the Germans attacked from the northwest, the Swedes harassed from the north, and the Lithuanians pressed from the west. Novgorod held its own against the Germans and the Swedes, but eastern and southwest Russia were overrun by Tartars and Lithuanians, who remained for a long time masters of the situation.

These new and difficult conditions, these struggles for self-preservation, brought out the very best qualities of the Russians and developed national heroes (such as Alexander Nevski, Daniel of Galich, Prince Dovmont, in Pskov) who knew how to rally the people in the fight for national preservation.

THE RUSSIA OF NOVGOROD

24. LORD NOVGOROD THE GREAT.—Lord Novgorod the Great included the city of Novgorod and the vast domains subject to it. The city, situated on the Volkhov River, had a "Business Quarter" on the right bank and a "Sophia Quarter" on the left bank. Each of these quarters was divided into "ends," two in one and three in the other, making five in all.[2] In the same way the

[2] The Business Quarter (*Torgovaia Storona*) derived its name from the *torg,* "trade," comprising the market square, commercial "courts" or halls, and arcades. This quarter was divided into two sections called "ends" (boroughs or precincts). The Sophia Quarter took its name from the famous Cathedral of St. Sophia, erected by Iaroslav the Wise. This quarter contained three "ends," and, besides these, had an inner fortress, or citadel, the *Dietinets.* It is believed that these various "ends" of the city had originally been separate villages which were later merged into one city, Novgorod (New City), with a common market place and the *Dietinets* in the center. Throughout the history of Novgorod the different "ends" of that city preserved their self-government.

territory under Novgorod was divided into five "fifths" (*piatiny*).[3]

This boundless area of Lord Novgorod the Great was sometimes spoken of as "the land of Novgorod," and sometimes as "the land of St. Sophia." Novgorod was the capital, and all other cities were outlying towns. The most important of these were Pskov, Staraia-Rusa, and Ladoga. During the thirteenth and fourteenth centuries, Novgorod and Pskov were the largest cities in Russia, but neither of them had a population of more than six or seven thousand households. In the eastern part there were no towns of any importance, only villages of from one to three hundred households.

25. GEOGRAPHICAL FEATURES OF LORD NOVGOROD.— With the exception of a few places in the southern *piatiny*, the soil of Lord Novgorod was not fit for agriculture. The population supported itself largely by hunting, fishing, and trading. It exchanged its products for those of the Baltic States, and these textiles, wines, and metals it bartered for the furs of the North, the grains of the Volga and the raw silk of the East.

In their pursuit of commerce, the Novgorodians penetrated the northern and northeastern parts of Russia, even beyond the Urals. They subjugated the natives, and exploited their forests, fishing grounds and salt mines. The independent trapper and small trader gave way in course of time to "merchant princes," the "boyars"

---

[3] (1) Obonega Piatina, Lake Onega to the White Sea;
(2) Vodskaia Piatina, Lake Ladoga to the Gulf of Finland;
(3) Shelon Piatina, Lake Ilmen and Shelon River;
(4) Derevskaia Piatina, southeast of Novgorod;
(5) Biezhetsk Piatina, along the watersheds of the Msta River and the tributaries of the Volga.
The four first mentioned were contiguous to the city of Novgorod, the fifth was a considerable distance away.

and large organized companies with their hundreds of servants, freemen and slaves, who went north and south, east and west in search of the materials of commerce.

There were several established water routes, with portages: a northern, by way of the Volkhov and Lake Ladoga; a southern, by the Msta, Lovat, Volga and Dnieper; a western, down the Volkhov, Lake Ladoga and Neva to the Gulf of Finland, or the Shelon, by way of Pskov to the Gulf of Riga. There was also an overland route to the west by way of Narva and Reval.

The trade with the West was at first in the hands of the "Gothic" merchants, men from Gothland, but during the thirteenth and fourteenth centuries it was taken over by the Hanseatic League of Northern Germany. The Germans in Novgorod had their own quarter, their own church, and their own exclusive corporation, or guild. The trade with the East was altogether in the hands of the Russians, and, judging from the numerous Arabian coins that are being dug up from time to time in Novgorod, there must have been considerable commerce with the Moslem world.

26. THE GOVERNMENT OF NOVGOROD.—During the tenth and eleventh centuries Novgorod was governed by the Grand Prince of Kiev through his representative, usually his son. But when, after the death of Vladimir Monomakh (1125), the princes weakened themselves by civil war, the Novgorod *vieche* demanded and obtained the right to select its own prince. Until the middle of the twelfth century, the Metropolitan at Kiev appointed the Novgorod bishop, but after that time the *vieche* was strong enough and rich enough to secure the right to name its own bishop from its own local clergy, leaving to the Metropolitan the benefits of investiture.

In the same way the *vieche*, little by little, gained the power of appointing the *posadniki* and *tysiatskie*, who had formerly been appointees of the prince.

In this manner Novgorod gained complete independence, complete self-government, with the *vieche* as the source of all power. It appointed and dismissed its highest officers; it made and unmade laws and treaties, and acted as the highest court of appeal. It transacted its business either at "Iaroslav's Court" in the Business Quarter, or the "Dietinets Square," in the Sophia Quarter. Every free citizen, the head of a household, had the right to come and vote. Questions were decided, not by counting heads, but by a general shout, which was regarded as "unanimously passed." In case of strong disagreement, the opposition set up a *vieche* of its own, and the two opposing forces settled their differences by a free-for-all fight on the Volkhov bridge. Under these conditions the *vieche* was not and could not be a deliberative body. It heard reports, approved or disapproved the recommendations or actions of its *Gospoda* (Council of Notables) or "*Herren*," as the Germans called it. This body was composed of the principal city officers, past and present, as well as other important citizens, and had at its head either the prince or the bishop. As time went on, the *Gospoda* became more aristocratic and more powerful.

On assuming office, the prince swore by the cross that he would "rule Novgorod after the ancient customs," that he would reside in the territory of Novgorod, that he would not appoint his friends to office, that neither he nor any member of his *druzhina* would acquire land or slaves in the domains of Novgorod, and that they would not engage in trade with the Germans. The prince was made to feel that he was an outsider. He was assigned quarters outside the city and was given to understand that the moment he misbehaved he would be shown "the way out of Novgorod."

Because he was an outsider, he was expected to play fair with all parties, to keep out of local feuds, act as mediator between quarreling factions, "to love the good and punish the wicked." As prince, he was the head of his own *druzhina* as well as of the military forces of the state; the head of the department of justice and administration. In practice he had, however, little power, for he could do little without first consulting the *posadnik*, a *vieche* appointee.

For his services the prince received "gifts," a definite amount of "tribute," the use of various public lands, and the right to hunt in certain reservations. In return, he granted to the citizens of Novgorod privileges in his own principality, the one from which he had originally been called to the throne of Novgorod.

The two other government officers, the *posadnik* and the *tysiatski*, were elected by the *vieche*, the one from the aristocracy and the other from the common people. The *posadnik* was at the head of civil affairs, with a court of his own, and was assisted by elected representatives of the various districts of the city; the *tysiatski* was in command of the city militia, with a court of his own, and assisted by military officers.

The Archbishop of Novgorod played an important part in the political life of the city. He was the head of the Council of Notables; he took a leading rôle in the meetings of the *vieche*, by giving or withholding his blessing to its acts; he acted as peacemaker when the *vieche* got into a fight. All negotiations with foreigners went through his hands; his seal was on all treaties; and to him foreigners turned for protection and redress. His residence near St. Sophia, as well as the cathedral itself, served as a meeting place for the Notables, as a state archive, and as a treasure house. The archbishop had vast church domains, and consequently a large staff of officials and even a considerable force of troops.

27. SOCIAL CLASSES AND CLASS STRUGGLE.—The inhabitants of Novgorod and its dependencies were divided into "better" and "lesser" people. In the first class were the boyars and the *zhitye* [3a] and in the second class the great mass of common people, the small traders, artisans, and laborers. In the *piatiny* the term "lesser people" was applied to the free and semi-dependent agricultural laborers.

Between the aristocratic rich and the free commoners there was constant strife. At first it was over the selection of the prince; later it was over class interests. Both tried to gain control of the *vieche*, and neither was particular about the means; the one packed the meetings, the other incited the rabble to attack and pillage the rich. The demoralization resulting from this class struggle was enhanced by the bitter feuds between the different boyar families, and sometimes one family and sometimes the other made common cause with the mob to down its enemy.

It was this turmoil and strife that caused the fall of Novgorod. The city became so weak that it could neither enforce obedience on the part of its provincial cities and dominions, nor defend itself against its outside enemies, Lithuania and Moscow. Conscious of the danger, but

[3a] The boyars were the wealthy families who had served the state with distinction; the *zhitye,* equally wealthy, were less aristocratic.

lacking the power to defend their independence in an open struggle, the Novgorodians tried to make an alliance with one of the two, but they could not agree among themselves even on this. The upper classes favored Lithuania, the lower, Moscow. It ended at last by Moscow's conquering Novgorod (1478) and absorbing it and all its territories.

28. PSKOV.—Pskov, situated on a rocky ledge at the confluence of the Pskova and Velikaia Rivers, was the principal provincial town of Novgorod. It was a western outpost and stood between the capital and the enemies from the west. This explains in part its importance. It started as a small fortress and, as the population overflowed the fortified area, walls were added until Pskov was as large as Novgorod. Inside the fortress stood the Cathedral of the Holy Trinity and the market place, and the same scenes were enacted here as in the capital. Like Novgorod it had provincial towns, about twelve in number, each a stronghold guarding Pskov.

The development of the Baltic trade had made Pskov so rich and powerful that it began to assert its independence of Novgorod. Finally, in 1348, by the Treaty of Bolotov, Novgorod recognized Pskov as its "younger brother." Thereafter, Pskov chose its own *posadniki* and princes, usually obtaining the latter from the Grand Principality of Moscow. Ecclesiastically, however, it remained subordinate to the archbishop of Novgorod. Its government was similar to that of the mother city, but class and property distinctions were less pronounced in Pskov than in Novgorod, and its *vieche* was better managed and more orderly. The peculiarities of the social organization of Pskov, and its legal and civic order, found expression in the independent Pskovian legislation evolved through the *vieche*. A monument of this legislation is the Pskovian Legal Code,[4] compiled in the fifteenth century, which served Pskov in place of the *Russkaia Pravda* of an earlier day.

The most celebrated and revered of the princes of Pskov were St. Vsevolod-Gabriel Mstislavovich, a grandson of Monomakh, and Dovmont, who had successfully defended the city in 1299, and controlled its destinies during the first period of its independence. As Moscow grew stronger, it fastened its hold on Pskov, and the princes of Pskov became, as it were, representatives of the Grand Princes of Moscow.

THE RUSSIA OF SUZDAL

29. SETTLEMENT OF SUZDAL TERRITORY BY RUSSIAN SLAVS AND FORMATION OF GREAT-RUSSIAN PEOPLE.— The name of Suzdalian Russia, or the Vladimir-Suzdalian Principality, is applied to the territory lying between the middle and lower Oka, on the one hand, and the upper and middle Volga, on the other, along the Kliazma and Moskva Rivers, tributaries of the Oka. This region was open for colonization, for the few scattered and primitive Finnish tribes were in no position to resist encroachments. At the dawn of Russian history there are already Slav settlements at Bielo Ozero, Rostov, Suzdal, and Murom (on the Oka). The cities of Vladimir (on the Kliazma) and Iaroslav (on the Volga) belong to the period of the Kiev princes. But until the end of the eleventh century all this northeastern territory was sparsely populated.

[4] *Pskovskaia Sudnaia Gramota.*

As a result of the Congress of Liubech (1097),[5] Suzdal was erected into an independent principality, and given to Vladimir Monomakh, who settled it on his youngest son Iuri,[6] and from this time forward the development of Suzdal, fostered by its princes, was rapid. Within a century it had become a powerful principality, with many flourishing cities, such as Moscow, Iuriev-Polski, Bogoliubovo, Tver, Kostroma, Galich-Merski, and others. The princes of Suzdal made special efforts to attract colonists from the older settlements by building roads through forests and swamps and by rendering other such facilities for travel. It was not long before many lines of settlers were making their way into the new country; those from Novgorod, Polotsk and Smolensk were drawn by the love of adventure and gain; those from Kiev were driven by the civil wars and the raids of the Polovtsy which devastated their homes.

The settlers from the south and the north brought with them their customs, place names, songs and stories. They married with one another and with the native Finns, and out of these intermarriages there emerged a new people, the Great Russians.

30. CHARACTER OF THE COUNTRY AND ITS EFFECTS UPON THE LIFE OF THE COLONISTS.—In the Suzdal region the men of Kiev and Novgorod found a country which differed greatly from their former homes. Though the sandy loam was not as fertile as the rich black earth in the Dnieper regions, it was yet much more fertile than in the Novgorod territory, and fertile enough to support the population. The forests offered various kinds of employment, such as apiculture, tar distillation, bast and fiber gathering, and hunting. But neither agriculture nor

[5] See Section 17.   [6] Called *Dolgoruki*, Long-Hands.

the forest industries as pursued there encouraged the growth of large cities, and for the most part the inhabitants lived in villages and hamlets.

Because the forests were dense the rivers became the highways of communication. The largest of them, the Volga and the Oka, skirted the boundaries of Suzdal, but numerous smaller streams penetrated into the very center of the principality. The immigrants settled along their banks and pushed out into the valleys. In Kiev the usual district consisted of a city with its surrounding countryside; in Suzdal, it was a river valley with its rural population. It is true that there were many cities in Suzdal, but as neither commerce nor industry attained any notable development, these cities were insignificant alongside those of the south, and were more like fortresses than centers of civilization.

Owing to the peculiar conditions of the colonization of Suzdal, the authority of its princes acquired, from the very beginning, great prestige. It was the princes who had built the cities, constructed the highways and the river crossings. When the settlers arrived in their new homes, they found the prince in full possession, and it was from him that they received the land; with him they signed their contracts; to him they paid taxes or "tribute" for its use; to him they were directly responsible; and to him they appealed in moments of danger. The prince was not only the sovereign, but the landlord, who had obtained title to the lands by right of a priority claim, and he could, therefore, dictate the conditions of occupation.

For similar reasons the institution of the *vieche* never grew in importance in Suzdal. In the cities which the prince built, the inhabitants were absolutely dependent on his will; and the old cities, Rostov and Suzdal, were not sufficiently strong to oppose him effectively.

These circumstances explain the power exercised by the princes of Suzdal, and show how they were enabled, as their principality began to fill up with settlers, to play such a part.

31. THE FIRST PRINCES OF SUZDAL.—Vladimir Monomakh made occasional visits to Suzdal, but otherwise paid little attention to it. His son, Iuri Dolgoruki, who had grown up here and had done much for the principality, may be called the first Prince of Suzdal. But even he could not free himself from the politics and feuds of his generation. He got into a fight for the title of grand prince, succeeded in establishing himself at Kiev (1154) and died there (1157).

Andrei Bogoliubski, his son, was a loyal Suzdalian. He helped his father in the north, fought by his side in the south, but when that conflict was over he turned his back on turbulent Kiev and the honors his father offered him there, carried off some of the holy ikons and went back to his own Vladimir. When Iuri died, Rostov and Suzdal took Andrei as their prince, regardless of the claims of his brothers, and in this way he became lord of the whole of Suzdal. He got rid of his brothers and the powerful nobles, he ignored the *vieches* of Rostov and Suzdal, and governed to suit himself.

Though Vladimir was a "provincial town" of Rostov, yet Andrei made it his capital rather than Rostov or Suzdal which had too much of the *vieche* tradition about them. But he spared no expense to make Vladimir the principal city of his principality. He fortified it, he erected fine stone churches,[7] especially the Uspenski Cathedral, which became the chief sanctuary for the whole region.[8]

Andrei was not content to be merely lord of his own principality; he was ambitious to be the ruler of the whole of Russia. He insisted on naming the prince of Novgorod and though that city defied and fought him, yet in the end it had to accept his dictation for he could starve it out by barring the way to the food supplies of the Volga. Against Kiev he sent an army which captured the city (1169) and returned to Vladimir loaded down with loot and the title of grand prince. He demanded submission from all Russian princes and those who refused quickly felt the force of his arm. His autocratic ways made Andrei many strong friends and bitter enemies. Those who favored a united and orderly country admired him, but those who stood for the old order hated him and assassinated him in 1175.

Andrei left no sons and immediately after his death there was a grand fight among the cities for supremacy and among the princes for the succession. Vsevolod, a young brother of Andrei, survived the struggle and established himself at Vladimir. He followed pretty much the policy of his brother and during his period of government (1176-1212) his word was law throughout Russia. So numerous were his warriors that the poet in the "Song

[7] The strikingly beautiful architecture of the oldest churches of Suzdalian Russia, with their remarkable sculptural adornments, has brought them great celebrity and fame. Their splendor and elegance bear testimony to the refined artistic taste and craftsmanship, as well as to the great wealth, of their builders, the princes of the twelfth and thirteenth centuries.

[8] Andrei placed in this Cathedral a wonder-working image of the Holy Virgin, which, according to tradition, had been painted by St. Luke.

of Igor's Campaign" says that Vsevolod could "splash the Volga dry with his oars, and empty the Don with his helmets."

This undivided authority came to an end with Vsevolod. His oldest son, Constantine, intimated that he preferred Rostov to Vladimir as a capital. This remark so angered the father that in the presence of the clergy and the *druzhina* he deprived Constantine of the right of succession and gave it to the second son, Iuri. When Vsevolod died the sons and nephews engaged in a civil war, and as neither side was strong enough to overcome the other, the fight ended in the restoration of the old order and the breaking up of the principality. The grand prince kept Vladimir, and the others held on to what they could and each was practically independent of the others. The old clannish system of succession, with brother following brother and nephew succeeding uncle, was restored. The only difference between Suzdal and ancient Kiev consisted in the fact that the cities of Suzdal had no *vieche*, and consequently their princes were absolute masters within their "appanages" (*udiely*), as their dominions now came to be called.

SOUTHWESTERN RUSSIA

32. PRINCIPALITIES OF VOLYNIA AND GALICIA.—At the same time that the principality of Suzdal in northeastern Russia was growing and gaining power, there began also the rise and prosperity of the territories of Volynia and Galicia in southwestern Russia.[9]

Volynia, with the city of Vladimir-Volynski as the

[9] About the year 1200 the two were consolidated into a single powerful principality.

capital, occupied the region along the right bank of the
Western Bug and extended through the upper reaches
of the Pripiat River as far as the Southern Bug. Its
name was derived from the ancient town of Volyn and
the tribe of the Volynians [10] who had lived there. It
had been subject to the princes of Kiev from the earliest
times, but from about the middle of the twelfth century
a line of local princes established themselves here and
reached out for more. Thus the older branch of the
Monomahk line acquired in Volynia a permanent "patrimony" and strove to add to this the older principality of
Kiev. Especial success attended the efforts of the son of
Mstislav Iziaslavich, Roman Mstislavich, who, after a
protracted struggle, won not only the throne of Kiev, but
also the principality of Galicia, bordering upon Volynia.

Its borderland position laid Galicia open to attacks
from Poles, Hungarians and nomads. Partly for this
reason it was not a desirable portion and was usually
given to one of the younger princes when there was nothing better for him in Russia. Towards the close of the
eleventh century Galicia, with Galich as the capital,
became a separate principality, and in the twelfth century, in the time of Prince Volodimirko and his son
Iaroslav [11] it grew into considerable importance. These
two princes succeeded in uniting the country under their
rule. They extended the boundaries of the principality
by conquest, they attracted settlers from Poland, Hungary, and Russia by offering fertile soil, they took advantage of the geographical position of Galicia to make it
a highway of commerce between western Europe and
Russia. By these means Galicia became prosperous and

[10] Buzhans and Duliebs.
[11] Sometimes called Iaroslav Osmomysl.

strong and in the "Song of Igor's Campaign" Iaroslav Osmomysl is ranked with Vsevolod.

After the death of Iaroslav there was a short period of anarchy which led to the extinction of his line and the conquest of Galich by Prince Roman Mstislavich of Volynia in 1199. He united the two principalities and his son Daniel Romanovich continued the work of consolidation.

The histories of northeast and southwest Russia have some points of similarity, but many points of difference. Both developed rapidly by the influx of settlers from neighboring states. But whereas Suzdal was surrounded by passive aboriginal tribes, Volynia-Galicia was encircled by aggressive Poles, Lithuanians, Hungarians, and Polovtsy. The princes of the southwest had to be ever ready to fight the one or the other, to combine with one against the other. In this way, foreign powers were brought into the affairs of Volynia-Galicia and they used their opportunities for their own advantage.

Another point of difference between the north and the south was their internal development. At Suzdal the prince succeeded in doing away with the city *vieche;* in the south the ruler failed to crush the powerful boyar aristocracy.

These two factors—interference of foreign princes and a turbulent aristocracy—led to the decline of Volynia-Galicia and to its conquest by the Poles and Lithuanians.

THE EPOCH OF THE TARTAR CONQUEST

33. THE COMING OF THE TARTARS.—When the decline of Kiev had run its full course and new centers, Novgorod, Suzdal, Galich, were appearing in its place,

the Tartars made their appearance in Russia. "There came a people," the chronicle tells us, "of whom nobody knew anything for certain, whence they had come, what was their speech, and of what race and what faith they might be."

The original home of the Tartars was Mongolia. Their scattered and savage clans had been welded together by Khan Temuchin, who assumed the title of Jenghiz Khan, *i.e.*, "Grand Khan." In 1213 he entered on his series of conquests by taking northern China. His armies moved westward, subjugating the people and devastating the country as they went along. After a time they came to the Caspian Sea, the southern shore of which they followed, then crossed the Caucasus Mountains, poured down into the steppes of the Black Sea, and came into conflict with the Polovtsy. These appealed to the princes of Kiev, Chernigov, Galicia and others to help them, and though the Tartars told the princes that they had no war with them they nevertheless joined the Polovtsy. The two forces engaged in battle on the river Kalka (1223), in which the Russians were crushed and the flower of their army annihilated. The Tartars followed the refugees as far as the Dnieper, then turned eastward and disappeared as suddenly as they had come.

In 1227 Jenghiz Khan died and his domains were divided among his descendants. One of them, Baty, a nephew, led a large horde of his subjects across Siberia, over the Urals, and fell on the Bulgars on the Volga. They were easily defeated and the road was open to the Russian possessions. The Russian princes were too much divided to coöperate and Baty had little difficulty in defeating one after another.

In the course of the winter 1237-38 the Tartars devastated the territories of Riazan, Moscow, Suzdal, Vladimir, and Tver. Some of the inhabitants were taken captive, others were massacred, and those who were left were made to pay tribute. On their way to the open steppes of the Polovtsy in the southeast the invaders were halted for a short time at the siege of the town of Kozelsk, the inhabitants of which put up a heroic defense. Apart from this, Baty met no opposition of importance.

After resting a year, Baty started on the warpath once more. He overran Pereiaslavl and Chernigov, sacked Kiev after a desperate fight (1240), subjugated Volynia and Galicia, and crossed the Carpathians into Hungary and Poland. By this time western Europe was alarmed and when the forces of East and West crossed swords in Bohemia, Baty found such strong resistance that he retreated. He retraced his march to the lower Volga and there founded Sarai, the capital of the "Golden" or "Kipchak" Horde Tartars.

34. TARTAR RULE IN RUSSIA.—The Russians were not dispossessed, for the Tartars preferred to live on the open grazing lands of the south. The Russians, nevertheless, felt the heavy yoke of the conqueror. Before taking office the Russian princes had to present themselves before the Khan and do homage, and during the first period they had to go even to Mongolia where the Grand Khan lived. A heavy and humiliating tribute was imposed on the people and at times the burden became so heavy that revolts broke out. Conditions grew better rather than worse as time went on. Little by little the princes secured the right to collect the Tartar tax in

their own territory and in this way saved their people from the outrages of the Tartar tribute collector.

It should be said to the credit of the Tartars that they did not interfere with the institutions of the Russians. Not only were they tolerant in religious matters but they also exempted the clergy from taxation and other onerous obligations. They left it to the princes to settle their own political questions, but when feuds broke out among them the Tartars took advantage of the opportunity to exercise their authority and to punish with a heavy hand. On the whole they did not disturb the old order and this circumstance helped the Russians to gather strength for the future struggle with their masters.

The Tartar conquest cut off Suzdalian Russia from Novgorod, where German influence was felt, and from Kiev and the southwest where Polish ideas were penetrating. This isolation and the shielding of western Europe from Tartar oppression explains the cultural backwardness and stagnation of the Great Russians during the thirteenth and fourteenth centuries, and the impress of Mongolian customs and manners upon their lives. This Tartar influence may easily be exaggerated. The Tartars lived apart, they had little to give, and even that little was at first resisted by the Russians because of the hatred of their conquerors. It was not until the fifteenth century, when friendlier relations between the two peoples were established, when the Tartars ceased to be masters and became subjects and had settled alongside the Russians, and intermarriages took place, that there came to be an interchange of customs, manners and ideas.

35. GERMANS AND LITHUANIANS.—While the Tartars attacked Russia from the east the Swedes, Danes,

and Germans advanced upon her from the west. The Swedes conquered Finland, the Danes took Esthonia, and the Germans colonized the lands at the mouths of the Western Dvina and the Niemen. With these territories in their possession the Swedes and Germans reached out for more, and by the middle of the thirteenth century were in open conflict with the Russian cities. The attacks of the Swedes were soon repulsed but the advance of the Germans was not so easily checked.

In the middle of the twelfth century north German merchants sailed into the Western Dvina and opened trade relations with the natives. Pretty soon afterwards missionaries came who baptized the Letts, Finns and the Lithuanians. But the natives did not take kindly to this treatment and at the first opportunity dived into the river "to wash off" the holy water. The Pope decided to establish a permanent mission and with that in view appointed Albert as Bishop of Livonia, gave him a staff of helpers and a small army of crusaders. They sailed up the mouth of the Dvina and founded the city of Riga in 1200. Two years later (1202) Bishop Albert founded the order of "Sword Bearers." [12] The new order was governed by a Master but was dependent on the bishop. With the help of these knights Livonia was conquered, the natives converted, and the country opened to German trade and settlement.

During the years 1225-1230 another religious order, the "Teutonic Knights," took possession of the region between the Niemen and the Vistula. It had come here at the invitation of Konrad of Mazovia, a Polish prince,

---

[12] "Gladiferi." The Knights wore a white robe with a red cross and sword on the shoulder.

who was anxious to have some one between him and the warlike Lithuanian Prussians. The newcomers had a disciplined military organization which gradually crushed the Prussians and turned their lands into a German territory in feudal dependence on the Emperor. In this manner the two orders, encouraged and supported by Pope and Emperor, firmly established themselves on the shores of the Baltic at the mouths of its important rivers.

The German invasion was quickly felt in Russia. In the first place the Germans pushed into the interior and after a hard fight seized the lands of the Prince of Polotsk along the Dvina, captured Iuriev (Dorpat) and secured temporary possession of Pskov. In the second place the German pressure on the Lithuanians forced the latter to fall back on the Russian settlements in Polotsk, Kiev, and Volynia.

36. North Russia. Prince St. Alexander Nevski. The Appanage System.—In 1238 Iaroslav Vsevolodo-vich, who became Grand Prince of Suzdal, set to work to rebuild the cities and to reëstablish order out of the chaos left by the Tartars. Making a virtue out of a necessity, he went to pay homage first to Baty on the Volga, then to the Grand Khan in Mongolia and there he died in 1246. He was succeeded by his brother and later by his sons, of whom Alexander Nevski is the best known.

Alexander Iaroslavich made a name for himself while Prince of Novgorod. In 1240 the Swedes invaded the principality by way of Finland and had come as far as the junction of the Neva with the Izhora. Here Alexander fell on them and defeated them so decisively that he has been known ever since as Alexander Nevski (of the Neva). The churchmen have interpreted this deed as a victory of the Orthodox over the Catholic Church, and have canonized the hero.

Soon after this the Germans captured Izborsk and Pskov, and came within twenty miles of Novgorod. Alexander drove them back to Lake Peipus, and there, on a cold day in the winter of 1242, engaged the main body on the ice and inflicted such severe punishment on the Sword Bearers that they were glad enough to let the Russians alone after that.

In 1245 Alexander took the field against the Lithuanians and forced them out of the territories of Novgorod.

When, soon after the death of his father (1246), Alexander became Grand Prince of Vladimir, he was faced with more serious problems than before. He realized that he was too weak to overthrow the Tartars and therefore submitted to them and urged all other Russians to do likewise. In 1263, as he was returning from a visit to the Khan, he was taken ill and died on the way, deeply mourned by the oppressed people as the man who had given his life "for the Russian land, for Novgorod, for Pskov, for the grand principality, and for the Orthodox faith."

Under the appanage system of the thirteenth and fourteenth centuries, the succession to the Grand Principality of Vladimir was still passed around, at least theoretically, among the members of the dynasty according to the old custom. But all the other principalities were no longer regarded as belonging to the dynasty but to the individual reigning princes, to do with as they pleased. He who obtained from the Khan the title of Grand Prince did not even move to Vladimir. He governed it from his own capital and was known by his own capital, Iaroslav of Tver, Basil of Kostroma, Andrei of Gorodets. As time

went on and these princely estates were cut up to provide for all the sons, each principality came to have its
own line of "grand princes," and a struggle ensued among
the various local princes for the headship of the line and
among the numerous local grand princes for the honor
of the title of Grand Prince of Vladimir and "all the
Russias." This fight demoralized Russia in every way
and resolved itself into a struggle for the survival of
the fittest.

37. SOUTHWEST RUSSIA. PRINCE DANIEL OF GALICIA.
—For twenty-five years Prince Daniel Romanovich was
engaged in fighting his neighbor princes and keeping
down his own unruly nobles. He had barely succeeded
in establishing himself firmly in his position when the
Tartar hordes swept over Volynia, Galicia and other
parts of southwest Russia under his control. When the
smoke had cleared away he commenced to rebuild the
devastated area. He invited colonists from Poland,
Hungary and Germany to settle his lands and encouraged
commerce with neighboring states. Outwardly he submitted to the Khan but at the same time schemed to free
himself from his yoke. He cast about for allies and
promised to unite with the Catholic Church if the Pope
would declare a crusade against the Tartars. The Pope
sent him a crown but no crusade, and therefore Daniel
turned for help elsewhere. He concluded an alliance
with Prince Mindovg of Lithuania but before anything
came of that the Khan got wind of it and forced Daniel
to destroy his fortresses.

Daniel had to give up the idea of fighting the Tartars
and pay attention to the Lithuanians who were encroach-
ing upon his territories. He invaded Lithuania a number of times and forced Mindovg to sue for peace and

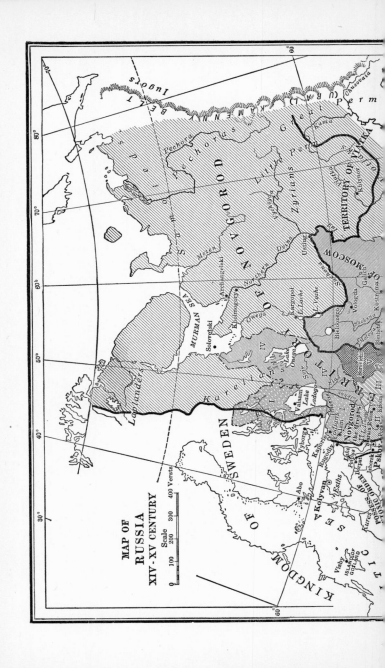

MAP OF
RUSSIA
XIV-XV CENTURY

Scale
0   100   200   300   400 Versts

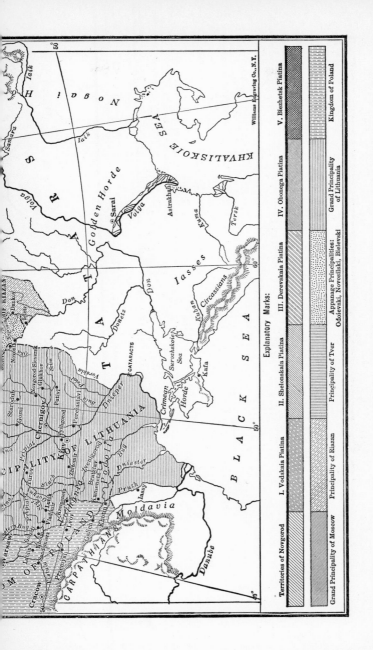

pay tribute. A marriage alliance was concluded between the two princely houses and in this way Russian influence increased in Lithuania.

Daniel, who died in 1264, holds a high place in Russian history. Like Alexander Nevski, his contemporary, Daniel Romanovich was a great soldier and an able statesman. He left to his descendants a better inheritance than Alexander, for southwestern Russia was farther from the Tartars and felt their oppression less than northeastern Russia. The same restlessness, the same feuds ruined the one and the other. But while in the north the struggle ended in a victory of one of the Russian princes, in the south the Russians fought, but the foreign powers got the spoils of war. About the middle of the fourteenth century, Lithuania seized Volynia, Poland took Galicia, and all the noble efforts of Prince Daniel Romanovich were undone.

CHAPTER THREE

THE GRAND PRINCIPALITY OF LITHUANIA

38. THE FIRST LITHUANIAN PRINCES.—During the thirteenth century the Lithuanian tribes, being hard pressed by the Germans, united for common defense under Prince Mindovg. He seized the Russian town of Novgorodok, on the upper Niemen, which he made his capital, and from there gradually extended his conquests until they included the Russian territories of Polotsk, Vitebsk, and part of Smolensk. Mindovg was a crafty warrior and statesman and made every means serve his end. He united with friendly Lithuanians against unfriendly Russians, with friendly Russians against unfriendly Lithuanians, and led both Lithuanians and Russians against the Germans. When it served his purpose he had himself baptized and accepted a crown from the Pope; when it was no longer to his advantage he relapsed into paganism. He fought Daniel Romanovich of Galicia until he exhausted himself and then he made an advantageous peace by proposing a marriage alliance between the two princely houses. He naturally had many enemies, especially among the Lithuanians, and they assassinated him in 1263. One of the men implicated in the plot was Prince Dovmont, who escaped to Pskov, where he was baptized, became the Prince of Pskov and successfully defended that city against invaders.[1]

[1] See Section 28.

The death of Mindovg was followed by civil war which lasted off and on until 1316, when Prince Gedimin came to power. He made Vilna his capital and from there ruled over a strong state extending from Polotsk to Kiev, one-third of which was Lithuanian and two-thirds Russian. Russian influence which made itself felt in the time of Mindovg became quite marked in the days of Gedimin, especially in the army, in diplomacy and in court circles where Russian was the language spoken. The two peoples intermarried, lived side by side, and were gradually becoming one. Gedimin signed himself "rex Litwinorum Ruthenorumque," king of both Lithuanians and Russians. This peaceable relation between the two nationalities, one pagan and the other Christian, this toleration in religious matters, explains the rapidity and ease with which Gedimin and his dynasty brought under their rule southwestern Russia.

Gedimin's two sons divided their father's kingdom, Olgerd taking the Russian, and Keistut the Lithuanian part. The two brothers stood by each other in their wars and succeeded in checking the Germans and in uniting virtually all of southern and southwestern Russia, including Kiev and Volynia.

39. Union of Lithuania and Poland. Iagailo.— Olgerd, who was looked up to by the Russians as the restorer of the Russian state along the Dnieper, died in 1377 and left a son, Iagailo, who had neither his father's ability nor his tact. Iagailo commenced his reign by falling out with his uncle and having him murdered in 1382, and followed it up by a marriage alliance with Poland which brought elements of discord into the Russo-Lithuanian state.

In addition to internal struggles among the nobles,

Poland was threatened in Galicia by the Lithuanians, and on or about the Baltic by the Germans. Under the circumstances Polish statesmen decided on a union of Poland and Lithuania which would not only remove one of the enemies, but would also make it possible to face the other with a stronger force. An alliance was formed and in 1386 Iagailo married Queen Jadwiga of Poland and became King Wladyslaw of Poland. From now on his interests are more Polish than Lithuanian. He not only removed the Lithuanian pressure on Galicia, but he also used Lithuanian forces to help the Poles reconquer Galician territory from the Hungarians. In 1410 a combined army of Lithuanians, Russians, and Poles so overwhelmingly defeated the Teutonic Knights at Grünwald and Tannenberg that the Order never fully recovered.

In accordance with the conditions of the alliance Iagailo became Catholic and authorized Polish priests to baptize his non-Catholic subjects. At once a religious question came up to disturb the harmony which had existed between the Lithuanians and the Russians. Until 1386 the pagan Lithuanians and Orthodox Russians lived side by side in peace, the culture and religion of the latter gradually spreading among the former. Had the process been allowed to go on, the two peoples would have become one. But when Iagailo became King Wladyslaw, Polish interests, culture, religion and nobility began to predominate at the expense of the Lithuanian and Russian and, as a result, bitter national, cultural and religious antagonisms developed.

40. Vitovt.—The leader of the opposition was Vitovt, son of Keistut. He had his troubles with Iagailo, but in the end made his peace with him and in 1392 was recognized as Grand Prince of Lithuania by Iagailo. Accord-

ing to the agreements between the Polish and Lithuanian aristocracies in 1401 and 1413, the union of their two countries was put on a dynastic basis, and Vitovt was nominally a vassal of Wladyslaw. But for all practical purposes Vitovt was independent and carried out his own policies, which were also the policies of Keistut and Olgerd. He added Smolensk (1395) to his other Russian lands in the east until the Lithuanian principality extended "from the Baltic to the Black Sea." He reached out for territory in the north and northeast, but there he came in contact with the Grand Prince of Moscow, who stoutly resisted him, and forced him to agree to make the Ugra River (branch of the Oka) the boundary of their domains. Vitovt even attempted to humble the Tartars, but was defeated.

Vitovt had the backing of his Orthodox Russian subjects and the anti-Polish factions in Lithuania. Had he adopted a Russian Orthodox policy, he might have created a Russian grand principality to rival and even to supersede Moscow. He did not do so because he needed the help of the Poles against the Germans; he did not adopt a Lithuanian national policy because the Lithuanians themselves were not of one mind. At the Polish-Lithuanian Congress held in 1413 it was agreed that the subjects of the Lithuanian Grand Prince who should become Catholic would have the right to hold office in Lithuania, and would have the same rights and privileges as Poles of the same classes. Many of the Lithuanians took advantage of this agreement, became Catholic and supporters of a strong Polish-Lithuanian Union. After this there were three distinct parties fighting for control —an Orthodox-Russian, an Old Lithuanian, and a Catholic-Polish. Each regarded Vitovt as its leader. He treated them all alike, but never allied himself with any one of them. When he died in 1430 he left them unreconciled and antagonistic.

41. The Lithuanian Principality After Vitovt. —After the death of the childless Vitovt the successors to the grand princely throne, chosen by the higher dignitaries of Lithuania, pursued an independent Lithuanian policy. The union with Poland remained only as an idea; but to abandon this idea entirely was impossible, for Poland and Lithuania needed each other's help against their common outside foes. Iagailo's youngest son, Kazimir (1440-1492), having been chosen Grand Prince of Lithuania in his childhood, and later King of Poland, united for a time the two countries. But upon his death Lithuania again separated from Poland and selected Alexander Kazimirovich as Grand Prince of Lithuania. When, however, in 1501 Poland elected Alexander as King it was agreed that hereafter the two states would elect one and the same ruler. In this manner was brought about the personal union dreamed of in 1386.

Notwithstanding the constant opposition to Polish union, *Polish influence continued to grow in Lithuania throughout the XV century*. Although the grand princes of Lithuania acted independently, they and their officials were of the Catholic persuasion and under the influence of Polish culture. As long as the appanage princes were still powerful, this did not greatly matter, for each prince governed his own province independently. If he happened to be Orthodox or Russian, his province did not feel the Catholic and Polish pressure. But during the XV century the authority of the Lithuanian grand Princes had greatly increased, the administration was more centralized, and the provincial princes became the lieutenants and servants of the grand prince. Catholics were favored at the expense of the Orthodox, and Poles over Russians. Government positions were filled with princes and boyars of the Roman faith (as a result of the union of 1413), and Orthodox Russians felt humiliated and wronged.

Some of the Russian nobles renounced Orthodoxy and embraced Catholicism and Polish culture with all they had to offer; others renounced their allegiance to the Grand Prince of Lithuania and attached themselves with their provinces to the Grand Prince of Moscow; still others, availing themselves of the ancient privilege to leave one lord for another, left Lithuania and entered the service of Moscow. In this manner Moscow was drawn into Lithuania, attacked her and threatened to take from her all Russian territories. As these attacks and threats increased, Lithuania was forced to cling closer and closer to Poland for protection.

Russian aristocrats and princes were not the only ones to suffer under the Catholic Government of Lithuania. During the first period of its history the Lithuanian-Russian principality had a Russian social organization, inherited from Kiev Russia. The provincial princes were surrounded by their *druzhina*, made up of free servitors and serfs. In the center of the rural district stood the city with its *vieche*, upon which depended the *volost*, or province, inhabited by a free peasantry (*smerdy*). According to the terms of the union, all Lithuanians converted to Catholicism lived under Polish law, that is, they were granted those privileges which were enjoyed by persons of the corresponding classes in Poland. But in Poland at that period was definitely established a peculiar feudal order, with sharply differentiated classes, the gentry (*szlachta*) dominating. The Polish gentry had gradually become the ruling class, with vast political and proprietary rights. This class had very few obligations towards the state, and it exerted its influence upon the administration of the country and the election of the kings. It enjoyed certain privileges in the ownership of land, and on its estates it was given unlimited power over the peasant serfs, who had no rights. These Polish conditions, advantageous to the nobility, but unbearable for the rest of the population, were finding their way also into the Lithuanian state when it began to grant to its Catholic subjects equal rights with the corresponding classes of Polish society.

In the Russo-Lithuanian state there was a class of nobles, boyars and others, who rendered military service in return for land. They did not, however, possess the same political rights and social privileges as the same class in Poland. Many of these Lithuanian nobles were quite willing to become Poles and Catholics in order to have the rights and privileges of the Polish *pans* and *szlachta*. They adopted Polish manners and customs; they kept the peasants in bondage; put themselves in possession of the land; and strove to be the politically dominant class. Furthermore, they served as the propagators of Polish influence in all domains of the political and social life of Lithuania. In this way the old order decayed and a sharp internal conflict began between the all-powerful nobility and the rest of the population.

BEGINNING AND RISE OF THE PRINCIPALITY OF MOSCOW

42. CAUSES OF THE ASCENDANCY OF MOSCOW.—It has been said already (sec. 36) that during the epoch of

the Tartar conquest the appanage system of princely rule had developed in Vladimir and Suzdal, and that it ended with the ascendancy of Moscow.

The principality of Moscow began its separate existence during the second half of the thirteenth century. According to tradition, Moscow had been founded by Prince Iuri Dolgoruki.[2] In the beginning the city of Moscow was a fortified place, built on the southern frontier of the Suzdal territory to protect it from Riazan and Chernigov in the south. Baty, on his way from Riazan to Suzdal and Vladimir, captured and sacked the city of Moscow en route. During the first century of its existence it was a possession of the Prince of Vladimir. Prince Alexander Nevski (sec. 36) left his youngest son, Daniel, in Moscow, and after that Moscow became a separate appanage of Daniel's descendants, and grew in strength and influence.

The primary cause of the ascendancy of Moscow was its *exceptionally favorable geographical position*. It was situated at a junction of several highways leading from south Russia to the north, and from the territories of Novgorod to those of Riazan. Colonists going north from the southern provinces passed through Moscow and settled in the neighborhood for a time at least before resuming their way farther north. In this way the Principality of Moscow was quickly and densely populated, and this furnished its princes with large resources; for the greater the density of the population, the larger the revenues. The Moskva River connected the upper Volga with the middle Oka, and the Novgorodians used this

---

[2] The chronicles mention the name of Moscow first in 1147 (and subsequently in 1156 and 1176, calling the place "Kuchkovo" and "Moskva").

route to ship to their own country grain, wax and honey from the richest sections of Riazan. The Moscow princes profited by this commercial traffic and their wealth gave them a great deal of power and lust for more territory.

Another reason for the rise of Moscow was the *ability and cleverness of the first Moscow rulers.* They knew how to take full advantage of their favorable position. The first two princes of Moscow, Daniel Alexandrovich and his son, Iuri, succeeded in obtaining possession of the whole course of the Moskva River by taking from the Prince of Riazan the city of Kolomna at its mouth, and from the Prince of Smolensk the city of Mozhaisk near its headwaters. In addition, Prince Daniel got the city of Pereiaslavl-Zaliesski by the bequest of the childless Prince of Pereiaslavl. The lands and riches of Iuri Danilovich increased to such an extent that he decided, as a representative of the oldest line of the stock of Iaroslav Vsevolodovich, to ask the Horde to recognize him as the head of the Grand Principality of Vladimir. This brought him into open conflict with the Prince of Tver. In the end, however, Moscow won out. In 1328 Iuri's brother, Ivan, nicknamed *Kalita* (the purse), gained the sceptre of the Grand Prince, and from that time on it remained in the hands of the Moscow dynasty.

43. GRAND PRINCE IVAN KALITA AND HIS IMMEDIATE SUCCESSORS.—Concerning the reign of Grand Prince Ivan Danilovich Kalita little is known. As soon as he ascended the throne, the chronicler informs us, "there was thenceforth a great quietness throughout the Russian land, and the Tartars ceased fighting against the Russian land." To the same prince is given the credit of obtaining the right to collect the *vykhod*, or tribute (sec. 34), for the Horde and thereby keeping the Tartars out of

Russian territory. The order and tranquillity in the dominions of Kalita attracted new settlers—both common people and distinguished boyars with multitudes of retainers. But his greatest triumph was the making of Moscow the capital of the Metropolitan of Russia.

With the decline of Kiev the question came up whether the Metropolitan should remain in the run-down city or seek a new residence. About 1300, after one of the Tartar raids on Kiev, Metropolitan Maxim settled this question by moving to Vladimir. The primate's removal to the north made the Princes of Galicia request the Patriarch of Constantinople to appoint a Metropolitan for southwestern Russia. The Patriarch, however, refused thus to split the Russian Church. Upon the death of Maxim he appointed the Volynian Abbot Peter as Metropolitan, and Peter followed the example of Maxim and made Vladimir his official residence. However, as Vladimir was no longer the capital of the Grand Prince, and was being fought over by the princes of Tver and Moscow, the Metropolitan was forced to take sides. He supported Ivan Kalita of Moscow, spent much time with him at Moscow, built there the famous Cathedral of the Assumption (Uspenski, modeled after the Uspenski Cathedral of Vladimir) and was buried there. His successor, the Greek Theognostus, definitely established the Metropolitan See in Moscow. Moscow came to be the religious and later the political center of all Russia. Tradition has it that in building the Cathedral of the Assumption, Metropolitan Peter predicted the glorious future of Moscow to Ivan Kalita, who at that time was not yet Grand Prince.

Such were the first triumphs gained by the Princes of Moscow by virtue of their farsightedness, favorable situation, and support of the clergy. The results of these successes began to tell at once. In the reign of Kalita (1328-1341) and of his two sons, Simeon the Proud (1341-1353) and Ivan the Red (1353-1359), Moscow began decidedly to dominate the other principalities. Ivan Kalita treated Tver, Novgorod and Rostov as he pleased. Simeon "the Proud," in the words of the chronicler, had "all Russian princes under his hand." Because of their strength, wealth and the support of the Tartars, the Moscow princes were in a position to preserve order and tranquillity, not only within their own domains, but throughout the territory of Vladimir and Suzdal. So important and desirable was this to the people, exhausted by the Tartar yoke and the internal troubles, that they gladly submitted to the authority of Moscow, and many boyars with their retinues from the south as well as from other parts of Russia entered the service of the Moscow princes. In this way they not only helped to swell the ranks of the armies of Moscow, but also improved their own conditions. To be a servitor and boyar of the Grand Prince was both more honorable and more profitable than to be in the service of any other prince.

The clergy was as loyal to the Princes of Moscow as the nobility. Alexius, a member of a distinguished Moscow boyar family, succeeded Theognostus as Metropolitan. During the reign of the weak Ivan the Red and the minority of his son Dmitri, Alexius practically governed the Moscow principality. He enjoyed great favor at the Horde and used his influence to advance the interests of Moscow. The Russian clergy followed in the footsteps of St. Alexius and always upheld the Princes of Moscow in their endeavors to establish in Russia a firm authority and stable order. Next to Metropolitan Alexius, mention should be made of the monk Sergius, the founder of the famous Troitse-Sergiev Lavra Monastery, north of Moscow. Sergius stood by Moscow in times of crises and lent his vast moral authority to the undertakings of her rulers.

Behind the boyars and clergy of Moscow were the common people. The fact that Moscow was noted for its domestic tranquillity, for its comparative freedom from outside attacks, and for its peaceful relations with the Tartars, induced many people to settle within its borders. The Moscow princes built villages and cities for the newcomers. They bought out the impoverished princes and small proprietors, and settled on their lands thousands of prisoners ransomed from the Tartars.

Up to the close of the fourteenth century, under Kalita and his sons, the growth of Moscow was only in the nature of external consolidation, by means of successful annexations. Later on, however, when the Princes of Moscow stood out as the champions of the whole of Russia against the Horde and Lithuania, Moscow became the center of national life and the Princes of Moscow, national sovereigns.

44. DMITRI DONSKOI AND THE BATTLE OF KULIKOVO. —The sons of Ivan Kalita reigned only brief periods. Simeon the Proud died of the plague, and Ivan the Red came to his end from an unknown cause when only thirty-one. Simeon left no children, but Ivan was survived by two sons. As the number of the princes did not increase, the lands were not divided up, the power of the princes was not weakened, and the title of the grand principality passed from one to another. Only after the death of

Ivan the Red, when no adult princes were left to succeed, was the firman for the grand principality given to the Princes of Suzdal. After two years the Metropolitan Alexius and the boyars succeeded in enlisting the support of the Khan, and regained the title for the young Dmitri Ivanovich, son of Ivan the Red. As soon as he became of age Prince Dmitri took the reins of government from the hands of the Metropolitan Alexius and the boyars into his own, and after that the affairs of state were managed with vigor and boldness. He took the stand that the title of Grand Prince, as well as the city of Vladimir, belonged to the Princes of Moscow. This question led to war with Tver and the intervention of Prince Olgerd of Lithuania on the side of Tver. Olgerd besieged Moscow, but was unable to take it and returned home, leaving his ally to fight his own battles. In 1375 Prince Michael of Tver concluded a treaty with Dmitri in which he acknowledged himself to be the "younger brother" of the Prince of Moscow and renounced all claims to the Grand Principality of Vladimir. In the same way Dmitri dictated terms to other princes of Russia. When, towards the close of his reign, the Novgorodians disobeyed him he declared war on them, reduced them to obedience and levied a heavy contribution of 8,000 rubles on them.

Under Dmitri, Russia for the first time risked open warfare with the Tartars and attempted to throw off their yoke. In their testaments and treaties the Russian princes often expressed the prayers "God free us from the Horde," "God take away the Horde." Simeon the Proud in his testament exhorted the brothers to dwell in peace, according to their father's will, "that the memory of our parents and of ourselves may not be forgotten, and that the candle may not go out." By this candle was meant the inextinguishable thought of national deliverance. However, as long as the Horde remained powerful and formidable, its yoke continued to oppress the Russian people. A struggle against the Tartars became possible only after protracted internal strife had started within the Horde, when one Khan murdered another, when rulers changed with extraordinary rapidity.

While these civil wars were in progress, the defeated factions fled to the north where they lived by plundering the Russian and Mordvinian settlements in the regions of the Oka and Sura Rivers. The Princes of Riazan and Nizhni-Novgorod, and Grand Prince Dmitri sent their troops against them. This resistance of the Russians aroused the Tartars and caused them to unite. In 1377 they defeated the Russians on the Piana River (tributary of the Sura), and ravaged Riazan and Nizhni-Novgorod. In retaliation, the Moscow and Nizhni-Novgorod troops laid waste the Mordvinian villages on the Sura where the Tartars had entrenched themselves. The struggle became relentless and bitter. Prince Mamai, having assumed the authority over the Horde and proclaimed himself Khan, dispatched his troops to Russia to punish the seditious princes. They overran Nizhni-Novgorod and Riazan and were on their way to Moscow when Dmitri Ivanovich encountered them in Riazan on the Vozha River, and defeated them (1378).

Both sides realized that the matter could not rest there. Tartar prestige had suffered by the Russian victory, and Mamai knew that he had either to renounce his domination over the Russians, or bring them into subjection by force. For two years he planned and schemed, gathered a large army and concluded a military alliance with

Prince Iagailo of Lithuania whereby their two forces were to unite in September, 1380, and attack the Russians. Dmitri took note of what was going on and made his preparations. He appealed to Novgorod and to other Russian cities for help, but without great success. His own people and his subject princes rallied around him, and they constituted a considerable force. The campaign against the Tartars was regarded as a religious crusade and was blessed by Abbot Sergius of the Troitsa Monastery. Dmitri took the field in August and advanced with his army towards the frontiers of Riazan with the expectation of blocking Mamai on his way to Moscow. On the march he was informed that the Tartars were marching westward in order to join the Lithuanians. Under the circumstances Dmitri decided not to wait for Mamai but to go in search of him and prevent his union with Iagailo. He came up with him on the field of Kulikovo near the Don River, and engaged him at once, for the Lithuanians were reported to be within one day's march. At first the fight went against the Russians; many of the leaders were killed; Dmitri was for a time out of the fight but in the end the strategy of the Russian prince won the day. Before engaging in the battle he had placed a strong reserve of forces out of sight, and at the critical moment ordered it to attack. The Tartars were taken by surprise, became disorganized and fled pell-mell from the field. The Russians pursued for a time and secured much rich booty. It was a great victory, but dearly paid for in Russian lives.

The Tartars did not give up without another struggle and this time they were successful. In 1382 they made a sudden incursion into Russia, took Moscow and other Russian cities, sacked and burned them, led thousands of the inhabitants into captivity and forced Dmitri to pay tribute and hand over his son as a hostage. Russia was not yet united enough, not yet strong enough to shake off completely the foreign yoke.

Notwithstanding the setback, the significance of Kulikovo was tremendous. The contemporaries regarded it as the greatest of all events and bestowed upon Dmitri the honorary title of "Donskoi" (of the Don). The military importance of the victory on the Don consisted in that *it destroyed the idea that the Tartar was invincible, and demonstrated that Russia had grown sufficiently strong for an open struggle for independence.* The Tartars gained the day in 1382 only because they had come unawares, Moscow having failed to notice them in time to take precautions. It was now generally understood that in a fair and open fight the Russians would whip the Tartars. The battle of Kulikovo was important from the political and national point of view in that *it gave an impetus toward a vigorous national consolidation under a single ruler, the Prince of Moscow.* The invasion of Mamai had been awaited in fear and trembling throughout the north of Russia. But while the Prince of Riazan concluded an agreement with the enemy, the Princes of Suzdal, Nizhni-Novgorod, and Tver remained neutral, and Novgorod the Great delayed in sending aid. The Prince of Moscow ventured forth alone and attacked Mamai in the wilderness, where he could protect not only his own appanage, but the whole of Russia. By this act Dmitri stood out as the champion of all Russia, the head of the whole nation and of all the other princes. After this Moscow was the obvious center of national unification, and the successors of Dmitri had merely to carry on his policy and consolidate into a compact whole

the appanages which were giving themselves freely into
their hands.

Herein lies the importance of the battle of Kulikovo.
It laid the ghost of Tartar invincibility, turned the
appanage prince of Moscow into a national Great-Russian sovereign, and hastened the process of national and
political consolidation in north Russia.

45. GRAND PRINCES VASILI DMITRIEVICH THE FIRST
AND VASILI VASILIEVICH THE SECOND, THE DARK.—
Dmitri Donskoi died when he was only 39 years old.
To his oldest son, Vasili, he left the grand principality
of Vladimir and a share of the Moscow appanage, and
to the other sons, the remaining cities and provinces. In
his testament he provided that: "If my son, Vasili, dies,
his appanage shall go to the brother next after him."
This was interpreted by Dmitri's second son, Iuri, as
giving him the right to succeed his elder brother to the
lands of Moscow as well as to the title of grand prince.
Others, however, differed with him and held that Dmitri
had in view only the eventuality of Vasili's dying childless. Generally speaking, the Princes of Moscow upheld
in their testamentary bequests the principle of family
inheritance (and not that of dynasty, or clan) of the
lands of the grand princes and of their own appanages.

In the reign of Grand Prince Vasili Dmitrievich
(1389-1425) Russia was twice invaded by the Tartars:
first, by Khan Timur-Lenk, or Tamerlane, who, however,
did not penetrate beyond the southern borders of Riazan;
second, by Prince Edigei. Edigei appeared suddenly,
laid siege to Moscow (1408), devastated the country,
laid a contribution upon Moscow and returned unscathed
to the Horde.

Vasili continued the hostilities which his father had

maintained with Lithuania. Both Russia and Lithuania were expanding in the region of the upper Dnieper and Western Dvina, and naturally came into conflict. In spite of the fact that the Grand Prince of Moscow was married to a daughter (Sophia) of the Lithuanian Grand Prince Vitovt, their quarrels led to open warfare. In the end they agreed that the Ugra, a left tributary of the Oka River, should be the boundary line between their dominions. Having made peace with his father-in-law, Vasili Dmitrievich entrusted Vitovt with the guardianship of his son, the Grand Prince Vasili Vasilievich.

Grand Prince Vasili Vasilievich, called the Dark (or blind), was ten years of age when his father died. His reign (1425-1462) was very turbulent and unfortunate. His uncle, Iuri Dmitrievich, claimed the title of grand prince for himself and upon the death of Vasili's guardian, Vitovt, Iuri and his sons fought Vasili Vasilievich for the possession of Moscow. This bitter feud lasted for about twenty years (1430-1450); Moscow changed hands frequently, but in the end Vasili Vasilievich gained the day and the principle of patrimonial inheritance from father to son triumphed over the ancient clan and dynastic order of succession from brother to brother. The overwhelming mass of the population, the clergy, and the boyars sided with Vasili Vasilievich, for they realized the advantages of a family succession which would lead to the establishment of that undivided authority which the country wanted.

While the Russians were carrying on their feuds, the Tartars were waging civil wars. The defeated factions were forced to seek homes elsewhere. Some found service with the Grand Prince of Moscow while others wandered from place to place and preyed on the Russian settlements. The leader of one of these bands was Khan Ulu-Mahomet. After devastating the Russian provinces on the Oka he built the city of Kazan, near the junction of the Kazanka River with the Volga, and founded a tsardom. With Kazan as a base he attacked the Russians, going even as far as Moscow in his raiding expeditions. Prince Vasili took the field against the Tartars, but was defeated and captured by them (1445). He was later released for a heavy ransom. When he returned from captivity he brought with him many Tartars. This displeased the Russians, who complained that he "liked the Tartars and their language beyond measure and treated the Christians without mercy." Vasili's unpopularity was taken advantage of by one of his rivals, who seized him and put his eyes out.

In the reign of the unfortunate Prince Vasili Vasilievich there were important developments in the life of the Russian Church. In 1439, at a Council of the Orthodox and Catholic clergy at Florence, a union of the Eastern and Western Churches had been proclaimed. The Emperor and the Patriarch of Constantinople had sought this union and were prepared to make all kinds of concessions in the hope that the Pope and the Western powers would come to the aid of the Greeks in their struggle against the Turks. The union left the Greeks in possession of their church ritual, but obliged them to recognize the Catholic doctrines and the primacy of the Pope. One of the members of the Council was the learned Greek, Isidore, a partisan of union who had been made Metropolitan of Russia a short time before this body met. As soon as he arrived at Moscow he commenced to prepare for the Council and departed for Florence with a large staff. While in Italy he was showered with favors by the Pope and worked zealously for union with the Latin Church. He returned to Moscow in 1441, reported the terms of the Union and urged its acceptance. But the Greeks had for centuries developed such a hatred against Catholicism among the Russians that they would have nothing to do with the union. Isidore was placed under arrest, but succeeded in escaping to Lithuania, and thence to Italy. At Moscow, it was now decided to break with the Constantinople Patriarchate, which had betrayed Orthodoxy, and to have a Russian metropolitan chosen by a council of Russian bishops. Under this new system, Bishop Jonas of Riazan was installed as Metropolitan of Moscow. At the same time other metropolitans, appointed from Constantinople, were inducted in the old Kievian metropolitan seat in southwestern Russia.

FORMATION OF THE GREAT-RUSSIAN STATE

46. GRAND PRINCE IVAN VASILIEVICH THE THIRD. SIGNIFICANCE OF HIS REIGN.—Vasili the Dark was followed by his son Ivan who played a prominent part in Russian history. Ivan Vasilievich had ability, determination, knowledge of the world, and practical experience, for he had been associated with his blind father in the government. At the outset of his career he had as neighbors and rivals the Princes of Iaroslav, Tver, Novgorod, and Riazan, but before he died he had brought their territories under his domination and had formed one Great-Russian State. He pursued the same policy in his own family, depriving his brothers of their appanages and special privileges, and limiting the territories and power of his younger sons. In short, in every way and in all things Ivan impressed upon his contemporaries the idea that the grand prince was an autocratic monarch to whom princes, as well as commons, were equally subject. The new idea of a national sovereign, exercising undivided authority, resulted in the establishment of a court ceremonial, a greater pomp and solemnity of manners, and the adoption of various emblems and symbols expressive of the exalted rank of the grand prince. In this way was accomplished, along with the consolidation of northern Russia, the transformation of the appanage prince of Moscow into an autocratic sovereign of all Russia.

Lastly, having become a national ruler, Ivan III adopted a national policy in the foreign relations of Russia. He shook off the last vestiges of dependence upon the Khan of the Golden Horde. He took the offensive against Lithuania and laid claim to all those Russian territories which had been in the possession of the Lithuanian princes since the days of Gedimin. In styling himself sovereign "of all the Russias," he meant to assert his right not only to northern but also to southern and western Russia. Towards the Livonian Order Ivan also maintained a firm, aggressive policy.

These acts, principles and claims make the reign of Ivan III stand out. The consolidation of northern Russia around Moscow had begun long before his time. Under Dmitri Donskoi its first signs had become apparent, but its actual accomplishment was due to Ivan. This is why Ivan III may justly be called the creator of the Moscow State.

47. The Subjection of Novgorod the Great and the Territories of Novgorod.—We have seen already that during the last period of its independent existence

a ceaseless strife had been going on at Novgorod between the upper and lower classes. This weakened it and rendered it an easy prey to its more powerful neighbors, Moscow and Lithuania. Every Grand Prince of Moscow attempted to control Novgorod and to have his own prince there at the head of affairs. More than once the insurbordination of Novgorod compelled Moscow to make war, to levy contributions, and reduce the Novgorodians to submission. Vasili the Dark sacked the city and forced the inhabitants to swear that they would remain loyal to him and would not shelter any prince hostile to him. The pretensions of Moscow to Novgorod drove the Novgorodians to seek the protection of Lithuania, which used the opportunity to subjugate the Novgorodians and to levy contributions just as Moscow did, without offering very much protection. Finding themselves between two such formidable enemies, and realizing the difficulty of maintaining their independence, the Novgorodians decided to form a permanent union with one or the other. Two parties sprang up in Novgorod; one drew its support from the common people and favored Moscow; the other was led by the boyars and worked for Lithuania. In the Grand Prince of Moscow the commons saw an Orthodox and Russian ruler, and in the Prince of Lithuania, a Catholic and a foreigner, while the boyars saw in the former a destroyer and in the latter a preserver of the old order and the old privileges. After the sacking of Novgorod by Vasili the Dark, the Lithuanian party at Novgorod gained the upper hand, and in 1471 Novgorod concluded a treaty of alliance with Kasimir, Prince of Lithuania and King of Poland, by which he bound himself to protect Novgorod against Moscow, to appoint his representative to Novgorod, and to respect all the liberties and ancient customs of Novgorod.

The news that Novgorod had gone over to Lithuania was regarded at Moscow as treason, not only to the Grand Prince, but also to the Orthodox faith and to the Russian people. It was in this sense that Grand Prince Ivan wrote to the Novgorodians, urging them to break with Lithuania and her Catholic king. When they refused, the Grand Prince summoned his army commanders, officials and clergy, laid before them the wrongs and treason committed by Novgorod, and asked them whether to declare war immediately or to wait until winter, when the rivers, lakes, and swamps of Novgorod would be frozen. It was decided to go to war at once. The campaign was regarded in the light of a religious crusade. As Dmitri Donskoi had taken up arms against the infidel Mamai, so, in the words of the chronicler, the Orthodox Grand Prince Ivan had gone out to fight these renegades who had forsaken Orthodoxy for the Latin faith. The war was of short duration. The Lithuanian help did not materialize; Novgorod was overrun, and the inhabitants had to sever their relations with Lithuania, pledge loyalty to Moscow, and pay a huge money contribution.

As soon as Ivan returned to Moscow the internal turmoil in Novgorod was renewed, and year after year different factions appeared before him in Moscow, appealing for redress of grievances. During one of these audiences two officials of Novgorod addressed the Grand Prince as *gosudar*, whereas up to that time the Novgorodians had addressed the Moscow Prince as *gospodin*. The distinction was very important. *Gosudar* was the title by which slaves and servants addressed their master, while *gospodin* was an honorary title. To the free people of Novgorod, however, the Prince was a *gospodin* and not a *gosudar*. It is but natural that Ivan made use of this slip of the tongue. When the Novgorodians repudiated the new title and replied that they had authorized no one to address Ivan in such a way, he charged them with duplicity, laid siege to the city and demanded unconditional surrender. The Novgorodians had little choice, and in January, 1478, they accepted the terms of the Grand Prince and sealed the oath by kissing the Cross. Novgorod, as a state, ceased to exist, and the bell which used to summon the *vieche* meetings was taken to Moscow. Hard upon the conquest of Novgorod the Great, Moscow also acquired the other territories of Novgorod.

At first Ivan abstained from harsh treatment of the inhabitants, but a year after the conquest, when there broke out a revolt and an attempt was made to restore the old order of things, the Grand Prince made the people feel his anger. Many of the boyars were executed, and many more were exiled to the Moscow territories in the east. Gradually all the "better people," *i.e.*, the higher classes of Novgorod, were deported and their lands confiscated and distributed among Moscow families which were settled in large numbers in the territory of Novgorod. In this way the aristocracy of Novgorod disappeared completely, and with it perished the very memory of Novgorodian liberty. The "lesser people," *i.e.*, peasants and other land laborers of Novgorod, were freed from the oppression of the boyars and organized in tax-paying peasant communes as in Moscow. On the whole, their condition was ameliorated, and they had no cause to regret the passing of the old order. With the passing of the Novgorod aristocracy went also Novgorod commerce with the West, especially after Ivan III banished the German merchants from the city. In this manner was destroyed the independence of Novgorod the Great. Pskov still preserved its self-government, but at the pleasure of the Grand Prince.

48. ANNEXATION OF THE APPANAGE PRINCIPALITIES. —The annexation of the appanage principalities to Moscow was actively continued under Ivan III. The Princes of Iaroslav and Rostov handed over their domains to the Grand Prince and entered his service as retainers and boyars. In this way all the small appanages were gathered together by Moscow, with the exception of Tver and Riazan. These two "grand principalities," which had once fought Moscow, were now on the decline. The last Princes of Riazan, the two brothers Ivan and Fedor, were nephews of Ivan III, who practically ruled Riazan for them. The Prince of Tver, Michael Borisovich, also took orders from Moscow, and his troops fought shoulder to shoulder with those of the Grand Prince in the campaign against Novgorod. In 1484-1485, however, the Prince of Tver established friendly relations with Lithuania in the hope of regaining his independence. When Ivan III heard of it he marched against him, drove Michael to Lithuania, and annexed Tver (1485). Thus was accomplished the final unification of Northern Russia.

By pursuing a national policy Moscow attracted Russians of the Lithuanian-Russian principality. The Viazemskis, Odoievskis, Novosilskis, Vorotynskis, and numerous other princes dwelling on the eastern frontiers of the Lithuanian State went over with their land to Moscow. This transference of allegiance from the Catholic ruler of Lithuania to the Orthodox prince of Northern Russia made it possible for the Moscow Princes to regard themselves as the sovereigns of the whole Russian territory. They argued that even that part which was under Lithuanian rule, although not yet united to Moscow, should be so united, by virtue of their common religion, nationality, and ancient dynasty of St. Vladimir.

49. FAMILY AND COURT AFFAIRS OF IVAN III.—At the same time that external changes were taking place, there were also internal transformations in the life of the Moscow Court. The first wife of Ivan III, a Princess of Tver, died in 1467, before Ivan had reached the age of 30. The Pope, who was interested in Moscow, offered to arrange a marriage between Ivan and Sophia Paleologus, the niece of the last emperor of Constantinople. When Constantinople was captured by the Turks (1453), Thomas, the brother of the slain Emperor Constantine Paleologus, fled with his family to Italy and died there. His children were brought up in the spirit of the Florentine Union, and the Pope hoped that a marriage alliance would pave the way towards a union of the churches. Ivan III sent his ambassadors to Italy and they brought the bride to Moscow where the marriage was solemnized in 1472. Although this marriage contributed little towards bringing about a church union, yet it had important consequences in other respects.

First of all, it encouraged and strengthened the relations that had already developed at that period between Moscow and the West, especially with Italy. In Sophia's train came highly trained Greeks and Italians [4] whose services were enlisted to build fortresses, churches, stone buildings, to cast cannon, to coin money and to under-

---

[4] These Italian immigrants were known in Moscow as "Friazin" (from "Friag" or "Frank"); in this way Moscow knew Ivan Friazin, Mark Friazin, Anthony Friazin, etc.

take diplomatic missions. One of the best known of these Italians was the architect Aristotle Fioraventi, who built the famous Uspenski Cathedral and the Granovitaia Palace. It was due to the labors of the Italians that the Kremlin was enriched with new edifices and greatly adorned. Ivan III also had Germans in his court but, with the exception of the doctors, the Germans did not play a prominent part at this time. Other foreigners visited Moscow from time to time, including Sophia's Greek relatives, and ambassadors from European rulers. For the reception of visitors and ambassadors a special ceremonial was adopted at the court of Moscow, entirely different from that which had been observed formerly on the occasion of Tartar embassies.

There was another side to this change that was not so beautiful. The Russians complained that since the coming of Sophia and the Greeks the country had been thrown into a state of confusion and disorder; that the Grand Prince was more haughty and less accessible; that he insisted upon visible tokens of homage; that he had a higher conception of his authority; that, having married a Greek princess, he regarded himself as the successor of the vanished Greek emperors, and took over their coat of arms—the double-headed eagle. In a word, after his marriage to Sophia, Ivan III became ambitious for power. This the Princess was made to feel, for he put her away in his old age. They quarreled over the question of the succession to the throne. Ivan III had a grandson, Dmitri,[5] and a son, Vasili, by Sophia, and he could not decide whom to name as successor. At first he decided in favor of Dmitri, and elevated him to the tsardom[6]

[5] Son from his first marriage, Ivan the Young, who died in 1490.
[6] Expressly to the *tsardom* and not to the Grand Principality.

in his own lifetime; but a year later he changed his mind, removed Dmitri, invested Vasili with the title of Grand Prince and associated him in the government. Each of the two candidates had cliques at court, and their fortunes went up and down; some of the boyars were even executed. The people of Moscow blamed Sophia for these disturbances, and accused her of undermining the good old customs and introducing vicious innovations in the life of Moscow, as well as having an evil influence on her husband and son. We must not, however, exaggerate Sophia's influence. Even without her the Moscow Grand Prince would have become conscious of his power and absolute authority, and relations with the West would have been established just the same. The entire course of Moscow history was tending to make the Grand Prince of Moscow the sole ruler of a powerful Great Russian nation and a neighbor of several European countries.

50. FOREIGN POLICY OF IVAN III. RELATIONS WITH THE TARTARS.—At the time of Ivan III there existed within the boundaries of present Russia three Tartar groups: the Golden Horde, the Crimean Horde, and the Kazan Horde. These three hordes were fighting one another, and Ivan III made use of their enmities to advance his own cause. He forced the Kazan tsar to become his subject; he induced the Crimean tsar to ally himself with him to fight the Khan of the Golden Horde whom he ignored and treated with contempt. The weak Khan of the Golden Horde, Akhmat, urged Lithuania to help him against Moscow, and, as nothing came of that, he tried it alone. In 1472 he appeared on the banks of the Oka, pillaged the country, but was afraid to advance upon Moscow. In 1480 Akhmat came as far

as the Ugra River where Ivan met him with a strong force. The two leaders faced each other, but neither dared to attack. Ivan ordered the capital prepared for a siege, sent Sophia north, and kept going back and forth between Moscow and the Ugra, afraid of the Tartars and of his own brothers. Ivan's cautiousness and slowness seemed like cowardice and made him unpopular. Akhmat remained on the Ugra through the summer and late fall, when snow and ice compelled him to return home. Soon after that he was slain in a feud, his sons perished in a struggle with the Crimean Horde, and the Golden Horde itself was broken up in 1502. Russia continued for three centuries longer to suffer from raids by Crimean, Nogai and other Tartars near the Russian border.

51. FOREIGN POLICY OF IVAN III. LITHUANIA AND LIVONIA. RELATIONS WITH THE WEST.—Lithuania was watching with uneasiness the rapid development of Moscow by annexation of territory and centralization of power, while she was growing weaker through internal dissensions because of the Polish union and the loss of the Russian Orthodox princes (and their territories) who went over to the Grand Prince of Moscow. Each year the antagonism between the states became sharper and, though Lithuania was not strong enough to declare open war, she yet encouraged Tver and Novgorod to resist Moscow, and incited the Tartars to attack the Russians. Moscow was waiting for an opportunity to assert her power and in 1492, when Poland elected John Albert as King of Poland and Lithuania chose Alexander Kazimirovich as Grand Prince of Lithuania, Ivan III attacked Alexander and compelled him to recognize the transference of the lands and allegiance of the Russian Orthodox

princes and to recognize him as the "Sovereign of all the Russias." The peace between the two princes was sealed by the marriage of Ivan's daughter, Helen, to Alexander, it being understood that she was to remain Orthodox. The Catholics at court made it so unpleasant for her that she complained to her father, who reproached his son-in-law. Another cause of bad feeling between the two rulers was the Catholic and Polish pressure on the Russian princes in Lithuania who sought the protection of Moscow. The situation became so bad that war broke out in 1500 and continued until 1503, when it ended in a truce. Russia was left in possession of all the principalities she had acquired, and with a claim on all other Russian territories still in the hands of Lithuania.

In this conflict Lithuania had the help of the Livonian Order, and Moscow, of the Crimean Tartars. Diplomatic relations were opened with Denmark, the Empire, Hungary, Venice and Turkey. Russia was gradually emerging from her obscure position and entering the circle of the European Powers.

52. GRAND PRINCE VASILI IVANOVICH III.—In the testament of Ivan III he made it clear that his oldest son, Vasili, was to have all the sovereign power. He was given sixty-six cities, and his four brothers thirty and small ones at that. Vasili alone had the right to coin money, to deal with foreign powers, to inherit the appanages of his childless relatives, and to his children alone belonged the title of Grand Prince. Vasili was sovereign, and his brothers and other relatives were his subjects. Such was the fundamental idea of Ivan III's testament.

Vasili III inherited the ambitions of his father, carried out his policies, and completed his work. Ivan had allowed Pskov to enjoy undisturbed its *vieche* and local self-government. Situated on the outskirts of the Russian territory, under the constant menace of Lithuanians and Germans, Pskov held firmly to Moscow, rendered obedience to her, and accepted a Moscow governor. The people of Pskov did not always get on with the governors and there were charges and counter charges. Vasili got tired of hearing complaints and in 1510 removed the Pskov *vieche* bell to Moscow, deported some three hundred Pskov families to Moscow, and sent to take their place an equal number of Moscow families.

A somewhat similar fate befell Riazan. In 1517 Vasili imprisoned the last Prince of Riazan and annexed his province. As in the case of Pskov, large numbers of the leading families of Riazan were transported to the provinces of Moscow, and Moscow people settled in their places. This was done in order to remove all possibility of revolt.

Lastly, there still remained the princes of the Sieversk provinces who had come over with their lands from the Lithuanian Grand Prince to Ivan III. Vasili III, taking advantage of their quarrels, drove them from their cities and annexed their possessions (1523). In this way all the so-called "appanages" were done away with, and there remained only ordinary princes, subject to the Grand Prince of Moscow, enjoying the same rights and privileges as his own Moscow boyars.

Vasili's foreign policy was a continuation of his father's. He encouraged Russian princes to leave Lithuania (the Glinski princes) and this brought on two wars. In 1514 Vasili III took Smolensk, a place of vast strategic importance, and forced Lithuania in 1522 to conclude a truce by which she surrendered Smolensk to Moscow until "eternal peace" or "final settlement."

This final settlement, however, was not reached for over a century, as Lithuania and Moscow were utterly unable to fix the boundaries of the disputed Russian provinces.

Relations with the Tartars after the fall of the Golden Horde were not improved. In the south the Crimean Tartars, and in the regions of Nizhni-Novgorod, Kostroma, and Galich, the Kazan Tartars and their Mordvin and Cheremiss subjects committed depredations. Harassed by these semi-nomads, the Russians could neither dwell in peace at home nor colonize the fertile black soil to the south of the Oka (the so-called "wilderness"), nor the wooded regions beyond the Volga, along the Unzha and Vetluga Rivers. The entire eastern and southern frontier population of the country lived in constant fear of the Tartars who sometimes managed to evade the Moscow troops and dash into the interior even as far as Moscow. It thus remained for Vasili III to guard his frontiers and sometimes to intervene in the internal affairs of the Tartars and strengthen his influence among them. He succeeded in doing so in Kazan, but the Crimea was too far away. The Moscow government tried to win over the Crimean Tartars by sending from time to time embassies bearing gifts. At the same time it took precautionary measures and stationed troops every summer along the southern boundary of the country (running along the bank of the middle Oka and therefore called at that time "The Bank"), to guard "The Bank" against southern raids.

As Vasili III's first wife, Solomonia, member of the boyar family of Saburov, had no children, he, with the sanction of the Metropolitan Daniel, forced her to enter a convent. His second wife, Princess Helena Vasilevna Glinskaia, a member of a Lithuanian family of exiles, bore him two sons, Ivan and Iuri. Ivan was only three years old when Vasili III died, less than sixty years of age. The last "Assembler of Russia" was domineering and vain, and lacked many of the fine traits of his father, Ivan III. Vasili loved power and praise, and his associates were people who favored and flattered him.

THE TRANSITION FROM THE APPANAGE SYSTEM TO AN ORGANIZED STATE

53. THE AUTOCRACY OF THE MOSCOW SOVEREIGNS, AND THE IDEA OF MOSCOW AS A THIRD ROME.—As we have already learned, Moscow was formed of the original Moscow principality and such other territories as were annexed from time to time. When they had nothing more than their appanage, the princes regarded it as their "patrimony," when they added Vladimir they looked upon it in the same light, and when they negotiated with Lithuania about the surrender of the old Russian cities they assumed the attitude that the whole of Russia was their "patrimony" handed down to them by their ancestors. The view that the prince was the proprietor of Russia and the inhabitants mere possessors spread downward and, in disposing of an estate, the seller used to say: "I have sold the land of the sovereign and of my possession." The part played by the princes in national unification made them national leaders and gave them national authority. They began to take themselves seriously and to act imperiously. Ivan III declined the royal title that had been offered him by the Emperor, unwilling to accept any outside "investiture" to rule his "own country." Foreign ambassadors reported that the power exercised by Vasili III was higher than that of any

other ruler of that time, and that the people of Moscow
likened their sovereign to God, saying: "We do not know
that, only God and the Sovereign know it."   Thus was
created in Moscow a powerful autocratic rule, patrimonial in its origin and national in its significance.

This took place at a time when the other Orthodox
countries were drifting towards their decline and fall.
During the close of the 14th and the beginning of the
15th centuries the Turks subjugated the Balkan Slavs,
threatened Constantinople, and finally took it in 1453.
After that date Moscow was the only Orthodox state
left with an Orthodox sovereign and independent Metropolitan.   Ever since the conversion of Russia, the idea
was accepted in Russia that all "Orthodoxy" (that is to
say, the totality of all Orthodox Christians) had from
time immemorial been united under the supreme authority of the Greek Sovereign ("Cæsar," "Tsar") and the
Greek Church.   Constantinople, the capital of the Greek
Tsar and Patriarch, was called by the Russians "Tsargrad" and looked upon as the metropolis of all "Orthodoxy."   Now that Tsargrad and all the eastern states
and churches were in the hands of the Turks, Moscow
was looked upon by the Russians as the center of Orthodoxy.   Ivan III and Vasili III regarded themselves as
heirs and successors to the Byzantine Emperors.   Ivan III
married a Greek Princess, adopted the Greek coat of
arms, and crowned his grandson Dmitri to the "Tsardom."   He, as well as Vasili III, occasionally called himself "Tsar."   This view was also accepted by the Greeks
and the Balkan Slavs who looked up to the Princes of
Moscow as the only defenders of the faith.   Whenever
they appealed for help and support against the Turkish
yoke they addressed the Russian princes as successors of

the Byzantine Emperors. The relation between Russia and Byzantium was an interesting subject in these days. On the theory of the divinely ordained oneness of the entire Christian world, a scholar of that period, a Monk of Pskov, Philotheus by name, wrote an epistle to Grand Prince Vasili III in which he tried to show that at first Rome was the center of the world; then came the second Rome, Constantinople, and lastly a third Rome, Moscow. "Two Romes have fallen," wrote Philotheus, "and the third stands, while a fourth is not to be." Such was the expression given to the idea of the world significance of "Moscow, the third Rome." They called the Grand Prince of Moscow "Tsar of all Orthodoxy"; Moscow, "the new city of Constantine" (*i.e.*, a new Tsargrad); and the Russian people, "New Israel," chosen by the Lord himself to stand at the head of all "Orthodoxy." Having accepted the idea of the transfer of the universal supremacy from Tsargrad to Moscow, the theologians attempted to prove it. They pointed out that in many instances sacred objects (the ikon of Our Lady of Tikhvin) had in miraculous ways passed over from Greece to Russia. They declared that the Apostle Saint Andrew had once been in Russia, blessed the spot upon which Kiev was founded later on, and prophesied that in Russia would flourish the true faith. From this evidence they drew the conclusion that the Russian Church derived its origin from the Apostles themselves and was, therefore, a worthy successor to the Greek Church. They next proceeded to show that the insignia of the Tsar's rank had been long since turned over by the Greek Tsar, namely by Constantine Monomachus, to Grand Prince Vladimir Monomakh from whom it had descended to the Grand Princes of Moscow. There actually existed (and still exists today) in Moscow a cap and shoulder cape worn by Monomakh which the Grand Princes put on at their coronation. Finally, the legend was revived that Rurik was descended from Prussus, brother of Emperor Augustus, and consequently the ruling dynasty of Russia was of Roman Imperial origin. By legends such as these, the idea became firmly rooted that Moscow was the foremost in all "Orthodoxy," that the Prince of Moscow was "Tsar of Orthodoxy," and that the Moscow Church ranked above the old Eastern Churches.

When the Moscow Princes convinced themselves of the truth of these teachings, they became ambitious to play the part of autocratic tsars. But this autocratic power did not suit all the people and was not recognized everywhere, and a movement against it became apparent among the Moscow boyars during the 15th century.

54. THE BOYARS AND THE PRINCELINGS; THEIR CLAIMS.—During the first period of Moscow ascendency there came to the front a class of boyars, or nobles, in the service of the prince. They showed their zeal and loyalty at all times, especially in the trying fourteenth century. On more than one occasion they governed for the incapable or minor princes and saw to it that the interests of the principality did not suffer. The prince, in turn, appreciated their help and rewarded the boyars. It is said that Dmitri Donskoi on his deathbed commanded his children to "love your boyars, honor them and do nothing without their counsel." It was so profitable and honorable to serve the Prince of Moscow that from the fifteenth century on many of the appanage princes from Northern Russia and many princes from Lithuania took service with him. Those who had appanages were allowed to keep them, and those who had

not were given land. These newcomers were expected to render military and other service to the prince, just as the Moscow boyars did. In the course of time jealousies grew up between the two classes of nobles, between the princes and the boyars, and between the different families. Those who traced their descent from Rurik or Gedimin, and those who had at one time held appanages regarded themselves as above the ordinary Moscow boyars, and demanded that they should hold the higher offices of state. By long drawn out disputes the princes and boyars would try to establish the relative seniority and rank of each princely and boyar family, and the custom of making appointments based on family rank became firmly rooted. A person would accept a position only when he had convinced himself that he would not be humiliated and subordinated to a person of equal or less distinguished rank. This custom of reckoning official position according to pedigree was known as *miestnichestvo*, *i.e.*, holding positions by rank.

In this manner there grew up in the fifteenth century a new class of boyars, at the head of which stood, by virtue of their "grand lineage," the descendants of the appanage princes who had become the subjects of Moscow. These prince-boyars never lost sight of their family tree, and even reminded the Prince of Moscow that they were of the same descent as he and should, therefore, be associated with him in the government. Neither Ivan III nor Vasili III, with their autocratic ideas, admitted their claims for a moment, and they did all they could to limit the power and independence of these princelings. They refused to consult them and managed the affairs of state with the aid of the trusted government clerks. If the princelings protested, they were banished, put into monasteries, and even executed. If they attempted to go over to Lithuania, they were charged with treason and desertion. The boyar-princes became domestic foes, and a problem.

55. SYSTEM OF LAND HOLDING AND SERFDOM.—In the appanage times, when the colonization of the northeast was in progress, social lines were not sharply drawn. At the head of the social ladder was the prince and his family, followed by the boyars and more important freemen. Between the prince on one side, and the boyars and freemen on the other, there was a definite understanding as to the conditions of their service. They acted as his civil and military officers; they were free to leave him for some other prince, losing their lands if they belonged to the prince, retaining them if they were their own. In addition to the boyars and freemen, the prince had directly depending on him large numbers of "men" slaves and bondsmen. They filled the ranks of his army, tilled his fields, and engaged in other enterprises. Frequently the prince invited poor freemen to settle on his land on favorable terms. This group formed a separate middle class, hardly serf, yet not wholly free, bound to the prince by terms of contract. All other persons living in the prince's domains were known by the general name of krestiane, or peasants, and were not directly dependent on him. These peasants were organized into communes, or mirs. They managed their own affairs, collected their own taxes and paid them to the prince. Every now and then he ordered a revision of the census, and accordingly increased or decreased the levy. The individual peasant had his dealings with the mir and not with the prince, and the latter was quite indifferent to the movements of the peasants, provided he got his money out of

the mir. Similar freedom of movement was enjoyed by the peasants on the boyar lands, for they held their land on the same terms as the peasants of the prince.

This loose social structure was affected by the change from the appanage to the national system. It will be remembered that the ruler of Moscow took the position that the lands of his subjects belonged to him and they could not, therefore, pass out of his jurisdiction. This put a stop to the transferring of land and allegiance from one prince to another. Each person owed military service to the prince for the land he held. When summoned to fight, princelings and boyars appeared with "entire" armies, while small proprietors appeared with "their own heads" or with a few others.

The wars with the Lithuanians, with the Germans in the Baltic, and with the Tartars, required larger forces than could be supplied in this feudal way. It was necessary for the prince to develop new military resources, and he did it by offering, at first, his own "palace" land and, later, state "black" land in return for military service. In time such holding became known as pomiestia, and the holder as pomieshchik. They were unlike hereditary patrimonial estates in that they reverted to the prince when service was no longer rendered.

By the beginning of the sixteenth century there were thousands of these pomieshchiks, particularly along the frontier, in the newly annexed territories, and even in the central provinces close to Moscow. For the administration of these lands a special pomiestnaia izba was created which was quite distinct from the bureau which looked after the patrimonial estates.

In addition to land, those holding by military tenure received, from time to time, allowances of money and, the more distinguished of them, kormlenia. That is to say, they were made governors of cities or provinces and given the opportunity to enrich themselves through *korm*, gifts and fees, legal and administrative. This new bureaucracy included high and low—princelings, boyars, large landholders, and even soldiers.

In view of the fact that the pomieshchik had definite obligations and had to furnish a definite number of men in time of war, he could not afford to let his peasants come and go as they pleased. He had the peasants and their lands registered in a special book, and demanded that they remain on the land on which they were registered. Those who were "unregistered" he tried to detain by advancing them money, seed and work animals, and by making them sign a contract not to leave until the debt was paid. It was not only the landlord, but also the mir who raised objections to the free movement of the peasants. It was not always easy to replace those who departed, and therefore those who remained had to pay the tax for the whole mir. This is how it came about that the free roving peasant of the appanage days was gradually forced to live in one place and obliged to pay tax to the prince, and, at the same time, work for the pomieshchik.

56. THE CHURCH LAND QUESTION. HERESY OF THE JUDAIZERS.—In the fifteenth century the numerous monasteries had so much land and so many peasants that it caused uneasiness both to the state and the church. Monasticism had its growth during the period of Tartar domination, when many people renounced the world and fled into the "wilderness." Around the hermitages and monastic colonies peasants settled, and numerous villages grew up. Large numbers of these monastic colo-

nies grew up in the regions of Kostroma, Galich, Vologda and Bielozersk. The princes were glad to give the monasteries title to the land and allow them to develop in their own way. In this manner the monasteries acquired much land and a great deal of wealth. Not all the members of these fraternities regarded this wealth in the same way. Some used it selfishly and wickedly, while others employed it for the good of the public. At the close of the reign of Ivan III, when the monastic estates had reached enormous proportions, and the darker side of monastic land ownership had become apparent, the whole church land question came up for debate. The discussion was led by two distinguished abbots, Joseph Volotski and Nil Sorski. The first was an ascetic and excellent manager, proficient in the literary field as well as in practical affairs, who had enriched his monastery and at the same time succeeded in preserving monastic discipline. He argued that wealth does not necessarily undermine the morals of a monastery, and that monasteries should go on increasing their wealth and employ it for worthy purposes. He said, among other things: "If no villages should be left to the monasteries, how would a noble person take monastic vows. And if there should be no elders (*i.e.* monks) of good family, whence would come the men for the Metropolitans, Archbishops, Bishops, and other positions of authority in the Church? And thus, if there should be no noble elders, the faith would also be shaken." His opponent, Nil, and his disciples, who came to be called the "Trans-Volga Elders," took the stand that monasteries should separate themselves from worldly affairs and have no wealth. Monks, he taught, should definitely abandon all temporal cares, live as hermits in the wilderness and devote themselves to the service of God. The question was debated at the general church council of 1503. The majority of those present sided with Joseph and drew up a resolution in favor of monastic land ownership. As a consequence, not only were monastic estates left intact, but continued to grow and multiply by gift, purchase, and money lending.

The materially minded faction of the clergy, taking their stand upon the writing of Joseph Volotski, established a regular school of monastic administrators and managers who came to be known as "Josephites." This school had, as its guiding principle, a determination to stand in well with the temporal powers. The Josephites became noted for their submissiveness and obsequiousness to the grand princes, and called down upon their heads the reproaches and denunciations of the austere Trans-Volga "non-acquisitive" monks, especially Abbot Vassian, a member of the princely family of Patrikeiev, and Maxim the Greek of Mt. Athos, who had been invited to Moscow to translate Greek books and reorganize the library of the grand prince. The conflict of the two factions grew more and more bitter and affected the religious and social life of that period. It finally ended in the decisive victory of the Josephites, and the imprisonment of Vassian and Maxim because they disapproved of the second marriage of Vasili III.

At this time there was another burning controversy which had its inception in Novgorod in 1471 and from there spread to Moscow. It is known as the "Heresy of the Judaizers" because a Jew, Zechariah, was one of its leaders. The Judaizers denied the Holy Trinity and the Divinity of Christ; they refused to honor the Holy Virgin and the Saints; they refused to bow before the

Holy Cross and ikons; and they observed the laws of Moses and kept Saturday instead of Sunday as a day of rest. Some of the heretical priests were brought by Ivan III from Novgorod to Moscow and installed in the court cathedrals of that city where they worked quietly and made many converts, even in high places. The heresy spread so fast that Archbishop Gennadius of Novgorod made complaints to Moscow, but the case was not pushed with vigor. In order to arouse the Moscow authorities Gennadius secured the coöperation of the influential Joseph Volotski. Joseph denounced the heresy vigorously and demanded the death penalty for the heretics. In this, again, he was opposed by the Trans-Volga monks, who wrote against such cruelty in the name of Christ. In this case, as in the dispute over the monastic lands, the views of Joseph won. At the general church council of 1504 the heretics were condemned to death, and many of them were burned at the stake.

Such were the principal subjects dealt with in the literature of Moscow at the close of the fifteenth and beginning of the sixteenth centuries. The Josephites supported the idea of autocracy and the established religious order, and were, in turn, supported by the grand princes.

CHAPTER IV

THE TSARDOM OF MOSCOW DURING THE XVI AND XVII CENTURIES

TIMES OF IVAN IV, THE TERRIBLE

57. CHILDHOOD AND YOUTH OF GRAND PRINCE IVAN
VASILIEVICH IV.—Grand Prince Vasili III died (1533),
leaving two young sons, Ivan and Iuri. Under the circumstances their mother assumed the reins of power.
She was an ambitious and suspicious woman, and put in
prison her uncle and the uncles of her children, and left
them there to perish. She, however, did not survive them
long, having been poisoned, so it is said, by her disaffected boyars. At that time (1538) Ivan was seven
and one half years of age, and Iuri five. In the past, as
in the case of Dmitri Donskoi, the regency was assumed
by the Metropolitan and the boyars who loyally served
the prince and principality. But times and manners had
changed since the fourteenth century, and the boyars of
the sixteenth century were more selfish than their ancestors. The Shuiskis fought the Bielskis for the control of
the government, and in this struggle they spared neither
Grand Prince, nor Metropolitan, nor common man.
They insulted the one, deposed the other, and oppressed
the third. It was in this atmosphere of intrigue, corruption and violence that Ivan IV grew up. In public the
boyars rendered homage to Ivan and his brother, but in
private they insulted them and neglected them, even in

the matter of food and clothing. This neglect, lack of respect, and open looting of the palace, filled young Ivan with bitter thoughts and lust for revenge. Even when a boy of thirteen he displayed cruelty and a love for torture. He learned to conceal his feelings and to deceive the boyars. He had but one friend in the world, the Metropolitan Macarius, a highly educated and gifted man. Macarius had a rich library and succeeded in persuading the young prince to read and to think of Moscow as the Third Rome, and of himself as the head of Orthodox "Tsardom." However, when Macarius attempted to soften the manners and cool the fiery and cruel passions of Ivan, he failed.

When he reached the age of sixteen Ivan announced to the Metropolitan and the boyars his intention to marry and to assume the crown of a *Tsar*. In 1547 he married an ordinary boyar's daughter (not a princess) from the family of Fedor Koshka, and had himself crowned as "Sovereign Tsar and Grand Prince."

58.—Ivan's reign opened auspiciously and gave much promise. His young wife turned his mind from base thoughts, and the priest Sylvester encouraged him in good deeds.

In 1550 Ivan summoned a council of church and lay dignitaries to reform the administration of justice and church government. A new legal code (Tsar's Sudebnik) was compiled in 1550, and the church manual (Stoglav) in 1551. In addition to these reforms other measures for the public good were put into force. The system of "kormlenia" (sec. 55) was abolished and the duties of the "kormlenia" men were entrusted to local men, the "rural elders," or to specially elected officers. These men were paid by the crown from a special tax which was levied to take the place of the kormlenia. In this way Ivan IV provided extensive local self-government except in matters of great importance. The only government appointees in the provinces were the *voivodes* in command of the garrisons, and the "town clerks" in charge of government property in the cities.

Certain military reforms were instituted. From the "lesser boyars" and noblemen Ivan IV selected, in 1550, one thousand of the best, gave them land in the vicinity of Moscow, and formed them into a special regiment known as the "Moscow Nobles" to distinguish them from the "Provincial Nobles." The army itself was organized on a new plan. Before this change the boyar militia of each district formed a distinct military unit. Ivan split up these units into hundreds, and appointed special officers over each. In addition, there was formed a special infantry with muskets (streltsi) and good artillery companies. In view of the fact that the system of holding office according to one's pedigree interfered with efficiency, Ivan made some reforms along this line also. Lastly there was a revision and equalization among the estates of the "pomieshchiks." Some of these landholders were granted money payments in addition to their land.

59. FOREIGN AFFAIRS IN THE FIRST PERIOD OF IVAN'S REIGN. WAR WITH THE TARTARS.—During the centuries of contact with the Tartars the Russians had learned their ways, their strong and weak points, and Ivan made use of this knowledge in his war with Kazan. In 1551 a large Russian army was sent against the Kazan Tartars and placed in such a position that one division protected the boundaries of Moscow from the Crimeans, while another moved towards Kazan and built the fortress of Sviiazhsk at the mouth of the Sviiaga River. In the

year following (1552) these tactics were repeated. One army was sent against the Crimean Tartars and another, led by Ivan, moved on Kazan. Kazan was surrounded and after stubborn resistance was taken on the second of October. In this campaign the Russian troops made use of powder for the first time to blow up the enemy's fortifications. Kazan was burned and plundered, the remnants of the Tartar garrison annihilated, the Tsar of Kazan, Ediger, captured and baptized, and the Tartar khanate overthrown. In the place of the Tartar city, Ivan built up a Russian Kazan in which he placed Russians. He permitted the Tartars to live only in the suburbs. Throughout the territory which had been ruled by the Tartar khans, fortresses were built (Cheboksary, Tsivilsk, Iaransk, Urzhum, Malmyzh, and—farthest of all—Ufa). All aboriginal tribes (the Mordvins, Cheremis, Chuvash, Votiaks, Bashkirs) were reduced to submission. Large tracts of land on the Volga and Kama were now opened to Russian colonization.

Having secured the headwaters of the Volga, Ivan became eager to take posssession of the mouth also. In 1556 the Russians conquered Astrakhan, founded on the ruins of the Golden Horde, which at that time was the capital of the feeble Nogai khans.

The conquest of the Tartar khanates was an important national achievement. Tranquillity was established along the entire eastern frontier; Russian prisoners in Tartar captivity were repatriated; enormous stretches of fertile land were acquired; a direct road was opened up by way of Viatka and the Kama River, to the country beyond the Ural Mountains; and lastly, the first triumph of Christianity over Islam, of Europe over Asia, had been won. Conscious of all the glory of these triumphs the Russian people celebrated them in their songs and made Ivan IV, the Terrible Tsar, their epic hero.

60. THE CHANGE IN IVAN IV, AND HIS BREAK WITH HIS ADVISERS.—Ivan IV had been accomplishing all these brilliant deeds with the aid of the circle of boyars chosen by Sylvester. To this circle belonged, among others, Aleksei Fedorovich Adashev, Prince Andrei Mikhailovich Kurbski, and several other lesser princes. These men worked in harmony until 1553 when misunderstandings and quarrels began to crop up. Ivan suspected (and not without reason) that Sylvester and the boyars were "shearing him of power" to "rule the Tsardom." When the Tsar refused to act on their recommendations they were resentful. They frowned upon his marriage with an ordinary boyar's daughter—marriage to a "slave" they called it. They quarreled with the relatives of Tsaritsa Anastasia, and in 1553 this enmity resulted in a serious clash. In that year Ivan IV was taken ill and, believing that he would not recover, he made his will. He left his Tsardom to his infant son, Dmitri, and asked the boyars to take the oath of allegiance to Dmitri at once. Some did, while others refused, arguing that, as Dmitri was still an infant, the actual regency would be exercised by his mother's family, and that they, as boyars, could not take orders from them. This procedure by members of his "chosen council" was regarded by Ivan as a plot against his son, and a move to put his cousin, Prince Vladimir Andreievich Staritski, on the throne. With great difficulty Ivan succeeded in compelling all the boyars to take the oath to Dmitri, but he never forgot their attitude. Soon afterwards he recovered his health, but Sylvester and his men never regained favor in the Tsar's eyes, though there was no open breach.

In 1560, after the death of his wife, a complete change came over the Tsar. New favorites appeared at his court, and with these he led a life quite beneath his dignity. The old advisèrs were removed. Sylvester was banished to a monastery, Adashev was sent to Livonia, and Kurbski fled to Lithuania. Other members of the council tried to make their peace with the Tsar, but only succeeded in stirring his wrath, indignation and cruelty.

61. SECOND PERIOD OF IVAN IV's REIGN. DOMESTIC AFFAIRS.—The persecution of the boyar-princelings was inaugurated by the Tsar with an extraordinary act. At the very close of 1564 he suddenly left Moscow, turned up at Alexandrovskaia Sloboda near the Troitse-Sergiev Monastery, and from there sent word (in January, 1565) to the capital that he had abandoned his Tsardom because of the treachery of the boyars. The Moscow people sent a deputation headed by the clergy, begging the Tsar not to forsake them. He agreed to continue in power on condition that he be allowed to "lay his ban" upon the traitors, to punish them, and to set up his own *oprichnina*, *i.e.*, "set up his own court and his own separate domestic establishment." In this manner there came into being the notorious *oprichnina*. In the olden times this name was applied to special appanage bequests to the widows of princes by their husbands. It was such a special arrangement that Ivan now made for himself. He founded a new "court," built new palaces, named new courtiers and servants, and selected a new "thousand" of noblemen, as had been done already in 1550 in Moscow (sec. 58). In order to support this new court he took for himself several cities and districts from which he obtained the necessary funds and supplies. The people who became members of this separate organi-

zation were popularly known as *oprichniki*, but Ivan himself called them "court people."

Once established, this organization set to work to crush the princely aristocracy—that group which regarded itself as having almost equal rights with the sovereign. In his new "court," to which he refused to admit the "traitorous boyars," he found the power and the means to proceed against them. He annexed to his personal establishment cities and districts which included the ancient patrimonial appanages of the boyar princelings, and administered them as if they were conquered territories. He deported from them persons whom he regarded as dangerous—usually the descendants of the appanage princes—and settled them along the frontiers, on the new land where there was no appanage tradition and where they would be harmless. In the place of the banished aristocracy the Tsar put the petty *oprichnik* landlords who were loyal to and dependent upon him. This destruction of the old nobility and shifting about of population ("sorting out folks" Ivan called it) continued for almost twenty years, during which time nearly half of the country was placed directly under him. The other half remained under the old system and was governed by the boyar council and called the *zemshchina*, and its inhabitants, *zemskie* people. In 1575 Ivan IV placed this half under a special "grand prince," one of his subjects, the baptized Tartar Tsar Semion Bekbulatovich, but he soon removed him to Tver.

The *oprichnina* ruined not only the princelings, but also all those who were forcibly deprived of their patrimonial estates and compelled to settle in new places. This system was, in itself, enough to stir the hatred of its victims. Its operation was rendered still more odious by its unparalleled atrocities, and by the torture and execution of those whom the Tsar disliked. At his command hundreds of "traitors" were decapitated. In 1570 the Tsar accused the inhabitants of Novgorod of treason. He made a regular war on them, massacred them without a semblance of legal trial, and treated them as if they were foreign enemies. During Ivan's lifetime the *oprichniki* throughout the country would break into private homes and commit all kinds of excesses in the name of stamping out "treason." Ivan, who came to be known as "The Terrible," was as bad as the worst of his men. He followed up his bloody executions by wild orgies, and the orgies, by prayers mingled with blasphemy. At Alexandrovskaia Sloboda he built something in the nature of a monastery, where his depraved henchmen, the monastic "brotherhood," wore black robes over their gaudy garments. From humble prayer the brotherhood turned to wine and bloodshed, mocking all genuine religious devotion. Metropolitan Philip of Moscow would not reconcile himself to the depravity of the court of the Tsar, and he denounced Ivan and his retinue. For this he was deposed by the Tsar from the Metropolitan See and deported to a monastery, where he was strangled to death in 1570 by one of Ivan's brutal *oprichniki*. Ivan did not hesitate to put to death his own cousin, Prince Vladimir Andreievich, whom he had suspected of plotting against him ever since his illness in 1553. Ivan the Terrible placed no restraints upon his cruelty and no curb on his passions. He abandoned himself to every imaginable dissipation and vice. Soon after the death of Tsaritsa Anastasia he married Maria Temriukovna, a Circassian princess from the Northern Caucasus, and when she died (1569) he took one wife after another until he

had married seven times. The clergy, having no right
to consecrate marriages of one and the same person more
than two or three times, was compelled to bestow the
blessings of the Church upon these unlawful matrimonial
alliances.

The extraordinary cruelty of the Tsar and his strange
behavior made it difficult to understand him. Some of
his subjects said that the Tsar was "playing with God's
people"; that he had divided his tsardom into two halves,
and commanded the one half (the *oprichniki*) to plunder
and murder the other. He was not, however, regarded
as an abnormal or insane person, but as a "man of wonderful reasoning."

Ivan the Terrible succeeded in ruining the aristocracy
by taking from them their appanages and giving them to
his favorites. In doing so, however, he weakened the
state, and almost desolated the central provinces of Moscow. The banished prince-boyars were followed by their
serfs, and, in many cases, by the free peasants who did
not take kindly to the new proprietors. These were not
the only reasons why the peasants migrated. The fields
of Kazan and the black earth south of the Oka were more
fertile than the soil which they were giving up; and last,
but not least, there was no reign of terror in those borderlands. The stream of migration from the central provinces continued during Ivan's reign, and towards its close
these regions had become so depopulated that the
Tsar found it impossible to raise enough soldiers and
sufficient revenue to carry on his wars. This explains
why his wars with Lithuania and the Swedes ended so
ingloriously.

During the second half of Ivan's reign measures were
taken to defend the southern frontiers and to settle the

so-called "wilderness" to the south of the Oka. The conquest of Kazan and Astrakhan aroused the Crimean Tartars and Turks; both demanded the restoration of the khanates, and prepared an expedition against Astrakhan and a raid on Moscow itself. In 1571, the Khan of the Crimea, following the same road which had been taken by Khan Akhmat in 1480, slipped by the Russian border troops and made a dash on Moscow which he subjected to pillage and fire. He tried it again the following year, but was defeated near the Oka and driven back. These raids forced Moscow to give serious thought to the frontier problem. The old forts along the bank of the middle Oka no longer served their purpose, for in the time of Ivan IV thousands of Russians had settled beyond that line. Many of these settlers were free "Cossacks" [1] who lived by fishing, hunting, plundering and fighting. They attacked without conscientious scruples Tartar and Russian, Mohammedan cities on the Black Sea and Orthodox towns in the interior. At times they made war on the Tsar by waylaying his diplomatic missions; at other times they entered his service and guarded them.

In 1571 a special commission was appointed in Moscow to study the frontier question. This body recommended that, in view of the fact that a sufficiently large number of these Cossacks were already living on the "frontier" south of the Oka, the government should take over that region. In accordance with this plan a number of fortified towns were built with military posts between them so as to keep the Tartars in view and in check. In addition to the men sent out from Moscow for service on the frontier, many Cossacks and other Russian set-

[1] They acknowledged no authority save that of their own chosen "ataman."

tlers were taken on. By the end of the sixteenth century the entire wilderness, as far as the upper Vorskla and Sieverski Donets, was dotted with fortresses and made safe for colonization. Those Cossacks who refused to submit to the authority of the state moved farther south on the lower courses of the Don and Donets and formed their own organizations with elected "atamans."

62. FOREIGN AFFAIRS IN THE SECOND PERIOD OF THE REIGN OF IVAN IV.—In 1558 Ivan IV began his famous struggle for Livonia. At that time Livonia included Esthonia, Courland, the Island of Oesel and other islands. Livonia was at this period in a demoralized state owing to the quarrels between the Archbishop of Riga and the Grand Master of the Order of Sword Bearers, and to the Reformation with its religious strife. Fully informed of this state of affairs, and appreciating its importance to Russia, Ivan the Terrible desired to get Livonia into his possession. For centuries the Russian commerce with the Baltic had gone through the Livonian ports of Riga, Reval and Narva. The Livonian merchants did everything they could to monopolize the whole trade and prevent Russian development. They kept Russians from the sea, and foreigners from Russia; they refused to let artisans and artists go through to Moscow, and prohibited the passage of silver, weapons and other material needed for Russian progress. Russia was weary of these tactics, and when she saw the demoralization of Livonia, and the possibility of its falling into the hands of a more powerful neighbor, she was determined to get it for herself and establish direct trade relations with Europe. In pursuance of this plan Ivan demanded the payment of tribute; in other words, the acknowledgment of Livonia's dependence upon Russia. Livonia

agreed to pay tribute, but as it failed to do so on time Ivan, in 1558, invaded it and started a war that lasted twenty-five years. The progress of this war was as follows.

In the course of the first two years the Russians devastated practically the whole of Livonia, with the exception of its most important fortified towns and castles. Unable to resist, but unwilling to surrender, Livonia fell to pieces and delivered herself up, piece by piece, to her Baltic neighbors who were more closely related by racial and religious ties. Esthonia accepted the sovereignty of Sweden; Livonia proper went over to Lithuania; the Island of Oesel became the possession of Duke Magnus of Denmark, and Courland was transformed from a church province into a temporal domain. Master Kettler of the Order became Duke of Courland, in feudal dependence upon the King of Poland. This ended the Livonian Order (1560-1561).

As soon as Sweden and Lithuania assumed the sovereignty of the territories, they demanded that the Russians evacuate their provinces. Ivan defied them, and the Livonian War became a Swedish and Lithuanian War. The war with the Swedes was not pursued energetically, for Ivan gave his attention to the Lithuanians. In 1563 he took the City of Polotsk, laid waste Lithuanian territory and continued to fight until the Lithuanians sued for peace and offered to cede Polotsk. In 1566 the Tsar convened at Moscow the *Zemski Sobor*, or national assembly, composed of the representatives of various classes of the people. The main object of the meeting was to discuss the advisability of peace or war with Lithuania, and it was voted that war should continue. It was carried on with success until 1576 when Stephen

Batory, a man of great military ability, was chosen to the Polish-Lithuanian throne (1576).

Batory opened a vigorous campaign against Ivan the Terrible at the very time when the Tsar's resources were low, owing to the depopulation of the central provinces. Batory recaptured Polotsk, seized the important fortress of Velikie Luki, but could not take Pskov. The Papal Nuncio Antonio Possevino offered to act as a mediator and peacemaker, and through his efforts a peace, or rather a truce, lasting ten years was concluded. By the terms of this agreement Ivan renounced his claims to Livonia and his conquests in Lithuania (1582). The Swedes, seeing how weak Ivan was, invaded Russia, captured the cities of Iam and Korela, and forced Ivan to make peace and to give up to them Esthonia and the cities named above (1583).

The long drawn out Livonian War was thus ended. Ivan's enemies were stronger and more numerous than he had anticipated, and his resources were less than he had hoped. However, the loss of this war does not in the least detract from the undertaking. Ivan understood Russia's need of the Baltic for the purpose of entering into direct relations with the more advanced West. Ivan's successors during the seventeenth century renewed the attempt to get possession of it, and Peter the Great at last succeeded in bringing this about.

In the reign of Ivan the Terrible occurred also two events which, although only incidental in his career, were of prime importance. These events were, first, the appearance of English ships at the mouth of the Northern Dvina, and, secondly, the conquest of Siberia by the Cossacks of the Stroganovs.

In 1553 three English vessels left the Thames in

search of a northern passage to China. Two of the ships were lost in the Arctic, but the third found itself at the mouth of the Northern Dvina. Its captain, Richard Chancellor, was taken to Moscow, where he was well received and encouraged to return. He came again, only this time with an official mission from the English Government to establish trade relations with Moscow. Two years later a Russian embassy was sent to London, and in this way began the trade of Moscow with England. English merchants set up their trading depots in many Russian cities, traveled all over the north of present-day Russia, became well acquainted with it and brought home descriptions of this territory. The English were followed by the Dutch, who had already opened commercial relations with the Russians in the little town of Kola on the Murman Coast. Towards the close of Ivan's reign there was a large and regular yearly fair established, also a flourishing seaport, Archangel, at the mouth of the Northern Dvina. Although the navigation season was only three months, and Archangel far from the chief markets of the world, Moscow did what it could to develop direct communication with Europe by way of the White Sea. There was a saying in those days "the vast ocean, the road that God Himself has built, how can one close it?" Anyone who dared and cared to go to Russia over this sea route could do so, but the road overland was closed by hostile neighbors who tried to keep Moscow down.

The expedition to Siberia was due to the private initiative of the Stroganovs, a wealthy Novgorod boyar family. This family had gradually acquired enormous territories on the Vychegda and Kama Rivers, and on the middle Ural, with the right to build trading stations and forts.

Stroganov hunters pushed farther and farther eastward until they reached Siberia. They were by no means the first Russians in this part of the world. Novgorodians had penetrated into this region as far as the Ob in the fourteenth century, and in the fifteenth century the voivodes of Ivan III took possession of the territories of Perm and adjoining lands up to the Ob. But owing to the strong opposition of the Nogai Tartars about Tobolsk, the Russians could make little use of their conquests. In the second half of the sixteenth century the head of this Tartar Khanate (known then as Sibir) was the energetic Khan Kuchum, who incessantly harried the Stroganovs, as well as those aborigines who were paying tribute to the Tsar. In 1582 the Stroganovs sent Ataman Iermak with a band of 840 adventurous Cossacks across the Urals. They came up with Kuchum on the Irtysh River, defeated him, captured his capital, Sibir, and put an end to the Sibir Khanate. Ivan IV was highly pleased with the outcome of this campaign, and followed it up by sending reënforcements and officers to take charge of the newly conquered territory.

TIMES OF TROUBLE

63. TSAR FEDOR IVANOVICH AND BORIS GODUNOV.—Ivan the Terrible died in the beginning of 1584. A year and a half before his death he quarreled with his eldest son, Ivan, and struck him a blow that caused his death. The throne of Ivan the Terrible, therefore, fell to Fedor, second son of Ivan and Anastasia. Fedor's ill health, gentleness and piety made him greatly beloved and revered by the people. He was, however, incapable of governing, and for that reason the boyar Nikita Romano-

vich, an uncle of the Tsar on his mother's side, acted as regent. Nikita Romanovich lived only a few months after assuming office, and when he died he was succeeded by Fedor's brother-in-law, the boyar Boris Fedorovich Godunov. The boyars did not like Boris; he was too young and not sufficiently aristocratic to suit them. They, with the Metropolitan Dionisius, set on foot an intrigue to get Fedor to divorce his childless wife, Irina, and marry another, hoping thereby to get rid of Boris and his sister. Godunov frustrated the plot, forced the Metropolitan to retire, and exiled some of the boyars, among whom were the princes Shuiski. This bold and successful move made it possible for Godunov to assume the title of regent in 1587. He had all the power and authority of a tsar, and, according to the testimony of his contemporaries, he used them to advance the interests of the state. Under his regency trade prospered, the state revenue increased, quiet and peace returned, and people found "consolation after the sorrows of the past." While ascribing this blissful state to the prayers of Tsar Fedor, the Russian people gave their due to the talents of Boris Godunov. They were unanimous in praising him as a wise ruler, and even his political enemies spoke well of him. No one had as yet a premonition of the swiftly approaching calamities.

Of the wars of Tsar Fedor the most memorable were the conflict with Sweden, ending in the restoration of the authority of Moscow over the cities of Ivangorod, Iam, Orieshek, Korela; the invasion of the Crimean Khan, who reached the gates of Moscow in 1591 only to be driven off; and, lastly, the final conquest of the Siberian Khanate. Among the measures of internal organization and government, the first place, in historical importance, belongs to the establishment of the Patriarchate in Moscow. Of far-reaching importance also were the decrees concerning the peasantry.

64. ESTABLISHMENT OF THE PATRIARCHATE IN MOSCOW AND DECREES CONCERNING THE PEASANTRY.—We have seen already (sec. 45) that after the Florentine Union the Moscow Metropolitan See separated from the Patriarchate of Constantinople. The Metropolitan of Moscow was no longer appointed by the Patriarch of Constantinople, but was chosen by a council of Russian bishops and archbishops, and consecrated at Moscow. Though he was ranked as Metropolitan, he regarded himself as superior to the Eastern Patriarchs, who were humbled and impoverished by the Turks. This superiority, actual and assumed, did not wholly satisfy the rulers of Moscow now that they were tsars and successors of the Byzantine Emperors. It seemed to them a matter of great importance that Moscow, "the Third Rome," should have a Patriarch as well as a Tsar, just as "the Second Rome" had had.

Since the fall of Constantinople representatives of the Orthodox churches in the East were in the habit of coming to Russia to appeal for "donations." In 1586 there came on such a mission no less a person than the Patriarch of Antioch (Ioakim). While this distinguished visitor remained in Moscow the question of setting up a Patriarchate there was discussed. The Patriarch promised to take up the subject with the other Eastern Patriarchs and was sent on his way with a rich donation. The Eastern Patriarchs, however, showed little enthusiasm for the proposal and did nothing. Two years after the visit of the Patriarch of Antioch there arrived at Moscow the Patriarch of Constantinople, Jeremiah. Godunov took up the question with Jeremiah, and they concluded an arrangement by which the latter consented to assume the office of Patriarch of Russia, and thereby establish a precedent. Godunov had no intention of letting this alien Patriarch assume too much power and, therefore, proposed that he take up his official residence at Vladimir. Jeremiah would not be set aside and the two argued back and forth. In the end it was agreed that Jeremiah should consecrate the Metropolitan Job as Patriarch of Moscow. The consecration took place in January, 1589. Jeremiah returned to his own home, and in 1590 convoked at Constantinople a council of Patriarchs, which approved and confirmed his action, and gave the new Patriarch the fifth place [2] in the assembly of Patriarchs.

In Section 55 was discussed the change in the land tenure in the central provinces, and the lowering of the status of the peasants. The condition of the latter grew worse in the reign of Ivan the Terrible, and many of them abandoned their holdings and went to the frontier to join the Cossacks or to take up new land on the Volga. So many of them moved away that the landlords became alarmed and made every effort, legal and illegal, to retain them. The peasants, however, persisted in leaving. Labor grew more scarce and the landlords resorted to all kinds of schemes, fair and unfair, to secure it. They either stealthily enticed the peasants from another estate by offering them more favorable terms, or secured their release by paying their indebtedness. In this kind of game the stronger and wealthier landholders had the advantage over the weaker and poorer.

In view of the fact that the government depended to a very great extent on the smaller landholders for its

[2] Constantinople, Jerusalem, Antioch, Alexandria, and Moscow.

military forces, it could not stand aside and see them ruined. It had to take action for this reason, and also because the "removal" of peasants led to quarrels, fights, and law suits without end. Beginning with 1592 decrees on the subject began to be passed. A new registration of the peasants on the estates was ordered. In 1597 a special decree provided that the courts should hear cases that had to do with "removals" since the beginning of 1592, and that all peasants who had left prior to that date should be regarded as free from their old masters. A five year period of limitation was thus provided for suits to recover fugitive peasants. Several other decrees followed, one of which prohibited the large landlords from taking peasants from the smaller ones; another prohibited the removal of peasants at all at certain periods prescribed by the government (interdictory years). The purpose of this legislation is clear, but it does not appear that any good came of it. The migration of the peasants continued, and complaints were as loud as ever about their disappearance. It is, however, important to note that the government was paying attention to the condition of the peasants and beginning to regulate the relations between the laborer and the landlord.

65. DEATH OF THE TSAREVICH ST. DMITRI IVANO-VICH, AND THE EXTINCTION OF THE MOSCOW DYNASTY. —Besides Tsar Fedor Ivanovich, Ivan the Terrible left another son (by his seventh wife Maria Nagoi), Tsarevich Dmitri, who was born in 1582. On the death of Ivan, little Dmitri was sent with his mother and her brothers, members of the noble family of Nagoi, to the city of Uglich. Their stay at Uglich virtually amounted to exile, for Uglich was governed by Bitiagovski, an officer appointed by the Tsar, who saw to it that the

Nagois did not make trouble. They resented their exile, made it uncomfortable for Bitiagovski, and taught the tsarevich to hate the government at Moscow which was responsible for their banishment. At noon on the 15th of May, 1591, the tsarevich's mother heard a cry in the courtyard, and when she rushed out she found her son with a mortal wound in his throat. In her frenzy she accused Bitiagovski of killing her son, and this so excited the crowd that they killed Bitiagovski, his son, and about ten others. As soon as Moscow heard of what had happened it sent an investigating committee, headed by Metropolitan Gelasius and Prince Vasili Ivanovich Shuiski. After making a thorough investigation, the committee reported that at the time of the tragedy the tsarevich was playing the game of "knife" with his playmates and, while so doing, fell in a fit, and inflicted upon himself the mortal wound. The reports exonerated Bitiagovski and charged the Nagois with inciting the mob to murder.

When the clergy and the boyars heard the report of the committee they banished the Nagois and compelled Tsaritsa Maria to go to a convent. Notwithstanding the report there were many people who believed that not only were Bitiagovski, his son, and his friends responsible for the death of the Tsarevich, but that Boris Godunov was the chief criminal. It was whispered about that Boris did away with the tsarevich in order that he himself might become tsar upon the death of the childless Fedor. The literature of that period has many different accounts of this event. Some of the writers accept the report of the investigating committee, while others, following the rumors, maintain that Dmitri was assassinated.

Whichever way one may view this matter, it should be borne in mind that at the time of the tsarevich's death, in 1591, Godunov had no reason to think that Tsar Fedor would remain childless. Indeed, soon after Dmitri's death a daughter, Theodosia, was born to the Tsar and lived one and a half years. It was only after her death (1594) that Tsar Fedor began to fail. He died childless on the 6th of January, 1598, leaving his wife, Tsaritsa Irina, "over all his states." Had she cared to ascend the throne, she could have reigned to the very end of her days. Instead she retired to the Dievichi Monastery, took the veil under the name of Alexandra, and declined to mix in worldly affairs. Thus came to an end the dynasty of Ivan Kalita. The people of Moscow had now to look around for a new sovereign.

66. The Ascension of Boris Fedorovich Godunov to the Throne.—Patriarch Job, who had been left the "principal personage" at Moscow during the interregnum, convoked a *Zemski Sobor*, or national assembly, at his residence, to choose a tsar. This assembly was made up of the higher clergy, the boyars in the tsar's council, and representatives from the official classes, as well as the commercial and industrial inhabitants of Moscow. Of the candidates under consideration two stood out, Boris Fedorovich Godunov and Fedor Nikitich Romanov, Tsar Fedor's cousin. The Patriarch favored Godunov and brought about his election in February, 1598. When Boris, who was with his sister at the Dievichi Monastery, was notified of his election he positively declined. A religious procession was made to the Dievichi Monastery, and the Patriarch warned Boris that if he persisted in refusing the clergy would close all the churches and stop the services. Only then, and after his sister had added

her entreaties, did Boris consent. Although the election of Boris had thus been a national and perfectly legitimate act, his enemies spread the report that he had secretly resorted to bribery and threats to secure the throne. At the same time, however, many of his contemporaries denied the charge and said that Boris had been elected because of his "wisdom and justice," and his "firm rule," and in recognition of his administrative ability and other merits. Though he accepted the election in February, Boris delayed his coronation until the first of September in order to convince himself that he would have popular support.

Those of the boyars whom he distrusted he either banished or put in places where they would do him no harm. Prince Bogdan Bielski was exiled to a remote spot on the Volga, Fedor Nikitich Romanov was sent to a distant monastery and became a monk (Philaret), and the Shuiskis and Golitsyns were appointed to posts far away from Moscow.

In governing the country Boris carried on the work he had begun under Tsar Fedor. He avoided foreign conflicts, and worked to build up the country. He was anxious to do away with usury and to protect the peaceful inhabitants from all oppressors. He befriended the common people and looked after their welfare. During the famine years of 1601-03 Boris distributed grain, and gave employment to the needy. His resources, however, were inadequate to take care of all the hungry, and the situation got out of hand. Hordes of famine stricken people, as well as bandits, wandered all over the country, plundering, burning and killing. Famine and highway robbery, in the words of the contemporaries, were "the beginning of the calamity" for Russia.

In his solicitude for the state, Boris attached a great deal of importance to European learning. He had in his service foreign artisans, military instructors and architects. He gave his son, Fedor, a very good education, and sent Russian young men to foreign countries in order to prepare them to become teachers for schools which he planned. In short, under Boris Godunov there had become apparent the drift of the Moscow Government toward closer relations with the enlightened West.

67. THE PRETENDER.—In 1603 rumors spread in southwestern Russia and Poland that Tsarevich Dmitri Ivanovich, who was supposed to have died at Uglich in 1591, was alive. The man who assumed this name, and who later was known as The Pretender, gave a vague account of how he had been saved from the hands of Godunov. He went to Poland where he became a Catholic. He was presented to the king, Sigismund III, who helped him to raise an army of Poles and Cossacks to regain the throne usurped by Boris Godunov.

When the news reached Moscow that a Pretender had made his appearance, the authorities there recalled that the name of Dmitri had been assumed by a fugitive monk, Gregory Otrepiev, who had lived at one time in the Kremlin and became well acquainted with affairs in Moscow. From Moscow, Otrepiev, with three other monks, fled to Lithuania and Poland, and pretended to be the Tsarevich Dmitri. Although Moscow communicated all these facts to Poland, no credence was given them, and The Pretender continued his activities unmolested. Some scholars are inclined to believe that The Pretender was the Tsarevich Dmitri, and that he had been saved by the Nagois from Boris' assassins. Others are of the opinion that the Pretender was not Otrepiev, but some other person in whose company Otrepiev had been traveling from Moscow to Poland. Still others claim that the Pretender was not even a Moscovite, but a native of Western Russia, trained by the Poles to play his part. It is more than probable that he was a Great Russian and used as a tool by the boyars who were opposed to Boris and allied with the Romanovs. The ringleaders of this intrigue assured the Pretender that when he was saved from assassination he was given a different name and concealed in a monastery until it was safe for him to come out. All the actions of the Pretender go to show that he looked upon himself as the real tsarevich; hence he did not fear being exposed as a Pretender.

In the fall of 1604, the Pretender left his headquarters at Sambor and started for Moscow. He met with little opposition until he came to Novgorod-Sieversk, where he was utterly routed and driven back to Putivl, the boundary line of the territories of Moscow. His agents gathered another force made up of soldiers of fortune, frontiersmen, Cossacks and garrison soldiers who were incited to rebel, and led it north once more to the fortified town of Kromy. The army of Boris followed the Pretender to this place and, while it was wearing itself out trying to take Kromy, Godunov died suddenly in April, 1605.

The throne of Moscow was now occupied by Boris' young son, Fedor, but the power behind the throne was his mother, Tsaritsa Maria Gregorievna (the unpopular daughter of the *oprichnik* Maliuta Skuratov). Maria had neither the ability nor the prestige of Boris, and the situation soon got out of hand. The smoldering hatred of the boyars towards the Godunovs now burst into a flame. The Shuiskis and Golitsyns, in common with other boyars, took up the cause of the Pretender, not because they believed in him, but in order to rid themselves, first, of the Godunovs, then the Pretender, and thus clear the way for a tsar of their own making. In accordance with this plan they appealed to the army to swear allegiance to the Pretender. At the same time Prince Vasili Ivanovich Shuiski, who had assured the public that the tsarevich was dead, now asserted that he was alive, and on his way to Moscow. This propaganda aroused the citizens to such an extent that a mob killed Tsar Fedor and his mother, and drove his sister Xenia to a monastery.

In June, 1605, the "true Tsar Dmitri" arrived at Moscow. As already stated, Dmitri had in all probability been prepared for the part of Pretender by certain boyars of Moscow who hated Godunov. In Poland he found support in the King, the Catholic clergy and the nobles. The King helped because he desired to weaken Russia through civil war; the clergy because it hoped to bring Moscow into the Catholic fold; and the nobles because they saw a chance to win fame and fortune. The success of the Pretender was due not so much to the Poles as to the Russians from the frontier, namely, Cossacks, discontented garrisons, banished princelings from the central provinces, and escaped serfs. These Russians had one feeling in common—hate; hate towards the old government, hate towards the Godunovs, and hate towards the "wicked boyars" who oppressed the common people. When this army, made up of so many conflicting elements, entered the territories of Moscow, there was trouble. The Moscow boyars saw the danger and tried to avert it by denouncing the Pretender. Prince Shuiski made still another public statement in which he declared that Tsarevich Dmitri was really dead, and that the present claimant was an impostor who should not be admitted into Moscow. He was no longer believed. He was put into prison, while the Pretender was received with joy as the true tsarevich.

68. REIGN AND DEATH OF THE PRETENDER.—After his entry into Moscow the Pretender appointed his own Patriarch, the Archbishop of Riazan, and had himself crowned. He sent for the mother of Tsarevich Dmitri, Martha the Nun, and received her as his own mother, while she greeted him in public as if he were her own son. On the occasion of his coronation all those who had suffered under Boris, the Nagois, Romanovs and others were allowed to return from exile. Although the Pretender had been converted to Catholicism while in Poland, and had promised the Pope and the King to introduce Catholicism in Russia, yet when he came to Moscow he made no secret of the fact that he was Orthodox, and did nothing to encourage the Jesuits who followed him about. He also failed to let the King have the Russian territories he had promised him, but offered to join him in a war against the Turks and Tartars. The Jesuits and the Polish diplomats were much dissatisfied with Tsar Dmitri. The only Poles whom the Pretender treated with consideration were the Mniszechs, the relatives of Marina Mniszech, for whose hand he was suing. In the hope that the Catholic Marina would exert some influence upon her husband, the Polish Government encouraged the marriage, and Marina and her father went to Moscow.

While The Pretender had caused disappointment in Poland, he found no favor at Moscow. Some of the foreigners who were in Moscow at that time report that

Tsar Dmitri was very intelligent and capable. Russian contemporaries are silent on this subject. They do, however, tell us that he little resembled a tsar, that he did not take a nap after dinner, and walked through the streets without a guard. They go farther and say that he was not even an ordinarily well-bred person, that he was not religious, did not observe the fasts, that he dissipated, and was too friendly with the Poles who had followed him. In a word, he had shocked Moscow by his lack of dignity and plebeian ways. Another complaint was that he made little use of the distinguished boyars, and ran the government with the aid of insignificant secretaries of Polish-Lithuanian nobles. All these things irritated Moscow, but the climax came at the time of his marriage. A great number of Poles had come to Moscow with the Mniszechs to attend the wedding and, as there were no hotels, they were lodged in private houses. The guests assumed an air of superiority and needlessly hurt the feelings of their hosts. The Russians put up with all these humiliations, but when on the day of the wedding the Poles were invited to the Palace and they were not even admitted to the Kremlin, it seemed as if their cup of woe were full and running over. In addition to all this, the populace was aroused over the fact that the new tsaritsa had not become Orthodox, and that the wedding itself had taken place, in defiance of custom, on the eve of a holiday (May 8).

This popular resentment against the Pretender and the Poles was turned to good account by the boyars. Prince Shuiski was let out of prison and he with his brothers and other boyars worked out a plot. Early in the morning of May 17, 1606, the conspirators sounded the alarm with the cry, "the Poles are killing the boyars," and directed the mob to the houses occupied by the Poles, while they (the boyars) broke into the palace. There they killed the Pretender and arrested Tsaritsa Marina and her followers. This accomplished, the boyars tried to stop the massacre of the Poles and the looting of the city, but before they succeeded in restoring order more than two thousand foreigners had been massacred.

69. VASILI IVANOVICH SHUISKI ASCENDS THE THRONE OF THE TSARS.—The disorder lasted two days. On the third, May 19, Prince Vasili Ivanovich Shuiski, ringleader of the plot, had himself proclaimed tsar by the mob in the Red Square. Tsar Vasili kissed the cross and swore that he would put no one to death, "without fair trial and with the participation of his boyars," would condemn no innocent person, and would listen to no denunciation without proof. In other words, he promised to govern his state differently from Ivan the Terrible, Boris Godunov, and the Pretender, under whom executions and proscriptions without any trial were of frequent occurrence. It was generally believed that this pledge had been exacted from Shuiski by the boyars, who, in this way, limited his authority. This oath, however, was pretty much a dead letter, for Shuiski was in reality a very arbitrary and vindictive ruler.

The position of the new sovereign was exceedingly difficult. Moscow was aware why Tsar Dmitri had been overthrown, but the other cities knew nothing as yet. It was necessary to inform the country at large of the reason for the murder of the Pretender and the choice of a new tsar. A detailed account was sent to the various cities, explaining, in the name of the sovereign and in the name of Martha Nagoi, the events at Moscow: the imposture and apostasy of the overthrown Dmitri; his secret relations with Poland and the Pope; his overthrow; the coronation of Shuiski, whose "pedigree" was even older than that of the former tsars of Moscow; and lastly, the discovery of the remains of Tsarevich Dmitri, which had been brought from Uglich and which God had glorified with incorruptibility and miracles because of the innocent martyrdom suffered from Boris Godunov. Tsar Vasili hoped that no further trouble and no new Pretender would have to be feared after such explanations.

70. THE TROUBLES UNDER TSAR VASILI.—Tsar Vasili's explanations failed to produce the desired effect. At many places they were not believed. Rumors were afloat that Tsar Dmitri had saved himself from the boyars, that he had escaped from Moscow, and would soon reveal himself. In the southern borderlands, where a ferment of rebellion in favor of Dmitri had existed a year or two before, the people again began to stir and to gather once more in support of Dmitri against his "wicked" boyar betrayers. As in the time of the Pretender's struggle with Boris, when Putivl was the former's chief stronghold, so now again, under Tsar Vasili, the same stone fortress became the center of the uprising led by the commander of the garrison, the voivod Prince Gregory Shakhovski. The rising spread very quickly, and by the fall of 1606 the country was up in arms and Russia was seething with civil war.

There were three distinct movements against Vasili: one was led by Bolotnikov, another by the Second Pretender, and still another by King Sigismund.

As a soldier Ivan Bolotnikov had fought against the Tartars, was captured by them and sold into Turkey, whence he escaped and returned, by way of Italy and Poland, to Russia where he took service with Prince

Gregory Shakhovski. Bolotnikov was really a leader of a social revolution. He aroused the peasants and serfs against the boyars and landlords, and promised to abolish serfdom and annihilate the "wicked boyars" and the rich in general. His enemies denounced him and his followers as "thieves" and criminals. In the autumn of 1606 Bolotnikov moved on Moscow at the head of an immense host of "thieves." On the way he was joined by nobles from Tula and Riazan, who did not at first understand that between them and the "thieves" there could be no friendship. They kept together, however, until they came close to Moscow. By that time the nobles realized that it was against their class interest to fight with Bolotnikov, and, therefore, at the first opportunity, they deserted him and went over to Vasili. With their aid Vasili defeated the "thieves" and drove them south. They made a stand first at Kaluga and Tula and later they all united at Tula where they were joined by Cossacks from the Volga, led by the Pretender Peter.[3] Vasili's troops surrounded Tula and flooded the fortress so that many were drowned. The others were captured and packed into prison, or given away as presents, or driven off. Prince Gregory Shakhovski was exiled, and Bolotnikov disappeared without a trace, having probably been executed.

At the time when Tsar Vasili was besieging Bolotnikov and his "thieves" at Tula, there was already another person in the city of Starodub-Sieverski who called himself Tsar Dmitri Ivanovich. He claimed to have saved himself from the boyars by escaping to Lithuania. As there was at that time a persistent rumor that Tsar Dmitri

[3] He called himself the son of Tsar Fedor but was the Cossack Ileiko.

was still alive, the new Pretender was taken seriously, although nobody knew at that time nor later who he really was. After the capture of Tula by Shuiski the Second Pretender gathered up a whole army of the fleeing "thieves" and added them to his Cossacks and other forces. In view of the fact that his Russian troops had the same revolutionary ideas as Bolotnikov, they were also called "thieves," and the leader the "Thief." In addition to his Russians the Thief had a considerable number of disaffected Lithuanian and Polish nobles, adventurers, and revenge seekers, among the latter being Marina Mniszech and her father. With this large force the Thief moved on Moscow, made his headquarters in the village of Tushino nearby, and in the summer of 1608 surrounded Moscow and cut off communication with the rest of Russia, with the exception of Riazan. In their encircling movement the "thieves" tried to take the Troitse-Sergiev Monastery. The monks put up a valiant defense and for sixteen months successfully repelled every form of assault. Not all the Russians displayed the same patriotic spirit. Many inhabitants of Moscow for one reason or another went over to Tushino and changed sides so often that they became known as "birds of passage."

In the Thief Vasili had a more formidable opponent than in Bolotnikov. An appeal was sent out to the commanders of garrisons to hasten to the relief of the capital, and Vasili's young nephew, Prince Michael Skopin-Shuiski, was ordered to Novgorod the Great to gather a Russian army and to ask the King of Sweden for help. The Swedes were induced to lend troops in return for the cities of Ivangorod, Iam, Koporie, Orieshek and Korela. While Skopin was engaged in Novgorod a movement of resistance against the Thief started in other parts of Russia. The Tushino bands which appeared on the Volga and beyond in order to subject that part of Russia to the Thief, thoroughly discredited themselves and their leaders by their plundering. To defend themselves the city population and the peasants organized and, under the leadership of military officers sent from Moscow, they were able to drive the marauders back towards the capital.

By the spring of 1610 Skopin had gathered a considerable army, made up of militia from different cities, and Swedish troops, and moved on Moscow. When the Thief realized the danger of his position he raised the siege, abandoned his camp, and retreated towards Kaluga.

While the Thief was yet undefeated Tsar Vasili had already a new enemy on his hands. The Swedish assistance to Tsar Vasili led to a declaration of war against Moscow by the Polish King Sigismund, who felt that an understanding between Russia and Sweden was against his interests. In the fall of 1609 Sigismund laid siege to the very strong fortress of Smolensk. He spent the whole winter there and wasted his resources in a vain attempt to capture it. He then demanded that all the Poles and Lithuanians serving in the army of the Thief should join him at Smolensk. Many refused, saying that they had conquered the Tsardom of Moscow for themselves and not for the king. Under the circumstances Sigismund got little help from Tushino. While he continued before Smolensk, Skopin raised the siege of Moscow. Vasili hoped to send Skopin against Sigismund, but the sudden death of this young and popular hero left the command of the army to Prince Dmitri Shuiski, brother of the tsar, a man of no ability. He started for Smolensk, but was surprised on the way at the village of Klushino by Stanislaw Zolkiewski, the commander of the Polish forces. Shuiski was defeated and retreated in disorder towards Moscow followed by Zolkiewski. This defeat aroused the Thief and he too moved on the capital. This new disaster was too much for the inhabitants. They rose against Tsar Vasili, deposed him (July 17, 1610), and forced him to retire to a monastery. The authority now fell into the hands of the boyars, and, as these governed in groups of seven members, the period of their reign has been called the "septemboyarate rule."

71. ELECTION OF THE POLISH ROYAL PRINCE WLADYSLAW TO THE THRONE.—Long before the overthrow of Shuiski, at the time when the Cossacks and Poles abandoned their camp at Tushino, a certain portion of the Tushinites had refused either to follow the Thief to Kaluga, or to return to Moscow under the rule of Shuiski. Among the more prominent of this group were the Saltykovs, and the Metropolitan of Rostov, Philaret Romanov. The last named had been carried by the Tushinites by force from Rostov to Tushino, and invested there as Patriarch of all the Russias. Philaret, the Saltykovs and their circle proposed to Sigismund that his son, Wladyslaw, occupy the throne of Moscow, on condition that he govern the country with the aid of the "Council of Boyars" and "National Assembly." The King agreed (February 4, 1610), but, since Vasili Shuiski was in power, nothing could be done.

When Vasili was overthrown and Zolkiewski reached Moscow, he informed the inhabitants of the agreement, and demanded that they recognize Wladyslaw as their tsar. The Moscow boyars were willing, but desired to summon delegates from the cities to elect Wladyslaw tsar. This was impossible, for the Thief blocked the way; therefore, a meeting was called in August, 1610, of all such representatives as were in the city. This body elected Wladyslaw, and drew up a charter stipulating that he embrace the Orthodox faith, govern the country through the mediation of the boyars and the National Assembly, and that Moscow remain independent of Poland and Lithuania (both in domestic and foreign affairs). Zolkiewski accepted all these conditions, and took the oath on behalf of Wladyslaw, and the Russians kissed the cross in token of allegiance to the royal prince. This election was by no means unanimously approved by the Russians. Some of them insisted that the tsar should be a Russian and suggested for the throne either Prince Vasili Vasilievich Golitsyn, or Michael Fedorovich Romanov, the son of Metropolitan Philaret.

A "Grand Embassy" was organized to go to King Sigismund to offer the throne to Wladyslaw. Zolkiewski saw to it that the chief envoys should be the most distinguished citizens of Moscow, namely, Metropolitan Philaret and Prince Vasili Vasilievich Golitsyn, the dangerous rivals of Wladyslaw. Accompanied by a large suite, the ambassadors "of the whole country" started for Smolensk. They were not yet aware that the King desired the throne for himself and that he had asked Zolkiewski to prescribe the oath of allegiance to him and not to his son. In vain did Zolkiewski write to Sigismund that this could not be done, that Moscow would under no condition accept him, a zealous Catholic and persecutor of Orthodoxy. As the king insisted, Zolkiewski left Moscow for Smolensk to plead with him. When this failed, he resigned his command and retired to his estate.

The king strove to gain his object and to influence the Grand Embassy, as well as the boyars who had remained at Moscow. Russians who had come to him from Tushino were appointed to various posts at Moscow to act in the name of Wladyslaw and himself. With the aid of these men and the Polish garrison, Sigismund intimidated the Moscow boyars (so that, in their own words, they "scarcely breathed"), and treated Moscow like a conquered city. The Russian envoys stood by the agreement entered into with Zolkiewski, and refused to yield anything in their negotiations with the King and the Polish nobles. An excuse was found for having them arrested, and they were deported to Poland. Hermogenes, Patriarch at Moscow, however, resisted Sigismund's agents in every possible way, and appealed to the citizens not to betray their faith and to stand by the agreement. All those Russians who realized the Polish menace rallied around the Patriarch, and were prepared to fight if necessary. As yet, however, these patriots did not feel the time auspicious for open war. They were afraid of a revival of the domestic troubles by the Thief, who was now at Kaluga waiting for the opportune moment to act in his own interest. Suddenly, however, the news reached Moscow that he had been killed by one of his own followers while out hunting (December 11, 1610).

72. THE FIRST POPULAR RISING AGAINST THE POLES AND ITS FAILURE.—On Christmas Day, 1610, Patriarch Hermogenes issued an appeal to the Russian people to rise up against Sigismund because he had broken his word and plotted against Moscow. When the commander of the Polish garrison learned of this appeal he placed Hermogenes and some of the boyars under arrest. It was

too late. The appeal had already gone forth, and all over the land enraged nationalists were marching on Moscow. By Easter, 1611, there was quite an army of them, and they besieged the Polish garrison in the Kremlin. The destruction of the outer city by the Polish garrison for defensive purposes, and the retreat of the Moscow Government, representing the Polish King, within the Kremlin, thoroughly discredited Sigismund in the eyes of the Russians. Nobody any longer obeyed the orders of the boyars and officials. To the Russians these pro-Polish boyars were traitors and national enemies, fighting for the Poles against the Russians.

In the place of this treasonable government another had to be set up. Elected deputies from the different units of the national army assembled in a general council and "on behalf of the whole country" formed a government to rule the army as well as the nation. At the head of it was a triumvirate composed of Procopius Liapunov, Prince Dmitri Trubetskoi, and Ivan Zarutski. This government was, however, of short duration. The national militia, made up of nobles, merchants, "thieves," Cossacks of the "Second Pretender," fugitive peasants and serfs, worked well enough together during the period of enthusiasm. As the siege progressed the class feeling, the old enmities and feuds broke out anew. At the meetings of "the whole country," or army council, the nobles denounced the lawless and turbulent acts of the Cossacks, and also demanded that fugitive serfs and peasants who had joined the Cossacks should be forced to return to their masters. The Cossacks, of course, took issue on both points. The triumvirate was not of one mind; Liapunov took the side of the nobles, while the other two men defended the Cossacks. At the first favorable opportunity the Cossacks assassinated Liapunov. This bloody act made the Cossacks so bold that they proceeded to abuse and to lord it over the nobles and other citizens, and forced them, in self-defense, to return home. When these had gone there were left in Moscow about ten thousand Cossacks—not enough to force the Poles to surrender, but too many for the welfare of Moscow.

73. SECOND RISING AGAINST THE POLES AND THE LIBERATION OF MOSCOW.—In the fall of 1611 Russia was in a desperate plight. The Poles were holding Moscow, Smolensk and other cities in the southwest, while the Swedes were occupying Novgorod and other Russian territory. There was no military force aside from the Cossacks and they were doing more harm than good. There was no government, no leadership, and no one knew just what to do. From all parts of Russia prayers went up, "God save Russia." In those terrible days it was the clergy who rallied the Russian patriots in defense of their country. Archimandrite Dionysius of the Troitse-Sergiev Monastery was tireless in his endeavors to unite the Russians against their enemies. He minimized class enmities, treated the Cossacks as patriots, and appealed to them, as well as to the nobles, to forget their feuds and work together for the salvation of their country. Patriarch Hermogenes, a prisoner of the Poles in the Kremlin, was equally tireless in his efforts. But he had no confidence whatsoever in the Cossacks. He knew that they had in their camp Marina Mniszech and her son, Ivan, "The Little Thief," whom they planned to put on the tsar's throne. By word of mouth and by letter he urged the Russian patriots not to trust but to fight the Cossacks. The cries and appeals of Hermogenes and Dionysius were taken up by the

clergy of the provinces, and partly through their efforts the towns were induced to work together for the national good.

The leadership in this national movement belongs to the city of Nizhni-Novgorod and to its patriotic citizen, Kozma Minin Sukhoruk. In September, 1611, he persuaded his fellow citizens to appropriate one third of the annual income of each house owner for the purpose of raising an army. When the money was raised Prince Dmitri Mikhaelovich Pozharski was appointed to organize the militia. The next move was to persuade the neighboring cities to follow a similar policy. In their correspondence the citizens of Nizhni-Novgorod made it clear that the army was to be used against the Poles and the Cossacks. In the course of the autumn and winter of 1611-12 many other cities in addition to Nizhni-Novgorod put their forces under Pozharski and entrusted their funds to Minin. The Cossacks in Moscow regarded this as an insurrectionary movement and prepared to crush it. In the spring of 1612 Pozharski moved his forces to Iaroslavl on the Middle Volga and summoned a national assembly of the clergy, boyars, and representatives of the cities. At Pozharski's request, this assembly assumed both the civil and military government of the country. It planned first to elect a tsar and then order a march on Moscow. Circumstances, however, necessitated a change in the plan.

In July, 1612, a report reached Iaroslavl that Sigismund was sending reënforcements to Moscow, and, to prevent their entrance to the city, Pozharski hurried towards the capital. The Cossacks were so hostile that it was necessary to camp some distance from them. At first they tried to assassinate Pozharski, but when that failed they became alarmed, and more than half of them, together with Zarutski and Marina Mniszech, fled to Astrakhan. The remaining Cossacks, under Prince Trubetskoi, attempted to come to terms with Pozharski. Before these negotiations were concluded the Polish reën-forcements came up and attacked Pozharski. In this bloody battle the Cossacks were at first little more than spectators but when they finally got into the fight the Poles were repulsed. After this victory Trubetskoi and Pozharski consolidated their departments and officials into a single government and did "all things in common." On October 22 the Russians took Kitaigorod, just outside of the Kremlin and four days later the Polish garrison, exhausted by hunger and fighting, surrendered to Pozharski. Moscow was once more free. To commem-orate this great event, the army erected the Kazan Cathedral on the Red Square.

74. Election of Michael Fedorovich Romanov as Tsar.—Immediately after Moscow was delivered, the Provisional Government of Princes Pozharski and Trubetskoi notified the different cities to send ten elected deputies from each city to the capital for the purpose of "choosing a sovereign." In January, 1613, the repre-sentatives of fifty cities arrived at Moscow, and, together with the citizens of the capital, formed an electoral con-vention. The first question to be taken up was the possi-bility of having foreign candidates for the throne. Wladyslaw and the Swedish Crown Prince Philip were considered and rejected. After the discussion it was agreed not to choose "a tsar among peoples of other faith," but to elect their own from "among the great families of Moscow." There were many "favored sons," and for a long time no agreement could be reached. The

Cossacks and the people from the provinces, who were in large numbers at the capital, were for the youthful Michael Fedorovich Romanov. They became so loud in their demands that on February 7, 1613, the convention for the first time voted in favor of Michael. It was however, decided to postpone the final choice until the opinion of the country at large and of the boyars who had not come to the convention could be ascertained By February 21 favorable news had come from the cities and the boyars. Therefore, on that day Michael Fedoro vich Romanov was solemnly proclaimed Tsar, and the members of the convention and the population of Moscow took the oath of allegiance to him.

The new tsar was not then at the capital. In 161? he and his mother, Martha Ivanovna the Nun, were kept prisoners in the Kremlin. Upon their release his mother returned to the monastery, while he went to his estate in Kostroma. While in Kostroma he almost fell into the hands of a lawless band of Polish soldiers or Cossacks He was saved by one of his loyal peasants, Ivan Susanin who after warning Michael led the bandits into the depths of the forest, where he perished with them Michael escaped to the strongly fortified Ipatiev Mon astery near Kostroma where his mother was, and there a deputation from the national assembly found him. Michael at first refused to accept the throne. His mother advised him not to accept it because she said the Russian people had "lost their firmness of spirit," and would probably do away with the youthful Michael as they had done away with Fedor Godunov, the Pretender, and Shuiski. After much pleading with him Michael Romanov yielded. On March 14, 1613, he gave his consent and then went to Moscow.

75. Significance and Consequences of the Times of Trouble.

As one studies the details of this stormy period its course becomes clear. The trouble started with the running out of the dynasty, but the real reasons for the upheaval are to be found in the prevailing discontent among all classes of the population.

The boyars and princelings were embittered against Ivan the Terrible and Godunov, and jumped at the first chance to regain their position at court and in the affairs of the state. From the death of Ivan the Terrible a *palace struggle* for the crown of the tsar had been going on among the different aspirants for power. By launching the Pretender against Boris Godunov, the boyars had provoked a *popular movement*. The Pretender found his main support among the Cossack class, made up of peasants and serfs who had left their homes on account of the oppression of their masters, the landlords. The Cossacks joined the fight, not so much to help the Pretender, as to get even with the nobles at Moscow, and to obtain from Dmitri all manner of rights and privileges. When the Pretender fell by the hands of the boyars, the Cossacks continued to fight, aiming straight at the overthrow of the entire system of serfdom under which the peasants and serfs were suffering and groaning. The palace struggle for power developed into a social war, the lower classes and the Cossacks being arrayed against the landlords and boyars.

This civil war destroyed all order. The Poles and Swedes took advantage of the "chaos"; the one power seized Moscow and Smolensk, while the other took Novgorod. The first attempt to expel the Poles from Moscow failed because the popular army was made up of too many mutually hostile elements. In the end the Cossacks drove off the nobles, but the Cossacks alone were not strong enough to capture Moscow. Then the nobles and citizens united in one army to fight the Poles, as well as the Cossack "thieves," and defeated both. Having liberated Moscow, they hastened to elect a tsar, and little by little put an end to the anarchy.

In this way the troubles that had been caused by the extinction of the dynasty at Moscow passed through three stages: (1) the struggle of the boyars for power and for the throne; (2) the struggle of the lower classes (Cossacks) against the higher (landlords); (3) the general struggle of the Russian people against the foreign enemies and domestic "Thieves."

This anarchy, having lasted nearly a quarter of a century, could not but leave a deep trace in the political and social conditions of Moscow. To begin with, the boyars, after starting these troubles, not only failed to achieve their object, but were themselves utterly ruined. Some of the leading boyar families disappeared, others became obscure and poor, while still others lost for a long time all their former influence. Greatly undermined by Ivan the Terrible, the power of the boyars was completely shattered by the Times of Trouble.

The Cossacks also failed to gain their object. No matter how often they revolted, they always lost. Finally, the main force of the Cossacks, led by Zarutski, fled from the country, while the remaining Cossacks surrendered to the national militia. Zarutski himself perished, and the Cossacks who remained in the "wilderness" and on the Don ceased troubling Moscow and tried to live in friendly relations with her. They set up on the lower Don something in the nature of an independent state governed by elected leaders, and occupied themselves with hunting, fishing, and fighting the Tartars and Turks.

With the aristocracy ruined and the Cossacks defeated, the chief influence in the State of Moscow fell into the hands of the lesser nobles and city middle class. It was their militia that had liberated Moscow, and it was their national assembly that had chosen Michael Romanov. They composed the tsar's own council (Boyars' Duma), as well as the staffs of officials who took up the administration of the country after the anarchy had ceased. These were some of the consequences of the Times of Trouble.

The government also felt most deeply the effects of these troubles. Former sovereigns had regarded the state as their private "patrimony," but the newly elected sovereign looked upon the state as a tremendous force that required a national council for its proper control. This is why the new tsar was loath to rule the country without the aid of a National Assembly. The entire history of Russia during the seventeenth century is deeply bound up with events of the Times of Trouble.

These were some of the significant and outstanding features of this period. They signalized the end of the old order and the coming of a new.

CHAPTER V

THE TIME OF TSAR MICHAEL FEDOROVICH ROMANOV (1613-1645)

76. BEGINNING OF HIS REIGN.—Tsar Michael was only seventeen years of age and in poor health when he took the throne. He had to depend on some of his relatives to help him govern, and of these the Saltykovs took the most prominent part. They were not always inspired by the highest motives, and removed from the neighborhood of the tsar all those who might stand in the way of their selfish ambitions. Trubetskoi and Pozharski, the leaders of the national militia, and many others who had had so much to do in restoring peace and order and putting the young monarch on the throne, were appointed to distant posts, or totally ignored. It is true that the tsar's council of boyars (boyar duma) met from time to time, but the real power, at first, was in the hands of a circle of court favorites. On the other hand the National Assembly (zemski sobor) exerted considerable influence and functioned uninterruptedly for ten years. The tsar insisted on having this body near him to help him pacify the country, to advise him in matters of legislation, and to give him moral support. Every important measure was approved by the assembly "on behalf of the whole country," and representatives of the assembly accompanied the tsar's officers on all important missions.

77. THE STRUGGLE AGAINST THE ENEMIES OF THE STATE.—At the beginning of the reign all the energy and resources of the government were used to get rid of the domestic and foreign foes. Ataman Zarutski and his band of Cossacks, who had fled with Marina Mniszech to Astrakhan for the purpose of setting up a Cossack state under Persia, quickly came to grief. A Russian force was sent against him, but before it got to Astrakhan the local inhabitants drove him off. Zarutski marched northward and, together with Marina Mniszech and her son "Tsarevich Ivan" or the "Little Thief," was captured on the Ural River. Zarutski and Tsarevich Ivan were executed, Marina sent to prison, and the Cossacks scattered.

The small lawless bands that infested the country were difficult to deal with. They were hard to come up with, and at times they combined into a considerable army and attacked the small force of regular troops sent against them. In 1614 a horde of these "thieves" under Ataman Baloven advanced up to the very gates of Moscow, but this boldness cost them dear, for they were badly beaten by the tsar's troops. After the destruction of Baloven's force there was little trouble from the Russian "thieves," but the Lithuanian and Polish marauders continued to devastate the country for some time. Another gang of "thieves" were the "Cherkasses" (Dnieper Cossacks), who, in their plundering expeditions, came even as far north as the White Sea. Gradually, however, the "thieves" were put down and order reëstablished.

In addition to fighting the Cossacks at home, Russia was carrying on war against Sweden and Poland. Sweden would not give up the Finnish coast, Novgorod and neighboring towns, and Russia was not strong enough to

take them away by force. In 1617, through the mediation of Dutch envoys and an English merchant, John
Merrick, peace negotiations were opened between the
Swedes and the Russians. A treaty of peace was concluded at the village of Stolbovo in 1617. Novgorod
and several other cities were restored to Moscow, and
the Finnish seacoast from Narva to the city of Korela
was left to the Swedes.

King Sigismund and his son would not give up their
claims to the throne of Moscow, but were not in a position to make their claims good. During 1617 and 1618
Wladyslaw invaded Russia and came as far as Moscow,
but could not take it. By this time both sides were
exhausted and ready to make peace. Peace commission-
ers representing the two monarchs met at the village of
Deulino (near the Troitse-Sergiev Monastery) and
opened negotiations. As Michael would not permanently
surrender Smolensk and the other Russian cities, and as
Sigismund and Wladyslaw would not surrender their
claim to the Tsardom, no peace was at this time possible.
Under the circumstances a truce for fourteen and one
half years was concluded. It was stipulated that
Smolensk and the Sieversk cities should be held temporarily by the King, and that the Poles should release
from captivity Metropolitan Philaret and all other
prisoners.

78. PHILARET ROMANOV AND HIS POLICIES.—In the
summer of 1619, Philaret Nikitich Romanov, father of
Tsar Michael, returned from captivity and was consecrated Patriarch. This office had been waiting for him
since the death of Patriarch Hermogenes (1612). Philaret was also given the title of "Grand Sovereign," the
same rank as that held by the Tsar himself. This gave

Moscow actually two sovereigns. Philaret, being the more experienced and having greater strength of character, took the lead, and, until his death (1633), he governed the state with enegry and firmness and without the assistance of favorites.

Very soon after assuming power, Philaret addressed the National Assembly on the condition of the country, and recommended for its consideration certain administrative and financial reforms. During the civil wars the local self-government institutions created by Ivan the Terrible (sec. 58) had almost completely disappeared. As military measures, the elected "Elders" were displaced by appointed military officers (voivodes), and these officials abused their authority and oppressed the people. Complaints against them did them no harm, for they had their confederates in the government bureaus at Moscow. In order to curb these voivodes a special department was created to look into the acts of these men. As this measure failed to cure the evil, the voivodes were recalled, and the inhabitants of the districts were allowed to elect their "elders" from the local nobility. Unfortunately there were not enough of these nobles to go around, for the few who were available were already in the military and civil service of the government. For a somewhat similar reason it was impossible to do away with the corruption and graft at the capital.

Philaret was equally unsuccessful in his efforts to bring about a more just distribution of the burdens of taxation. In 1619 a census of the country was taken in order to determine the kind and amount of service each landholder should render the state. On the basis of this survey assessments were made, but the results were not entirely satisfactory.

79. SOCIAL AND ECONOMIC CONDITIONS.—The government reorganized the landholding system of the nobility. It took the lands from those who showed themselves incapable and failed to render state service, and added them to the estates of those who were performing their obligation. To the last category of nobles the government gave money also. Widows and orphans of nobles who had died in the service of the state were given small sections of land as pensions. It was more difficult to regulate the relations between the landlords and their laborers. The ruined peasants were ever on the lookout for a chance to improve their miserable condition. They went from the small estates to the large ones of the boyars or monasteries, or else to the free prairies of the Don. To cope with this situation, a decree was issued entitling the landlords to reclaim their fugitive peasants not only up to five years, as had been the case under Boris Godunov, but ten and even fifteen years after they had escaped. But this was only of small help, and the nobles did not cease petitioning the government for a law that would permanently bind the peasant to the estate.

In the reign of Tsar Michael, when the taxation was heavy, many people, especially in the cities, tried in various ways to evade paying. One of the forms of this evasion was to convey the land to a boyar or monastery while retaining possession and enjoying the benefits of ownership. Such transfers of land and consequent reduction of taxable areas made the burden of the remaining taxpayers in the mir heavier. These men petitioned the tsar to put an end to this practice, but in view of the fact that the parties concerned observed the forms of the law little could be done to stop it.

There were still other ways of dodging the payment of the taxes, either in whole or in part. At that period only "plowed land" was assessed, and in view of that fact, as well as the destruction of crops caused by lawless gangs, many people cultivated a minimum amount of land. To check this evil, the government changed the "acreage" to a "household" tax. It made each peasant household pay irrespective of the arable area.

In order to increase his revenue, which he so greatly needed, the Tsar encouraged foreign commerce. In 1614 he granted the English and Dutch merchants the right to trade anywhere in Russia, the latter on the payment of low duties, and the former without any payment of duty. Under these special privileges the foreigners made great headway, but it was pretty much at the expense of the natives, who could not stand the competition. Not only foreign merchants, but foreign specialists of all kinds, were encouraged to come to Russia. The Times of Trouble showed the need of close contact with the West, and the need of armies equipped and trained on the model of Europe. For this purpose foreign military officers were engaged, and foreign scientists employed to prospect for metals and to build foundries and arsenals. Foreign physicians, foreign artisans, and even foreign scholars were needed and employed in Moscow. Towards the close of Michael's reign there were about one thousand Protestant families in the "German" suburb of Moscow.

80. THE WAR WITH POLAND AND THE PROBLEM OF AZOV.—In 1632 King Sigismund of Poland died, and the Russians decided to take advantage of the inter-regnum to regain Smolensk. An army of 32,000 troops was hurried to Smolensk and surrounded this strong for-

tress. For eight months they besieged it in vain, and, by the end of that time, the newly elected King Wladyslaw came to its relief. He defeated the Russians and obliged them to make peace in the summer of 1634. The Tsar agreed to let Poland keep Smolensk and other Russian cities captured by Sigismund in the Times of Trouble, and the King renounced his claim to the throne of the Tsar.

No sooner was the war with the Poles brought to an end when another one loomed up with the Turks and Tartars. As of old, Crimean Tartars attacked the Russians on the frontier, and the Don Cossacks the Tartar and Turkish settlments on the Black Sea and the Sea of Azov. The Tsar, the Khan and the Sultan built fortresses to defend their peoples, but they were not able to control the lawless gangs, though each accused the other of inciting them.

In 1637 a large army of Cossacks captured the city of Azov, massacred the inhabitants, and reported the deed to the Tsar. He refused to approve their action, for he feared trouble with Turkey. In 1641 a Turkish army tried to recapture Azov, but met with little success. The Cossacks realized that unless the Tsar helped them it would only be a question of time before they would be compelled to surrender the place. They, therefore offered Azov to him if he would send assistance. He hesitated, realizing the risks, and finally laid the matter before the National Assembly which met in January 1642. This body voted in favor of accepting the offer of the Cossacks, but at the same time declared that they had no money, and that the corrupt officials in the provinces and in the capital were a greater evil than Turk and Tartars. When he heard the opinion of his deputies, the Tsar notified the Cossacks that he could not help them. After sacking the place the Cossacks withdrew and Azov became once more a Turkish city.

In the reign of Michael friendly relations were established between Moscow and the capitals of Western Europe. England lent the Tsar twenty thousand rubles, and helped him to make peace with Sweden; Austria undertook to bring about peace between Russia and Poland in 1615; France negotiated for trade privileges in Russia. A marriage alliance was arranged between Irina, the daughter of the Tsar, and Crown Prince Waldemar of Denmark, but because of religious differences the plan had to be abandoned.

THE TIME OF TSAR ALEKSEI MIKHAILOVICH
(1645-1676)

81. BEGINNING OF HIS REIGN AND THE RIOTS OF 1648.—In the summer of 1645 Tsar Michael died and was succeeded by his sixteen year old son, Aleksei. The young man called to his aid his tutor the boyar B. I. Morozov, a self-seeking, domineering person. Morozov gathered about him men of his own type, and together they oppressed the people. The situation grew worse when, early in 1648, the Tsar and his tutor married into the same family, and a number of new relatives and office seekers were brought into the government. Their abuses became so flagrant that in June, 1648, a riot broke out in Moscow, and the city was in a turmoil for several days. Morozov was sent out of the city by the Tsar, but many of his confederates were killed and their houses

plundered and burned. Other aggrieved cities also turned against their oppressors, and for a time the whole nation was in turmoil.

After this open insurrection the nobles of Moscow petitioned the Tsar to bring order and system into the existing laws. The youthful sovereign who supposed that all was going well was amazed at these outbreaks. He learned for the first time how Morozov had abused his confidence, and after this would have nothing more to do with him. In his place he put the boyar Prince Nikita Ivanovich Odoevski, a very able and intelligent man. Aleksei also decided to make changes in the bureaucratic system.

82. THE SOBOR CODE OF LAWS OF 1649.—In July, 1648, the Tsar summoned the Boyars' Duma and the Patriarchal Council and deliberated with them on the means of restoring order and justice in the country. After discussing the subject it came out that one of the causes of the maladministration of justice was the ignorance of the laws. The old Sudebnik of 1550 had never been published and could only be copied, the Kormchaia Kniga (sec. 12) was so bulky that no one even thought of copying it, and the supplementary laws were known to very few. This general ignorance gave the judges a chance to do as they pleased. "The law is like a wagon shaft, it turns in whichever direction you push it" became a common saying. To remedy this evil a committee of five, headed by Odoevski, was appointed to collect all the laws (Sudebnik, Kormchaia Kniga) and supplementary decrees since 1550, arrange them in order, prepare a new and complete code, and submit it to the Zemski Sobor.

The Sobor assembled on September 1, 1648. One hundred and thirty cities sent representatives. These included both taxpayers and petty nobility. They met apart from the Boyars' Duma and clergy. After hearing the report of Odoevski the representatives made their recommendations on the old and the new laws. Most of these suggestions and proposals were accepted by the Tsar and were incorporated into Odoevski's code.

The most important among the new enactments were the following: the clergy was deprived of certain judicial privileges and forbidden to acquire more land; the boyars and clergy were forbidden to settle their peasants and serfs in special suburbs near the towns, and to accept fictitious transfers of land (sec. 79); the urban communities were given the right to reclaim the land that had fictitiously gone out of the mir (sec. 79), and to expel all persons not members of the mir; the nobility was allowed to reclaim its fugitive peasants without any limit of time; foreigners were not allowed to trade anywhere in Russia outside of Archangel.

On close examination it is clear that the small nobility and the city people gained most from these laws, and were loud in their exclamation that "Now the sovereign is merciful, doing away with the oppressors in the tsardom!" The clergy and boyars were less enthusiastic, and said that the new laws were inaugurated "for fear of mutiny among the common people, and not because of real justice." The great mass of common people lost out. Peasants were tied down to the soil of their oppressive landlords, and were classed as criminals if they left. And thus the new laws, passed for the benefit of the middle classes, only served to embitter the upper and lower classes.

The work of the National Assembly in connection with the compilation of a code of laws came to an end in 1649, and the new code, known as the "Code of the National Assembly," or Sobornoie Ulozhenie was printed (1650) in what was at that time considered an enormous edition (2000 copies) and distributed throughout the country.

83. Copper Money and Its Consequences.—Tsar Aleksei hoped to pacify the nation by his Code, but one year after its publication a serious insurrection broke out at Pskov and Novgorod. It was caused by the shipment of money and grain to Swedish territory through Novgorod and Pskov, in accordance with certain provisions of the Treaty of Stolbovo (1617). The inhabitants of these two cities disapproved of the act, accused the boyars and voivodes of treason, and attacked the officers and foreigners who were concerned with this export of money and grain. After a short time Novgorod quieted down and submitted to the authorities, but Pskov offered resistance for several months. The Tsar did not wish to cause any bloodshed, and turned the matter over to the National Assembly. This body sent a special deputation to Pskov which persuaded the inhabitants to return to order and obedience, and give up the ringleaders.

Five years later the government had another uprising on its hands. While war was being fought with Poland, and the Tsar was in Lithuania (1654-5), a terrible plague broke out. So many people died of it that trade ceased, agriculture was neglected, and the whole economic machinery came to a standstill. It was difficult enough in normal times to raise sufficient money to carry on a war, but it was almost impossible under the demoralized conditions that existed in that year. The importation of silver also fell off, owing to the decline of foreign commerce, and there was no bullion for the mint. Under the circumstances the government decided to mint copper money of the same size as the silver coin, and give it the same value as silver, though it was worth only one-twentieth as much. Beginning with 1656, copper money commenced to circulate in large quantities. For two years all went well and then rumors spread that the copper coins were being counterfeited, that the officials of the mint were striking coins for themselves and their friends, and that the government itself was circulating too much of this copper money. As a result of these rumors the copper coin depreciated, and the cost of living, in terms of copper money, went up.

The government became alarmed. It issued an order that all payments to the state treasury should be made in silver, but, at the same time, the treasury paid its bills with copper. This created a panic; the value of the copper coin sank still lower, the cost of living went up still higher so that the poor began to cry out "We are perishing utterly and dying of hunger; they do not sell for copper money, and we have no silver." In 1662 the poor of Moscow rose in open rebellion, marched to the village of Kolomenskoie, on the outskirts of the capital where the Tsar was, and demanded the surrender of the boyars whom they believed responsible for the general misery. Aleksei calmed this group of excited people by promising to investigate, but pretty soon another mob arrived, more furious and riotous than the last. When persuasion failed to quiet them, guns were turned on them and many were killed. This act quieted the populace, but did not remedy the evil. "Without silver money everybody expects total ruin through the copper money," the Tsar was assured by the representatives of the trading and artisan classes; and "If this money is going to remain any longer, we, too, must perish from it." In 1663 the copper money was withdrawn and entirely prohibited, and in its place the government put into circulation silver from its reserve.

84. THE MOVEMENT OF RAZIN.—The hard times of the last fifteen years caused many people to escape to the little Cossack towns of the Don. The Don Cossacks, however, refused to take all these fugitives into their "Circle" as equals, and to share with them their rights, privileges, resources, and the supplies which they received from the Tsar. The new arrivals, because of their poverty, were nicknamed "naked," and they were in a most pitiful condition. Cultivation of the soil was forbidden by the Cossacks (who feared it might lead to serfdom), and the hunting and fishing grounds were monopolized by the old settlers. Under the circumstances there was nothing left for the newcomers to do but work for the Cossacks for their keep. Instead of abundance and freedom, the refugees found hunger and bondage. It is no wonder that they became restless and desperate.

Formerly, before the outlet of the Don was barred by the city of Azov, it was easy to go to sea and plunder the Tartars and Turks along the coast. Now that this opening was closed, the eyes of the "naked" Cossacks turned towards the Volga. They organized (1667) under the leadership of Stepan (Stenka) Razin and proceeded down the Volga, looting right and left all the way down to the Caspian Sea. From there they went on the Ural River where they spent the winter, trading and fraternizing with the Kalmyks. In the following year (1668) the Cossacks (about 2,000 in number) led by Razin attacked the Persian settlements along the Caspian (from Derbent to Resht), captured enormous spoils, and forti fied themselves for the winter on a small island near the Persian shore. In the spring of 1669 the Cossacks returned to the Don by way of Astrakhan, a Russian city. The Tsar's officers were afraid of these Cossacks and let them pass. When Razin returned to the Don, covered with fame and loaded with booty, he became a person of importance. All kinds of destitute and desperate characters offered to join him, and in a short time he had three thousand followers. He planned another expedition, but this time it was not against the Persians, but against the Tsar and his boyars. He counted on the support of the lower classes who were embittered by the suffering they had endured during the last few years.

In the spring of 1670 Stenka Razin attacked the voivodes of the Tsar on the Volga. It now became manifest that the lower classes and even the Tsar's soldiers sympathized with the audacious ataman and were ready to make common cause with him. Razin captured the cities of Tsaritsyn, Astrakhan, Saratov, and Samara. Voivodes, nobles, and people of the upper classes in general who fell into his hands were tortured and murdered, and their homes pillaged. Even the churches were not spared. The "rabble" of the cities united with the Cossacks against the "better people." From the towns the insurrection spread to the country, and landlords and government officials were massacred. From a mere Cossack revolt it grew into a nation-wide rebellion, spreading over an enormous territory along the middle and lower Volga. Razin insisted that he was loyal to the Tsar and that his movement was directed against the boyars, the landed nobility, and merchants who oppressed the common man.

By slow stages Stenka moved up the Volga. At Simbirsk he was met by the Tsar's troops, composed of the new regiments trained by foreign instructors, was routed and forced to flee. He was captured on the Don by the domiciled Cossacks and sent to Moscow where he was executed in 1671. His army broke up into numerous bands, and it took several years to restore peace and order in the rebellious territory.

85. PATRIARCH NIKON.—During the reign of Tsar Aleksei the church, as well as the state, passed through a crisis. It started soon after the election (1652) of Nikon to the Patriarchate. Nikon was of humble origin, but highly gifted both in body and in mind. He studied in a monastery and, when his education was completed, was married and became a country priest. His eloquence and attractive personality led to his rise, and to his transfer to the capital. After serving ten years in Moscow, he persuaded his wife to enter a convent, while he went to a monastery on the White Sea and became a monk. He soon became abbot and, while administering the duties of his new office, came in contact with the Tsar. Nikon made a deep impression on Aleksei, who brought him to Moscow and promoted him step by step until, in 1652, he caused his election to the highest office of the Russian Church. Nikon would not at first accept the high dignity, and consented only after the Tsar and all the people present at the Cathedral had tearfully promised "to obey him in all things like a chief, and shepherd, and father." Nikon interpreted this promise literally. His appointment as "Grand Sovereign" by the Tsar strengthened in Nikon the idea of his own importance. When, in 1654, the Tsar left for the Polish front and entrusted the affairs of state to Nikon, he acted as if he were the sovereign himself.

86. Banishment and Deposition of Patriarch Nikon.—According to the contemporaries, Nikon commenced to "stand high and ride far." He was fond of displaying his power, and insisted upon tokens of respect and submission from every one. One of his former friends reproached him with these words: "What honor is there for thee, holy father, in being feared by all? Nothing is heard any longer of the tsar's sovereign power. Everybody is afraid of thee, and thy envoys are feared more than the tsar's." The fact that the Patriarch managed the affairs of church and state with vigor and ability did not make him any friends. He was hated by the clergy, by the nobles, and even by the family of the Tsar, on account of his pride, ambition, and domineering ways. All his enemies realized that as long as Nikon enjoyed the favor of the Tsar they could do nothing to him. They, therefore, proceeded to set Aleksei against him by calling to the Tsar's attention the arbitrary acts of the Grand Sovereign. During the years of war on distant battlefields, Aleksei had developed a great deal. He was able to take a detached view of things, and to think for himself. As he watched from the distance he became less and less pleased with Nikon. For a period he gave him the benefit of the doubt, but as time went on the relations between these two men became more and more strained. Finally, in 1658, the break came. His name was taken off the Court list, and he was no longer invited to appear there. Finding himself treated with contempt, Nikon, on July 10, 1658, after having said mass at the Uspenski Cathedral, set out for the Voskresenski Monastery, about forty versts from Moscow. Nikon departed without giving up his office, and though he urged the clergy to elect another patriarch, he made

it clear that he was still the head of the church. Having a patriarch already, the clergy could not elect another. In order to deal with this matter, a church council was called, but this body split over the question whether a council had the right to depose a patriarch. Interestingly enough the Tsar sided with the party that held that the council had no such power. After debating the matter it was decided to refer it to a "Grand Council" made up of representatives of all the Orthodox Churches. At the end of 1666 the Grand Council convened. There were present about thirty of the most distinguished Eastern churchmen, including the Patriarchs of Alexandria and Antioch. As the time of the meeting of the Grand Council was approaching, Nikon became aggressive. He started for Moscow to reoccupy his throne, but was immediately turned back by the Tsar. He then attempted to enter into direct relations with the patriarchs, and sent them charges and complaints against everybody, including the Tsar, his government and his new code of laws. These papers were intercepted and later used as evidence against him. When the Council went into session Nikon was summoned to appear before it to face the Tsar and to state his case. He took the stand that the church is higher than the state, the patriarch above the tsar. "In temporal affairs," he said, "the tsar and prelate are not above each other, but in matters spiritual, the grand prelate is higher than the tsar." He condemned the new code of laws because it restricted the church and subjected the clergy, in certain cases, to the civil courts. Whatever theoretical merits Nikon's arguments may have had, it is clear that they had no foundation in Russian life. In Russia the clergy had never sought, had never acquired great temporal power, and had never played a prominent part in the state. The Patriarch's reasoning appealed neither to the laymen nor to the clergy, and was interpreted as a move on his part to obtain power.

In writing the verdict the Eastern Patriarchs said that the patriarch should in all things be "obedient" to the Tsar. The Russian prelates took exception to that. They claimed that in state matters the Tsar was supreme, and in church affairs the Patriarch, and their view was finally accepted by the Grand Council. Nevertheless the sovereigns of Moscow held to the idea of the Eastern Patriarchs that the Tsar was over the patriarch and gradually subordinated the church to the state. Nikon was unanimously condemned, deposed from office, and exiled to a distant monastery. In 1681, being then seventy-six years of age, he was permitted to return to the Voskresenski Monastery to spend his last days. He never completed his journey, for he died on the barge that was conveying him down the Volga.

87. THE CORRECTION OF THE LITURGICAL BOOKS IN THE TIME BEFORE NIKON.—Before the introduction of printing under Ivan the Terrible, religious books in Russia were copied by hand and, as a result, many inaccuracies and even absurdities crept into the text. At the Stoglav Council of 1551 this matter was touched upon, and a recommendation was made that the clergy make the necessary corrections. Two years later it was decided to set up a "Publishing House" for the publishing of uniform, verified and corrected texts. In 1563 such an establishment was opened, but it quickly came to grief and closed because of disagreement on what was correct. It was reopened after the Times of Trouble when there was a great scarcity of religious books and it was impera-

tive that new ones be issued. This time, too, the correctors could not agree on many points and accused each other of heresy.

The service books in use were translations from the Greek, made at different times and by different people. It was of no use to compare the different translations with each other, because they did not agree. The only thing to do was to compare them with the original; but unfortunately there were few originals, and few people who could read them.

That was not the only problem. In the course of time certain rites and customs had found their way into the Russian service which were not in the Greek. The Russians made the sign of the cross with two fingers, the Greeks with three. In reciting the Creed the Russians said: "I believe in the Holy Ghost, the True Lord and Giver of life," but the Greeks left out the word "true."

These and like differences had been going on so long that they had become strongly established, and had come to be considered as important and as sacred as any other part of the church service. It was of no use to argue that the "Greeks did not do that" because the usual reply was "the Greeks have lost the purity of the faith," that Moscow alone had the true and pure faith, dogma, and ritual, and that the Russians had always been able to please the Lord, save their souls, and bring their land to the highest state of piety and greatness.

Patriarch Philaret and his immediate successors faced the problem and tried to solve it in an intelligent manner. They sent men to the Balkans and to Kiev (at that time a center of Orthodox theology) to collect manuscripts and books, and to observe the religious services. At the same time they invited scholars from Greece and Southwest Russia to teach the Russians to read the originals, and to help with the translations and corrections. In this manner considerable progress was made during the first half of the seventeenth century in the revision of the prayer book. This very revision stirred up all kinds of theological disputes. Those who blindly followed the unrevised texts accused the foreign scholars of mutilating and distorting the true text.

88. NIKON'S REFORM AND THE CHURCH SCHISM.— Before Nikon became patriarch he belonged to a small circle of scholars interested in the subject of reform. These men realized that there were inaccuracies in the Russian books, and that they should be corrected, but they refused to admit that the Russians were altogether in the wrong, or that they had much to learn from the Greeks or the monks of Kiev. If any changes or reforms were to be made, the Russians themselves would make them. After he had assumed the responsibilities of the patriarchate and had given serious study to the whole question, Nikon came to the conclusion that the Greeks had preserved Orthodoxy in all its purity. Having convinced himself on this point, he insisted in his usual arbitrary and dictatorial manner that the sign of the cross should be made with three fingers and that religious images should be painted after Greek models. By his lack of tact, by his preference of alien "correctors" over the native, he aroused national antagonism, and turned against him many of his former friends. They protested to the Tsar, and denounced his acts as unorthodox and anti-national. This angered him and he exiled the leaders, but their protest was not in vain. Their opposition influenced Nikon to convene a church council. In 1654 this body met at Moscow and took up the pro-

posed corrections which Nikon submitted, and almost unanimously accepted them. Nikon did not stop there, but referred his whole program of reform to the Eastern Patriarchs. In 1655 the Patriarch of Constantinople sanctioned and blessed, in the name of the Greek Church, everything that the Russian Patriarch had done. Nikon made the most of this victory, but by doing so he played into the hands of his opponents. They charged him with submitting a Russian affair to a foreign authority, and subordinating the Russian Church to the Greek.

As long as Nikon remained in power he saw to it that corrected books were printed and distributed, and that the clergy lived up to the new ritual, especially in the matter of making the sign of the cross with three fingers. When he left Moscow in 1658, however, there was no one to push the reforms. His enemies then made use of his unpopularity and organized a movement against the "innovations"—a movement which had as its chief motive the restoration of the "Old Belief." So serious did the agitation become that the Tsar, in 1666, convened the Russian clergy to express itself on the whole subject of innovations. This body gave its hearty approval of the Nikon reforms, condemned the opposition, and anathematized and banished a number of its ringleaders. When the Grand Council met in 1667 it took the same stand on the reforms, and declared the "Old Believers" to be heretics and dissenters. The Solovetski Monastery, a wealthy and famous place in North Russia openly rejected the reforms. When persuasion failed, troops were ordered against the monastery, and for eight years (1668-1676) the monks held out. Their firm "stand for the Old Belief" left a deep impression in North Russia, and made many converts. One of the problems of the Old Believers was how to secure priests. They solved it in different ways. Some persuaded the "Nikonian" clergy to join them, while others made a virtue out of a necessity and did without priests. The "priestless" portion split up into small groups, some of which were quite fanatical.

89. CULTURAL DEVELOPMENT.—Soon after the Times of Trouble, intercourse with the outside world grew rapidly in Russia. Merchants, doctors, engineers and army officers came from the West, while learned theologians and scholars came from Greece and Little Russia. The influence of these foreigners spread beyond their narrowed spheres to the court, the home and the school. Indeed it became so noticeable that it divided Moscow society.

There were many who feared to borrow anything from the outside, who were anxious to preserve the ancient national customs unaltered. The representatives of this nationalistic and conservative tendency held that "Moscow is a third Rome," its people a "New Israel," and the Tsar the sovereign "of all Orthodoxy." They claimed that true religion had been preserved only in Russia, and that it ought to be maintained rigidly and unimpaired; otherwise Russia, like Rome and Greece, would perish.

There was another group of men who refused to take seriously the claims of the nationalists that Moscow was the only Orthodox and divinely favored country. The misfortunes of the civil wars of the early seventeenth century proved to them that God was not particularly mindful of Russia, and the foreign wars of the same period taught them that their neighbors were better educated, richer and stronger than the Russians. They saw that the Greeks were more learned in matters ecclesiastical, and the Western Europeans more skilled in military affairs, handicrafts, and commerce. The learned men of Kiev who came to Moscow, though remaining Russians and Orthodox, were yet farther advanced culturally, because of a proper Western training, than the men of Moscow. Observing these facts, many Russians realized that they had been deceiving themselves, that their national pride had led them astray, and that they would have to learn from the foreigners and borrow from them everything useful and agreeable.

At first only a very few were drawn to the Western ideas and customs, and they were looked upon as apostates and traitors, and punished. Later, however, many powerful advocates of cultural reform made their appearance. Among the more important of these was Fedor Michaelovich Rtishchev who had studied theology under the monks of Kiev and supported their endeavors at Moscow. Another champion of the new learning was the Chief of the Diplomatic Office, Afanasi Lavrentievich Ordin-Nashchokin. He was an admirer of the European systems of government, as well as the social and economic theories of that period (especially protectionism), and was eager to do everything in the State of Moscow "according to the example of the outside, foreign lands." He was not willing, however, to go so far as to imitate every trifling detail, for in his private life he remained a gentleman of the old school. "What care we for foreign custom?" he said. "Their dress is not for us, and ours is not for them." On the other hand, his aide in the Diplomatic Office, the boyar Artamon Sergievich Matveiev, was a great admirer of everything Western European, and he had his entire domestic establishment

organized on the "German" or "overseas" pattern, even
to a theatre. Matveiev was a close friend of Tsar Aleksei
Mikhailovich, and interested him in European ideas.
The succeeding Chief of the Diplomatic Office, Prince
Vasili Vasilievich Golitsyn, was still more progressive
than his predecessors and dreamed of most extensive
reforms.

Following the example of these distinguished persons,
and under their high patronage, the society of Moscow
gradually adopted new customs and ideals. Foreign
dress, household objects, musical instruments, and pic-
tures were introduced in Moscow. At the Diplomatic
Office foreign books were translated, and extracts made
from foreign newspapers. European learning was cultivated, and exerted such a powerful appeal that some
people even fled from the country in their search for
knowledge. An official of the Diplomatic Office, Gregory
Kotoshikhin, made his way to Sweden, where he wrote
an interesting description of Moscow.[1] On the other
hand, people from Western Europe came in ever greater
numbers to Moscow to secure positions in the government service, or to engage in trade. The Catholics made
an attempt to start their propaganda and, with that end
in view, sent in 1659 a learned Croatian Catholic priest,
Iuri Krizhanich. He claimed to be Orthodox and expressed a desire to teach at Moscow. He was, however,
suspected, and forced to leave. After his escape he wrote
a book on Moscow which won him great fame.

A vast cultural change was thus in progress in Russia.
The old ideals were passing, and new ones were rising
and gaining influence. Little by little the Russian people
were emerging from their national isolation and exclu-

[1] "Concerning Russia in the Reign of Aleksei Mikhailovich."

siveness, and entering into active relations with more advanced nations.

90. FOREIGN AFFAIRS UNDER TSAR ALEKSEI MIKHAILOVICH.—Beginning with 1654, Tsar Aleksei Mikhailovich carried on long and stubborn wars against Poland and Lithuania over Little Russia, or the Ukraine.[2] In this struggle Russia reconquered Smolensk, the Sieversk territories, and Kiev, together with the parts of the Ukraine situated on the left bank of the Dnieper. The tide had now turned. Until now Poland and Lithuania had taken the offensive against Moscow, but under Tsar Aleksei Russia forced the fight and put enfeebled Poland on the defensive.

The wars with Sweden and Turkey grew out of the struggle with Poland. The Swedish War (1656-1659) was indecisive, each of the belligerents retaining its possessions. The Turkish War did not go beyond a few minor engagements on the left bank of the Dnieper. Tsar Aleksei died early in the year 1676, and peace was concluded with the Turks by his son, Tsar Fedor (1681).

LITHUANIA AND POLAND IN THE XVI AND XVII CENTURIES

91. THE LUBLIN UNION OF 1569. ITS SIGNIFICANCE AND CONSEQUENCES.—We have learned already (sec. 41) that Polish influence, notwithstanding the constant striving of Lithuania for independence and separation from Poland, continued to grow in Lithuania after Vitovt. This growing influence was spread by the Catholic grand princes and Lithuanian nobility (szlachta).

[2] The Polish possessions on the middle Dnieper where the Russian inhabitants had seceded from Poland and were eager to unite with Orthodox Moscow.

o whom it was advantageous to establish Polish ways
n their Lithuanian principality. The preservation of
he old order, on the contrary, was championed by the
Lithuanian aristocracy, the Orthodox princes and nobles
(pans). When hard pressed by their Catholic sovereigns, many of them either became subjects of the princes
of Moscow (sec. 51), or else defended their faith, their
rights, and the independence of their country at the
Lithuanian "*Seims*," *i.e.*, diets of the nobility. Until
he middle of the sixteenth century the Lithuanian aris-
ocracy, notwithstanding the growing Polish influence,
had been able to hold its own, and to defend the independence of the principality from all Polish attempts to
unite Lithuania more firmly to the crown of Poland.

About the middle of the sixteenth century, the situation
changed. Lithuania went to war against Moscow over
Livonia (sec. 62) and met with reverses. Ivan the Terrible captured Polotsk, devastated the greater half of the
Lithuanian principality, and threatened it with further
conquests. In former times the Lithuanian aristocracy
was not averse to submitting to the authority of Moscow,
but it was different at this period. They feared Ivan the
Terrible and, rather than submit to him, they appealed
for aid to the Polish Government.

At this time the childless Sigismund Augustus was
King of Poland and Grand Prince of Lithuania. With
his death the line of the Jagellons came to an end, and
he question of succession to the thrones of Poland and
Lithuania arose. Should the two countries preserve
he dynastic union, should they have a real union, or
should they dissolve the union altogether? King Sigismund Augustus and the Poles desired a real union and,
taking advantage of the difficult position of Lithuania,

the king and the Poles launched a vigorous campaign in favor of a permanent union. Up to 1569 their efforts were in vain, but in that year, at the Diet of Lublin, the opposition of the Lithuanian patriots was broken and after some stormy debates and quarrels, an act was drawn up providing for a single, inseparable state, the so-called "Rzeczpospolita" or "Republic."

By the Union of Lublin the southern half of the Lithuanian Principality, namely, Volynia, Podlachia, Podolia, and the territory of Kiev became a part of the Kingdom of Poland. The rest of Lithuania remained a separate "Principality" in a "real" or permanent union with the Crown. This was a severe blow to the once powerful State of Lithuania. By taking advantage of the temporary weakness of Lithuania and the strife between the aristocrats and nobles of that country, Poland simply seized half the territory of Lithuania, on the ground that the area in question had long formed part of the possessions of the Polish Crown. From now on the two countries had in common an elected King, a Diet (legislative body), and a Senate (administrative body). Each of them, however, retained its own laws, armies, and local institutions.

Soon after the Union of 1569 Sigismund Augustus died (1572), and a period of "kinglessness" followed while the election was going on. At first the Diet chose Henri de Valois (who later became King Henri III of France), but so restricted his power in favor of the nobility that he quickly tired of the honor, and returned to France. In his place, Stephen Batory (1576-1586) was chosen king, likewise with limited authority; and he in turn, was followed by Sigismund III of the Swedish royal house of Wasa. Under these elective rulers the political power of the state was concentrated entirely in the hands of the nobility, with the exception of a few cities which had the right of self-government. It shared with the king the right of supreme authority. According to the law, the nobility could refuse obedience to the king and even make war on him if he violated their rights and liberties. In short, the nobility had become the absolute master of the Commonwealth, and had almost ruined it. Still, they boasted of their "golden freedom" and openly declared that there was only one class in the country— the "szlachta nation." The Catholic clergy alone succeeded in preserving its independent position; the rest of the population lost all influence in the political life of the country.

The transfer of Russian territories from Lithuania to Poland, and the final triumph of Polish influence in Lithuania was followed by grave consequences for the Russian inhabitants of the Commonwealth. First of all, after the formation of the Union, the question of establishing a church union arose. In the second place, the peculiar features of the Polish aristocratic system bore hard on the common people. The church union, as well as the increasing burdens of serfdom, produced great discontent among the Orthodox-Russian inhabitants, and stirred up a sharp conflict within the Commonwealth.

92. THE CHURCH UNION. THE RELIGIOUS STRUGGLE AND THE ACTIVITY OF THE CHURCH FRATERNITIES. —After the Union of Lublin the idea of subjecting the Orthodox provinces of the Commonwealth to the authority of Rome seemed quite feasible. It was the time of the great religious agitation in Western Europe. The Reformation had alienated many nations from Catholicism, and the Popes were making strenuous efforts to sup-

press the Protestant movement. In this struggle agains
Protestantism the Papacy received powerful suppor
from the Jesuits. As soon as Protestantism showed sign
of life in the Commonwealth, the Jesuits were called i
to fight it and quickly suppressed the movement. The
opened free schools for the training of the children, com
posed scholarly theses against the heresy and in defens
of the Catholic dogma, preached brilliant sermons, an
held public debates on religion. These measures prove
more effective than direct persecution, and Protes
tantism in Lithuania was soon weakened and disappeare
almost completely. Having vanquished the Protestan
"schism," the Jesuits turned next upon the othe
"schism," Orthodoxy, and with the same weapons. The
took every opportunity to expose the deplorably chaoti
state of affairs in the Orthodox Church in the Common
wealth, and assured the Orthodox people that it would b
very easy to cure all their ills by the simple process o
accepting union and acknowledging the supremacy o
the Pope. This idea found its clearest expression in th
work of the learned Jesuit, Peter Skarga, "On the Unit
of God's Church Under One Shepherd" (1577).

The condition of the Orthodox Church in the Com
monwealth was not satisfactory. In the fifteenth cen
tury, after the Florentine Union, the West Russia
Church had seceded from the Metropolitan See of Mos
cow and set up an independent metropolitan at Kiev
By doing so this Church lost the powerful support o
the princes of Moscow and found itself in complet
dependence upon the Lithuanian sovereigns, all of whom
were Catholics. Efforts to establish the union witl
Rome, which were dropped after Metropolitan Isidore'
attempt at Moscow, were constantly being renewed i

Lithuania. Failing to bring the Orthodox people into the Union, the Catholic government deprived them of its protection and looked upon the Orthodox Church coldly and even with hostility. It appointed to the bishoprics persons who were notoriously unfit for this high pastoral office, and it restricted the rights and material resources of the Orthodox churches and monasteries. The Orthodox people felt wronged and humiliated. Some emigrated to Moscow (sec. 41), and those who remained in Lithuania attempted, with the means at their disposal, to defend their faith and their Church from persecution and internal disintegration.

Naturally, the leading protectors of the Church were the Orthodox appanage princes, and their example encouraged the common people to defend and care for their persecuted Church. Under the law, both the landed nobility and the townspeople had the right to exercise a "patronage" over their churches and monasteries. They helped to elect the lower clergy, watched over the intactness of church property, looked after orderliness in church affairs, exposed abuses of prelates and other clergy, and defended the interests of the Church before the government. The parishioners of the churches formed ecclesiastical *fraternities*, which in the large cities (Lemberg, Kiev, etc.) became rich and powerful, and exercised a noticeable influence upon the administration of the Church.

This interference by the laity greatly irritated the higher clergy—those prelates whom the king selected because they advanced the interests of the government and were indifferent to the welfare of the Church. These prelates were more like temporal dignitaries in their way of living, and the more they were censured by their congregations, the more they sought the protection of the Catholic authorities. Finally, at the close of the sixteenth century, these ecclesiastics decided to bring about a union with the Catholic Church in the expectation of securing complete papal and royal protection, and independence of their congregations. In 1591 some of these bishops declared to King Sigismund III their readiness to accept the Union. They next persuaded the Metropolitan of Kiev (the aged and weak-willed Michael Rogoza) to join them. They followed this up by sending a mission to the Pope, petitioning him to take the West Russian Church under his headship.

This happened in 1595. In the following year this affair became a matter of public knowledge and aroused great indignation among the Orthodox, who were opposed to the Union. A church council was then called at the city of Brest, attended by the Uniates who had submitted to the Pope, and by Orthodox who were against the Union. Owing to the strong differences of opinion the council broke up into two bodies. One, led by nearly all the bishops, accepted the Union and became Uniate; the other, made up of the clergy and laity who refused to obey their bishops, took an oath never to forsake the Eastern Church. The King ruled that the decision of the Uniate council was binding on all others, and that the Orthodox Church ceased to exist in the kingdom. In this manner the triumph of the Union was achieved in Western Russia.

Since Orthodoxy was legally abolished, it followed that the propagators of that faith were rebels against the ecclesiastical powers and heretics. Orthodox churches, especially those in the rural districts that had not accepted the Union, were closed or sometimes leased out to Jews.

The Orthodox were deprived of their political rights, were looked upon as mere "plebeians," their faith was styled "plebeian," and they were treated by the higher classes as unworthy of notice. The Orthodox, inspired and led by such men as Prince Constantine Ostrozhski, the Metropolitan of Kiev, and the clergy resisted all efforts to crush the faith of their fathers.

But the chief support of the persecuted Orthodox Church was derived from the fraternities in the cities, and from the larger monasteries (the Pecherski Monastery at Kiev). By their combined efforts there were founded at Kiev and other Russian cities printing presses and schools of theology, especially the "Mogilian Academy." With sermons and books the Orthodox faith was kept alive. In this way did the Orthodox Church answer the Union and the persecutions. The Catholic pressure in Southwestern Russia gave rise to a vigorous intellectual movement, promoted Orthodox theological scholarship, and brought forth a literature in defense of Orthodoxy. The learned monks of Kiev rendered important services not alone to their native Western Russia, but to Moscow as well, when they went there as teachers.

93. FORMATION OF THE COSSACK SETTLEMENTS ON THE DNIEPER. COSSACK INSURRECTIONS.—The transfer of the Russian lands along the Dnieper from Lithuania to Poland, in 1569, led to the rapid spread of Polish institutions in these territories. The Polish nobles moved out on this "border" ("ukraina"), and established serfdom. In this frontier country the Poles came in contact with the Cossacks: Moscow Cossacks on the Don (Don Cossacks), South Russian Cossacks on the Dnieper (Dnieper Cossacks, sometimes called Ukrainian or Cher-

kas Cossacks), on the right bank of the Dnieper below Kiev.

These Dnieper Cossacks lived by farming, fighting the Tartars, and by plundering. They resented the intrusion of the Polish nobles (who intended to turn them, like the peasants, into serfs), and retreated deeper into the steppes beyond the reach of the newcomers. On the islands of the lower Dnieper, beyond the cataracts of this river, the Cossacks built small fortified towns which came to be known as the "Stronghold Beyond the Cataracts," or "Zaporozhskaia Siech." They formed a single community, or "*kosh*," with an elective chief "*kosh ataman*," and successfully resisted aristocratic landlords and savage Tartars.

All the attempts of the Polish Government to subjugate the Cossacks and induce them to abandon their raids into Tartar and Turkish territory proved vain. The more the nobles persecuted the Orthodox Church and oppressed the peasants, the faster flowed the stream of Russian immigrants from Poland to the Ukraine, and the larger grew the number of Cossacks. The Polish kings tried to enlist them in the government service by forming them into special Cossack regiments, by giving them land, by exempting them from the authority of officials and landlords, and by granting them self-government. These enlistments took care of only a very small portion of the Cossacks, for their number was constantly increasing. The newcomers brought with them their hatred of the Church Union, hatred for serfdom, and hatred for the Polish Government. But the act which brought on the rebellion was the effort of the government to suppress the lawlessness of the Cossacks, and make them either serfs or obedient soldiers.

Towards the close of the sixteenth and beginning of the seventeenth centuries the Cossacks started to make trouble for Poland. They attacked, expelled or exterminated the Polish nobles in the Ukraine, freed the peasants and enrolled them in Cossack bands. They invaded Polish territory, and with fire and sword laid waste the land. They ravaged the coasts of the Black Sea, and burned and looted even under the walls of Constantinople.

Much of this happened when Sigismund was attempting to take Smolensk and make himself Tsar of Moscow. He was not in a position to stop the Cossacks. They had become so formidable that their hetman, Peter Sagaidachny, was, for all practical purposes, the ruler of the Ukraine, and the protector of Orthodoxy. He saw to it that no wrong was done to the Orthodox people of Kiev, and was even instrumental in having the Orthodox Metropolitan See restored to Kiev. All these events, of course, could not but greatly irritate the Poles and, at the very first opportunity, they turned on the Cossacks. The Polish army gradually got control of the situation. It occupied the whole Ukraine, executed many of the Cossacks, deprived the others of self-government, and reduced them to serfs. This occurred in 1638, in the reign of King Wladyslaw. The Cossacks stood it for ten years and then, under the leadership of the famous Bogdan Khmelnitski, went on the warpath.

94. BOGDAN KHMELNITSKI AND THE SECESSION OF LITTLE RUSSIA.—Bogdan Khmelnitski, born of a wealthy family, had served with the Cossacks since early youth, and had attained distinction as an officer. He got into trouble with the Poles and ran away from their service. Then he organized a force of Zaporogian Cos-

sacks and Crimean Tartars, and led them in 1648 against the Polish army. The Poles were routed and Khmelnitski became master of the whole of Southwestern Russia, including Galicia. An attempt was made to negotiate peace but, as Khmelnitski regarded himself as the champion of the entire Orthodox population, while the Poles looked upon him and his Ukrainians as rebels, the negotiations fell through. The war was renewed (1649), and led to a treaty of peace signed near Zborow. It stipulated that the number of enlisted and registered Cossacks should be 40,000; that no Polish troops should enter the Ukraine; that Jesuits and Jews should not be permitted to reside in the Ukraine; and that Orthodoxy should become dominant.

This was a great triumph, but not a complete liberation from Polish rule. The Polish nobility with its serfdom, Catholicism, and the Uniates were still in power. Large numbers of disgusted Cossacks emigrated to the east, to the Donets River in the territory of Moscow. The Poles were equally dissatisfied with the treaty, and had no real desire to carry it out. Hence a new war was started (1650) which turned out disastrously for Khmelnitski. He was forced to consent to an unfavorable peace. Realizing that he was not strong enough to fight the Poles alone, and that he could not depend on the Tartars, he appealed to Tsar Aleksei to take Little Russia under his high protection. The matter was referred to the National Assembly which, after deliberating for some time (1651-1653), finally decided to take over Little Russia. In January, 1654, the annexation of the Ukraine to the State of Moscow was consummated at a meeting of the "General Rada," or Popular Assembly, at the city of Pereiaslavl. The "Rada" shouted in chorus: "We want to belong to the Eastern, Orthodox Tsar!" Under the terms of the treaty with Moscow, the Ukraine retained the right to elect the chief of the Cossacks, the right to self-government, and the right to maintain direct foreign relations, except that there could be no dealing with the King of Poland and the Sultan of Turkey without the knowledge of the Tsar.

95. THE STRUGGLE BETWEEN MOSCOW AND THE POLISH REPUBLIC OVER THE UKRAINE.—In the spring of 1654 the war of Moscow against Poland and Lithuania began. The Russian armies captured Smolensk in 1654, and the cities of Vilna, Kovno and Grodno in 1655. At the same time Khmelnitski occupied Lublin, the Swedes invaded Great Poland, and it seemed as if the end of the Commonwealth had come. The only thing that saved it was the quarrel between Moscow and Sweden. Loath to see the Swedes succeed, Tsar Aleksei concluded a truce with the Poles and launched a campaign against the Swedes which, however, proved unsuccessful.

After the death of Bogdan Khmelnitski (1657) an insurrection broke out in the Ukraine. The treaty of annexation was differently understood by the Russians and Ukrainians. The Tsar regarded the Ukraine as annexed territory and the Ukrainians as his subjects, while the hetman of the Cossacks looked upon the Ukraine as an independent state. The Tsar sent in his officers and garrisons to the Ukraine to keep the unruly Cossacks in hand. The Cossack leaders naturally resented it, and planned a secession from Moscow and a new understanding with Poland, though the mass of common Cossacks opposed the restoration of the Polish rule. A bloody civil war then broke out in which the Russian troops, though at first defeated (1659), were in the end victorious.

This Cossack war was merely an incident in the struggle between Russia and Poland, which dragged on ten years (1657-1667) and ended with the truce of Andrusovo. Poland retained Lithuania and the Right (Dnieper) Bank Ukraine; Russia kept Smolensk, the Sieversk territory, the Left Bank Ukraine, and Kiev on the right bank of the Dnieper.

Under this treaty the Ukraine was cut in two, a fact which displeased the Cossack leaders both in Poland and Russia. They conceived the idea of uniting the two parts under the Sultan, and went so far as to acknowledge his authority. This step drew the Turk into Ukrainian affairs, and led to war between Turkey and Russia.

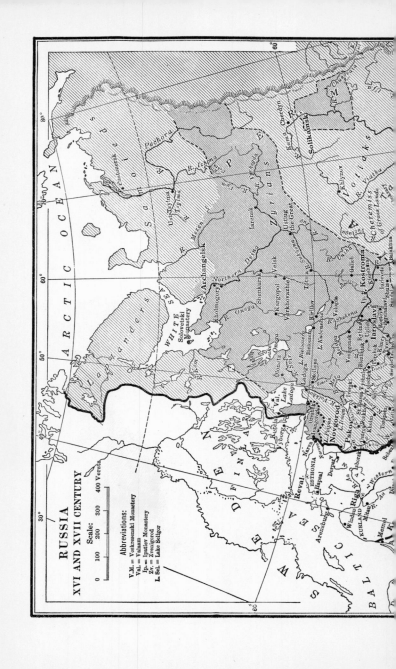

RUSSIA
XVI AND XVII CENTURY

Scale:
0   100   200   300   400 Versts

Abbreviations:
V.M. = Voskresenski Monastery
Val. = Valaam
Ip. = Ipatiev Monastery
Zv. = Zvenigorod
L. Sel. = Lake Seligor

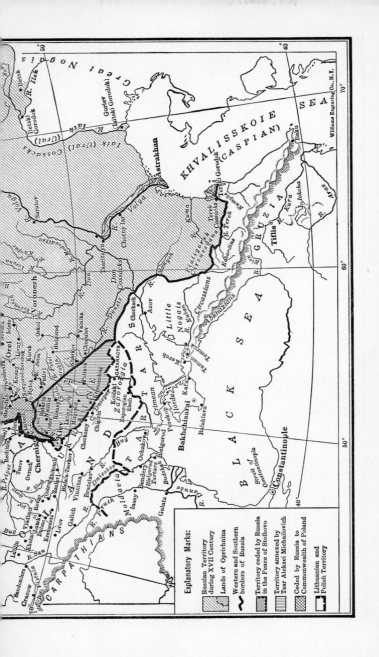

Explanatory Marks:

Russian Territory during XVII Century

Lands of Oprichnina

Western and Southern borders of Russia

Territory ceded by Russia in the Peace of Stolbovo

Territory annexed by Tzar Aleksei Michailovich

Ceded by Russia to Commonwealth of Poland

Lithuanian and Polish Territory

KHVALISSKOIE (CASPIAN) SEA

GREAT NOGAIS

Great Nogais

BLACK SEA

GRUZIA

CARPATHIANS

TARTARY

MOLDAVIA

UKRAINE

Zaporozhia

Constantinople

Astrakhan

Tiflis

Baku

Don Cossacks

Terek Cossacks

Iaik (Ural) Cossacks

William Engraving Co., N.Y.

PART TWO

CHAPTER VI

FORMATION OF THE RUSSIAN EMPIRE

EPOCH OF THE REFORMS OF PETER THE GREAT

96. TSAR FEDOR ALEKSEIEVICH.—Tsar Aleksei Mikhailovich died early in 1676, in his forty-sixth year. He left two sons, Fedor and Ivan, by his first wife, Maria Miloslavski, and one son, Peter, by his second wife, Natalia Naryshkin. Fedor and Ivan were sickly; Peter, on the other hand, was in the best of health. Under such circumstances, the Miloslavskis and Naryshkins became deeply interested in the question of succession, even while the Tsar was still alive. When Tsar Aleksei died and was succeeded by the fourteen-year-old Fedor, the Miloslavskis had the more prominent Naryshkins either exiled to distant parts, or banished from court. Pretty soon, however, the Miloslavskis and Iazykov and Likhachov, the two personal favorites of the Tsar, got into a bitter fight which lasted until Fedor's death in 1682.

97. THE EVENTS OF 1682.—Ivan, though physically weak and mentally backward, should have succeeded his brother; but, as a result of the court feuds, the two

favorites brought about the election of Peter, on the
plea that Ivan was incapacitated. The Patriarch and
the boyars, who disliked the Miloslavskis, gave their
blessing and approval to his act. This procedure was
illegal from two standpoints; first, they had no right to
pass over the oldest son, and second, the National Assembly had not been consulted. This was an issue which
the Miloslavskis seized upon and made the most of.
Sophia, sister of Ivan, a very energetic and ambitious
woman, organized a plot to overthrow her enemies and
get the power in her own hands.

At this time a military organization known as the
Streltsy garrisoned Moscow. These soldiers were well
organized, enjoyed special privileges, lived with their
families in parts of the city specially reserved for them,
and were a power to reckon with. Occasionally they
took the law into their own hands. This was true soon
after the death of Fedor when the *Streltsy* attacked their
officers and committed other lawless and predatory acts.
The government was afraid of them and had to close its
eyes to their deeds. It was to them (the *Streltsy*) that
the Miloslavskis appealed against the boyars who had
"strangled" Tsarevich Ivan.

On May 15, 1682, an armed mob of these troops came
to the Kremlin Palace. Tsaritsa Natalia took both Tsar
Peter and Tsarevich Ivan out to the "Red Staircase" of
the palace to show the mutineers that both were alive
and well. Ivan himself tried to calm the rioters, assuring
them that no one had attempted to murder him and that
he had nothing to complain of. He failed to pacify
them. They broke into the palace and, before the eyes
of Peter and his family, brutally put to death many of
his relatives. From the palace the rioters went to the

city where they tortured and killed the boyars and others listed by the Miloslavskis until all "traitors" were done away with. After the massacres were over the rebels became frightened at their own act, and demanded that the memory of their deeds against the "traitors" be honored by the erection of a special column celebrating the murders. They further demanded that Ivan should reign jointly with Peter, and that the regency during their minority should be exercised by Tsarevna Sophia and not Tsaritsa Natalia. All these demands were complied with. Sophia assumed power and proceeded to get even with her enemies and to reward her friends.

The Miloslavski faction had thus achieved complete success, but they had started something they could not stop. Some fanatical "Old Believers" saw their opportunity now to profit by the agitated state of mind of the country to abolish the innovations of Nikon (sec. 87). They worked on the *Streltsy* and incited them to rise in defense of the "Old Belief," and at their bidding a solemn council of the clergy was convened in the summer of 1682 to discuss questions of religion. The schismatics behaved with much self-confidence, not to say insolence, and when the session was over the Old Believers announced with much joy that they had won the victory. This caused such an agitation that Sophia asked the *Streltsy* officers to seize the schismatics, and put some of them to death. The movement was thus suppressed and the quarrel over the two faiths temporarily silenced, but new troubles soon broke out.

A rumor was spread at Moscow that Prince Khovanski, Commander of the *Streltsy*, was scheming to put the two Tsars and Sophia to death and make himself Tsar. Khovanski behaved tactlessly, making it appear as if he were the only person capable of holding the riotous *Streltsy* in check. The family of the Tsars, including Sophia, was afraid to remain at the capital and went to live at its summer residence, surrounded with troops composed of noblemen. Khovanski and his son were then summoned to appear before the regent, were charged with many evil designs, and put to death. This bold act, as well as the knowledge that an armed force was being sent against them, broke the courage of the *Streltsy*, who pleaded guilty to all their mutinies, and requested that the memorial column that had been erected to celebrate the Fifteenth of May should be destroyed. At the close of 1682 Sophia and Ivan returned to their palace at Moscow, but Peter and his mother continued to live in the villages near Moscow, most of the time at the village of Preobrazhenskoe.

98. Education of Peter the Great.—The year 1682 exerted a most powerful influence upon the character and life of Tsar Peter Alekseievich. During the lifetime of his father, Peter was the spoiled child of the court, and after Aleksei's death Tsar Fedor showered love and care upon him. At the age of five Peter learned to read and write. When he had attained these accomplishments he was placed under the guidance of a monk from Kiev who taught him grammar, Latin and Greek, philosophy, dialectics, and the other studies of the period. But before Peter had gone very far Tsar Fedor died, the insurrection broke out, and he had to move out to the country. His education came more or less to a standstill, for his mother refused to accept the teachers the government selected, and Sophia was inwardly pleased that Peter's education was neglected.

The revolt of the *Streltsy* and the immediate consequences of it left a black and indelible impression upon the child Peter's mind. He saw his relatives butchered before his eyes; he experienced all the agonies of expected death; he lived in fear and trembling, first, from the *Streltsy*, and later from Sophia. As a result of these experiences, he became suspicious of the court and every one connected with it.

Peter's life in the villages on the outskirts of Moscow was very simple. Like most healthy boys he liked to play and, in choosing his playmates, he made no distinction between the children of boyars and the sons of peasants. They played war, built fortresses, and formed military companies. He took his "playing soldier" seriously and, as he grew older, he formed two real regiments from the soldiers of the villages of Preobrazhenskoe and Semenovski. In his artillery practice and fort building he realized his lack of knowledge of mathematics, and the only people who could teach the subject to him were the foreign officers in the Russian army.

The relations between Peter and these foreigners were quite natural. The court was full of foreigners—doctors, artists, artisans, and gardeners. Preobrazhenskoe, the village to which he moved after leaving the court, was close to the "German suburb." Although his mother, Natalia, distrusted the monks of Kiev and Russian teachers, yet she had no fear of foreigners, and whenever something had to be done at her residence, or whenever Peter wished to know something, she sent for the foreigners. In this way it came about that Peter depended on the Germans to help him build his fortress; on the Dutchman Timmerman to teach him arithmetic, geometry and fortification; and on another Dutchman, Brant, to instruct him in the art of sailing. Under the influence of his games and of his foreign instructors, Peter became little by little a soldier and a sailor. He did not obtain the ordinary scholastic education of his time, but acquired instead some special, unusual knowledge, and showed some queer preferences which were not at all what was expected of a tsar. This youthful sovereign represented a cultural type that was quite uncommon in Moscow.

There were many things in Peter that were criticized: his lack of education and training, his passion for boats and ships, and his friendship for foreigners. Peter became a frequent visitor in the German suburb, where he made friends and thoroughly enjoyed himself. He became especially friendly with the Scotchman Gordon, who served as a general in the Russian army, and with the Swiss Lefort, another officer in the army. Lefort was rather gay and lighthearted, and he and Peter sometimes behaved in a way to shock the average Russian. After what has been said it is clear why Peter had no systematic education and training, and why, instead of the usual theological and scholastic studies, he acquired military and technical knowledge, why he disliked the ancient customs and usages of the Moscow court, and preferred the ways of the foreigners.

Until he grew to manhood, affairs of state and court had no attraction for Peter. He devoted himself entirely to the "games of Mars and Neptune." No one thought that he had ability. Moscow spoke of him as a young man of whom nothing sensible was to be expected. His mother, Natalia, in order to get him to take a more serious view of life, picked out a bride for him, Eudoxia Fedorovna Lopukhina, and married him off in 1689. But neither his mother nor his wife could, for any length of time, keep him away from his soldiers and his boats. Thi was the man Peter when, in 1689, he reached the age of seventeen—the age that gave him the right to reign, and his mother and her relatives began to urge him to be a man and to assert his rights against Sophia.

99. Rule and Deposition of Tsarevna Sophia.— Sophia began to rule in 1682 and continued to do so for seven years. The power behind the throne was Prince V. V. Golitsyn, with whom Sophia had become so intimate as to cause gossip. Generally speaking, it must be said that the domestic policy showed very notable humanitarian features. It was even said that Golitsyn planned great reforms, including the liberation of the peasants. In foreign relations the most noteworthy event was the treaty with China. During the seventeenth century the Russians had crossed all of Siberia to the shores of the Pacific, and occupied Kamchatka and the Amur River. No resistance had been offered to the Russians by the small and barbarous native tribes in the north, but the Chinese on the Amur put up a fight. The hostilities were settled in 1689 by the Treaty of Nerchinsk, under which the Russians gave up the banks of the Amur to the Chinese.

In 1686 a permanent peace was concluded with the Polish Commonwealth, on the basis of the truce of Andrusovo of 1667 (sec. 95). King John Sobieski of Poland, hard pressed by the Turks, agreed to the permanent surrender of Kiev in return for Russian help against the Turks and Tartars. In virtue of this agreement, Prince V. V. Golitsyn made two campaigns against the Crimea (1687-1689), but failed on both occasions. These failures, at the very time when Peter became of age, were seized upon by the enemies of Sophia to overthrow her and put Peter in her place. She saw the danger and attempted to avert it by having herself made *permanent* autocrat and co-regent with her brother. At Sophia's suggestion Shaklovity, head of the *Streltsy*, and his agents set to work to get the Streltsy to petition Sophia to have herself crowned Tsaritsa. Their proposal was coldly received by the troops and, when it became known, it discredited the parties concerned. This was the moment when the enemies of Sophia decided to act.

In the summer of 1689 the quarrels between Tsaritsa Natalia and Sophia became so bitter that both sides prepared for the worst. Sophia surrounded herself at Moscow with a guard of Streltsy for fear of assassination. The air was full of suspicions and alarms. One night in August 1689, a false report reached Preobrazhenskoe that Streltsy were being sent from Moscow to kill the Tsar. Peter was dragged out of bed, put on a horse and, with his clothes under his arm, dashed away to a neighboring forest. There he dressed himself and went on to the Troitse Sergiev Monastery. This shock affected his whole nervous system—henceforth his face twitched, his hands shook, and his gait was unsteady. Peter was joined in the monastery by his mother, wife, boyars, his "play" regiments, and companies of Streltsy, as well as regular troops who had come over to his side. When he felt himself strong enough, Peter demanded that Sophia explain the nightly assemblies of the Streltsy, and invited the boyars of Moscow to come to him. Public opinion was in favor of Peter, and Sophia's cause seemed lost. Patriarch Ioakim turned against her, the boyars followed, and finally the Streltsy deserted. Sophia was sent to a convent, Golitsyn was arrested, and Shaklovity and some of his confederates were executed. In a special message Peter called upon Ivan "to rule the Tsardom himself"; but, as Ivan was quite incapacitated, Peter and his friends became the real rulers.

100. The Period of 1689-1694.—The coup d'etat of 1689 made little change in Peter's life. He continued as before to drill his regiments and to sail his ships. The only difference was that he now navigated them on the vast White Sea, while formerly he sailed them on the small Lake of Pereiaslavl. State affairs he left to his mother, the Patriarch, and their circle. He did not always approve of their policy, but for the time being he did not openly oppose. They differed in their attitude towards foreigners; Peter was friendly to them, the Patriarch hostile. In Sophia's reign Ioakim was kept in a rather humiliating position, while the Kiev scholars were given the place of honor, and allowed to spread their teaching. Ioakim called a church council which cast suspicion upon the orthodoxy of the Kiev clergy and deprived the monks and scholars of Kiev in Moscow of their privileged position. Other foreigners were regarded in the same evil light by the Patriarch, and made very uncomfortable; some were even persecuted. Ioakim died in 1690, and his successor, Adrian, was of the same type of mind. Natalia stood back of the Patriarchs, and as long as she lived Peter let her govern as she thought best.

101. Campaigns Against Azov. The Navy. The "Companionships" and the Grand Embassy.—The death of his mother (1694) forced Peter, now twenty-two years of age, to devote himself to government affairs. In fulfillment of the treaty of 1686 with King John Sobieski, a fresh war against the Turks and Tartars had to be undertaken. Peter had seen the failure of the two previous campaigns in the south, and decided that, instead of wasting his forces in the Crimea, he would

attack the Turkish fortress of Azov at the mouth of the Don.

In the spring of 1695 Peter, to conceal his real purpose, sent a large army to the lower Dnieper to threaten the Crimea, while he, with another force, moved down the Don and the Volga against Azov. The siege of Azov dragged on till the fall of 1695 without any success, because the besieged received supplies and reënforcements by sea. Peter, who took a deep interest in the military operations, realized the causes of his failure, and went to work to remove them by building a navy that would blockade Azov. At Voronezh, Moscow and other cities, work was started, and by spring a "sea fleet" of thirty naval vessels, besides hundreds of small craft, was ready at Voronezh and elsewhere. In the summer of 1696 a Russian army and navy surrounded the fortress of Azov and captured it. This was a great and unexpected success. Peter, Gordon, Lefort and their associates proved that they could perform deeds of valor as well as play games.

This victory spurred Peter's ambition, and suggested to him vast projects. He conceived the idea of building a large navy and forming a European combination with the view of driving the Turk from Europe, and immediately set to work to carry out this idea. He was now in a better position to do what he liked since he was now the sole ruler, for Tsar Ivan died in 1696.

The building of the new navy assumed the character of a special national duty. The order was given that the land owners should deliver by the year 1698 a certain number of full-rigged and armed ships [1]; and that the city

[1] Secular estates at the rate of one ship for 10,000 peasant households, and church lands at the rate of one ship for 8,000. The land

inhabitants together should furnish twelve vessels. In the same brusque, direct and arbitrary fashion Peter settled the technical problems. Shipyards were built at Voronezh, and shipbuilders and all kinds of technical workers were invited thither from foreign countries. To train native sailors, seamen, and shipbuilders for the future navy of his country, Peter (1697) sent fifty young nobles abroad to study "navigation science." If the "companionships" were felt as a burden by the people all over the country, the latter measure made the whole aristocracy at the capital fairly groan.

Peter's next step was to bring about an alliance of the Christian Powers against the Turks and Tartars. For this purpose he sent a "Grand (Extraordinary) Embassy" to the courts of Germany, Holland, England, Rome, and Venice. Lefort and F. A. Golovin were appointed the Ambassadors and furnished with a large suite, which included the Tsar himself under the name of "Corporal Peter Mikhailov of the Preobrazhenski Regiment." Before going, Peter turned over the affairs of state to his uncle, Lev Naryshkin, his tutor, Prince Boris Golitsyn, and to other trustworthy subjects.

The political schemes and personal acts of the young sovereign aroused opposition and complaints were made that he was amusing himself to the detriment of the people. Feeling against him was so strong that there was a plot on his life. It was discovered before he went on his journey and drastically put down. The ring-

owners were called to Moscow to form "companionships" in order to apportion the cost among themselves. It was estimated that a ship would cost 10,000 rubles, or 1 to 1.20 rubles per household—quite a large amount for those days. The total cost of the new navy (up to 50 ships) was placed at half a million rubles—equal to one fourth of the annual revenue of the crown.

leaders were executed, others were exiled, and the Streltsy who were involved were transferrd from Moscow to **Azov** and the Lithuanian-Polish frontier.

PETER'S JOURNEY ABROAD

102. THE FOREIGN VOYAGE OF PETER THE GREAT.— The foreign voyage of Peter the Great had much influence on his life. He acquired much useful knowledge, became used to the more civilized ways of European life, and accepted the European point of view. Furthermore, the journey of the Tsar stimulated the intercourse between Russia and the West, and led to a greater exchange of men between the two parts of Europe. Hereafter, many Russians went to live and study in foreign countries, and hundreds of foreigners came to Russia. Lastly, Peter's contact with European politics made him give up the impracticable dream of driving the Turks back to Asia, and adopt the more practical one of fighting Sweden for the possession of the Baltic seaboard.

The Grand Embassy departed from Moscow in the spring of 1697. At Riga the Swedish authorities met the Russians very stiffly; in Courland they were received more cordially, and in Prussia they were given a most hospitable welcome. Elector Frederick refused to go to war against the Turks, and advised the Tsar to fight the Swedes instead. From Prussia the Tsar proceeded to Holland. On the way he met and spent the evening with the wife and mother-in-law of Elector Frederick. These ladies have left an interesting account of his appearance and conduct. They were impressed with his intelligence and vivacity, and lack of good manners. "He is very good and very bad," they said. The same impression of a remarkable but ill-disciplined person was made by the Tsar also in Holland.

In Holland Peter left the embassy, and went to the little Dutch town of Saardam, noted for its shipyards, to work as a common ship's carpenter. The citizens of Saardam had no difficulty in identifying the Tsar, because of his huge stature and the peculiar shaking of his head of which they had heard. He became an object of curiosity and this so disgusted him that he left after eight days and went to Amsterdam. Here he was less annoyed. At one of the largest shipyards Peter was employed as an ordinary mechanic for more than four months and, as he said, "Through my own efforts and skill I built a new ship and launched it." He was not yet content with his knowledge, for in Holland ships were built according to "long practice," and not according to scientific theory. In order to get his theory, Peter went to England, for he had heard that "in England this art is just as perfect as any other, and it is possible to master it within a short time." He secured a position in the government shipyard at Deptford, and "after four months finished this science." In addition to the "navigation business," Peter, while in Holland and England, made a study of museums, factories, hospitals and other public institutions.

After his work in England Peter returned to Holland, and then went, together with his embassy, to Vienna. Wherever the Grand Embassy turned with its proposal of a general war against the Turks it met with failure. In Western Europe an intensive struggle had commenced between the Hapsburgs and Bourbons, and nobody was interested in the Turks. The German Emperor, who was at that time fighting the Sultan, was trying to make peace with him in order to throw his forces against France. Dissatisfied with the Emperor, Peter was about to start for Venice, when he was hurriedly recalled to Moscow by the news that the Streltsy had revolted. On his way back to Russia he passed through Poland and met the new king, Augustus (the Elector of Saxony). The two monarchs struck up a friendship which developed into the idea of an alliance against Sweden.

103. THE FIRST REFORMS AND THE SUPPRESSION OF THE STRELTSY.—When he arrived at Moscow in 1698, Peter did not stop at the palace, but went directly to his own village of Preobrazhenskoe. He did not allow family ties to interfere with his plans. His wife, Eudoxia, was ordered to retire to a monastery, and his son, Aleksei (born in 1690), was turned over to the care of his sister, Tsarevna Natalia.

At the very first reception of the members of his court at Preobrazhenskoe, Peter commanded them to wear thereafter the short European dress, and to shave their beards. He did not hesitate to cut with his own hands the beards and coats of such as were unwilling to obey. The clergy and peasants were allowed to wear their beards, but the city population could do so only after purchasing a "beard license." Another innovation was the introduction of a new calendar. Hitherto time had been reckoned from the creation of the world, and New Year's Day was the first of September. After celebrating New Year's Day of 7208 (under the old reckoning) on September 1, 1699, Peter ordered that in the future the calendar should date from the birth of Christ, and the beginning of the year should be January 1.

Together with these first steps in his cultural reforms, Peter inaugurated his terrible reprisals against the

Streltsy. Their insurrection in 1698 was caused by discontent with the conditions in which they found themselves after their transfer from Moscow to Azov and the Polish frontier. They saw clearly the hostility and distrust which the Tsar felt for them, and they realized that they were being punished and had little to expect in the future. When their complaints and petitions were left unanswered, they lost patience, mutinied and started for Moscow to join their families. Regular troops and artillery were ordered against them, and at the very first encounter the *Streltsy* laid down their arms and fled. They were captured; some were executed, and others were thrown into prison.

Peter, on his return, found that the *Streltsy* revolt had not been sufficiently investigated, and that the offenders had not been sufficiently punished. A new investigation was started. Under torture, some of the *Streltsy* testified that they had been incited to revolt by Sophia. Although this accusation was not fully substantiated, Peter accepted it and denounced his sister to the elected representatives of the people (whom he invited to meet at the palace), and ordered that Sophia become a nun. The *Streltsy*, as an organization, was disbanded; two thousand of their number were executed in different parts of the capital; the others were dismissed from their regiments and forbidden for ever after to enlist in the army.

104. The Great Northern War. First Years of the War.—In 1699 Peter began to make preparations for war against the Swedes. He entered into an alliance with Augustus II, the Saxon-Polish King and Elector, and with King Christian of Denmark. His allies convinced him that the time was most convenient for the opening of hostilities, since the very young and irre-

sponsible Charles XII had been installed on the throne of Sweden. Peter, however, hesitated to take up arms as long as a state of war existed with the Turks. In August, 1700, he was informed that his ambassadors had succeeded in concluding peace at Constantinople, and that Azov had been ceded to Russia. At once his armies were ordered to march to the Baltic, and the famous Swedish War which was destined to last twenty-one years was on.

In his struggle to reach the shores of the Baltic Sea, Peter the Great was following out the policy of his predecessors on the throne: Ivan the Terrible (sec. 62); Tsar Fedor Ivanovich (sec. 63); and Vasili Shuiski (sec. 70). By the Treaty of Stolbovo in 1617 (sec. 77) Russia was forced to surrender the Baltic shore, but she had never reconciled herself to the loss. Every statesman realized that Russia must have direct maritime intercourse with Central Europe, and that sooner or later a war would have to be waged for it. Tsar Aleksei had been absorbed largely in the affairs of the Ukraine, and in his struggle with the Poles and Turks. Under Peter the Great the troubles in the South had been settled at last, and Russia was in a position to direct her attention to the shores of the Baltic.

Peter sent his troops to the Gulf of Finland and besieged the Swedish fortress of Narva. The war had not been going on very long when it became quite evident that the youthful and supposedly easy-going Charles XII had enormous energy and military skill. As soon as the allies opened hostilities, he attacked Copenhagen and compelled the Danes to sue for peace. He next turned on the Russians at Narva, where Peter had an army of 40,000 men. On November 19, 1700, Charles threw himself on the Russians, created confusion in their ranks and drove them towards the river Narova. As there was only one bridge, some of the Russian soldiers sought safety in swimming across the river and perished in great numbers. Only the "play" regiments of Peter (the Preobrazhenski and Semenovski) made a stand at the bridge and gallantly crossed the river after the rest of the army had fled. Charles captured the artillery and fortified camp of Peter. Instead of pursuing the Russians and invading Russia, Charles marched against his third foe, King Augustus. This was a blunder on his part, for while Charles (in the words of Peter) "got stuck in Poland," the Tsar reorganized his army and made ready to fight again.

Before this battle Peter went to Narva to inspect the army. He found it poorly drilled, insufficiently clad and fed, and short of powder and ammunition. He found also that his Russian soldiers and his foreign officers did not get on together. As Charles approached, Peter went to Novgorod to fortify it, thinking the Swedes would invade Russia. Peter took the defeat of his army at Narva in the same spirit as he did the first failure at Azov. In the course of the winter of 1700-1701 he succeeded in gathering a new army and casting about 300 new guns, using church bells for that purpose when copper was not obtainable in any other way. At the same time he concluded a new treaty with King Augustus against their common enemy.

After this treaty Peter's army fought on two fronts. One Russian army was kept in Poland and Lithuania to threaten the Swedes and keep them from exerting all their strength against Augustus. Another army invaded the Finnish coast, as well as Esthonia and Livonia, and step by step established itself there. In 1701 and the succeeding years the Russian cavalry, under the command of Field Marshal Boris Petrovich Sheremetev, "visited" and ravaged these regions, twice defeated the Swedes who opposed them, and captured the ancient Russian cities of Iam and Koporie. Peter himself joined the army in the fall of 1702, and took the Swedish fortress of Noteborg which he renamed Schluesselburg ("key city" to the sea). In the spring of 1703 the Russians descended to the mouth of the Neva and captured the Swedish fortress of Nyenschanz, at the junction of the Okhta and Neva. Below this place Peter built, in May, 1703, the fortress of St. Peter and St. Paul, and outside its walls he laid the foundations of the city of St. Petersburg. This gave to Peter a fortified outlet to the sea, which he at once utilized. On Lake Ladoga (more precisely, on the Svir River) sea-going ships were hastily built and launched in 1703, and in the fall of that year work was begun on the naval fort of Kronstadt, which became the base-port of the new Baltic fleet. Finally, in 1704, the powerful Swedish strongholds of Dorpat (Iuriev) and Narva were captured. In this way Peter obtained an outlet to the sea (St. Petersburg), and also protected this outlet by fortresses from the sea (Kronstadt), and land (Narva, Iam, Koporie). In permitting Peter to get such a start, Charles made an irreparable mistake.

105. THE GREAT NORTHERN WAR. THE YEARS 1707 AND 1708.—At the beginning of 1707 Augustus was forced to terminate his struggle against Charles XII, to leave Poland, to go to Saxony and there sign such a treaty as the conqueror dictated. Charles was now free to turn against Russia with his powerful and, as yet, in-

vincible army. Peter's position was very critical. His allies had been vanquished, and he had to face the victor alone. What made matters worse were the domestic troubles that had broken out, due in large part to the hardships of the long war. As early as 1705 there occurred a revolt at Astrakhan against the "boyars and foreigners"; this was followed by an uprising among the Bashkirs beyond the Volga, and finally by the insurrection of the Don Cossacks.

We have seen (sec. 84) how serious was the trouble caused by the homeless and desperate Cossacks on the Don and Volga in the time of Stenka Razin. No sooner was this movement put down than a new one (in favor of the "Old Belief") developed. The domiciled Cossacks stood for law and order, and wanted the bars put up against the many "thieves" who were coming to the Don from the other parts of Russia. The "thieves," however, continued to come, for life in Moscow was hard, and the Don offered liberty and the opportunity to free themselves forever from serfdom and the hardships of peasant life. Though the Cossacks did not approve of the newcomers, yet they would not surrender them. "No extradition from the Don!" was their invariable answer to the attempts of Moscow to recover fugitives. After the Azov campaigns, in which the Don Cossacks had rendered important aid, Peter praised and rewarded them, but demanded that they should extradite those who came to the Don from the interior. This demand offended the Cossacks, for it was a violation of their ancient rights, and they paid no heed to it. Peter now resorted to a measure that had no precedent. In 1707 he despatched troops to the Don to search out and bring back such persons as had arrived there lately. Thereupon the homeless and destitute elements revolted and, after annihilating the Tsar's soldiers, turned and defeated the domiciled Cossacks, and raised the whole country of the Don from Azov to Tambov against Moscow. Peter was compelled to send a large army to the Don which succeeded in suppressing the insurrection in 1708.

In addition to all these troubles in Russia proper there were others in the Ukraine. In 1707 Peter learned that the Ukrainian Hetman, Ivan Mazepa, was maintaining treasonable relations with King Stanislaw of Poland. At first Peter would not believe the denunciation, but when it was repeated the following year by trustworthy persons, he ordered an investigation. The charges were not sustained, and the accusers were handed over to Mazepa who had them executed.

Though he cleared himself Mazepa was guilty. To understand his motives one must know something of the situation in the Ukraine. The political and economic condition there was unstable and alarming. There was constant strife between the Cossack "Elders" (sec. 95) and the common Cossacks and townspeople. The Elders were anxious to preserve the autonomy of the Ukraine so that they could lord it over the other classes and, therefore, resented the intervention of Moscow which the common people, the inhabitants of the cities, and sometimes also the clergy, called for. Mazepa, who became Hetman in 1687, was able to hold in check and conciliate the different social elements, and, at the same time, look after the best interests of Moscow. But when Charles XII defeated Augustus, installed another King in Poland, and was about to turn on Peter, Mazepa was placed in a difficult position. Everybody expected to see Moscow crushed, and the Cossack leader had to decide whether the Ukraine should remain loyal to Moscow and share the hard lot of the vanquished, or make common cause with the Swedes and secure her independence. This is how and why Mazepa decided to enter into secret negotiations with the Poles and Swedes.

Such was the situation at the time of the Swedish invasion of Russia. Insurrections of the native tribes living on the Volga and beyond; uprisings of the Don Cossacks, danger of defection in the Ukraine, and the fear of attack by the Tartars and Turks in the south. So terrible did the danger seem to Peter that he sometimes took no pains to conceal his discouragement.

At the very beginning of 1708 Charles captured the city of Grodno where the Russian troops were stationed, and then marched to Moscow. He had under him more than 40,000 seasoned fighters and expected, in addition, to be reinforced by General Loewenhaupt with 16,000 men, munitions and supplies from Livonia. On their way to the Dnieper the Swedes defeated the Russians near the village of Golovchino, and at Mohilev they took the bridge leading across the Dnieper. Peter expected them to move on Smolensk, but instead they turned south to the Ukraine to unite with Mazepa. Loewenhaupt with his army was now left in the rear of Charles, and hastened to join him. Peter prevented their junction by attacking (September 1708) Loewenhaupt on the Sozh River, annihilating more than one half of his army, and capturing his entire transport train. This defeat of his general left Charles without powder and provisions. He was equally unfortunate in his relations with Mazepa. Before the latter could make a move the Russian general, Menshikov, learned of his treachery, started for him and almost captured the traitor. Mazepa fled to Charles, and the Ukrainian insurrection was averted. Charles and Mazepa went into winter quarters in the Ukraine (between Romny and Gadiach), where the Russian armies soon encircled them. The population of the Ukraine remained loyal to Moscow and treated the Swedes as enemies.

The campaign of 1708 thus ended without any success for Charles XII. His reliance upon Mazepa had proved vain, and his expectation of reënforcements equally vain. Peter, on the other hand, had many reasons for rejoicing. His army had an important victory to its credit; the Ukrainian insurrection had been smothered; and the Don rebellion suppressed. His spirits rose, and he looked forward with confidence to the future.

106. THE BATTLE OF POLTAVA.—In the course of the winter 1708-9 Charles made several vain attempts to shake off the Russians and clear a path to Moscow. In the spring he left his winter quarters, went down to the Vorskla River and commenced to lay siege to Poltava, one of those frontier posts built to meet possible Tartar attacks. If they should succeed in taking it, the Swedes would be able to proceed to the "wilderness" and thence either march on Moscow or deal directly with the Tartars and Turks. There was still another possibility. They might go by way of Bielgorod to Voronezh and seize the Russian ships and grain. Unfortunately for Charles he had little gunpowder and ammunition for bombarding the place, and his assaults were broken against the gallant defense of the garrison.

Under the circumstances the siege of Poltava dragged on and gave Peter time to come to the relief. On the morning of June 27, 1709, the Swedish army of 30,000, led by Charles, and the Russian army of 42,000, commanded by Peter, engaged in a battle. By noon the fight was over; the Swedes were routed; half of their army was either killed or captured, and the other half took flight towards the Dnieper and into the clutches of the Russian general, Menshikov. Charles, wounded and bleeding and half unconscious, was saved and carried across the Dnieper and from there to Turkish territory. The Battle of Poltava cost him dear. Before this event Sweden enjoyed the hegemony over the Baltic Sea and in general over Northern Europe, but after it this leadership went to Russia. This is what gives that battle its importance in the history of Russia and Europe.

The tremendous significance of the victory of Poltava was clearly realized, not only by Peter, but by all the enemies of Charles, both open and secret. Peter followed it up by seizing the Swedish possessions (Riga, Reval, Pernau and Viborg) on the Finnish and Baltic coast. Denmark and Saxony declared war on Sweden, Poland drove out Charles' nominee to the crown, and recalled Augustus of Saxony. Sweden, attacked by her enemies and abandoned by her king, seemed about to perish. Instead of returning to Sweden Charles was busy in stirring up the Turkish Sultan against the Russian Tsar.

107. THE CAMPAIGN OF THE PRUTH AND THE END OF THE GREAT NORTHERN WAR. THE PERSIAN WAR.— The efforts of Charles XII in Turkey proved to be successful, and at the close of 1710 the Sultan declared war. Peter did not wait to be attacked, but marched south, where he was assured that the appearance of his troops on the Danube would cause all the Orthodox inhabitants of those regions to rise against the Turks. He had, more-

over, the definite promises of the princes (hospodars) of
Moldavia and Wallachia that they were ready to help
the Russians.

Prevailed upon by all these promises, and expecting,
in addition, help from King Augustus, Peter placed himself at the head of an army of 40,000 in the spring of
1711, and started south. One bitter disappointment
after another followed him. Augustus sent no reënforcements, the hospodars had not prepared the provisions
they had promised, and the Turks, long prepared for the
campaign, met him with a force of 200,000 men and
surrounded him on the Pruth River. Hungry, thirsty,
and weary from marching across the torrid steppe and
fighting off attacks, the Russians would have been forced
to surrender had not the Turkish Commander-in-Chief
(the Grand Vizier) consented to open peace negotiations.
By the treaty which was concluded Peter gave back to
the Turks Azov and the surrounding territory which he
had obtained from them by the Treaty of 1700. It was
a humiliating concession, but Peter felt that he had ex-
tricated himself very successfully from the captivity and
disgrace which had threatened him and his army.

Now that he had peace in the south, Peter redoubled
his efforts in the north. In 1714 he routed the Swedish
navy at Cape Hangoudd (Gangut in Russian) in southwestern Finland, occupied the Aland Islands, and threatened Stockholm itself. Together with his allies Peter
operated along the southern shores of the Baltic, in Germany, whence the Swedes were finally expelled in 1716.
These combined operations, however, brought Peter into
a conflict with his allies. The Germans and Danes were
afraid that he would establish himself in Germany permanently, and he was greatly dissatisfied with the slow-

ness of their operations. He decided to get a new ally, Louis XV of France, and with that in mind he visited Paris in 1717. Peter was cordially received and entertained, but failed in his mission, for France declined to take a hand in Baltic affairs.

After this Peter opened direct negotiations with Charles XII, who had returned to Sweden from Turkey. Peace parleys were started on the Aland Islands, but were interrupted by the death of Charles in 1718, and entirely broken off immediately afterward by the Swedish Government which concluded peace with its enemies in Germany and with Denmark, and renewed the struggle with Russia. It was, however, too weak to put up much of a fight. In 1719 and during the following years the Russians invaded Sweden by sea, and devastated the country all the way up to Stockholm. In 1721 peace negotiations were renewed once more, at the small town of Nystad, and on August 30 a treaty was signed. Sweden ceded to Russia forever Livonia, with Riga; Esthonia, with Reval and Narva; Ingermanland and part of Karelia, with Viborg; Russia restored Finland and, in addition, undertook to pay a large sum of money.

The long struggle thus ended with the decline of Sweden and the rise of Moscow. Peter was overjoyed at this peace, and noisily celebrated the victory, first, at his "paradise"—Petersburg, and later at the capital —Moscow. On October 22, 1721, the anniversary of the freeing of Moscow from the Poles in 1612, Peter, at St. Petersburg, assumed the title of "Emperor of all the Russias" and changed the former "Grand States of the Russian Tsardom" into an "Empire of all the Russias." The Senate, in recognition of his merits and achievements, conferred upon the emperor, in addition to his imperial title, those of "The Great" and "Father of His Country."

In 1722, immediately following the close of the Northern War, Peter declared war on Persia. A Russian army started south from Astrakhan, and occupied the Persian cities of Derbent and Baku. In 1723 Persia concluded peace and surrendered to Peter the western seaboard of the Caspian, which he needed in order to enter into relations with the East and India.

It is clear that all the wars fought by the Tsar had for their object the winning of the seacoasts—the Black Sea (Azov), the Baltic, and the Caspian. Peter, far-seeing political genius that he was, realized the importance of the open sea in international intercourse and the progress of civilization.

108. DOMESTIC REFORMS OF PETER THE GREAT.—In considering the political reforms of Peter the Great we must not imagine that he supplanted, by one stroke, the old order of Moscow with a new European system in accordance with a single, definite scheme. Peter was not able to adhere to any preconceived plan, or to observe any strict consistency, because all his reforms and all the administrative and social changes which he introduced had to take place under the pressure of military contingencies and needs.

The Swedish War was a long drawn out affair, extremely difficult, exhausting, and fraught with great perils. It absorbed all his energy and time to get troops and resources for the fight. He was always on the move —from the White Sea to the Danube, from St. Petersburg to Voronezh. The army was his first care, and military reforms received first attention; the army needed money and hasty changes were made in the system of taxation to meet that want. Under the pressure of military necessity Peter introduced a number of innovations, which gradually destroyed the old order without, however, creating a new one, and the result was chaos in the administration. After the Battle of Poltava and the campaign of the Pruth Peter felt more confident and safe, and he undertook to complete in a proper manner everything that had been done thus far in haste and piecemeal.

It should be kept in mind that, in reorganizing the life of the various classes of the population and the forms of administration, Peter had no intention whatever of changing the fundamentals of the existing régime. The supreme autocratic power, in his reign, remained exactly the same as it had been under his father, Aleksei. No important change was made in the position of the social classes: they were not endowed with any new rights, nor released from their former obligations. In brief, that type of state which had been evolved prior to Peter was not altered by him. All of his reforms aimed merely at perfecting the existing order by giving it the more civilized outward forms of the West. His only essentially radical reform was in the administration of the Church for, with the abolition of the patriarchate, the Church was brought into complete subjection to the State.

109. ORGANIZATION OF THE SOCIAL CLASSES.—We know already (secs. 55, 58, 79) how the class of service men was organized. It consisted of "Moscow Nobles" and "City Nobles." The first were the aristocrats, the governing class, and occupied the highest positions at court. They were in charge of the government bureaus and chancelleries, were sent on missions, acted as voi-

vodes and commanders of armies. The second class, "City Nobles" and "Lesser Nobles" formed the mass of the gentry. They served in the cavalry town militia, and were the backbone of the field army of the state. All service men were provided with estates by the government, and sometimes money and yearly salaries. Some of these people had their patrimonial estates, but this did not prevent them from seeking government land, in addition. Among the service classes were numbered the garrisons (Cossacks, *Streltsy*, artillerymen) who were settled in the suburbs of the towns they garrisoned and provided with pasture and other lands. In the seventeenth century regular troops were treated in the same way as the classes just named, and given definite places of residence. These "foreign model troops" were complemented by the conscription of the so-called "idle people," that is, men without any definite occupation. This was the military organization that Peter found when he became Tsar.

The struggle with the Swedes demanded a regular army and Peter little by little transferred all the noblemen and service men to the regular service. Every service man, from the aristocratic nobleman of Moscow down to the last gunner of the artillery, was enlisted, and had to serve either in the army or the navy. Not more than one third of the members of each family of the nobility was permitted to enter the civil service. Service was for life, and everyone had to begin at the bottom and work up. In view of the fact that now everyone, from the highest to the lowest class, had to serve on an equal footing, the old classification no longer served the purpose and was done away with. All men, whether aristocrats or plebeians, started at the lowest rungs of the ladder with the possibility of reaching the highest. The order of such promotion was clearly defined by a "Table of Ranks" (1722). It divided all the government positions into fourteen ranks or *"chins."* The principle of individual merit now triumphed over aristocratic "lineage."

By doing away with the old order of service and compelling all the nobles to enter the regular army regiments, Peter rendered the condition of the nobility difficult in many ways. They not only had to spend their whole life in the government service, but they had also to learn to read, and to acquire some knowledge of mathematics; otherwise they would get no promotion and would be deprived of the right to marry. Furthermore, Peter restricted the rights and privileges of the nobility in the matter of land ownership. He would no longer grant the nobles land, but paid them a salary for their service. By the law of 1714 he also prohibited the splitting up of estates. When a noble died his estate passed to the oldest son, unless another son was named in the testament, but under no circumstance could it be divided among all the children. It was but natural that the nobility should complain and try in every way to evade the heavy burden, but Peter held them to their obligations and punished severely every attempt to shirk. Only to the highest, ancient nobility did he grant one substantial concession. He permitted the young men of this class to enter his own favorite guard regiments—Preobrazhenski and Semenovski—stationed at St. Petersburg. Towards the close of Peter's reign these two regiments were almost entirely made up of nobles, and the companies that composed the regiments bore the names of the princely families. But even these aristocratic guards were not allowed to idle. They were entrusted with various missions, sometimes of the greatest importance, and became competent and trustworthy officials.

The urban classes represented a very small and poor element of the population prior to Peter's time. City life, with its commercial and industrial activity, had scarcely existed in the State of Moscow. A few cities in the north had large populations and wealth, but nearly all others were, as Peter himself had said, "houses in ruins." It was only in 1649 that legislation was passed making the city inhabitants a class distinct from the rest of the taxpaying population.

In his foreign travels Peter had seen rich and cultured industrial and commercial cities, and he learned that trade and industry were looked upon as the chief sources of national prosperity. The contrast between what he had seen in Western Europe and what he found in Russia on his return made a deep impression on the Tsar, and he determined to repair his "ruined house" and create in his own country an economically strong and active urban class. With this object in view, he exempted the townspeople from some of their obligations in connection with government commercial and industrial establishments, and gave them more self-government. In 1720, the office of "Chief Magistrate" was established to deal with the urban classes throughout the empire. All cities were divided into different categories according to population, and the population was divided into "regular" and "irregular" citizens. The "regular" citizens formed two "guilds" or corporations: the first was composed of the representatives of wealth and intelligence; the second, of small traders and craftsmen. The craftsmen, in turn, formed associations, or craft guilds. The "irregular citizens" were mostly unskilled laborers. The city government was in the hands of the "regular citizens," who elected the mayor and legislated in the municipal councils. Every city was subject to the authority of the "Chief Magistrate" at the capital.

These were the measures adopted by Peter to develop city life. But owing to the more or less primitive condition of his cities, and the strain of the wars, the result of his efforts was rather a disappointment, and the cities of Russia remained for some time longer in the backward state in which he found them.

Far-reaching reforms were made in the condition of the peasantry. At one time taxes were levied on "plowed ground," but as this led to a reduction of the cultivated area, it was changed in the seventeenth century (secs. 55, 79) to a tax on (peasant) "households." The taxpayers got round the new legislation by crowding several "households" into one. Peter met this evasion by substituting a "soul" tax for the "household" tax. In 1718 a census was taken of all taxable citizens in the city and country. This census was later revised and became the basis of the new taxation system. According to the "revision" there were five million taxable persons, and on each person privately owned an assessment of seventy-four kopeks a year was laid, but on persons on crown land a somewhat higher rate was levied.

The new system of taxation had no particularly important consequences for the crown peasants, but it had important and evil consequences for the other peasants. On every landlord's estate there dwelt side by side peasants and serfs. Originally the peasants lived on his fields, and the domestic serfs at the manor house. But in the seventeenth century (or thereabouts) the landlord, in order to get all the labor he could out of his serfs, commenced to settle them in separate cottages "beyond the manor" and made them cultivate the land. In ancient times the serfs, as private chattels, had not paid any taxes, and had no dealings with the state. Seeing, however, that the "people beyond the manor" differed in no wise from the peasants, the government at the close of the seventeenth century taxed them also, even though they were not classed as peasants. When the census was made up Peter ordered that all serfs, manorial and others, should be entered as taxpayers, like peasants. No distinction was made between them. They came to be classed together as "landlords' subjects." Since the landlord had to pay for both peasant and serf and the government made no distinction between them, he too treated them as one class. In this way the eighteenth century transformed the peasants from government taxpayers into the absolute slaves of their masters.

We thus see many changes in the condition of the various social classes during the closing years of Peter's reign. The nobles had their privileges reduced; the city inhabitants had theirs increased; and the peasants had their burdens made heavier. Peter was not thinking of classes, but of service, not of rights, but of duties. Each individual was a cog in the machine; he lived "for the cause of the sovereign and the nation," and was obliged to give himself and his wealth to the state.

110. MILITARY ORGANIZATION.—Peter the Great has been credited with founding a regular army in Russia. This, however, is not quite correct. Already under Tsar Michael, a few regular regiments on foreign models had been organized at Moscow (sec. 79). Peter did not originate any new army, but he brought about reforms that were important and far-reaching.

Peter gradually abolished the old army. After the revolt of 1698 he disbanded the *Streltsy*. A little later he did the same thing with the special cavalry of the nobility, by forcing the nobles to join the regular regiments. He increased the number of regular army regiments by the incorporation of Cossacks, *Streltsy* and garrison soldiers until they came to be the only existing field army. The regiments were recruited from the taxpaying population (one recruit for every twenty households) and from the young nobility. In short, Peter introduced universal liability to compulsory military service. Only the families of the clergy were not subject to conscription. Soldiers were taken from their homes and occupations, and sent wherever the authorities desired. As there were not enough barracks to shelter all, many of the soldiers were billeted on the civil population.

The results of the army reforms and organization were most striking. At the end of his reign Peter's army numbered 200,000 regular troops and 75,000 Cossacks; and his navy consisted of 48 large warships, 800 smaller vessels, and 28,000 sailors.

111. THE GOVERNMENT.—Before Peter's time the government of Moscow was a strong centralized bureaucracy. The Council (Duma) of Boyars met from time to time, with or without the Tsar, to discuss matters of state and to make recommendations. These recommendations the Tsar issued as decrees (ukaz), and they became laws. The Duma had under it many departments (sometimes as many as forty) with a boyar at the head and a staff to assist him. There was a department of foreign affairs, a department of military affairs, a department of Siberian affairs, and so on. The government was strongly centralized and through its appointive offi-

cers, like the voivod, it reached directly or indirectly, every citizen.

Peter the Great ceased to convoke the Duma of Boyars, preferring to discuss informally all important affairs and laws with his trusted friends and favorites. The Duma was not needed, for it was held that whatever the emperor wills is law. To direct the current affairs of the administration, and to act as a supreme court of justice, Peter founded in 1711 a "Governing Senate." The Senate, composed of a small group of persons appointed by the sovereign, did not itself legislate; it merely published the laws which the Tsar transmitted to it. This Senate watched over the propriety and legality of the acts of the administration, and rendered decisions on administrative and judicial questions which were referred to it. In 1722 Peter created, in conjunction with the Senate, a special "Procuratorship," with a Procurator General at the head, to watch over the legality of the acts of all governmental institutions, including the Senate, to be the "eye of the sovereign," and to act as a connecting link between the Tsar and the Senate. The Procurator-General had his staff in the capital and in the provinces. Besides this open control, a secret service system was set up to "find out secretly, denounce, and expose" abuses on the part of government officials. In addition to the general supervision and direction of the administration, Peter turned over to the jurisdiction of the Senate those affairs of the old government departments of Moscow which were not allocated among the newly created "colleges" or boards. Thus, for instance, the Senate had charge of numerous matters relating to the nobility. The old departments were replaced by twelve new colleges (army, navy, foreign affairs, commerce, finance, justice industry, mining, etc.), and these began to function in 1718. Each college had its president, vice-president, and staff. The "college" system of administration was borrowed from the Scandinavian countries and Germany and Peter had a very high opinion of it.

In 1708 Peter introduced the "gubernia" as an administrative unit by combining "districts" (uiezds) into provinces, and provinces into a "gubernia." At the head of the gubernia was a governor (responsible to the Senate); at the head of the province was the "commandant" (formerly called voivod); and at the head of the district was the "Landrat," or county council or councilor of the nobility. It should be noted that Peter did not succeed in reducing the administration of the several "governments" (gubernias) to uniformity, nor did he manage to carry to completion the planned reforms; and, as a result, there was a certain degree of chaos in local administration, both in his own day and later.

Though the names of the institutions changed, there were no great fundamental changes. Just as before Peter's reign, so during his own time, the inhabitants of country or town had over them elected authorities, and through them they were subject to the authority of the voivod and governor, and they in turn to the Senate, (and, in certain matters, to the "colleges") in place of the former departments and the Duma.

In Peter's reign, just as in the time of his fathers, the country was ruled by appointed officials at the top, and by elected authorities at the bottom, and the whole machinery of the government was held together by a bureaucracy. Under Peter the old unity was somewhat broken up. Formerly the voivod governed every inhabitant of his district; now, the towns are subjected, not to the authority of the voivod, but to the "Chief Magistrate." Previously all voivodes were under the control of the departments; now, the governors and voivodes are subjected to the direct authority of the Senate and not the colleges. The Senate exercises its authority over the colleges, governments, and cities, separately in each case. In short, the administration had become far more complicated than before.

112. FINANCIAL MEASURES.—Prior to Peter, half of the government revenues came from direct taxation, and the other half from indirect and proceeds from the sale of government goods. Peter increased the income from direct taxation (sec. 109) by the introduction of the capitation tax. He also increased the indirect taxes by raising the tariff, and by devising new sources of revenue. Legal documents had to be written on a special paper sold by the government. Licenses of all kinds were required; beard licenses, bath house licenses, etc. In its need for revenue the government was always on the lookout for something to tax. It had a set of officers whose main duty was to think up new taxation. Peter also introduced a new coinage. Before his time coins of small denominations were Russian and of larger denomination foreign (Iefimki or Joachimsthaler). Peter minted rubles and half rubles, and made the ruble equal to one "iefimka" (instead of two as before). As a result of these various measures, the annual state revenue went up from 2,500,000 rubles (in the old currency) to four times that amount (in the new currency).

This increased revenue was a hardship on the people. In addition to the money payment, they had, during the years of warfare, to supply the government with soldiers, horses, vehicles, and laborers. Peter realized only too well the extent of the burden he had placed upon the nation, and he thought that he would promote its prosperity by the "balance of trade," by increasing the inflow of precious metals into the country through exports. With this object in view he built canals and developed commerce in every way by land and by sea. He urged the Russian merchants to combine in associations, and advised the nobility to invest in commercial enterprises. In order to have something else besides raw materials to export, the Tsar encouraged industries. More than once he erected factories, started them going, and then turned them over to the control of private capital. He also tried to develop the natural resources, and had his mining engineers prospecting. They made a very valuable survey of the minerals of the Urals, and a report on the coal deposits in South Russia.

Peter was consciously and actively trying to increase the national wealth, and to increase production. This is why he applied the system of Protectionism, and took a personal interest in every branch of national trade and industry. By a series of decrees he prescribed the methods of working ores, the way to harvest the grain, to protect the forest, to cultivate tobacco and silk, to improve the breed of cattle, and to manufacture linen. He published from time to time foreign market prices, so "that one may know where an article is cheap and where dear."

113. THE CHURCH ADMINISTRATION.—Peter's acts, his dislike of the ancient customs of Moscow, and the "foreign" nature of his reforms, aroused against him the fanatics of the old order. The "Old Believers" hated him and called him the Antichrist; many of the "Nikonians" could not reconcile themselves to him and protested

against his actions and behavior. All these malcontents looked to the Patriarch for guidance. Ioakim, who was Patriarch in Peter's youth, had been very much at odds with the Tsar on the question of foreigners; and though Patriarch Adrian (1690-1700) was less stubborn and uncompromising than Ioakim, he made no secret of his disapproval of the young monarch's actions. Similarly opposed to Peter were the other prelates. The famous Mitrofan of Voronezh lent his support to Peter in his struggle for Azov, but openly condemned him for favoring the ways of the foreigners.

Under such circumstances, Peter, at the death of Adrian (1700), hesitated to choose a new patriarch. He entrusted the functions of the office to Stephen Iavorski, Metropolitan of Riazan. This arrangement worked so well from Peter's point of view that he let it go until 1721, when he was ready to introduce his church reform. By this reform the patriarchate was abolished and replaced by an ecclesiastical college, called the *Synod*, made up of the higher clergy. At the head of the Synod was a President (Stephen Iavorski), who was assisted by two vice-presidents, councilors, assistants, secretaries, and a High Procurator. In religious matters the Synod exercised the authority of the patriarch, but had no power in civil affairs. It was one of the many government colleges and, as such, was subject to the control of the Procurator-General and the Senate. In this way did Peter dispose of the problem of church administration, radically destroying the very possibility of conflicts between the representatives of the sovereign and the ecclesiastical power.

In 1701 the church peasants were transferred, together with the church estates, to the Secular Department of

Monasteries which administered them. All those living on church lands, with the exception of the families of the clergy and church officials, became subject to military service. The jurisdiction of the church courts was limited: many cases were transferred to the secular courts, and representatives of the temporal authority began to take part in the work of the ecclesiastical courts. Finally, in 1724, Peter, realizing the hostility of the monastic orders, put them under strict control and abolished entirely the institution of itinerant or wandering monks.

114. EDUCATION.—Peter's great dream was to bring the blessings of education to his people. It was one of the reasons why he fought for a window to Europe, why he befriended foreigners, and why he reorganized his state on the European model. He had great enthusiasm for education, and on a private seal he had engraved these words: "I belong to those who seek knowledge and are willing to learn."

His whole life was spent in acquiring knowledge and putting it to practical use. He obliged others to do the same. His military officers, as well as his civil servants, were compelled to go to school in order to become more proficient in their work. A number of technical and special schools were founded to teach foreign languages, mathematics, navigation, engineering, and bookkeeping. It would be wrong, however, to assume that he did not appreciate the importance of a broader mental training. He did everything that he could to raise the cultural level of Russian society. He ordered translations from foreign books, and insisted that the translations be made in simple language and printed in a type invented by himself and easy to read. To keep his subjects informed of what was going on in the world, he started in 1703 the first Russian newspaper, the Moscow News (Moskovskiia Viedomosti). In 1724 Peter created an Academy of Sciences to promote research in the arts and sciences.

Peter gave consideration, not only to the training of the mind, but also to the polishing of manners, and the developing of more refined social intercourse among the Russian people. The first step in this education was the change in dress and outward appearance, and the second was instruction in how to behave in public. Peter ordered the translation and printing of a book of etiquette entitled "The Honorable Youth's Mirror, or The Rules of Worldly Manners." To give his people an opportunity to put into practice their knowledge he planned all kinds of public celebrations, in which he himself took prominent part. He was particularly fond of street masquerades representing characters from mythology or the races of the world.

The most original means used in improving public manners under Peter were the so-called "parties," arranged at the command of the Tsar at the homes of distinguished and wealthy citizens. These parties were open to all nobles and "distinguished" citizens and their families, and they had to come whether they wished to do so or not. At these gatherings they had a chance to dance, to play games, to carry on polished conversation and to display table manners.

115. FAMILY AFFAIRS OF PETER THE GREAT.—Peter completely undermined his health in the fall of 1724, when he caught a cold trying to save some soldiers who were drowning at the mouth of the Neva. He was ill during the early part of the winter, growing gradually

worse until, in January, 1725, he had to take to his bed. On the 28th of that month he died.

The family life of Peter was not altogether ideal. He was not happy with his first wife, Eudoxia Lopukhina, and he put her away in 1698. After their separation Peter took his eight-year-old son, Aleksei, from his mother and put him with his aunts. The child missed his mother, and grew to dislike and fear his father whom he saw but rarely. Aleksei lived in an atmosphere that was hostile to Peter, that disapproved of his ways and of his foreign ideas, and consequently Aleksei refused to study, refused to do the things his father recommended. There was no companionship between father and son, no heart to heart talks. Peter thought Aleksei was lazy and tried in various ways to get him interested in something, tried to make a European out of him, but Aleksei resisted all his efforts. Peter thought that he would make a man out of his son by getting him a wife, and so he married him off to a German Princess, Sophia Charlotte of Wolfenbuettel. She soon died, however, leaving an infant son, Peter (1715).

Peter became thoroughly discouraged over his son and finally demanded that he either turn over a new leaf, or give up his right to the succession. Aleksei renounced the throne, and then fled from Russia to the Emperor of Germany, Charles VI, to whom he appealed for protection. Peter, however, sent some very clever men who persuaded the Tsarevich to come back. When he returned an investigation was started to find out what were the motives of his flight. It was discovered that Aleksei and his companions were in a plot against Peter, and they were brought to trial. According to the law, every conspiracy against the Tsar was punishable by death, and the judges, composed of the highest dignitaries of the empire, sentenced them all, including Aleksei, to capital punishment. The sentence was never executed, for the Tsarevich died at the fortress of St. Peter and St. Paul (1718).

In 1712 Peter married Catherine Alekseievna, a woman of humble origin who had been taken prisoner at the time of the Northern War. She was a woman of ability and tact, and a real helpmate. Peter appreciated her fine qualities, and had her crowned in 1724. They had two daughters, Anna and Elizabeth. Shortly before Peter's death Anna was betrothed to the Duke of Holstein. Among the members of the Tsar's family were also his nieces, daughters of Tsar Ivan. One of these, Anna, was married to the Duke of Courland, and the other, Catherine, to the Duke of Mecklenburg.

At the time of Peter's death, the imperial family, with the exception of Tsarevich Peter Alekseievich, consisted entirely of women. This explains why, in 1722, Peter the Great changed the law of succession so as to give him the power to name his successor, regardless of dynastic ties. To justify the Tsar's act, one of the church dignitaries wrote a treatise called "The Legality of the Monarch's Will."

116. THE PERIOD OF THE FAVORITES (1725-1741). —Peter did not make use of the law of 1722 and when he died the question of succession was undetermined. Peter's grandson, Tsarevich Peter Alekseievich, was only ten years of age, and none of the ladies could present specially good claims. Some said that Peter had crowned Catherine so that she might succeed him; others insisted that Peter had been most anxious to leave his throne to his daughter, Anna. In short, no one knew who should succeed and there was no legal way to settle that question.

Under the circumstances the group of very able men with whom Peter had surrounded himself and who had helped him took the matter in hand. This circle was made up of individuals from different classes of society: boyars (Golitsyn, Dolgoruki, Repnin, B. P. Sheremetev); nobles (Apraxins, Naryshkins, Golovkins, Tolstoys); men without titles (Menshikov, Iaguzhinski, Shafirov); and foreigners (Ostermann, Bruce, Münnich). Peter had selected them because of their ability and had trained them to carry out his policies; they knew better than anyone else the mind of the monarch and who was best qualified to carry on his work.

At the moment of Peter's death these personages gathered at the palace to discuss the succession. The old nobility, led by Prince Golitsyn, favored young Peter Alekseievich, partly because of his imperial descent, while Menshikov, together with other dignitaries who, like himself, could not boast of aristocratic lineage, championed the claim of Catherine. Menshikov was clever enough to have the Guard regiments appear at the palace at the right moment and declare themselves on the side of the empress. This settled the matter. Catherine was put on the throne and Menshikov, naturally, became the power behind the throne.

This was the beginning of the period of favorites which lasted from 1725 to 1741. Life at court became nothing but a succession of intrigues, acts of violence, and palace revolutions. It is not surprising, therefore, that the period of the "favorites" has left a very odious impression on the Russian people.

117. IMMEDIATE SUCCESSORS OF PETER THE GREAT. —The principal events in the life of the court and the government during this period were the following.

When Empress Catherine entrusted her favorite, Menshikov, with the fullness of power, the other dignitaries became very envious. They were led by Prince D. M. Golitsyn, an old aristocrat, who still remembered conditions as they had been before Peter's day. Golitsyn argued that Peter had made a mistake when he abolished the Duma of Boyars and he proposed that a similar institution, endowed with legislative powers, be created to check the influence of any one "powerful person." Golitsyn had enough support to have his proposal enacted into law and a new institution, the Supreme Privy Council, composed of six persons (among whom were Golitsyn and Menshikov) came into being (1726). It was superior to the Senate and Synod, and discussed with the Empress all domestic and foreign affairs before she acted on them.

In theory it looked as if a new order had dawned, as if the empress had submitted to the guidance of the Supreme Councillors, but in practice the old system continued in force, for Menshikov was in control of the Council. In order to make his position at court more secure he persuaded Catherine to name Grand Duke Peter Alekseievich heir to the throne, and to arrange a marriage between his (Menshikov's) daughter and the future Tsar. When Catherine died (1727) the twelve-year-old Peter II ascended the throne and went to live with Menshikov. Menshikov had outwitted all his opponents and thought he had nothing more to fear. He began to act arrogantly, as if he were the sovereign himself. His enemies, however, had not given up the fight against the powerful upstart. Prince Ivan Dolgoruki succeeded in insinuating himself into the good graces of the young emperor and persuaded him to exile Menshikov and his whole family to the Arctic regions.

Russia, however, gained little by the change of "powerful persons." The Dolgorukis were as arbitrary and as selfish as Menshikov, but less original. They, too, arranged a match between Peter II and one of the Dolgoruki princesses and with the same object in mind. Unfortunately for them they were a bit careless. On the occasion of the coronation they allowed the young emperor to enjoy and expose himself more than was good for him. He became ill, caught the smallpox, and died January 1730, without making his will.

According to Empress Catherine's last testament, the throne should have gone to one of Peter the Great's daughters. But the members of the Supreme Privy Council (chiefly Golitsyns and Dolgorukis) set aside this will and named as successor Anna of Courland, daughter of Tsar Ivan. The electors reasoned that Anna, not having the best kind of claim to the empire, would be willing to agree to limitations of her power in favor of the Council. Without communicating with the other high dignitaries of the empire, the Supreme Councillors drew up a set of "conditions" which they sent to Anna at Mitau to sign, with the understanding that she would give them out as her own idea. The most important of the conditions were these: (1) not to appoint a successor, (2) not to govern without the consent of the Supreme Privy Council (which from now on was to choose its own members and appoint officials to all the most important posts), and (3) to delegate the authority over the army and the Guard regiments to the Supreme Privy Council.

Owing to the prolonged stay of the imperial court at Moscow there were then in that city all the regiments of the Guard and a large gathering of the nobility. Rumors about secret "conditions" presented to Anna caused excitement and indignation. The nobility regarded these underhanded dealings as a plot on the part of the boyars to set up "ten arbitrary and powerful families in the place of one autocratic sovereign." When the news reached Moscow that Anna had accepted the offer of the throne and that she herself had "promised most emphatically" to abolish the autocracy and to rule the country in conjunction with the Supreme Privy Council, the nobles demanded and secured permission to meet and discuss the whole question. They were of one mind in opposition to the Supreme Councillors, but could not agree whether to restore autocracy to its former place or restrict its power in favor of the whole nobility. Several bills embodying the various proposals were drafted by the nobles and submitted to the Supreme Privy Council. But as this body would take no action the nobles came in large numbers to Anna as soon as she arrived (February 25, 1730) at Moscow and urged her in a rather boisterous fashion to "renounce the conditions," and look into the bills that they had submitted. Anna replied that as soon as they agreed among themselves as to what they really desired and presented their request in an orderly manner she would consider it. After more discussion the faction that favored a restoration of autocratic power won over the other and all together petitioned the empress to "assume the autocracy," "destroy the Supreme Privy Council," and "restore the Senate to its rights." Anna was only too willing to do what she was asked and with her own hand tore up the "conditions" she had signed.

With the abolition of the Supreme Privy Council its members lost all influence. Anna distrusted both the boyars and the nobles because each class, in its own way.

had contemplated depriving her of power in its interest. She, therefore, chose her councillors from a small group of personal friends, mostly Germans, who had come with her from Courland. The most influential of this new group of favorites was von Biron and next to him the Loewenwold brothers. They, in turn, surrounded themselves with other Germans who were already in Russia. Ostermann was placed at the head of civil affairs and Münnich of military, and each of them appointed his particular Baltic friends to positions under him. Two additional Guard regiments were formed (the Izmailovski and the Cavalry Regiment) with Baltic Germans as officers to counter-balance, as it were, the Preobrazhenski and Semenovski regiments. In this way a German bureaucracy was built up and Germans began to play a leading part in Russian affairs.

The period of Biron's rule seemed to the Russian people terrible indeed. Biron had no love for Russia or the Russians and his idea of statesmanship was to furnish the empress with plenty of amusements so as to stand in well with her. Taxes were squeezed out in merciless fashion and landlords, as well as the local government officials, were held accountable for the arrears of the peasantry. Those who made complaints were dragged off to the "Secret Chancellery" where they were tortured and subjected to the most cruel punishments. Biron was, of course, fully aware that he did not have the good-will of the people and was therefore afraid of insurrections. To avert them, he encouraged denunciations and developed a regular system of spying. The "Word-and-Deed" men, as the informers were called, had a free hand both as to the persons to arrest and the methods of conviction. Biron persuaded Anna to rid the country, by exile or execution, of members of the old families—the Golitsyns, Dolgorukis, Iusupovs and other princes—even though none of them harbored any evil designs against the empress herself. The slightest opposition to Biron was certain to provoke his reprisals. The Cabinet Minister Artemus Volynski was condemned to death (1740) because he had denounced the favorite of the empress. Biron's method of government came to be known as "Bironism," which implied cruelty and selfish exploitation of the country combined with a system of secret denunciations.

This German domination lasted ten years. During this period the country was suffering from oppression and fear of denunciations, while the court was living in luxury, pleasure and extravagance. Balls and masquerades, hunting parties and other amusements followed one another without intermission. Anna's idea of amusements seems strange to us. Her court was filled with silly jesters and queer misshapen freaks with whom the empress loved to play. Once there was built an ice palace on the Neva in which a noisy mock wedding was celebrated. The life which the empress led soon undermined her health and she died in 1740, leaving the throne to her niece's son, Prince Ivan Antonovich of Brunswick Bevern, a mere infant. Since the baby emperor was unable to rule in person Anna appointed Biron (who had just been elected Duke of Courland) regent.

The Russians put up with Anna as empress because she was, after all, a daughter of a Tsar, but they would have nothing to do with Biron as regent. So intense and outspoken was the opposition to him that Field Marshal Münnich, with the aid of the Preobrazhenski Guard arrested Biron and turned over the government to the emperor's mother, Anna Leopoldovna (niece of Empress Anna).

When it became evident that this new regent also leaned on the Germans, the Russians set on foot a plot to overthrow the government. Soldiers and officers of the Guard appealed to Elizabeth, daughter of Peter the Great, to rescue the throne from Germans. "Little Mother," they said, "we are all ready; we are only waiting for your orders." The plotters were assisted by Marquis de La Chétardie, the French Ambassador at St. Petersburg, who was eager to get rid of the German influence in the Russian Court. He and Elizabeth's French physician, Lestocq, added their pleas to that of the Guard and finally persuaded her to attempt a coup d'état. On the night of November 25, 1741, Elizabeth went to the barracks of the Preobrazhenski Regiment, and thence, with a company of Guardsmen (later known as the "Bodyguard Company"), to the palace, arrested the Emperor Ivan and his parents, and proclaimed herself Empress of Russia. The downfall of the Germans was hailed with general rejoicing.

This brought to an end the "period of favorites." It is interesting to note the course of its development. It started with the unaristocratic Menshikov, was followed by the boyar Dolgoruki, and ended with the foreigners. All the different groups associated with Peter had their turn. In the fight for power these favorites and their court factions sought help and support among the Guard. It was with the backing of the Guard that Menshikov put Catherine on the throne, that the nobles crushed the Supreme Privy Council and restored autocracy, that Münnich arrested Biron, and that Elizabeth became empress. In short, it was the Guard that either supported or overthrew certain personages or the political order itself. Since the Guard, as we have learned (sec. 109), was composed of the nobility, the controlling influence at the capital was plainly of that class. *This growth of the political influence of the nobility forms the most important and significant feature of the period of favorites we are now studying.* It was destined to have far-reaching historical consequences.

118. DOMESTIC AFFAIRS (1735-1741). In the domestic affairs of Russia during the period of the favorites we must note, first of all, certain changes in the administrative methods that had been established under Peter the Great. It has been shown already that the creation of the Supreme Privy Council did away with the post af Procurator-General and greatly reduced the importance of the Senate and Synod. The Supreme Privy Council was first intended by its creators to act as a curb on the favorites, and later as a check on the autocracy itself. The Council supplied the lack of the legislative organ which Peter abolished (Duma of Boyars) without creating another to take its place. It was the Supreme Privy Council that had charge of the entire government of the state owing to the personal inactivity of Catherine 1 and Peter II. Because the Council had attempted to limit the authority of the monarch it was done away with (1730), and the rights of the Senate and the post of Procurator-General restored. But almost immediately afterwards another institution, the Cabinet, was created, very similar to the Council. It was found necessary under Empress Anna to concentrate the administration in the hands of one body since the empress herself shirked affairs of state.

In this manner the system of Peter the Great was

augmented by a supreme legislative body. Subsequently other changes were introduced in the administration, especially of local government, with a view to making it less complicated. A great deal had to be done to reconstruct the state along economic lines, for the country had been ruined by the burdens of the wars of Peter the Great and by the cruel and selfish oppression of Biron.

The status of the different social classes underwent some changes during the period of the "favorites." The condition of the nobility was bettered by a reduction of its obligations to the state and an extension of its privileges in land ownership. This improvement may be explained by the growing influence of the nobles through the Guard.

In 1730, at the time of the revolt against the "little scheme" of the Supreme Councillors, the Moscow nobles formulated their own ideas of a political system which would protect the interests of their own class. The nobility, boyars and ordinary nobles, was to participate in the government, to have its terms of service reduced to twenty years, special schools for its children, and the right to divide up its estates as it pleased. In return for helping her secure autocratic power Anna rewarded the nobles by granting them most of their demands. Nobles were to serve not more than twenty-five years and could retire at the age of forty-five. In case of large families one of the sons might be exempted from service entirely. Nobles could bequeath their land to all their sons, and, furthermore, crown lands as well as patrimonial estates became the property of the nobles. At St. Petersburg there was established a "Cadet Corps" (otherwise known as the "Land Army Corps of Nobles"), for young noblemen. Graduates of this school received commissions in the army and were not required to begin at the bottom. These three measures greatly improved the condition of the nobility.

The peasants, on the other hand, especially those on private estates, were worse off than before. The government of Empress Anna had little consideration for the peasants and piled on them heavier and heavier burdens. It gave the owners of the soil more and more power over the laborers. There was no law that entitled the landlord to attach his peasants to the soil but this was done so generally that it was accepted as law. The landlord looked upon his peasants as his "subjects" and treated them as his slaves. A peasant had no rights of his own; he could have no direct dealings with the government. The landlord was free to transfer his peasants from one estate to another and in case of insubordination he could invoke the help of the government.

119. Foreign Affairs (1725-1741).—In the reign of Empress Anna (1732) the cities on the Caspian Sea which had been taken from Persia under Peter the Great (sec. 107) were given back because the Caspian climate proved fatal to the Russian troops.

Russia intervened in Polish affairs. After the death of King Augustus II (1733) each of the neighboring powers attempted to place upon the throne of Poland its own candidate. Russia favored Augustus III, the Elector of Saxony, but the Poles elected Stanislaw Leszczynski, the old ally of Charles XII of Sweden and the enemy of Peter the Great. Anxious to keep out Stanislaw, a Russian army was sent into Poland which drove the king to Danzig and eventually caused his downfall and the election of Augustus III (1734).

During the reign of Empress Anna Russia fought a

long-drawn-out war (1736-1739) with Turkey. It
started because of the raids of the Crimeans on the Russian frontier provinces. Field Marshal Münnich invaded
and laid waste the Crimea, captured the important Turkish fortress of Ochakov (which closed the outlet to the
sea from the Dnieper and Bug), crossed the Pruth and
defeated the Turks near the village of Stavuchany, in
the neighborhood of the city of Khotin. But this long
and exhausting struggle was not ended by an advantageous peace, because Austria, the ally of Russia, had
suffered heavily in this war. Under the terms of the
treaty concluded at Belgrade in 1739, Russia obtained
considerable areas in the steppe of the Black Sea but
failed to win the seaboard and the right to maintain a
navy in the Black Sea.

Both the intervention in Poland and the war with
Turkey were in line with Peter's policies; but the way
they were carried out would have shamed the emperor.
The siege of Danzig was listless and the Turkish campaign dragged. There were endless intrigues and bicker-
ings among the factions in the army and at court. Foreign powers took advantage of this demoralization, not
only to get control in Russian affairs, but to name even
the ruler. There was a "Holstein Party," an "Austrian
Party" and a "French Party," and between them they
succeeded in bringing on a war between Sweden and
Russia in 1741.

EMPRESS ELIZABETH PETROVNA (1741-1761)

120. General Tendency and Character of
Elizabeth's Reign.—When she ascended the throne,
Elizabeth removed all the influential Germans from gov-

ernmental affairs and placed Russians in their places. The "Brunswick Family" was banished to the city of Kholmogory; Ostermann and Münnich were exiled to Siberia; Biron was brought from Siberia and kept at Iaroslavl. Notwithstanding the profound resentment against the Germans none were put to death and none tortured. These two features of Elizabeth's rule—patriotism and kindliness—were noted everywhere and gained for her the affection of the people.

The new empress announced that she would restore the methods of Peter the Great but neither she nor, with some rare exceptions, her collaborators had a very clear idea what these methods were. Generally speaking it must be said that Elizabeth had little interest and even less knowledge of state affairs. As a child she had no occasion to meddle in politics, and when she grew up she was purposely kept at a distance from the capital. When she was later recalled to court she was watched, and dared not show the least interest in serious things. These experiences made her suspicious and irritable and, at the same time, indolent and apathetic. When she was finally prevailed upon to head the palace revolution and become empress she developed a fondness for power without a corresponding fondness for work. After she had abolished the Cabinet Elizabeth left the running of the government to the Senate which, contrary to the laws of Peter the Great, assumed legislative as well as administrative functions. Like Anna, Elizabeth had her favorites, but they were in the Senate, and, as the senators acted in her name, she raised no objections.

Elizabeth's senatorial system of government prevented any one man from getting control. Her favorites were, on the whole, as indolent, as good natured and as little interested in politics as Elizabeth herself. They were willing, but not quite able, to restore the system of Peter, even if such a restoration had been desirable and possible. As "Peter's daughter" and as a restorer of Russian rule, Elizabeth was loved and respected. Under her tranquil and humane reign Russia recovered from "Bironism," lived without fear for the morrow, and gathered fresh strength for the coming epoch of glorious conquests and reforms. Therein lies the historical importance of Elizabeth's era and the secret of her popularity.

121. DOMESTIC AFFAIRS (1741-1761).—Elizabeth's Senate did not make radical changes or undertake vast projects; it confined itself merely to moderate reforms as they were needed. It gave serious attention to the affairs of the Church and the welfare of the clergy. It did much for education. At St. Petersburg there was founded in 1747 a university in connection with the Academy of Sciences, and in 1755 another university was opened at Moscow. The last named being much more centrally located made considerably more progress than the first mentioned. In addition to the universities numerous preparatory and special schools were established in different parts of the empire.

In the economic field the most noteworthy event was the establishment of government banks (one for the nobility, another for the merchants) which lent money at the rate of six per cent. Internal customs barriers were abolished. Provision was made for a census of taxpayers to be taken every fifteen years and two such censuses were actually taken—one at the beginning of Elizabeth's reign and the other at the end. Elizabeth consistently refused to confirm a death penalty. On several different occasions she commuted the sentence of capital punishment to hard labor.

The attitude of the Senate with respect to the nobility deserves particular notice. The Senate took the stand that only noblemen had the right to have landed estates, and, furthermore, that only those were noble who had noble lineage. By these regulations state service no longer conferred nobility. The nobles became an exclusive class desiring privileges but shirking obligations. In the time of Elizabeth they started an agitation to have themselves entirely exempted from all state service.

122. FOREIGN AFFAIRS (1741-1761).—When Elizabeth became empress she found a war with Sweden on her hands. The Swedes were unsuccessful from the start and were gradually forced back to Finland. In 1743 they agreed to make peace and ceded Russia the Finnish territories east of the Kuno River.

While Elizabeth was on the throne Austria and Prussia were at war and each of them tried hard to enlist Russia on its side. Prussia's efforts at the Russian Court were seconded by the French diplomats, especially Marquis de La Chétardie and the empress's French physician, Lestocq. Austria, on the other hand, was favored by the Russian Chancellor of the Empire, Bestuzhev-Riumin, who greatly feared the rapid rise of Prussia and the aggressive schemes of her "precipitate" king, as he nicknamed Frederick II. After some years of struggle and intrigue Bestuzhev-Riumin had his way; de La Chétardie was expelled from Russia, Lestocq was banished from court, and Russia allied herself with Austria against Prussia in the Seven Years' War. It started in 1756 but Russia did not come into it until a year later. In

1757 General Apraxin marched into Eastern Prussia where he defeated the Prussians sent against him, but failed to follow up his victory. For this he was dismissed and brought before a tribunal. Elizabeth suspected that Apraxin was disinclined to fight because he feared that she might soon die and her successor would be the pro-Prussian Grand Duke Peter Fedorovich. Chancellor Bestuzhev-Riumin himself also fell under this suspicion and was dismissed from service and banished to his country estate. After this house cleaning in the army and foreign affairs the war was prosecuted with greater vigor under the direction of a palace "conference" of the highest dignitaries of the empire.

In the years following (1758-1760) the Russian armies occupied Eastern Prussia and then invaded Brandenburg. In a bloody engagement (1758) at Zorndorf, near the Oder River, the Prussians defeated the Russians with great loss and forced them to retreat. But in the following year (1759) (again near the Oder, not far from the city of Frankfurt) the Russians almost annihilated the Prussians at Kunersdorf and just missed capturing Frederick. In 1760 Russian troops occupied Berlin for a short time and imposed a contribution upon the city.

Prussia's resources were completely exhausted by the war, and the only thing that saved Frederick was the death of Empress Elizabeth which occurred on Christmas Day, 1761. Elizabeth's successor, Emperor Peter III, immediately brought the war to an end, restored all that had been taken from Frederick and concluded with him not only a treaty of peace but an alliance. Russia thus at once lost the fruits of her victories, which had cost her so much in men and money,

123. THE QUESTION OF THE SUCCESSION.—Immediately after her accession, Empress Elizabeth named as
her successor Peter the Great's grandson, Karl Peter
Ulrich, Duke of Holstein, a son of Anna Petrovna. An
embassy was sent to the city of Kiel to bring the fourteen-
year old boy to Russia. He reached St. Petersburg in
1742, was baptized into the Orthodox Church as Grand
Duke Peter Fedorovich, and proclaimed heir to the
throne. He married Sophia Augusta, a sixteen year old
German princess, who was recommended by Frederick
the Great. Sophia Augusta was the daughter of a Prussian general belonging to the line of the petty princes of
Anhalt-Zerbst. The young girl was brought to St.
Petersburg and taken into the Orthodox Church as Catherine Alexeievna. After their marriage (1745) the young
couple lived aloof from state affairs, under the supervision of people especially appointed to look after their
"little court" and to train them for the dignities and
responsibilities that awaited them. In 1754 a son was
born to them, Grand Duke Paul Petrovich, who was not,
however, left in the care of his mother, but taken under
the personal charge of Empress Elizabeth.

Peter was not without a certain amount of intelligence,
but his actions at times made one doubt his sanity. Education made no impression on him for he could not
remember anything. He was most tactless. He had no
love for Russia and said so; he admired Frederick of
Prussia and cheered his victories. Orthodoxy and Protestantism formed in him a strange medley, and he was
unable to tell precisely which of the two he believed in.
When he was in his cups, which was often enough, he
committed shocking breaches of etiquette and all kinds
of pranks. He regarded himself as a military genius, but

had not the slightest idea of military affairs. He took himself very seriously and treated all those with whom he came in contact with contemptuous arrogance. As he grew older he grew worse, and it became quite obvious that he would not be able to govern the country.

On the other hand, as the years went on, Catherine displayed a brilliant intellect and unusual ability. At the court of Elizabeth she found herself removed from relatives and friends, surrounded by strange people, and bound to a husband whom she very soon learned to despise. Notwithstanding these circumstances Catherine never lost her composure. She made use of her leisure to read and study. From light reading she turned to more serious literature, and in a short time she had familiarized herself with French literature, especially the works of Montesquieu, Voltaire, and the "Encyclopædists." For intellectual force and breadth of education, Catherine was the most conspicuous personality at the court of Elizabeth, and the simple little girl had grown into a remarkable woman.

The birth of Grand Duke Paul was followed by far-reaching consequences for the court. It was manifest that the heir-apparent, Grand Duke Peter, with his incapacity and lack of Russian patriotism, would never be in a position to rule the country. Under the law of 1722 (sec. 115) Elizabeth was free to substitute Paul for Peter and in that case Catherine, as guardian of Paul, would attain an important place in the government. Elizabeth's high dignitaries saw the possibility of such an event and commenced to draw Catherine into their intrigues and schemes against her husband. When Bestuzhev-Riumin and Apraxin were punished in 1757 it was as much on account of their secret correspondence with Catherine as on account of the war. Catherine came very near being arrested and exiled from Russia in connection with this affair. The Empress knew that Peter was not fit to hold power and yet she could not bring herself around to entrust Catherine with it. She hesitated and wavered until death came, and settled the question in favor of Peter.

124. PETER III.—The first acts of Peter III made him some friends. He pardoned many, among them Biron and Münnich, who had been banished in the time of Elizabeth, and abolished the "Secret Chancellery" that had been established in the reign of Anna. Lastly, by his manifesto of February 18, 1762, he freed the nobles from compulsory state service, but expressed the hope that they would continue to serve, and would instruct their children in the "polite sciences."

But the good effect of these measures was offset by others less praiseworthy. Peter's foreign policy aroused bitter antagonism. All felt humiliated at the way the war with Prussia ended, the way the Russian victory was thrown away. It was felt that Peter was pursuing a personal rather than a Russian policy. This impression was confirmed when the Emperor proposed a war against Denmark because that country was suspected of having designs on his Holstein possessions. The enormous influence which the King of Prussia and his envoy had gained at the Russian Court seemed disgraceful to Russian patriotism.

Peter's treatment of the clergy and the nobility serving in the Guard was enough to stir up a sense of wrong. He did not understand the teachings and the ritual of the Orthodox Church and went out of his way to mock the service. He endeavored to close private chapels and to deprive the clergy of the right to manage their lands and peasants. The clergy made a strongly worded complaint against this persecution but Peter laid it aside without further thought. His attitude towards the members of the Guard was insulting. He called them "Janissaries," ridiculed them, and because he feared them he scattered them among the regular army regiments. Peter lavished all his care and devotion on his Holstein troops. Instead of the simple and comfortable Elizabethan soldier dress he clothed them in the expensive and uncomfortable Prussian uniform.

Peter's personal conduct seemed plainly intolerable to every one. "He is not at all like a sovereign," people complained. Childish pranks would alternate with vulgar dissipation. He was drunk a good part of the time. He insulted his wife Catherine in public. Even before he started divorce proceedings he had already chosen her successor. It became more and more obvious that Peter was incapable of governing and a danger to the state. It seemed as if the worst period of the German domination in Russia had been revived under his rule, and that "Bironism" had been restored.

Of this ill-feeling towards Peter III, Empress Catherine made excellent use. As soon as Empress Elizabeth died and even before she was buried Peter celebrated by getting beastly drunk and shocked everybody by his indecent actions. Catherine, on the other hand, went into mourning and behaved as a woman in her position should under the circumstances. Peter never concealed his German sympathies; Catherine always showed her Russian leanings. He never missed an opportunity to insult her;

she always carried herself modestly and properly. But she was, at the same time, taking an active part in the preparations for a revolution in her own favor.

The conspirators were court officials and young officers of the Guard, but while the former acted cautiously the latter proceeded boldly. At the head of the officers were the two Orlov brothers, Aleksei and Gregory. During the summer of 1762 Peter lived at Oranienbaum, and Catherine at Peterhof. Early in the morning of June 28, the Orlovs secretly conveyed Catherine to St. Petersburg and had her proclaimed empress and absolute ruler, with Grand Duke Paul as heir. All the troops took the oath of allegiance to Catherine, and the populace rejoiced. The dignitaries at the Winter Palace had to accept what was done and abandon their intention of proclaiming Paul Tsar, with Catherine as regent. On the evening of June 28, Catherine marched at the head of her troops against Peter. When the Emperor saw himself abandoned he abdicated on June 29. He was then sent to the Ropsha estate in charge of Aleksei Orlov and here, before Catherine could decide what to do with him, Peter died. It is supposed that he was killed in a drunken brawl, but the country was informed that the former Emperor had died of the colic.

CHAPTER VII

EXPANSION OF SERFDOM AND ARISTO-CRATIC PRIVILEGES

THE TIME OF EMPRESS CATHERINE II
(1762-1796)

125. GENERAL IMPORT AND LEADING FIGURES OF THE REIGN OF CATHERINE II.—The reign of Empress Catherine II was one of the most remarkable in the history of Russia. Because of the domestic reforms and great conquests in her reign Catherine II has often been called the continuer of Peter the Great's work. In internal affairs she accomplished remarkable results. She reformed the provincial administration and endowed the nobility and city inhabitants with self-government. In her foreign policy she won notable triumphs. She annexed the Crimea and the northern shores of the Black Sea, regained the Russian provinces held by Poland, and acquired Courland. Because of her extensive territorial acquisitions she is sometimes referred to as "The Great." The era of Empress Catherine II is equally noteworthy because of its cultural progress. Her government was enlightened, liberal and humane. The philosophical ideas of this empress left their mark not only upon legislation and politics but also upon the literary movement of her time. "The Age of Catherine" had its definite

and distinct character, not only in the field of Russian politics but also in Russian literature.

Catherine II was distinguished by her great ability to select able men and make proper use of their talents. This is why so many capable statesmen gained prominence in her time. "Of the glorious flock of Catherine's eagles," as Pushkin called them, some achieved great military distinction and others acquired fame as legislators and reformers. Among Catherine's collaborators the following should be noted:

Count Nikita Panin, a most capable and astute diplomat, assisted Catherine in directing Russia's foreign policy which the Empress took under her personal charge. Panin had been tutor to Grand Duke Paul in Elizabeth's reign. Catherine continued to employ him in that office and at the same time entrusted him with the College of Foreign Affairs. After Panin, at the close of Catherine's reign, foreign relations were in the hands of Count A. A. Bezborodko.

The Orlov brothers took a prominent part in domestic affairs. During the first few years of her régime there was a persistent rumor that the Empress was going to marry Gregory Orlov. In the second decade of Catherine's reign the Orlovs gave way to Gregory Alexandrovich Potemkin. He was an unusually intelligent and original person, apt to change easily from feverish activity to sluggish indolence, from daring schemes to fainthearted irresolution. The object of his greatest solicitude was the development of southern Russia, the so-called "New Russia." Catherine appreciated Potemkin's loyalty and "excellent mind" and rated him above all her other aides. Besides the Orlovs and Potemkin, Catherine was surrounded by less influential but not less capable and remarkable men in various branches of the administration. Among the last group were Prince Viazemski, the Procurator-General of the Senate, Count Sievers, Governor of Novgorod, with whose aid Catherine carried out her internal reforms, and Ivan Ivanovich Betski, adviser of the Empress in educational problems.

In the wars of Catherine many leaders of great ability came to the front. In the first rank were Counts P. A. Rumiantsev and A. V. Suvorov-Rymnikski ("Prince of Italy"). Suvorov never lost a battle. He was original in his military method and individual in his personal conduct. He won the loyalty and affection of his soldiers by mingling with them freely and by his unpretentious ways. Many of the Russian generals who later fought Napoleon received their training under Suvorov. Among the noted seamen of Catherine's time were Spiridov, Greig, Seniavin and Aleksei Orlov.

126. DOMESTIC AFFAIRS—BEGINNING OF CATHERINE'S REIGN AND THE COMMISSION OF 1767-1768.— Catherine devoted the first years of her reign to a study of the country and its system of government. She traveled in different parts of Russia, selected her collaborators and tried to gather all the threads of the administration within her own hands. The Senate, which under Elizabeth had exercised much power, was divided into six departments, each having a definite sphere of activity. At the head of the Senate as a whole Catherine appointed a Procurator-General with instructions not to allow that body to overstep its authority. At the same time Catherine also freed herself from the influence of individuals at court who now and then made an attempt to control governmental affairs under the youthful and, as they imagined, inexperienced Empress. Notwithstanding all

her tact and intelligence, it required several years for the Empress to establish herself in power firmly.

In 1765 Catherine set to work energetically to accomplish the principal object she had aimed at ever since her accession to the throne, that is to say, "that each government department shall have its own special functions and regulations so that good order shall be maintained in all things." Catherine thought that it was possible to promote law and order by perfect legislation. At that period the problem of new legislation was very much discussed. Beginning with Peter the Great all Russian sovereigns had emphasized the need of drafting a "new code" to take the place of the antiquated "Ulozhenie" of 1649. Under Peter the Great special committees were appointed to draft a new code, either by collecting the Russian laws or by copying foreign legislation (Swedish), but these committees never finished their task. In the succeeding reigns these attempts were continued. Anna and Elizabeth invited elected representatives of the nobles and merchants to assist these legislative committees. At last towards the end of Elizabeth's reign the committee had a plan for a legal code and when Catherine became empress this committee was still at work revising and redrafting the original draft.

Like all rationalist philosophers of her day, Catherine believed that a political and social order should be created in accordance with "reason" and not on the basis of old and obsolete laws, dictated by ignorance or adopted under the stress of the Tartar rule. She argued that a more perfect legislative system ought to be set up on the principles of the new philosophy and the actual needs and desires of the people. Before drafting her perfect system she made a careful study of the abstract principles and in order to determine the needs and desires of the people she planned to summon an assembly representing all classes.

After studying the ideas of the new philosophy, Catherine wrote her famous "Instruction" or "Mandate" (*Nakaz*), which was to guide the "Committee for Drafting the Project of a New Code." In this instruction the Empress set forth her general views upon all the principal problems of legislation. She pointed out that Russia because of her size was in particular need of a single, powerful, autocratic government. She discussed the condition of the various social classes, the objects of legislation, the question of crime and punishment, man's rights and duties as a citizen, problems of education, religious tolerance, and many other such theoretical questions.

The Instruction contained twenty chapters, subdivided into more than five hundred paragraphs. In composing this mandate Catherine made use of Montesquieu's "L'esprit des lois," Bielfeld's "Institutions politiques," and other political works of that period. Her views upon the nature of crime and the purpose of punishment were based upon the treatise of the Italian Beccaria "On Crime and Punishment," just then published. As a result of her investigations her Instruction embodies the most advanced, liberal and humane ideas of her day. In her autocratic government all citizens were equal before the law. The Instruction sponsored the principle of a separation of power; it repudiated torture and questioned the wisdom of capital punishment and cruel penalties. Catherine spent two years writing the Instruction and discussing it with her friends. Her liberal spirit alarmed her courtiers and they attempted to keep it in restraint. It was due to their influence that Catherine published only a part of her Instruction. It was printed in 1767 in four languages (Russian, French, German, Latin) and distributed in Russia and in foreign countries.

Towards the end of 1766 Catherine summoned deputies from the nobility, city inhabitants, and free rural population to the sessions of the Committee for Drafting the Project of a New Code. Peasants on private estates were not represented and the lower clergy shared in the elections in the cities as other citizens. The only special representatives of the clergy as a class were the prelates selected by the Synod. The deputies were requested to bring from their constituencies special mandates setting forth their needs and demands. As long as the deputies were occupied with the work of the Committee they were assured a salary and special personal privileges. In addition to this protection the government freed them forever from corporal punishment, torture and the death penalty. Thus was created the Committee, or Commission, which, according to the idea of Empress Catherine, was to find out the needs and desires of the nation, harmonize them with the lofty principles of the Instruction and draft a new, more perfect code of laws for Russia.

The sessions of the Commission were solemnly opened at Moscow in the summer of 1767. Half a year later it was transferred to St. Petersburg where it continued its deliberations for another year. The work of the Commission was directed by its President, or "Marshal," A. I Bibikov, and a special executive committee. Gradually numerous subcommittees were appointed to work on special problems. At the close of 1768 the sessions of the Commission were interrupted and the deputies given permission to go home; but the subcommittees continued their labors many years more. Although the undertaking was not completed the deputies were never again reassembled. After one and a half years of legislative work the Empress came to the conclusion that it would be impossible to draft a code of laws by debate in a large and more or less ignorant representative assembly. Such a task could be done much better by expert jurists, after which it should be submitted to the representatives of the people for approval. In dismissing the deputies Catherine did not by any means abandon the undertaking. Though the legislators had not passed any laws, yet their speeches and views were quite helpful to the Empress in her dealings with her subjects.

127. DOMESTIC TROUBLES. THE PUGACHEV REBELLION. During the seventies of the eighteenth century central and eastern Russia had many serious economic problems and troubles. They were brought on in great part by the heavy taxation and the severe military service of the wars since the middle of the century. But it was not the government alone that was oppressing the people. The landlords were abusing their peasants more and more until they reached the point of revolt.

These peasants realized very clearly that they were not the slaves but the subjects of the sovereign. In the beginning of the eighteenth century a peasant named Pososhkov, a contemporary of Peter the Great and the author of some remarkable treatises, put forth the doctrine that "the real proprietor of the peasant is the All-Russian sovereign, and the landlord has only temporary use of him." In these words Pososhkov pointed out the ancient connection existing between the landlords' state service and the relation of the peasants to the landlords. According to this doctrine the sovereign lent the peasants to the lord to work for him so that he might serve the state. It followed, therefore, that as soon as the lord ceased to serve the state he no longer had any right over the peasants.

As time went on the landlords served less and finally on February 18, 1762, they were entirely freed from service. But the peasants were not freed from their work. After this manifesto granting the new privileges to the nobility, the peasants in many places rose in open revolt, saying that as the landlords no longer had compulsory service they no longer had any right to require compulsory labor from the peasants. The revolt assumed such proportions that it was found necessary to send troops to suppress it.

In 1771 an epidemic at Moscow attained extraordinary proportions and every one who could do so left the city. The Government offices were closed, stores and shops were locked and all work came to a standstill. The populace became panic-stricken and refused to comply with the instructions of the physicians and the authorities to take the simplest precautions. Instead of doing what the doctors told them the people gathered in front of the image of the Holy Virgin near the Kremlin and prayed. Realizing that the disease must spread worse than ever through this congested crowd, Archbishop Ambrose had the image removed. The infuriated mob turned on the Archbishop and killed him and proceeded to pillage the Kremlin itself. Before order was restored by armed force about one hundred people had lost their lives.

While this deadly epidemic was spreading in the center of Russia a grave popular uprising similar in many respects to the movement of Stenka Razin was developing among the Cossacks on the Ural River. We have noted already (sec. 105) how the last vestige of Cossack independence had been lost on the Don after the insurrection of Bulavin, and how the remaining followers of this leader had scattered in all directions. But the Cossacks themselves with their traditions of freedom and hatred for the authority of the state were not crushed. They left the Don and settled on the Kuban, Terek, Ural, or wherever they could fish, hunt, fight and plunder. The government was right on their heels, however. In the course of the eighteenth century it gradually took over the territory along the Ural River and brought the natives as well as the Cossacks under its control. This was a repetition of the things that had been done before on the Don. In 1771 the Cossacks rose in revolt but were put down and cruelly punished. Some were banished to Siberia, others forced into the army, and their Cossack organizations subjected for an indefinite period to the military authorities. But severe reprisals had no effect in pacifying the rebels; they merely increased their sullen resentment and at last drove them to another revolt.

The leader of the Ural Cossacks was Emelian Pugachev, a fugitive Don Cossack who had vagabonded in different parts of Russia and was familiar with the inside as well as the outside of prisons. In 1773 he came to the Ural and gave himself out as Emperor Peter III. The death of Peter was so sudden and of such a suspicious character that almost immediately afterwards several impostors appeared. Peter was too well known in Central Russia to arouse any enthusiasm to put him back on the throne, but in the far distant Urals and among an oppressed people burning with hate and a sense of cruel wrong one tsar was as good a pretext for a revolt as another. In a short time Pugachev gathered a force of about 25,000 made up of Cossacks, religious dissenters, serfs, miners, Tartars, Kalmyks, Bashkirs, and other discontented groups, each with its particular grievance and particular object to attain. With the guns and ammunitions captured Pugachev equipped his army and led it down into the Volga valley. As it advanced it aroused the brutalized serfs against the lords, the common soldiers against the officers, the debtors against the creditors. Pretty soon the countryside was ablaze with the flame of burning manor houses, factories and cities, and the air filled with the cries of the families of nobles, merchants, and imperial officers as they were being tortured and murdered. A panic seized the population of the Volga and it soon spread to other parts of Russia even to the capital. Catherine sent General A. I. Bibikov to suppress the rebellion but she could not give him much of a force because of the war with Turkey and Poland and the danger of an uprising at Moscow. When Bibikov arrived at Kazan, the center of the rebellion, he was struck by the chaos and panic that reigned there. People were not thinking of defending themselves but of escaping. He assembled the local nobles, encouraged them to arm themselves and furnish means for resistance. With troops thus collected and with the militia of the nobility he overcame Pugachev and drove him with his bands back to the Ural Mountains. The revolt was now beginning to subside but before it was entirely put down Bibikov died.

In the spring of 1774 the rebellion broke out afresh. Pugachev again appeared on the Volga at the head of his Cossacks, but refused to engage in an open fight with the government forces. He moved swiftly from place to place, seized towns and incited the peasants everywhere to attack the landlords. He appeared suddenly under the walls of Kazan itself and, although he failed to capture the fortress, he put the city to the torch and eluded pursuit. He reappeared at Penza, took Saratov and marched on Tsaritsyn. By this time Catherine was so frightened that she recalled General Suvorov from the Turkish front and put him on the trail of the Cossack leader. Pugachev was forced from the Volga plain into the Ural Mountains where he was betrayed by one of his followers. He was sent to Moscow and there executed (1775).

The failure of this revolt was a deathblow to the free Cossacks. They lost completely their former independence and became a frontier militia commanded by the Tsar's officers. The peasantry, too, was brought to submission. Stringent measures were taken against the seditious mass of peasants, and all those who participated in the revolt were cruelly punished. The Empress herself in spite of her desire to be as humane and as merciful as possible was determined, above all things, to preserve law and order, and she therefore approved of the harsh measures.

128. REFORMS OF 1775 AND 1785.—In 1775 Empress Catherine issued her so-called "Institutions for the Administration of the Provinces." When she began her reign there were in Russia about twenty "Gubernias" or "governments." These were divided into "Provinces" and these, in turn, into "Districts," or "*Uiezds*." An "*Uiezd*" comprised a district that had come into being a long time ago and it usually consisted of the lands of an ancient appanage principality or of rural communities with some city for a center. These gubernias, provinces and districts differed considerably from each other in area and

population. Empress Catherine proposed to replace this obsolete division of her empire by one more modern. Under the law of 1775, a gubernia was to have a population from 300,000 to 400,000 and a district from 20,000 to 30,000. On this basis new gubernias were formed until they numbered fifty at the close of Catherine's reign. In like manner the number of uiezds or districts in each government was increased. As there were not enough cities as centers for the newly formed districts, villages and hamlets were turned into uiezd seats. In this way a new administrative division of the empire was made on the basis of statistics in the place of the old historical division.

In each government (gubernia) capital the following institutions were established: 1. A "Government Administrative Board," presided over by the Governor to "administer the entire Government by virtue of the law, in the name of the Imperial Majesty." 2. A "Crown Chamber," presided over by the Vice-Governor to have charge of all financial and economic "crown" matters. 3. Two "Chambers of Justice," one for civil and the other for criminal cases to exercise supervision over the lower courts. 4. A "Court of Conscience" or equity to try cases of juvenile delinquents, insane and unintentional offenders, and to settle disputes by arbitration instead of formal legalistic methods. (This was the first court of this kind in Russia.) 5. A "Department of Social Welfare," to look after the public schools, hospitals, almshouses and prisons. The members of the courts and the social institutions just named were elected by the several classes of the population.

In each district seat there was established a "Lower Country Court," corresponding to the "Government Administrative Board," to have charge of the administration and police in the district. It was composed of a chairman, known as the *"Ispravnik"* or "Captain," and two members who were chosen by the nobility of the district. In the towns the maintenance of law and order was entrusted to the *"Gorodnichie"* who were appointed by the central government. Elective tribunals of justice were also organized in the governments and districts for each class of inhabitants separately.

Such was the organization of the new local institutions of 1775. It was built up on a new and modern principle of separation of powers. All these institutions were organized on the collegiate principle. The local inhabitants were given a big share in the local administration. All classes participated in judicial matters by sending their chosen jurors to the courts of their particular class, as well as to the "Courts of Conscience." Moreover, all classes sent their representatives to the "Departments of Social Welfare," to take part in matters affecting the improvement of social conditions. Lastly, the nobles were granted the right to elect the officers of the district (the Lower Country Court). It may be said that under the law of 1775 the entire local administration assumed the character of self-government functioning under the control of the crown administration (the "Government Administrative Boards" and "Chambers.") In this respect Catherine gratified the desires of the several classes expressed in her Legislative Commission of 1767-1768.

The institutions for the administration of the "Governments" established in 1775 are of the greatest importance not only because they provided a better organization and administration for the rural section of Russia, but also for the reason that they exerted a most powerful, even though indirect, influence in other spheres of Catherine's political activity. The creation of the new institutions deprived the old "Colleges" at the capital of many of their functions and they died a natural death. In having the several classes take part in the "Government" and District administrations, new rights and new obligations were laid on them and, in order that they might properly perform them, they had to be provided with a new organization.

The new organization of the several social classes was determined by special charters granted to the nobility and the cities in 1785.

Under the charter of 1785 the nobles in each "Government" formed a separate corporation with the right of assembly. Once in three years they met at the "Government" capital to hold elections and discuss their affairs. They chose from their own number "Marshals" of the nobility for the entire "Government" and its several Districts as well as other officers for the institutions of the "Government." The nobles could address the Governor, the Senate, and even the monarch, with petitions regarding their affairs. According to the Charter of 1785 a nobleman was exempt from compulsory state service, from the payment of taxes, and from army conscription. Corporal punishment could not be inflicted on a noble. He could be tried only in the courts of the nobility and by his peers. His title of nobility was shared by his wife and by his children, and could not be taken from him without due process of law and then only by the Senate and with the consent of the sovereign. A nobleman had absolute right of ownership over his land and all that was on it including peasants. He was at liberty to engage in trade and industry. All these privileges and rights granted to the nobility in 1785 represented the last stage in the general progress of this class. Under Peter the Great the nobility had few privileges; under Empress Anna (sec. 118) it raised itself somewhat; under Elizabeth it became an exclusive aristocracy (sec. 121); under Peter III it was exempted from compulsory service (sec. 124); and now, under Catherine II, it was transformed into a privileged class with vast powers of self-government and great administrative influence, both in the gubernia and district.

Simultaneously with the charter of the nobility a "Municipal Statute" was granted to the cities. Like the nobles the city inhabitants formed a "Municipal Corporation" with the right to own property, to assemble and petition the Governor. At these assemblies the citizens deliberated on public affairs and elected the Mayor and other municipal officers, including the judges of the courts. Municipal business was managed by the Mayor with the aid of the "Six-Vote Council" (made up of one representative from each of the six different categories of city inhabitants). The division of merchants into guilds, and of artisans into craft associations (sec. 109) established by Peter the Great was preserved. We should note, however, that Catherine's efforts on behalf of the cities were almost as fruitless as Peter's. Poor in resources, still very backward, and lacking a sense of unity, the city inhabitants found no opportunity to form a genuine, united "urban community" and to develop real self-government.

129. THE PEASANT QUESTION.—In view of the fact that Catherine attempted to improve the condition of the nobility and urban population one might suppose that she did something for the peasants. It is true that

among her papers there is some evidence to show that Catherine had given serious thought to the question of peasant emancipation. In her Instruction she says, "We must not too suddenly, and by sweeping legislation, make a large number of freed peasants." It would seem that she had in mind to free the children of peasants who were born after the granting of the charter of the nobility, but this idea, like so many others of this nature, was never acted upon. The Empress tried to create a public opinion in favor of emancipation by stimulating discussion on the subject and by encouraging the nobles to take the initiative but her efforts in this direction were not successful. She kept wavering between a desire to do the humane thing and the necessity of standing in well with the nobles. This explains why her attitude on the serf question was so inconsistent. She improved the lot of about one million peasants on church lands, she prohibited free men and freed peasants from becoming serfs, and prohibited the sale of peasants during military conscription; but at the same time she presented her friends with crown lands having on them about one million serfs. In her day serfdom was legalized in Little Russia, and the lord obtained the right to send his peasant to hard labor in Siberia because of "mutinous behavior." It is generally admitted that in her reign the status of the serf was lower than ever before. He had now come to be a mere thing and the power of the lord over him was as absolute as that of master over slave.

That this evil should provoke the condemnation of the more enlightened and humane elements of society at that period is but natural. There was considerable agitation on the subject which the Empress at first encouraged privately and publicly. At the beginning of her reign there was founded at St. Petersburg the "Free Economic Society" with the object of promoting useful knowledge in agriculture; but at the suggestion of the Empress this organization started a discussion of serfdom, offered a prize for a treatise on the subject, and awarded it to one written in favor of emancipation.

Hand in hand with the expansion of serfdom went the protest against it, but it was a philosophical protest and nothing more. People said that the economic organization would break down without unpaid peasant labor, that the existing social order would collapse if millions of serfs were freed at once. At first Pugachev's uprising and later the French Revolution were held up as illustrations of what would happen if emancipation should take place. Even Catherine lost faith and enthusiasm in her ideals at the sight of these bloody deeds. When the nobleman Radishchev, who had been educated abroad, published (1790) a book, "A Journey from Petersburg to Moscow," in which he made many sharp comments upon the system of serfdom, Catherine exiled him to Siberia.

130. MISCELLANEOUS MEASURES.—From the preceding pages it will be seen that Empress Catherine did not always succeed in carrying out her intentions and living up to her ideals. She set out to formulate a perfect code of laws in the spirit of the liberal philosophy of her age and ended by creating a number of local institutions on the principle of separation of powers. She promised liberty and equality before the law to all citizens but gave it to the nobility only. This failure of Catherine's program has been justly ascribed to the fact that she greatly depended upon the support of the nobles. She could not lead them where they would not go. Where

its own class interest was not affected the nobility did not raise any opposition and Catherine could try out her ideas and usually did it with great success. Thanks to her broad culture her government always stood high in European educational affairs, expressed itself in language that was precise and beautiful, and worked steadily for the common good. In this sense Catherine's rule had an educational influence upon the society she governed and many of her measures earned enduring fame.

1. Among such measures those dealing with education, worked out by Catherine in common with General Ivan Betski, are noteworthy. Peter the Great emphasized the value of practical education (sec. 114); Catherine pointed out the importance of education in the development of character. She said: "A mind that is merely adorned or enlightened by science does not yet make a good and honest citizen . . . the root of all evil or good is in character training." Catherine thought that the first step in her new educational system should be the bringing up of a "new breed, or new fathers and mothers," in educational institutions in charge of experienced educators, separated from family and society—far from contact with the uncultured members of society. With this idea in mind the "Institutes" (boarding schools) for young ladies were founded ("Society for the Training of the Daughters of the Nobility" or Smolny Institute) in 1764, having separate classes for the daughters of the nobility and for those of ordinary citizens; and the "Cadet" schools for the training of young boys. The opening of these institutions marked the beginning of a boarding school system in Russia. In 1782 a special "Committee for the Establishment of Public Schools" prepared a well-ordered plan for the establishment of schools open to all classes. It contemplated the opening of a "small public school" in each District seat, a "main public school" in each "Government" capital, and at the top of this educational ladder four universities. This plan was very admirable but it was beyond the financial resources of the government to carry out. Not one of the four universities was founded and onlv here and there were public schools opened.

2. In the economic field Catherine pursued a policy entirely different from that of her predecessors. Peter the Great regulated trade and industry even to the minutest details, but Catherine, under Adam Smith's teaching, adopted (1782) the policy of "laisser faire, laisser passer." While she no longer directed and controlled trade and industry she continued to watch over them and aid them in their further development. She improved the credit system by closing the banks for special classes of the population of Elizabeth's time (sec. 121) and opening one "State Loan Bank" which lent money at the rate of 5 per cent.

In the time of Catherine paper currency came into use in Russia. It began in 1768 when a bank with a capital of one million rubles was established to issue "assignats." At first only a small amount of these bills was put in circulation and as they were redeemable in coin there was no difficulty in getting them accepted. As time went on the government issued more and more of them to cover running expenses with the result that they depreciated and the cost of living went up.

3. Most remarkable and valuable were the endeavors of Empress Catherine in the domain of public health. A special "Medical Commission" was established to co-operate with the Governors in providing cities with physicians and drug stores. It was one of the obligations of the local departments of "Social Welfare" (sec. 128) to establish "welfare institutions," hospitals, and homes for the sick and the feeble-minded. Vaccination, just started in Europe, was introduced into Russia, and the Empress herself, with her son, was vaccinated, to encourage her subjects to do likewise.

131. LITERARY MOVEMENT UNDER CATHERINE II.— The first seeds of European enlightenment planted by Peter the Great had borne fruit already in the reign of his daughter, Elizabeth. In her day Russia produced three writers of note: Lomonosov, Trediakovski, and Sumarokov. Under the influence of these men and the spirit of Elizabeth's court the study of French became popular in Russian society. Catherine was an ardent student of French literature.

When she became empress she did not give up her studies; she became the disseminator of French tastes and ideas. She not only read but wrote much on various subjects, from fairy tales and light comedies to treatises on government and pedagogy. The example of the Empress had its good effect. With the beginning of Catherine's reign there was a remarkable increase in literary activity. Several journals made their appearance ("Miscellany," "The Drone," etc.) which offered the Russian public some edifying reading matter. One of the methods adopted by these journals to make vice unpopular and culture popular was to satirize the one and uphold the other. The Empress herself collaborated in the "Miscellany" and had a great liking for journalistic polemics. While the vogue for periodicals soon passed, the literary movement did not come to a stop. There appeared on the literary horizon such great writers as Derzhavin and

Vonvizin (Von Wisin), followed by a whole pleiad of poets and dramatists of secondary magnitude. All of them were in one way or another encouraged by the enlightened Empress.

The intellectual awakening caused by Empress Catherine manifested itself in other than literary ways. It was at this time that Free Masonry began to spread in Russia. The Masonic lodges were exclusive and surrounded with an air of mystery, rites and ceremonials. Admission to these organizations depended upon the passing of various initiation tests. In the idealism and symbolism of Free Masonry people who were inclined towards mysticism and opposed to dry rationalism found a moral satisfaction. The first Masons in Russia were people of Catherine's circle and she befriended them. But later she began to suspect them of political motives, prohibited the movement and imprisoned some of the leaders.

Catherine aided the development of historical research and publications. Under her patronage and with her assistance Novikov published in twenty volumes a collection of ancient Russian documents under the title of the "Ancient Russia Library." The Academy of Sciences commenced the printing of the Russian annals, or chronicles. At this time was also published the voluminous "Russian History" of V. N. Tatishchev, a contemporary and collaborator of Peter the Great. A still larger work under the same title, "Russian History," was completed and published by Prince M. M. Shcherbatov to whom the Empress threw open the state archives. Prince Shcherbatov was not only a historian but also a publicist. He was rather critical of the conditions and manners of his time and preferred the old Russian customs.

Compared with the period that preceded it the reign of Empress Catherine II was one of great cultural awakening. The enlightened and humane views of the Empress, the liberal spirit of her "Instruction," the deep public interest aroused by the Commission of 1767-1768, the privilege of self-government conferred upon the higher classes by the laws of 1785, and the unprecedented expansion of literature and journalism gave to the "Age of Catherine" an unusual luster, and made the Empress exceedingly popular. This popularity was not diminished even by the change that came over Catherine after the outbreak of the French Revolution, for the same change had come over the public. Catherine was able to enjoy until her death the respect of her subjects, a respect which on more than one occasion was expressed in the endearing term "Little Mother Catherine."

132. FOREIGN AFFAIRS—THEIR GENERAL PROGRESS AND LEADING PRINCIPLES.—In the progress of Empress Catherine's foreign policies two periods of equal duration, divided approximately by the year 1779, may be noted. In each of these periods the Empress was guided by a clearly defined plan of action. At first she felt attracted by the "Northern System" which consisted of the formation of a permanent alliance of the states of northern Europe (Russia, Prussia, Poland, Sweden, Denmark and England) to offset the alliance of Austria and France. With this idea in mind Catherine turned all her attention to the affairs of Poland. But before she could carry out her policy there she was compelled to fight the Turks. Polish and Turkish affairs took up the first period of Catherine's political activity and added considerable territory to her empire. After studying the

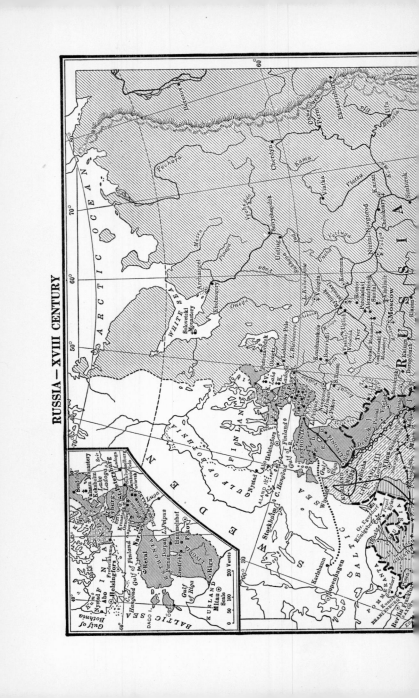

RUSSIA—XVIII CENTURY

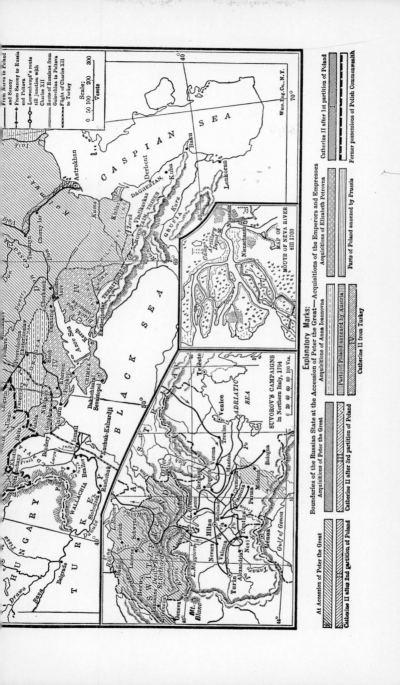

Explanatory Marks:

From Narva to Poland and Saxony
From Saxony to Russia and Poltava
Loewenhaupt's route till junction with Charles XII
Route of Russians from Golovchino to Poltava
Flight of Charles XII to Turkey

Scale;
0 50 100 200 300
Versts

Wm. Eng. Co., N.Y.

MAP OF NEVA RIVER
till 1703

MOUTH OF NEVA RIVER

SUVOROV'S CAMPAIGNS
in Northern Italy, 1794
0 20 40 60 80 100 Vls.

Boundaries of the Russian State at the Accession of Peter the Great.—Acquisitions of the Emperors and Empresses
At Accession of Peter the Great
Acquisitions of Peter the Great
Acquisitions of Anna Ioannovna
Acquisitions of Elizabeth Petrovna
Catherine II after 1st partition of Poland
Catherine II after 2nd partition of Poland
Catherine II after 3rd partition of Poland
Part of Poland annexed by Austria
Catherine II from Turkey
Parts of Poland annexed by Prussia
Former possessions of Polish Commonwealth

"Northern Accord" she became convinced that it was impossible to reconcile and combine the utterly divergent and mutually hostile interests of the northern European powers. Then, too, she discovered that Russian interests obliged her to go her own way.

In 1779 Russia and Austria formed an alliance against Turkey having for its foundation Catherine's famous "Greek Project." This project aimed to drive the Turk from Europe, to set up at Constantinople a Greek empire with an Orthodox sovereign, and to partition the remaining Turkish territories and islands among the European powers. This program and alliance led to wars with Turkey and Sweden and trouble with Poland. From these new wars Catherine emerged triumphantly and with considerable territorial gains, but her "Greek Project" remained a project and nothing more. Catherine's foreign policy did nevertheless strengthen Russia and was in line with the efforts of Peter the Great.

133. FIRST PERIOD OF FOREIGN RELATIONS. POLAND (1763-1773).—Immediately after she became ruler Catherine put an end to the close relations between the Russian court and Frederick II of Prussia which Peter III had maintained (sec. 124). She did not, however, resume the war against Prussia, but preserved a firm and absolute neutrality.

Events in Poland demanded Catherine's close attention. King Augustus III of Poland was growing old, and an interregnum was approaching. From the Russian point of view it was very important that the Polish king should be a friend of the empire. Moreover, since about the middle of the eighteenth century the domestic turmoil in Poland had become so violent that it looked at times as if the kingdom might fall to pieces and intervention might be necessary. An invitation for such intervention was actually extended to Catherine. In the beginning of her reign the Empress was petitioned by the White-Russian bishop, George Koniski, to protect the Orthodox inhabitants in Poland against individual and government outrages and oppression.[1]

It has been said already (sec. 91) that the principal cause of trouble in Poland was the unwillingness of the nobility to recognize the authority of the King and to admit that the lower classes had any rights. They shared with the King the government; they obeyed him or not as they pleased and sometimes they formed "confederations" among themselves against him in defense of their privileges and liberties in accordance with the law of the land and the inalienable right of the noble. Under these conditions the King was practically powerless and had to rely chiefly upon his personal resources. These were, however, never adequate to break the stubborn opposition of the ruling class. On the contrary the King was often forced to seek help and support from foreign courts to maintain himself in power. This "liberty" ruined both the country and the nobles. Alongside of the great nobles lived poor small landowners always ready to curry favor with their aristocratic neighbors and do their bidding. In this way it came about that some of the more important magnates had a large group of obedient dependents. The Diet was transformed into

---

[1] The Orthodox were not allowed to build or even to repair Orthodox churches; Catholics censored Orthodox prayerbooks; special taxes for the benefit of the Catholic clergy were imposed upon the Orthodox communicants; the Orthodox were subject to the authority of a Catholic ecclesiastical tribunal; finally Orthodox Russians were denied the right of holding public office and to become deputies of the Diet.

an arena for selfish and petty struggles between individuals and factions while the important interests of the country were neglected.

The Diet lost the character of a really serious representative assembly. According to the rules of procedure every measure had to be passed by a unanimous vote to become law. At a time when orderly procedure was still strong at the Diet the problem of unanimity was treated seriously and conscientiously. But in the eighteenth century when factional strife was keen it was easy enough to block and kill any measure by persuading one member of the Diet to exclaim "I do not agree." This custom granting to every deputy the right to veto (liberum veto) utterly ruined the work of the Diet. It was impossible to carry through any reform that counted because there was always some one who objected.

The inevitable consequence of this system was a full sway of arbitrariness and violence in public life. Since the government had little power, might became right and the stronger oppressed the weaker. The magnates quarrelled among themselves; neighbor abused neighbor; landowners oppressed the peasant-serfs; nobles lorded over the city inhabitants and the Jews; Catholics and Uniates persecuted the Orthodox and Protestants. Nowhere could the victims find any redress for their wrongs, any protection for their rights, property, and life. It is not to be wondered at that under these conditions people looked for protection from foreign governments. This condition of affairs gave the neighboring sovereigns an opportunity to intervene in the domestic affairs of Poland.

King Augustus III died in 1763. In accordance with the wishes of Catherine the Diet elected to the throne a native Pole, Count Stanislaw Poniatowski, who took the name of Augustus IV. He was a personal friend of the Empress and Russian influence was strong in the Polish court. After the complaint of Bishop George Koniski, Catherine and Frederick of Prussia asked Augustus IV that the Orthodox and Protestants in Poland should have the same rights as the Catholics. When the question was brought before the Diet it refused to give its approval to these rights.

Catherine met this refusal by instructing her ambassador in Poland to advise the Orthodox and Protestant nobles to form a "confederacy" for the protection of their rights. In a short time three such confederacies were formed: Orthodox, Protestant, and Catholic (those who favored toleration). Another attempt was made to carry the measure through the Diet and when that failed a Russian army was sent to Warsaw, and a demand made on the king that he arrest the Catholic opposition in the Diet. When several of the leaders were seized and carried off to Russia the Diet yielded. In 1767 a special law was passed which granted full equality with Catholics to the nobles of the other denominations, but made it clear that Catholicism was the dominant faith and that only a Catholic could become king. This was a most important reform. Its proper execution was guaranteed in 1768 by a special convention entered into by Russia and Poland by which Catherine pledged herself to protect the political organization of Poland and Lithuania. This pledge established, as it were, a Russian protectorate over Poland and gave Russia the right to control the domestic affairs of a neighboring state.

Empress Catherine thus brought about a complete revolution in the political and religious situation within Poland. It was hardly to be expected that the nobles would reconcile themselves to the forcible measures against the Diet and the King. A number of confederacies were formed in Poland (with headquarters at the city of Bar) "for faith and liberty," that is to say, in defense of the Catholic Church and the Diet and against the Russian protectorate. In this struggle the confederates of Bar did not spare the Orthodox inhabitants and thereby brought on the revolt of the "Haidamaks." [2] The Haidamaks rose in defense of their "faith and liberty" and massacred with unparalleled cruelty Catholic priests, Polish nobles and Jews, and destroyed entire cities. The King had no means at his disposal to defend himself or to enforce the law against the confederates or to suppress the revolt of the Haidamaks. He asked Catherine for troops to restore order which she, on the strength of the convention of 1768, sent.

The Russian troops quickly suppressed the movement of the Haidamaks, but it took them a long time to put down the confederates. Detachments of the confederates moved from place to place, pillaged and plundered, but refused to accept open battle. Both France and Austria aided the confederates and that rendered the struggle more difficult. Finally the Polish Government itself declined to coöperate with the Russian troops. As the fight dragged on Austria and Prussia became directly involved and they, too, despatched troops to Poland. When Suvorov finally defeated the confederates and captured the city of Cracow it became clear that the days of the confederacy were numbered. The powers did not recall their armies from Poland and asked reparations for the

[2] A name given to the roving bands of peasants, in many respects like the Cossacks of the sixteenth and seventeenth centuries, who lived on the right bank of the Dnieper.

losses and disturbances they had suffered. As a result of these negotiations Prussia appropriated Pomerania and part of Great Poland (the territories lying between Brandenburg and Prussia); Austria annexed Galicia; and Russia acquired White Russia.

This division of Polish territory took place in 1773 and is known as the First Partition of Poland. Catherine was not quite satisfied with the result. She thought that Prussia and Austria got a great deal more than they deserved, considering the little work they had done. She felt particularly aggrieved that Austria had secured territory that was fundamentally Russian.

134. FIRST PERIOD OF FOREIGN RELATIONS. TURKEY (1768-1774).—At the time that Russia was suppressing the Polish confederates and the Haidamaks Turkey declared war (1768). The pretext was the border raids of the Haidamaks, but the real cause was the anti-Russian influence of France upon the Turks. The French urged the Turks to attack while Russia was occupied in Poland and encouraged them to hope for success. This new enemy merely doubled the energy and determination of the Russians and they took up the challenge.

In the very first year of the war (1769) the Russians struck the Turks a heavy blow at the fortress of Khotin. This success was followed by others in 1770. On the Larga and Kagul rivers, near the Pruth, Count Rumiantsev with remarkable skill routed the many times superior forces of the enemy. Especially important and brilliant was the victory of the Kagul because it opened the way to the Danube and beyond. While the land battles were taking place the Russian navy, under Count Aleksei Orlov, was despatched from the Baltic to the Mediterranean. Orlov stirred up a revolt among the Greeks of the Peloponnesus against the Turks. In the naval engagement which took place in the Straits of Chios and the Bay of Tchesme the whole Turkish fleet was burned to the water's edge.

It was on land rather than on sea that the issues of war were decided. After their defeats by the Russian army the Turks no longer dared operate north of the Danube but confined themselves to a defense of its banks. More than once Rumiantsev managed to cross the river to besiege its fortresses but lack of provisions made long operations beyond the river impossible. On one such occasion (1774) he came as far as Shumla while his advance force reached the Balkans. In recognition of this extraordinary exploit of the first Russian crossing of the Danube and carrying the war into the very heart of Turkey Rumiantsev was honored with the titles of Field Marshal and "Zadunaiski" (Beyond-the-Danube). No less successful was the second Russian Army under Prince Dolgoruki which conquered the entire Crimea. The Turks at last realized that they had lost the war and decided to bring it to an end.

In 1774 peace was concluded between Russia and Turkey in the village of Kuchuk-Kainardji on the right bank of the Danube. The terms of this treaty were as follows: 1. All the Tartars living on the northern shores of the Black Sea and on the coasts of the Sea of Azov were recognized as independent of the Turkish Sultan. 2. Russia obtained Azov, Kerch (with Ienikale) and Kinburn (in other words, the outlets of the Don, Bug, and Dnieper, together with the Straits of Kerch). 3. Russian subjects and traders secured the special protection of the Turkish authorities. 4. Turkey undertook to pay to Russia an indemnity of four and one half million rubles. This peace was very advantageous to Russia.

135. THE CRIMEA AND NEW RUSSIA (NOVOROSSIA) 1774-1787.—The acquisition of the outlets of the Dnieper, Bug, Don and the Straits of Kerch gave Russia control of the Black Sea region and the Crimea. It is true that the treaty of Kuchuk-Kainardji made the Khanate of the Crimea independent but its independence was of no great value, closely surrounded as it was by Russian fortresses and far removed from Moslem neighbors. A few years later the Tartars got into a fight among themselves and one of the factions called for outside help. A Russian army marched in, restored peace, and took over the government. In 1783 Russia formally annexed the Crimea under the name of Taurida.

The annexation of the Crimea, the northern shores of the Black Sea and Azov freed South Russia from the constant menace of the Tartars and gave Russia immense stretches of almost uninhabited fertile soil and a seaboard indented with bays and harbors. All that this country needed to make it prosperous was peace and settlers and these it soon had. Immediately after the conclusion of the peace with the Turks Catherine put an end to the Zaporogian Siech (sec. 93), the stronghold of the lawless Cossack adventurers on the Dnieper. Now that the Tartars were subdued the usefulness of the Cossacks was over. There was danger that they might involve the country in a war. During the troubles in Poland they protected and aided the Haidamaks in their raids on Poland. In 1775 Catherine's troops broke up this nest and drove off the Cossacks. Some crossed the Danube into Turkish territory, others settled on the Kuban, and still others wandered in different directions. After the country had been rid of these Russian and Tartar rovers the Empress undertook to attract peaceful settlers to New Russia (Novorossia). Potemkin was appointed Governor of New Russia and made his headquarters at Ekaterinoslav, a city which he built and named in honor of the Empress. Along the mouths of the rivers he built forts (Kherson, Nikolaev) and constructed shipyards. Sebastopol he turned into a naval base. He brought settlers from northern Russia and from Germany. He granted vast tracts of land to Russian nobles who moved south with their peasants. He established agricultural stations to determine what crops were best suited to the soil and climate. In a very short time Potemkin made a civilized country out of the wilderness and then he invited the Empress to visit his beloved Novorossia.

In 1787 Catherine set out to see her favorite. She was accompanied by a large suite of important persons, including foreign ambassadors. On the Dnieper she was met by Poniatovski, King of Poland, and Joseph II, Emperor of Austria. Potemkin saw to it that the Empress should not be bored on the way. Her journey was just one succession of festivities. Thousands of people were driven long distances to meet her Majesty and tell her how glad they were to see her. But what chiefly impressed Potemkin's guests were not his cultural achievements but the great navy which had sprung up on the Black Sea within a few years. It was plain that Russia had gained a firm hold upon the new territory.

136. SECOND PERIOD OF FOREIGN RELATIONS. TURKEY AND SWEDEN, 1787-1791.—The annexation of the Crimea and the military preparations on the shores of the Black Sea had a direct connection with the "Greek Project" that occupied Catherine and Potemkin. Linked

with the same project was also the alliance of Russia and Austria against Turkey (1779). The Turkish Government realized the danger and decided to declare war before Russia had completed her armaments. In this move Turkey was encouraged by England. England resented Catherine's declaration (1780) of "armed neutrality" at the time of the American War of Independence and her proposal that neutral powers should form an alliance to protect their merchant ships from seizure by the belligerents. England was the greatest offender in this respect and therefore opposed the alliance and never quite forgave Russia for suggesting it.

At the very time that Catherine was making her journey in New Russia and the Crimea, Turkey decided to open hostilities (1787). The first months of the war were not favorable to the Russians. A storm destroyed the fleet on the Black Sea which greatly discouraged Potemkin and he failed to put vigor into the fight. Military operations dragged on for a year and a half around Kinburn and Ochakov (sec. 134) until, at last, Ochakov was taken by the Russians after a bloody assault. Soon after Potemkin handed over the command to Suvorov and the latter started out against the Turks on the Danube. His very name put life and confidence into the Russians and despair into the Turks. Suvorov won victory after victory. In 1790 he stormed Izmail, the strongest Turkish fortress on the Danube, and took possession of the river crossings. By this time the Russian navy had recovered from its great disaster and was operating successfully at sea. It looked as if Suvorov would march on Constantinople. This possibility frightened the Turks and made them willing to talk peace. Russia, too, was exhausted for she did not receive the promised support from her ally, Austria. In the treaty signed between the belligerents at Jassy in 1791 Turkey ceded to Russia the fortress of Ochakov, the territories lying between the Bug and Dniester Rivers, and recognized her right to the Crimea. For the time being the "Greek Project" had to be shelved, the more so as the chief advocate of this project, Potemkin, died in the course of this war.

Russia's alliance with Austria and the growing coolness towards the "Northern System" (sec. 132) turned Prussia and Sweden against her. Prussia confined herself to undermining Russia's influence in Poland, while Sweden, thinking the time opportune because of the Turkish War, came out openly against her (1788). In 1788-1789 the Swedish fleet failed in its attempts against St. Petersburg, and the Swedish army did but little better. The Russian army and navy were equally weak and ineffective. In 1790 the war came to an end by the Peace of Verela, which left the frontiers of the two countries unchanged.

137. SECOND PERIOD OF FOREIGN RELATIONS. POLAND, 1791-1795.—Russia was barely out of the Second Turkish War when she was called upon to intervene in Poland. The First Partition of Poland aroused the Polish nobility and made them realize that they and their system were chiefly responsible for the tragedy and that without reform their country would surely perish. After studying the various forms of government and the teachings of the French philosophers the Polish reformers drafted a constitution for Poland. This Constitution was passed by the Diet without discussion and debate on May 3, 1791.

Under the "Constitution of May 3," the throne of Poland was made hereditary. The executive power was vested in the king and his ministers and the legislative power in the Senate and the Diet. The Diet was made more democratic by the admission of deputies representing the urban classes. The *liberum veto* was abrogated and a majority vote was sufficient to pass a measure. Serfdom was not abolished but the landlord had the power to emancipate or improve the lot of his peasants. Religious freedom was proclaimed but the Catholic Church retained its predominant position in the state. The Constitution was moderate and a distinct step in advance, but it was nevertheless opposed by all those who were anxious to preserve the domination of the magnates and turbulent lesser nobles.

Immediately following the promulgation of the new Constitution the reactionaries formed a powerful confederacy at the little town of Targowica to protect their old rights and privileges. The confederates sent envoys to Catherine with the request that she defend the old order in the Commonwealth as she promised to do by the Treaty of 1768. In compliance with this request an army marched into Poland and Lithuania and occupied Warsaw in 1792. Not to be outdone King Frederick William II of Prussia sent his troops into the western provinces of Poland. In 1793 there was a Second Partition of Poland. In a special manifesto it was explained that the anarchy in Poland had grown to be such a menace and was so clearly related to the terror of the French Revolution that Russia, Austria and Prussia saw no other way of restoring order than by narrowing down the boundaries of Poland. To give a stamp of legality to the Partition a Diet was assembled at Grodno and asked to approve the act. This body agreed to cede the Russian territories to Russia but refused categorically to surrender genuinely Polish territory to Prussia. After lengthy wrangling with the Russian and Prussian envoys the members of the Diet decided to remain absolutely silent and refuse to make any answer to the questions put to them by the President of the Diet and the diplomats. After this "dumb session" had continued for some time the presiding officer ruled that "silence gives consent" and announced the cession of the territory in question.

By the second partition Russia obtained Volynia, Podolia, and the territory of Minsk; Prussia received Danzig and the territories of Great Poland (1793). What was left of Poland went back to the form of government prior to the Constitution of 1791. For all practical purposes Poland became a dependency of Russia, for the King could declare no war and conclude no peace without the consent of Catherine. Warsaw was occupied by a Russian garrison.

The Polish nobles could not reconcile themselves to such a state of affairs and commenced an agitation both inside and outside of Poland in favor of the restoration, the independence and the integrity of Poland. At Warsaw and Cracow secret committees were formed which incited the inhabitants of both the annexed and un-annexed territories to rebel. In 1794 there were revolts at Cracow, Warsaw, Vilna, and in other cities. At Warsaw a provisional government was set up which arrested the King, declared war on Russia and Prussia, and proclaimed General Thaddeus Kosciuszko dictator and commander-in-chief of the army. The Russian garrison of Warsaw was compelled to evacuate the city with heavy casualties.

Catherine at once sent her best forces to put down the uprising. Suvorov made a rapid march to Warsaw and ordered General Fersen to do likewise with those regiments that had survived the Polish massacre. In the battle of Maciejowice, near Warsaw, Fersen routed the enemy, captured Kosciuszko, and Suvorov took Praga, a suburb of Warsaw (1794). After the revolt was put down by the Russian and Prussian armies, Russia, Prussia, and Austria partitioned among themselves what was left of the Polish-Lithuanian lands (1795). Russia took Lithuania and Courland, and Prussia and Austria divided the remaining territories.

One cannot but admire the extraordinary triumphs of Catherine. In 1767 the representative assembly which she convoked at Moscow bestowed upon her the title of "The Great." She made no use of the title and it was never associated with her name as was the case with Peter the Great. But whenever her territorial acquisitions are mentioned the title of "Great" is often associated with her name as with Peter's because in her foreign policies Catherine the Great was the direct successor of Peter the Great.

From its very inception the policy of unification was as follows: 1. To fight the Germans and Swedes in the West to obtain the natural frontier of the seaboard; (2) to fight Lithuania in the southwest for the possession of the intervening Russian territories; (3) to fight the Tartars and Turks in the south and southeast for the freedom and safety of Russia's existence. Until Peter the Great there was little to show for the struggle. His genius and determination enabled him to reach the open sea. This struggle exhausted him and his resources and forced him to leave the completion of the task in the south and southwest to his successors. Catherine took up the fight where Peter left off. She recovered the Russian territories, except Galicia, held by Poland, and extended the Russian frontiers down to the Black and Azov Seas. Peter the Great solved one of the age-old problems of Russian politics and Catherine the other two. Therein lies the importance of the celebrated "Age of Catherine." From Catherine's time Russia enters upon a new era and begins to pursue new objects.

EMPEROR PAUL PETROVICH (1796-1801)

138. EMPEROR PAUL.—Paul was born in 1754. The first few years of his life were extraordinary in that he scarcely knew his parents. Elizabeth had taken him from Catherine and brought him up herself. At the age of six he was entrusted to the care of a tutor, the well-known Nikita Ivanovich Panin, with whom he remained even after his mother became empress. The child continued to live separated from his mother, he saw her very rarely and was timid and frightened in her presence. Catherine apparently had no love whatever for her son. As he grew older the antagonism between mother and son increased. He held her responsible for the death of his father, Peter III, and disapproved of her actions and those of her associates. Catherine could see nothing good in Paul and regarded him as hopelessly incapable. She refused to acquaint him with the affairs of the government, or to entrust him with official missions. By his marriage to Sophia Dorothea, a princess of Würtemberg (known by her Orthodox name as Maria Feodorovna), he had a son (1777), Alexander, whom Catherine took away to bring up with the intention of bequeathing the throne to him and not to Paul.

Paul's position grew worse as the years went by. He

was opposed and even insulted by his mother. He finally withdrew with his family to Gatchina and Pavlovsk, the estates which Catherine had presented to him, and led a retired family life. His chief occupation was the drilling of a few hundred soldiers. He was nervous and irritable and when things did not suit him he had fits of violent rage. The constant chafing under the restraints imposed upon him, the fear of losing the throne, the frequent humiliations and indignities at the hands of Catherine and her court embittered him. When he ascended the throne at the age of forty-two, Paul was a broken man, physically, mentally and spiritually.

139. DOMESTIC AFFAIRS UNDER EMPEROR PAUL.— Catherine's intention to keep Paul from the throne was not carried out. As soon as he became Emperor he inaugurated a series of radical changes at court, in the government, and in the army. Catherine's favorites were sent away and new men took their places. Paul disapproved of his mother's system of government and feared the influence of revolutionary France. His idea was to strengthen his authority and discipline in the state. Unfortunately he had neither experience in actual government nor political knowledge, and as a consequence his efforts were not altogether successful. He did not substitute a better system of government for that of Catherine but brought about confusion and irritation.

In place of the uniforms of Catherine's army Paul introduced the uncomfortable German uniform. He drilled and paraded his soldiers to the point of exhaustion, he punished them until they bled, but did not make an efficient fighting force out of them. The hardships of the service caused the nobles to avoid it and stirred their discontent. Suvorov made no secret of his disapproval of the new régime and was banished to his estate. Officers who were unable to meet the exactions of the new service were exiled to Siberia. Army service lost all its attraction and ceased to be regarded as something honorable.

Paul felt that Catherine had lessened the authority of the tsar and undermined the foundations of real law and order by her indulgence to the nobility and her liberalism. He therefore endeavored to restore the empire to its former autocratic régime. He began by regulating the order of succession. In place of Peter's law of 1722 Paul substituted (1797) a "Statute on the Imperial Family," which (1) established the order of succession to the throne "by natural right," or primogeniture, and (2) defined the so-called "appanages" (estates and revenues) of the imperial family, as well as the order of mutual relationships within the imperial household, and the titles and coats-of-arms of the grand dukes. To administer the "appanages," there was created a special "Department of Appanages." Lands and capital under its jurisdiction were set apart from the other lands and revenues of the crown. By thus placing the problems of the dynasty upon a stable basis a constructive piece of legislation was passed. This was, however, the only definite law promulgated by the Emperor. All his other ideas to enhance the sovereign power and to set up a strict and orderly system in state affairs failed utterly. Paul contemplated a restriction of the rights of self-government which Catherine had granted to the several classes and blocked the operation of the charters of 1785. In those places where the institutions of 1775 did not already exist they were not introduced. Paul reduced the number of the "Governments" created under Catherine and restored the antiquated "Colleges" (sec. 128).

All these changes failed to give a new system of administration or to bring about law and order. On the contrary they created general confusion and discontent. Paul knew how to tear down but not how to build up. He was not methodical in his work; and his acts were as often the result of impulse and anger as of reason and good will. In 1797 he issued the so-called "landlord servitude" (*Barshchina*) decree which said that peasants could not be forced to work for their masters on holidays or more than three days a week. While limiting serfdom with one hand Paul extended it with the other by making unusually generous gifts of land to individual noblemen, with the result that about 600,000 crown peasants on these lands were turned into serfs. It is easy to understand why the peasants who hoped for so much from him became restless and rioted. Paul's measures, aiming largely to destroy the vast influence of the nobility in the government and restore the splendor of the autocracy, created the impression of something very indecisive and inconsistent, something opposed not alone to the régime of the late empress but to Russian interests in general.

Especially severe were the measures of the Emperor to combat the influence of the French Revolution. Catherine had already formed an alliance with England, Austria, and Prussia, and ordered Suvorov to prepare an army for war against the French. She prohibited her subjects from having any intercourse with France and would allow only Frenchmen of the old régime to enter Russia. Upon his accession Paul revoked the order for the contemplated campaign of Suvorov, but at the same time made still more harsh the police regulations against the "Jacobin spirit." Not only was direct intercourse with France prohibited and punished, but intercourse with other countries of Western Europe was likewise made difficult and practically impossible. Russian subjects could not go abroad, and foreigners could not come to Russia (without a special permit from the tsar). The importation of literature and music (notes) was prohibited and none could be published in Russia without the authorization of the censor. Nothing was allowed to be worn which suggested France and the French Revolution. Woe to him whom Paul suspected of "pernicious freethinking." Because of its harshness Paul's rule has been called the "Reign of Terror."

In the course of time the Emperor's irascibility and cruelty began to assume a plainly pathological character. Empress Maria Feodorovna found it more and more difficult to calm and allay the outbursts of violent rage from which her husband was suffering. Commencing with 1798, Paul began to abuse his wife and his sons, Alexander and Constantine, and this treatment of his own family became a subject for serious political discussion. He came to be regarded as a dangerous enemy of the dynasty. A plot was set on foot, led by Count Pahlen, Military Governor of St. Petersburg, to remove the mentally unbalanced emperor from power and put him under the guardianship of Alexander. When the plotters arrived at the palace to propose his abdication Paul met them with stubbornness and violent anger and in the struggle that followed he lost his life (March 11, 1801).

140. FOREIGN POLICY OF EMPEROR PAUL AND THE CAMPAIGNS OF SUVOROV.—When he took the throne Paul announced that Russia would have no more war, that his subjects would have "their much needed and desired rest" from the anxieties and sacrifices of Catherine's military enterprises. While he was making these speeches

the French conquered Holland, Belgium, Switzerland, nearly all of Italy, were making ready to invade Egypt and planning the restoration of Poland. Wherever the French came, there they set up democratic and republican governments either by direct annexation of territory to France or by forming republics allied to the French Republic. The French Revolution was becoming a menace to Europe, both as a destroyer of governments and as a conquering power. It aroused against itself all the powers of Europe. In 1798 there was formed against France a coalition of five powers—England, Austria, the Kingdom of Naples, Turkey, and Russia. The immediate causes of the break between France and Russia were: the French seizure of the Island of Malta which was under Russia's protection; the encouragement given by the French to the Polish patriots; and the alarming news of a French invasion of the Black Sea.

Paul ordered the Russian fleet to proceed from the Black Sea to the Mediterranean. With the aid of the Turkish navy the Ionian Islands were captured from the French. From Greece the Russians sailed to Italy and preyed on the French wherever they could. At the same time Paul sent an army under Suvorov (who was recalled from banishment for this purpose) to aid Austria. Suvorov's plan was to drive the French from northern Italy and follow them to France. He opened his campaign at Verona (1799) and in the course of a few months he had driven the French out of Italy and was ready to invade France. Just then he received orders to go to Switzerland.

When Paul asked Suvorov to take charge of the army he gave him freedom of action. But the Austrians did not. They were constantly interfering and obstructing.

After the Italian campaign Suvorov desired to invade France, but the Austrian War Council insisted that he should first free Switzerland from the French. Paul was won over to the Austrian idea and Suvorov had to obey.

Of all the allied troops in Switzerland there remained only the Russian Corps of General Rimski-Korsakof at Schwytz. After inconceivable hardships Suvorov got his army over the St. Gotthard Pass, marched them through the gorges of the Reuss River across the so-called "Devil's Bridge" and emerged from the south at the Vierwaldstaetter Lake. Here he learned that Rimski-Korsakof had been routed by the French and forced to withdraw, and that the French were waiting for him (Suvorov) at Schwytz. Suvorov knew that the French force under General Massena was almost four times as large as his own exhausted army and therefore abandoned the plan of marching to Schwytz. He turned to the right, and came out at Lake Constance. On this march his brave troops repeatedly drove back the French forces that attempted to bar their passage. Suvorov's march across Switzerland won the admiration even of his foes; and his generals, especially Bagration and Rosenberg, achieved no less fame.

Suvorov remained undefeated and his army was saved; but Switzerland was now left entirely in the hands of the French. Paul held Austria responsible for this state of affairs and dissolved the alliance with her (1800). At the same time he broke the alliance with England. The Russian Auxiliary Corps that had been fighting the French in Holland shoulder to shoulder with the English was suffering reverses and a great shortage of food and clothing. Paul was so incensed against England for neglecting his troops that he prepared to attack her by land and sea. He issued orders for the Don Cossacks to invade India, but his death halted this expedition and the Cossacks were called back.

Beginning with 1800 there was a growing rapprochement between Russia and France which led to peace. Napoleon showed great solicitude and humanity in his treatment of the Russian prisoners of war and this won the gratitude of the Emperor.

RUSSIA—XIX CENTURY

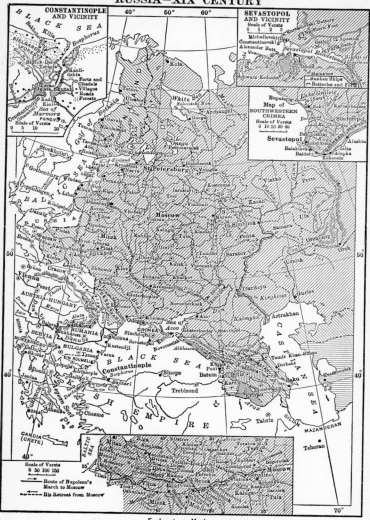

Explanatory Marks:

FRONTIERS OF RUSSIA AT THE ACCESSION OF PAUL THE FIRST:
At Accession of Paul I.   Acquisitions of Paul I.   Acquisitions of Alex. I.

ACQUISITIONS OF THE EMPERORS:
Acquisitions of Nicholas I.   Acquisitions of Alex. II.

CHAPTER VIII

PREDOMINANCE OF FOREIGN AFFAIRS OVER INTERNAL ADMINISTRATION

EMPEROR ALEXANDER THE FIRST, "THE BLESSED" (1801-1825)

141. EDUCATION AND CHARACTER OF EMPEROR ALEXANDER I.—Alexander the First was born in 1777 and was taken by Empress Catherine and brought up as her own son. Alexander developed into a handsome and highly gifted youth and Catherine spoke of him as "my own Alexander." She planned to train and educate him in her own ideals and make him her successor. She placed him under the care of General N. I. Saltykov and appointed a Swiss, Frederick Caesar LaHarpe, his tutor. Catherine issued a set of "Instructions" for the education of her grandson. His teachers were told to train the prince "in accordance with the laws of reason and the principles of virtue." LaHarpe had a great influence over Alexander and the two became close friends. The Swiss teacher was a liberal and a republican, and he made his pupil see the beauty of political freedom and equality and the ugliness of despotism. The two together looked forward to the near future when Russia would have a democratic form of government and serfdom would be

no more. Alexander was also influenced by the literary tendencies of his day and acquired a sentimental outlook upon life and an extraordinary gentleness of manner and address. All who came into contact with him were charmed by his kindliness, cheerfulness, courtesy and sociability. Happiness and joy seemed to be the daily portion of the young Grand Duke. He was not, however, as happy as he looked. His position between his father and his grandmother was unnatural. Catherine's plan to make him her successor turned Paul against him. Alexander tried to keep the good will of both, to treat grandmother and father with equal deference, and to conceal from both his real thoughts and sentiments. He became a master in the art of simulation, never losing his self-composure and always retaining his cheerfulness and friendliness. This is why he was often called the "Charming Sphinx." It was as impossible to resist his winning smile as to learn what was behind it.

142. Beginning of the Reign of Emperor Alexander I.—The death of Paul took Alexander by surprise. Immediately after that sad event the young monarch moved with his family from the scene of the tragedy to the Winter Palace. He issued a proclamation in which he promised to govern the nation "according to the laws and after the heart" of Catherine the Great and to "follow her wise intentions." This was interpreted to mean that he would not continue the harsh régime of his father. During the very first days of his reign he repealed all the irritating orders of Paul, restored the charters of 1785, and granted amnesty to all who had been condemned, exiled, and imprisoned without regular trial. The pleasing personality of the young monarch, his kindliness and courtesy, and his genuine mourning over the tragic death

of his father made a deep impression on his people and won him the name of "angel" which he retained to his very end.

Alexander entrusted the administration to officials of Catherine's time and to his personal friends who thought and felt as he did. Four (Kochubei, Novosiltsov, Stroganov and Adam Czartoryski) were especially close to him. These men met from time to time at the palace to discuss informally with the emperor all matters of state. This group was sometimes referred to as the unofficial, or intimate "Committee" from the fact that the emperor had jestingly spoken of it as the "comité de salut public," alluding to the revolutionary institution of that name in France. Stroganov kept a record of what took place at these gatherings and this diary has been preserved.

With the advice of this committee Alexander carried out all the measures of the first few years of his reign. One of the things done by the emperor at this time was the restoration of the Senate as the highest administrative and judicial body in the empire. Under Catherine the power of the Senate had been greatly restricted (sec. 126) and Paul had not thought it necessary to restore it. In place of the antiquated "Colleges" Alexander in 1802 created eight "Ministries" (war, navy, foreign affairs, interior, justice, finance, commerce, and education). Each Ministry had its Minister who was given full authority over the work of his department and held responsible for every act. To insure unity of purpose the Ministers met as a "Committee of Ministers." Occasionally the Emperor attended these meetings. Alexander set up the so-called "Permanent Council" of twelve members to deliberate on important affairs of state. In this way the Emperor reorganized the central government which had been disrupted by the local reforms of Catherine the Second.

Alexander's "intimate committee" devoted serious thought to the improvement of the condition of the serfs. After restoring to the higher classes the rights and privileges of which Paul had deprived them the young emperor wished to do something for the emancipation of the peasants. But the difficulties in the way of emancipation were as great now as they had been in the time of Catherine. All the committee did was to publish the law on the "Free Agriculturists" (1803) which gave the landlords the right to free their serfs, provide them with land and make "Free Agriculturists" out of them. It was hoped that this measure would gradually wipe out serfdom, but as a matter of fact less than 50,000 peasants were made "Free Agriculturists" in the reign of Alexander.

During the two years that the "Intimate Committee" functioned the Emperor convinced himself that while it had high ideals and good intentions it lacked practical experience and knowledge of Russian conditions and it could therefore do little to transform the political and social order. He called its meetings less and less often, took its advice rarely, and allowed it to die a natural death. Alexander had found a new counsellor, one who dreamed his dreams and anticipated his visions. This man was Michael Mikhailovich Speranski (1772-1839).

143. SPERANSKI.—Michael Speranski was the son of a village priest. After completing his education at the "Main Seminary" (Academy of Divinity) of St. Petersburg he became private secretary to Prince A. B. Kurakin. Speranski's ability, education and capacity for work quickly attracted general attention. When the new Min

istries were organized (1802) he was offered a place in the Ministry of the Interior, and he quickly became the right hand man of the Minister Count Kochubei. In 1806 Speranski came under the notice of the Tsar who was greatly impressed by his talents and the two became closely associated in the work of reform which had concerned the emperor for some time. Speranski was eminently fitted for the task. In addition to the qualifications already mentioned he had made a careful and penetrating study of the eighteenth century economic and political treatises and, being a self-made man, knew just how far these European theories could be applied to Russian life. It was this combination of the theoretical and practical, which the Intimate Committee lacked and Speranski had, that made him such a rare and valuable man. Alexander asked him to draw up a plan for the reorganization of the empire, to supervise the compilation of a new legal code, and to advise him on all important current state affairs.

The proposed political reorganization of the state was based on the principles of strong centralization and division of functions. At the head of the State stood the Sovereign and a State Council. The Ministers and their subordinates in the provinces executed the laws, the Senate and its lower courts interpreted them and the State Duma made them. The State Duma was composed of delegates from the Government (gubernia) Duma, this Duma of delegates from the District Duma the District Duma of delegates from the Township Duma, and this body of all the landowners from the township. Each department of government at the center and each local institution and officer in the empire had definite and limited functions.

Alexander was very enthusiastic about this reorganization and proceeded to put it into effect. On January 1, 1810, he organized the State Council and made Speranski its secretary. But that was as far as the reforms went. Alexander became frightened, suspicious, undecided and Speranski's plan was allowed to die.

Hand in hand with his work on the general reform scheme Speranski directed the labors of the "Law Committee" which prepared a new civil code on the lines of the Napoleonic Code. This code was submitted to the State Council where it was decently buried.

As adviser to the Emperor in administrative affairs Speranski devoted much time to the study of financial problems, diplomatic affairs, and the reorganization of Finland which had been conquered by Russia. He also revised and improved some of the institutions which came into being at the beginning of Alexander's reign, and in particular the Ministries. These changes were embodied in the new law on Ministries, "General Statutes of the Ministries" published in 1811. The number of ministries was increased to eleven by the addition of the Ministries of Police, Ways of Communication, and State Control. Speranski's activities and his rapid elevation made him many personal and political enemies. The general charge against him was that he favored the French. N. M. Karamzin, one of the most brilliant and famous literary men of the period, submitted a memorandum to the Emperor on "Old and New Russia," in which he pointed out that Speranski's French measures were destroying the old order in Russia. Although Speranski denied the accusations his enemies insisted that they were true. When Napoleon was about to invade Russia the Emperor lent ear to these complaints and removed

Speranski from the post of Secretary of State. A little later he banished him from the capital, first to Nizhni-Novgorod and afterwards to Perm. Only at the close of Alexander's reign was Speranski permitted to return from this exile.

When the Emperor had the enthusiasm the "Intimate Committee" had no practical plan, and when Speranski offered a plan Alexander lacked the courage to carry it out. Speranski managed, however, to improve the central organs of government and to consolidate the bureaucracy so that they functioned smoothly for years after.

144. ALEXANDER'S FOREIGN POLICY UNTIL 1812.— When he came to the throne the Emperor intended to preserve a neutral attitude in the European wars. He stopped the warlike preparations against England and resumed diplomatic relations with Austria. This change of attitude greatly displeased France, but for some time the two states preserved an openly friendly intercourse. This became more and more difficult to maintain as Napoleon grew in power. His insatiable ambition greatly irritated Alexander, and his ruthless tactics towards Central and Southern Europe seemed a dangerous and inadmissible thing. Russia protested but Napoleon paid no attention and pursued his own arbitrary course in Germany and Italy. Alexander was more or less forced to unite with Austria and England in a war against Napoleon.

In 1805 the Russians, commanded by Michael Golenishchev-Kutuzov, marched westward to join the allies, but before the scene of war was reached Napoleon had defeated the Austrians. In order to avoid an unequal contest the Russians withdrew to the north of Vienna. Alexander was not satisfied with this result and urged

Kutuzov to engage Napoleon. In the battle which took place at Austerlitz the Russians were badly defeated and forced to retreat to their own country.

In the following year (1806) the Russians made a military alliance with the Prussians, but before the allies joined their forces the French routed the Prussians in the battles of Jena and Auerstädt, and occupied Berlin as well as the Prussian territories as far as the Vistula. King Frederick William III of Prussia withdrew with his court to Koenigsberg in order to be close to the Russians. The Russian army under Bennigsen offered a stubborn resistance to the French, repulsing them in a great battle near Preussisch-Eylau. But in the summer of 1807 Napoleon was able to defeat the Russians near Friedland and drive them back to their own country. The whole Kingdom of Prussia was now in Napoleon's hands.

Soon after the battle the two monarchs, Napoleon and Alexander, met on a raft on the river Niemen, near Tilsit, to discuss terms of peace. Alexander tried to save Prussia but succeeded only in part. A large portion of Polish Prussia was formed into a Duchy of Warsaw and given to Saxony; another portion, Bialystok, was handed over to Russia and the remainder was handed back to the King of Prussia under humiliating conditions.

Russia emerged from this unsuccessful war without losses but with very little to be proud of. In addition to the treaty of peace Alexander formed an alliance with Napoleon. The basis of this alliance was the recognition of Napoleon's right to exercise control in Western Europe and Alexander's in Eastern Europe, especially in regard to Sweden and Turkey. Both sovereigns agreed upon joint action against England, and Alexander accepted Napoleon's "Continental System" which meant that Russia would have no commercial relations with England and would close her ports to English ships. The peace and alliance of Tilsit were ratified in the following year (1808) by the two emperors at Erfurt. This marked the period of closest friendship between Russia and France.

A natural consequence of the Tilsit Alliance was Alexander's war against Sweden. The occasion for this war was afforded by the Swedish refusal to join the alliance against England. During 1808 and 1809 the Russian troops, after a series of stubborn battles drove the Swedes from Finland. In the winter (1808-09) the Russian troops marched across the frozen sea and occupied the Aland Islands and then moved on the Swedish mainland. By the Treaty of Frederikshamn in 1809 Sweden ceded to Russia the territory of Finland up to the Tornea River. Even before peace was formally concluded Alexander occupied Finland and proclaimed its union with Russia. In the spring of 1809 Alexander summoned a Finnish Diet at Borgo and promised to preserve the existing institutions and "the religion, fundamental laws, rights, and privileges" of the inhabitants of the "Grand Duchy of Finland."

Turkey's hostility to Russia, which had never ceased since the time of Catherine II, had grown still more during the first few years of Alexander's reign. Open warfare broke out in 1806 and continued with interruptions until 1812. Napoleon at first inclined to support Turkey, but after Tilsit he gave Russia a free hand in the Balkans. The Russians repeatedly crossed the Danube and in 1811 Kutuzov delivered a crushing blow to the Turks at Slobozia, on the left bank of the Danube and forced them to sue for peace. By the Treaty of Bucharest (1812) Russia obtained Bessarabia.

Thus it came about that Alexander, who at first fought Napoleon, found himself compelled later to form an alliance with him and to engage in wars which he had neither foreseen nor planned. When in 1809 Napoleon again defeated the Austrians Alexander sent an auxiliary corps to support the French against his former Austrian allies. This sudden volte-face of Alexander's policy caused general surprise and disapproval in Russia. The appearance of a French Embassy at St. Petersburg, its unconventional and self-assured behavior, and its influence upon Alexander caused resentment and indignation among the Russians. The breaking off of commercial relations with England not only injured private commerce but reduced the income of the state and forced it to issue paper money with its accompanying evils. It can be easily imagined how this added fuel to the fire. To make matters even worse there was a rumor current that Speranski was secretly preparing reforms in the French spirit. Public opinion was greatly aroused against the French and Alexander realized that his policy was not popular.

Napoleon complained that Russia was not enforcing the Continental System and was lukewarm in her support against Austria. Napoleon, however, had little right to throw stones. He did practically nothing to help the Russians against the Turks. While professing friendship for Alexander he was encouraging the Poles to hope for a restoration of Poland. He seized the German possessions of the Duke of Oldenburg, uncle of Alexander, and annexed them to France. Contrary to the provisions of the Treaty of Tilsit he annexed Holland and the shores of the North Sea as far as the Elbe. He had no right to do this without the consent of Alexander. Napoleon was occupying more and more German territories in the East and pushing his garrisons nearer and nearer Russia.

Since 1810 Alexander felt that the alliance with Napoleon was a mistake, that the only result of it was discontent, commercial crisis, financial chaos, loss of self-respect, and a menace to the peace of his country. He grew colder towards Napoleon and began to prepare for war. Napoleon was also getting ready to settle the issues on the battlefield. Both sides tried to keep their military preparations secret and accused each other of harboring unfriendly designs and trying to break the peace.

War between the two countries was brewing. Its cause lay in the profound contradictions existing between French and Russian policies and between the rival personal ambitions of these two monarchs. Napoleon aimed to dominate the world, to make of Russia, as he did of Prussia, a dependency of France, and to treat the Tsar as he did the King. Alexander felt his importance and had ambitions of his own to play a great part in the world's affairs. Under the circumstances a clash was inevitable.

145. THE PATRIOTIC WAR OF 1812.—Already in 1811 everybody predicted a rupture between Russia and France. Alexander had made his preparations, but decided not to take the offensive. More than 200,000 Russian troops were stationed along the Niemen under General M. B. Barclay de Tolly and Prince P. I. Bagration. Emperor Alexander himself was with the army at Vilna.

It was a serious blunder to scatter the troops over such a great distance. Napoleon saw the importance of it and hastened to divide the Russians. In June 1812, and without a declaration of war he led his army of 600,000 across the Niemen to Kovno and from there to Vilna. Here he stopped for a month and a half to reorganize. This move of Napoleon divided the Russian forces. Alexander and his staff realized the superiority of Napoleon and the danger of engaging him. After consultation it was decided that Alexander should leave the scene of war and go to Moscow and St. Petersburg to take in hand the general direction of the national defense, and that Barclay de Tolly should become commander-in-chief.

Realizing the impossibility of direct combat with Napoleon's forces, Barclay de Tolly retreated towards Vitebsk and Smolensk and ordered Bagration to do likewise so as to effect a junction with his forces. The wisdom of such strategy had been demonstrated by Peter the Great in his Poltava campaign against Charles XII (sec. 105). It tended to strengthen the retreating army by fresh recruits and supplies and weaken the pursuing force by drawing it farther and farther from its base. Others besides Barclay de Tolly knew this, but he was the one who saw more clearly than the rest precisely how this retreat should be made and where it should halt. He very adroitly avoided all serious engagements with the pursuing enemy and kept up the morale and the physical condition of his army at the same time. At Smolensk the two Russian armies formed a junction and spoiled Napoleon's plan.

This successful strategy of Barclay de Tolly satisfied neither the Emperor, nor the people, nor the army itself. They felt it to be a disgrace to have it appear as if the army were afraid to meet the enemy in open combat.

Some went so far as to accuse Barclay de Tolly of cowardice and even treason. The clamor for the dismissal of the old general became so persistent that Alexander yielded to it and appointed Kutuzov in his place.

Before this dismissal took place Alexander ordered Barclay de Tolly to fight. In obedience to this order and yielding to the pressure of public opinion the Russians engaged the French at Smolensk. For several days the battle raged and it became quite evident that the Russians were not yet strong enough to measure their strength with Napoleon. Under the circumstances Tolly ordered the abandonment of Smolensk and resumed the retreat towards Moscow. While this retreat was on (August 16) Kutuzov arrived at headquarters. On the 26th of August he had a battle with Napoleon near the village of Borodino and convinced himself that Barclay de Tolly had been right.

The Battle of Borodino was destined to be one of the most sanguinary in history. On the Russian side about 110,000 soldiers took part in the battle and about 130,000 on the side of the French; and when the day closed about 100,000 were either killed, wounded or missing. All day long Napoleon charged against the Russians and succeeded in forcing their lines back a few hundred yards. In the evening the French abandoned the redoubts they had taken and returned for the night to their own camp. The Russians spent this night on the battlefield. Both sides had managed to capture guns, banners, and prisoners, and each regarded itself as the victor. Kutuzov planned to resume the attack the following morning, but when he found that half of his army had been lost in the battle of the previous day he decided to retreat and preserve the remnant from slaughter.

Hard upon the heels of the Russians were the French. They hoped to capture Moscow and bring the war to an end. In the village of Fili, on the outskirts of Moscow, Kutuzov held a council of war which agreed to abandon Moscow without a fight and starve out the enemy. Count T. V. Rostopchin, Governor-General of Moscow, who had at first called upon the inhabitants to organize armed resistance, now urged the people to evacuate the city. On the second of September Napoleon made his entry into the deserted capital. He had hardly settled himself before the city was set on fire and almost completely destroyed.

Contrary to French hopes no peace resulted from the occupation of Moscow. Napoleon's attempts to open negotiations failed. Alexander had firmly resolved not to lay down his arms as long as there was a single enemy soldier on Russian soil. Napoleon found himself in a most difficult position. Winter was on him and he had neither winter quarters nor provisions. While Napoleon was becoming weaker Kutuzov was growing stronger by reënforcements of men and supplies from the south. The Russian army was near enough to Moscow to keep the French in check, to prevent them from foraging, and from moving either north or south. To make the situation still worse the French army became disorganized and demoralized by the long march and the battle of Borodino. Napoleon decided to abandon the burned and pillaged city of Moscow, spend the winter in Smolensk and Vilna and resume military operations in the following spring. He was strengthened in his decision by the news that the Russians had defeated Marshal Murat at the village of Tarutino.

About the middle of October the French retreat commenced. To avoid the now hungry route over which he came Napoleon set his course for Kaluga but Kutuzov forced him back. The Russian army kept alongside the French, falling on it whenever a favorable opportunity presented itself. Napoleon's army quickly became a mob in flight. Its stay at Moscow and its looting had greatly undermined its discipline. It lacked the most indispensable supplies but was overburdened with loot, and many of the regiments except the "Guard" looked like bands of highway robbers. Napoleon's invasion had aroused a real national feeling. Armed with such weapons as they had the Russians attacked the straggling French detachments and harassed them unmercifully in every conceivable manner. The retreating French suffered especially at the hands of the small detachments of regular and Cossack cavalry which waged a guerrilla war and gave them no rest. In addition to all these miseries was the cold weather. The French were without warm clothing and substantial footwear and already exhausted by famine they froze to death by the hundreds and thousands. At Borisov the Russians made an attempt to surround what was left of the French army but failed, and Napoleon got across the Berezina and reached Vilna. That city offered neither food nor protection and Napoleon moved on with some 15,000 or 20,000 men, all that was left of his great army. Thus ended Napoleon's campaign in Russia.

146. THE STRUGGLE FOR THE LIBERATION OF EUROPE. THE HOLY ALLIANCE AND THE CONGRESSES.— There were many people in Russia who believed that the expulsion of Napoleon would end the war and bring Russia peace. Kutuzov himself evidently shared this opinion. Emperor Alexander, however, was eager to take

advantage of Napoleon's defeat to break his power altogether and deliver the other countries of Europe from his oppression.

At the Emperor's command the Russian armies crossed the frontier close on the heels of the French and launched the struggle for the liberation of Europe. Alexander called the German nation to arms against Napoleon and the first to respond was Prussia, then came Austria. Sweden and England also joined the coalition. Napoleon was not idle in the meanwhile. By the summer of 1813 he had raised a new army and now met his enemies on the Elbe. After numerous stubborn engagements (Luetzen, Bautzen, Dresden, Kulm) a decisive battle was fought at Leipzig, lasting four days. Napoleon lost this "Battle of the Nations" and was compelled to retreat with enormous casualties beyond the Rhine. Germany was liberated. On Christmas Day of 1813, one year after Napoleon had been driven from Russia, Alexander was able to proclaim to his troops that he was marching into France.

Exhausted by the Napoleonic Wars, France was not in a position to offer serious resistance to the huge armies of the allies. On March 31, 1814, Emperor Alexander and the King of Prussia made their solemn entry into the French capital. The French Senate, voicing the discontent of the nation at the heavy burdens imposed by the policies of Napoleon, declared that he had lost his right to the imperial throne. Napoleon abdicated at Fontainebleau and received from the allies the Island of Elba. In recognition of his great services the State Council, Holy Synod and Senate proposed to the Tsar that he assume the title of the "Blessed" (1814). While no direct acceptance of this offer was received from Alexander this title was later officially bestowed upon him.

The Congress of Vienna met in 1814. After settling first the affairs of the less important states the monarchs of Russia, Austria, and Prussia discussed the question of indemnifying their own countries for the sacrifices and losses they had sustained in the Napoleonic wars. This was to be done mainly at the expense of what had once been Poland. Alexander desired to bring all the territories of Poland under his scepter, but the allies refused to agree to this. For a time it looked as if a war might break out among them. Finally, however, they came to an agreement by which Russia got nearly the whole of the Duchy of Warsaw, under the name of the "Kingdom of Poland," Prussia secured Posen, and Austria obtained Galicia.

While the Congress was in session news came to Vienna (1815) that Napoleon had escaped from Elba and was in France. Once more the allied armies were set in motion towards the French border; but before the Russians could reach the scene of action Napoleon was defeated by the English and the Prussians at Waterloo. The Russian army was sent to France, nevertheless, and remained there until order and quiet were entirely restored. On his second visit to Paris Alexander conceived the plan of the "Holy Alliance," to include the European Powers.

The act of the "Holy Alliance" (September 1815) declared that the allied sovereigns had resolved to "subject" the entire system of their mutual relationships "to the supreme truths dictated by the eternal law of God the Saviour," and to be guided in their political relations "by no other rules but the commandments of this sacred faith, the commandments of love, truth, and peace."

They bound themselves mutually to dwell in perpetual peace, and always "to render one another aid, support, and succor," and to govern their subjects "as fathers of their families," in the same spirit of brotherly love.

Emperor Alexander was impelled to this act by a high religious devotion and a sincere desire to introduce Christian principles into the political life of Europe. But his allies, especially the Austrian diplomats led by Metternich, took advantage of the new alliance for purely material purposes. The obligation of the sovereigns to aid one another under all circumstances was interpreted as an obligation to intervene in the domestic affairs of the various countries. The practice of "intervention" was greatly extended as a result of the international conferences which met after that of Vienna from 1818 to 1822 at Aix-la-Chapelle, Troppau, Laibach, and Verona, for the purpose of amicably settling international disputes in accordance with the principle of the "Holy Alliance." Among other questions, the sovereigns and diplomats at these conferences discussed the internal troubles of Spain, Italy and the Balkans and decided to intervene, if necessary, with armed force. In the name of the ideals of the "Holy Alliance" all national movements were now suppressed and unpopular and unworthy rulers supported. Even the revolt of the Christian Greeks against Turkish oppression was at first looked upon as an inexcusable insurrection against the lawful sovereign. Alexander was ready to perceive in this revolt "a revolutionary sign of the times," and did not think himself justified in intervening even in behalf of his own oppressed co-religionists.

This activity of the "Holy Alliance" (its narrow legitimistic views and the principle of intervention) excited the peoples of Europe against it, and the Alliance became known as a reactionary force opposed to all progress. Alexander's noble aims were utterly distorted in practice.

During the concluding period of his reign Alexander devoted himself wholeheartedly to the reorganization and pacification of Europe, personally directing diplomatic affairs and attending the European conferences. As he had formed very close contact with the political spheres of Western Europe since the German war of liberation, a circle of non-Russian advisers and collaborators grew up around him (the Corsican Pozzo di Borgo, the Greek Kapodistrias, the Germans Stein and Nesselrode). Alexander entrusted these men with high and responsible positions, and they exerted vast influence in Russian politics. So far did this predilection of the Emperor for foreigners go that it gave occasion for grumbling in Russian court and army circles.

Alexander's particular attention during this period was devoted to Polish affairs. Having annexed the "Kingdom of Poland," he granted to its inhabitants an independent political organization provided for by the "Constitutional Charter" of 1815. This made Poland, as it were, a separate state with an army and a government of its own. The executive power was vested in a "Council" of Ministers presided over by the Viceroy of the Kingdom of Poland. The legislature which met every two years was made up of a Senate, representing the clergy and nobility, and a Chamber of Deputies, representing the people as a whole. The Diet had its first session in 1818 and it became at once evident that this body was opposed to Alexander's scheme of government. The Polish patriots were not satisfied with the Charter but desired the restoration of Poland as it was prior to the partitions. Alexander's policy could not go as far as this, and he therefore felt deeply chagrined and irritated at the Polish aspirations. Towards the close of his reign he even began to limit the rights that had previously been granted to the Poles.

147. LAST YEARS OF ALEXANDER'S REIGN.—The great events of 1812 made a very strong impression upon Alexander. The Napoleonic War had wrought a complete revolution in his views. During the first period of the war, when his armies were rapidly retreating before the invincible hosts of Napoleon, and when the ancient capital itself had to be surrendered to the enemy, Alexander was living in constant fear. One minute he was full of despair and resignation and the next minute he was burning with determination to go on with the fight. Napoleon's failure filled Alexander's heart with a profound gratitude for this dispensation of Providence. Indifferent until then in matters of religion, he now began to show a deep piety and a strong leaning towards mysticism. He looked upon himself as the insignificant, frail and mortal instrument in the hands of God to punish Napoleon for his arrogant ambitions and lust of power. After his experiences in Western Europe and as Alexander grew old the enthusiasm and ideals of his youth no longer appealed to him. He lost all interest in life and at times acted as if he were weary of it. He became suspicious and distrustful, and the only persons who had any power to influence him were queer people such as Baroness Kruedener and Archimandrite Photius, or reactionaries.

Foremost among this last named group was Count

A. A. Arakcheev. While ignorant and rude he gave the impression of being honest and devoted and these traits won him the confidence of Alexander. During the latter years of the Emperor, when all his former friends had been dropped one by one, Arakcheev gained enormous influence. He acted the part of a Prime Minister and stood between the Emperor and the outside world. Because of his rudeness and dictatorial manner Arakcheev was generally hated. Under his rule the administration of the empire recalled the days of Emperor Paul. Harsh conditions of military life, a contempt for education, and an irresponsible abuse of authority irritated and alarmed every one. It was useless to complain because Alexander would not believe the charges against his favorite.

Arakcheev gave much attention to the establishment of the so-called "military colonies." The crown peasants as well as soldiers from the regular army were colonized in certain regions as "military colonists." They were forced to cultivate their land and train for regular army service at the same time, and their children inherited their obligations. The object of these colonies was to replenish the regular army easily, cheaply and efficiently. Neither of these objects was attained. These settlements cost a great deal of money and proved to be a failure. The settlers were harshly treated, their whole life was regulated by military discipline and harsh regulations. They naturally chafed and often rebelled under these restrictions. They were poor farmers and worthless soldiers.

While the civil and military administrations were controlled by Arakcheev, Prince A. N. Golitsyn had charge of educational and ecclesiastical affairs which were combined in one department, the "Ministry of Ecclesiastical Affairs and Public Instruction." The old Ministry of Public Instruction, established in 1802, had done much to advance the cause of education in Russia. Universities had been founded at Dorpat (1802), Kazan (1804), and Kharkov (1804), and a Pedagogical Institute at St. Petersburg. In nearly all the provincial capitals, "gymnasiums" (high schools) were opened, and in the chief cities of the districts (*uiezds*) parochial schools. In addition to these a new type of educational institutions, "lyceums," was founded which combined parts of the curricula of the "gymnasiums" and the universities. With the growing number of schools the Ministry of Public Instruction itself kept on expanding and developing.

In 1817, however, under the influence of the ideas of the "Holy Alliance" and the consequent spirit of reaction, this Ministry was reorganized. It was combined with the ecclesiastical department so that "Christian piety should always serve as the foundation of genuine enlightenment." Prince Golitsyn, noted for his mysticism, was put at the head and instructed to correct the faults of the universities and other educational institutions, to stamp out "false reasoning" within their walls, and to combat the liberal spirit of literature through the censorship. The Prince himself was a humane and gentle person, but some of the officials in his department were intolerant and they launched a relentless persecution against everything which to them seemed like "atheism" and "freethinking." Obstructions were put in the way of the newly founded universities so that they would not spread the spirit of opposition and imbue their students with "the subtle poison of disbelief and hatred for the legitimate authorities," as the German universities were supposed to do. The severity of the censorship was increased to an unusual degree. The statutes of all educational institutions were subjected to revision.

The new tendency in public instruction failed to yield the expected results. The pious purpose of the Ministry was not achieved, since its methods in most cases were those of high-handed and ignorant arbitrariness combined with violence. Instead of developing genuine piety the Ministry fostered hypocrisy, deceit and bigotry. Finally Prince Golitsyn had to face a series of accusations of lack of orthodoxy (by the Archimandrite Photius) and was compelled to leave his post.

The oppression by Arakcheev and others like him excited general discontent. It was clear that Emperor Alexander had lost faith in the ideals of his youth and had given free rein to undisguised reaction against all the reforming endeavors that had once been so attractive to him. The gloomy and dejected spirit of the Emperor imparted a note of sadness to the last years of his reign.

148. SOCIAL MOVEMENTS OF ALEXANDER'S TIME.—
The Napoleonic War of 1812 and the foreign campaigns of 1813 and 1814 had a powerful effect upon the spiritual development of the educated Russian nobility. As a result of the legal privileges granted them by Catherine II and of the severities of Paul the Russian nobles had ceased seeking military careers. The Patriotic War brought the nobles back into the army and the war of the liberation of Europe gave them an opportunity to get acquainted with conditions in other countries. Heretofore it was only rarely that Russians went beyond their own border, but after their first visit to Paris, London

and Berlin they traveled abroad more and more. They came in contact with the intellectual movements of the age, with the German idealistic philosophy, with the French social teachings, with the English political agitation and their whole point of view changed. They returned home with boxes crammed with books, heads full of ideas and hearts aching over the shortcomings and backwardness of their own country.

Two tendencies manifested themselves in Russian society as a result of this acquaintance with Western conditions. One was towards a study of Russian history and conditions in the light of the modern German philosophy; the other was political—a desire to introduce the most modern and liberal European methods and institutions into Russia. The stronger the reaction and "Arakcheevism" became, the more vigorous became the efforts of these people to introduce democratic and social reforms in Russia. Almost immediately after the return of the army from abroad the better educated officers commenced forming political groups with the object of training their members in political and social ideas and paving the way for representative government and economic changes. The members devoted themselves to self-improvement and carried more humane manners and customs into their official activities and social relations. They led exemplary lives, treated their soldiers kindly and taught them to read and to write.

Among numerous groups of this kind, which sometimes were of a Masonic character (sec. 131), particular importance was gained by the Union of Salvation organized in 1816 and which changed its name to Union of Welfare in 1818. This society was divided into two sections, a Northern and Southern.

The Northern Union had its headquarters at the capital and its leading members were the Muraviev brothers, Prince Trubetskoi, and the poet Ryleev, while the Southern followed the Second Army in southern Russia and was guided by Colonel Pestel. Both sections of the Union were in constant touch with each other and pursued the same common object of bringing about forcibly a revolution in Russia. As regards the system to be set up after a successful revolution the members were not of one mind. Some favored a limited monarchy, others a republic similar to that of the United States. In view of the fact that their program contemplated a revolution their deliberations, conclusions and plans had to be secret.

Notwithstanding their secretiveness the government knew of the existence of these organizations almost as soon as they were formed. Alexander was rather kindly disposed towards the members. They reminded him of the days of his youth when he dreamed dreams. "It is not for me to punish them" he told those who urged him to take measures against the young men. As the plot thickened Arakcheev made another effort to secure Alexander's consent to suppress the revolutionary movement. He sent the Emperor a long report of the conspiracy and pointed out its dangers, but before the report reached its destination Alexander died (1825).

149. DEATH OF ALEXANDER THE FIRST. THE SUCCESSION TO THE THRONE. THE DECEMBRISTS.—In the autumn of 1825 Alexander went south with the Empress Elizabeth who was ill and needed a milder climate. He found a comfortable place for her at Taganrog and left her there while he went to the Crimea on a tour of military inspection. While traveling about he took a bad cold. He failed to rest and to take care of himself, and,

as a result, complications set in and he died November 19, 1825.[1]

As Alexander left no children (having lost his two daughters in their infancy) his successor should, under the law of 1797 (sec. 139), have been his eldest brother, Constantine. This is how the high dignitaries who had accompanied Alexander to Taganrog regarded the matter, and they therefore sent word of Alexander's death to *EMPEROR* Constantine, who was at the time in Warsaw. The same view was held at St. Petersburg. Immediately after he had received the news of Alexander's death Grand Duke Nicholas, a third son of Emperor Paul, took the oath of allegiance to Emperor Constantine. But Constantine did not want the throne and had renounced it already in 1823. Alexander had accepted his renunciation and transferred the right of succession to his next brother, Nicholas. Only two or three people knew of this renunciation. Alexander sealed up the original papers dealing with this act and deposited them at the Uspenski Cathedral at Moscow, and placed copies of them in the Senate, Synod and State Council at St. Petersburg. On the outside of the envelopes he wrote, "To be kept until I request them, and in case of my death to be opened prior to any other act." So closely was this secret guarded that Nicholas himself was unaware of the high destiny that awaited him. From occasional hints

[1] There is a story that Alexander did not die at Taganrog but disappeared mysteriously and reappeared a few years later in western Siberia as "Fedor Kuzmich," and that he lived there until 1864. As this mysterious Fedor Kuzmich never divulged his real name his identity has never been established with certainty. He was not Emperor Alexander. It is said that he was either the naval officer Semion Veliki or a member of the Horse Guards, Fedor Uvarov, and a Mason. But this is still mere conjecture. The only certainty is that it was not Alexander.

by his brothers he surmised that there had been some change in the order of succession but just what he did not know. Upon Alexander's death the envelopes at St. Petersburg were opened and the contents read. Even then Nicholas did not think it proper to accept the throne without first hearing from Constantine and making sure of the renunciation. Owing to this lack of understanding Nicholas took the oath of allegiance to Constantine at the Capital, while Constantine swore allegiance to Nicholas at Warsaw. Russia found itself with two emperors at once, neither of them anxious to ascend the throne, and each imploring the other to take it.

This confusion in the imperial family could not be concealed from the inhabitants of St. Petersburg. The members of the "Northern Union" who had been dreaming so long of political revolution decided to utilize this confusion to further their own aims. They started propaganda among the troops in the hope of securing their support. They made the soldiers believe that Constantine had met with foul play and urged them not to take the oath to Nicholas and to demand a constitution.

The circumstances attending the military riot provoked by the conspirators were as follows: On receipt of a letter from Constantine, in which he reiterated positively his renunciation and refusal to come to St. Petersburg, Nicholas decided to assume the power and issued a manifesto on December 14, 1825, calling upon the army and civilian inhabitants to take the oath of allegiance to him. In two regiments there were a number of soldiers who refused to take the oath. They marched with their arms to the place agreed upon in front of the Senate building and massed themselves about the monument of Peter the Great. They were followed by the sailors of the Guard and by the common people, who joined them in shouting "Hurrah for Constantine! Hurrah for the Constitution!" When they had repeated that a number of times they did not know what to do next. Their leaders failed to appear on the scene owing to various misunderstandings among themselves. Meantime Nicholas had moved his Guards against the rioters and surrounded them on all sides. Before taking harsh measures the Emperor tried persuasion. He asked the higher clergy to talk to the mutineers, but they failed to make any impression on the mob. He then sent Count Miloradovich, the Governor-General of St. Petersburg and popular hero of 1812. He made a stirring appeal to the soldiers not to make any trouble and seemed to win them over when someone fired a shot and killed him. After this the cavalry was ordered to charge and disperse the mob and later the artillery was turned on it. The sight of blood proved too much for the rioters and they dispersed quickly. During the night the dead were removed, order was restored in the streets, and many participants and ringleaders of the movement were arrested. Almost at the same time the "Southern Union" attempted to organize an armed revolt by marching on Kiev, but they were soon halted and arrested.

An investigation was started. Two days before the riot at St. Petersburg Nicholas had received from Taganrog the report on the revolutionary movement with the names of the leaders, which had been prepared for Alexander I (sec. 148). More than one hundred persons were arrested and tried by the Supreme Criminal Court made up of members of the State Council, Senate, and Holy Synod. This trial revealed in all its details the political movement directed against the dynasty and autocracy.

The court sentenced almost forty of the accused to death, and the others to exile and forced labor. But the Emperor mitigated the harshness of this verdict by limiting the capital punishment to the five leaders of the "Unions" and banishing the others to Siberia. Only those of the Decembrists [2] who survived Nicholas I were finally amnestied by his successor, Alexander II (1856).

EMPEROR NICHOLAS I (1825-1855)

150. PERSONALITY OF NICHOLAS THE FIRST AND CIRCUMSTANCES OF HIS ACCESSION TO THE THRONE.— Nicholas I, born in 1796, was almost twenty years younger than his brother Alexander I. The two saw each other rarely, had little in common and were educated differently. No one supposed that Nicholas would ever be emperor and nothing was done to prepare him for that position. Nicholas preferred playing soldier to studying, and as he grew up he gave a great deal of his time to the army and very little to the court and politics. He married Alexandra, daughter of King Frederick William III of Prussia, led a very happy family life, and cared for nothing beyond his family and service.

About six years before his death Alexander said something to Nicholas about a high destiny awaiting him. Nicholas did not fully grasp the meaning of these hints, but acted on them and began to prepare himself by a course of reading for this destiny. Alexander kept his brother at a distance as before and Nicholas had no real training in government until he became emperor. Thus it was only natural that when the news of Alexander's death reached the capital and the courtiers (Prince A.

[2] They take their name from the date of the plot—December 14.

N. Golitsyn) told Nicholas about his right to the throne he hesitated to accept it.

The circumstances attending Nicholas' accession were most turbulent and were destined to have far reaching consequences both for the sovereign and the state. In writing to his brother Constantine, Nicholas said he had won the throne "at the price of his subjects' blood." Throughout his reign Nicholas remembered his "friends of the fourteenth December," as he referred to them in conversation. He took part in the examinations and investigations of their case and had the opportunity to give careful thought to the circumstances of this affair.

The very first conclusion he arrived at was that the nobility was politically unreliable. A very large number of the members of the "Unions" were nobles and from now on Nicholas distrusted the nobility as a whole and suspected it of striving for political domination. He would not govern the state with the aid and through the instrumentality of the nobility as Catherine had done. He pushed the nobles aside and surrounded himself with a bureaucracy of obedient officials regardless of their social status. Under his rule the centralization of government was greatly consolidated under the Ministries and their agents.

Another conclusion which Nicholas came to as a result of the Decembrist affair was that the country desired and needed reforms. The complaints of the Decembrists about the miserable condition of the peasants, the lack of good laws, the corruption of the judges, the highhandedness of the officials and the ignorance of the masses revealed real evils in Russian life. These evils must be done away with and he himself as autocrat must do it.

Hence we note at the beginning of his reign a vigorous activity and reform of the administration, justice, and finances, as well as an attempt to ameliorate the condition of the serfs.

We thus observe that the young monarch, although poorly prepared by training for state affairs, was none the less open minded. The events attending his accession led him to favor a bureaucratic and autocratic form of government. He was fully alive to the need of reforms and intended to carry them out without the aid of either the public or the nobles.

The nobility shunned the bureaucracy of the new government. Hundreds of noble families had lost some of their members in the Decembrist uprising and they feared persecution for being merely related to the leaders of the movement. Not since the days of Peter the Great and Empress Anna had there been such a shake-up in society. The flower of the aristocratic youth perished in exile, and this loss affected not only the frame of mind but also the power of the nobility. The whole class was crushed and it withdrew from public life. Between the government and society there occurred thus something in the nature of a complete break and estrangement. The removal of the nobility made it easier for Nicholas to inaugurate his bureaucratic régime, but at the same time it raised a silent and determined opposition to his measures of reform regardless of their merits.

151. MOST IMPORTANT DOMESTIC ACTIVITIES OF NICHOLAS I.—Immediately upon his accession Nicholas removed from office the famous Arakcheev and the other favorites and mystics of his brother. New statesmen were called in, among whom were Speranski, Kochubei,

and other collaborators of Alexander during his younger years. Nicholas put these men to work on reforms. A special secret committee (known as the "Committee of the Sixth of December 1826"), under the chairmanship of Kochubei, was organized to examine the state papers left by Emperor Alexander and make a general "revision of the state administration." In the several years of its activity this committee drew up plans for the reorganization of the central as well as provincial government and prepared, in addition, an elaborate scheme to regulate the relations of the various social classes of the empire and to improve the condition of the serfs. On the basis of this recommendation a law regulating the social classes was submitted to the State Council and approved by it, but was never published owing to the revolutionary movements of 1830 which frightened the reformers. Similar fates awaited many of the other proposals of this Committee. On the whole its labors were absolutely wasted.

While the committee was discussing a general plan of reform the government put into force a number of practical measures to improve the administration. The following are most worthy of notice: (1) The organization of "His Majesty's Own Chancellery"; (2) the publication of the Code of Laws; (3) the abolition of paper money; (4) measures for the improvement of peasant life; (5) the improvement of public instruction.

(1) His Majesty's Own Chancellery existed prior to Emperor Nicholas without, however, playing a notable part in the administration of the state. It served merely as a private cabinet, or office, of the sovereign for such cases as he chose to take under his personal care. Under Nicholas there were so many such cases that it was necessary to increase the scope of his chancellery and divide it

into four permanent sections.[3]   Throughout his reign Emperor Nicholas followed the custom of taking personal charge of matters that were of especial interest to him.   Hence his chancellery began to play a most important part in the administration of the empire.

(2) We have learned already (sec. 126) that during the eighteenth century the attempts to arrange the existing laws in better order had failed.   Similar failure had attended the efforts of Speranski (sec. 143).   Soon after he came to the throne Nicholas ordered the Second Section, with which Speranski was connected, to undertake the work of codification.   Speranski collected all the laws that had been published since 1649 and organized this collection into a code.   This method of procedure was recommended by the Emperor, who said he did not wish Speranski "to make new laws," but only "to collect and bring into order those which already exist."   In 1833 the work of Speranski was completed and brought out in two

[3] The First Section executed the personal orders and instructions of the monarch, submitted to him papers addressed in his name, and announced his decisions.

The Second Section, formed in 1826, systematized the laws of the empire.

The Third Section, also dating from 1826, had charge of the highest police powers of the empire. Its officials were to "watch that the peace and the rights of the citizens should not be violated by any one's individual authority, or by the rule of the strong, or by the pernicious tendencies of the evil-minded." In course of time this surveillance of general law and order grew into a surveillance of political ideas and the Third Section took the place of the secret chancelleries for political affairs which had existed in the eighteenth century (sec. 117, 124).

The Fourth Section was organized after the death of Empress Maria Feodorovna, in 1828, to take the place of her chancellery for the administration of the educational and benevolent institutions which Emperor Paul had turned over to her after his accession. All such institutions as a whole (institutes, schools, asylums, almshouses, hospitals) were later combined under a "Department of the Institutions of Empress Maria."

separate editions: (1) "Complete Collection of the Laws of the Russian Empire" (from 1649 to 1825) and (2) "Code of Laws of the Russian Empire." From these laws and decrees was taken all that could be made use of and put under various subjects and issued as a "Code of Laws." Thus was accomplished the great and difficult task of compiling the code. It was done successfully, thanks to the simplified procedure and the talents and energy of Speranski. Collecting and systematizing the old Russian legislative material was easier and simpler than appropriating and adapting foreign laws to Russian conditions, or "composing a new Ulozhenie" on abstract principles.

(3) Nicholas inherited from Alexander financial disorganization. The struggle with Napoleon and the Continental System undermined the economic foundations of the Russian Empire (sec. 144). Increasing issues of paper currency were at that time the sole means of covering the deficits which kept unbalancing the budget year in and year out. Between 1807 and 1816 more than five hundred million paper rubles were put into circulation, and during that time the value of the paper ruble fell from 54 kopeks to 20 kopeks silver. This fluctuation and depreciation necessitated the keeping of two sets of accounts, one for paper and the other for silver. Sellers and buyers usually agreed beforehand whether payments were to be made in paper or coin. This was like buying on margin, and led to speculation and fraud. At Moscow in 1830 one large silver ruble was worth 4, a ruble in small silver 4.20, and a ruble in copper 1.08 paper rubles. In this confusion the poorer classes and those who knew little of such transactions were cheated. There was no stable rate of exchange for paper currency, and

the attempts of the government to establish a "rate for the common people" were not successful. The efforts of the government to reduce the issue of paper did not have the results expected because it did not call in the millions still in circulation.

Nicholas' Minister of Finance, E. F. Kankrin, set to work to accumulate a gold and silver reserve with which to redeem the paper currency and substitute a new legal tender. Among other measures he organized a bank of deposit. This bank took on deposit gold and silver in coin or bullion and issued to the depositors "deposit notes," which had the same value, ruble for ruble, as silver. These banks were quite popular and the deposit notes came to be used more and more in business transactions. Equally successful was the sale of government bonds which paid small interest and were accepted as legal tender. These deposit notes and serial bonds furnished the crown with a valuable metal reserve and familiarized the public with new forms of paper currency which did not fluctuate in value.

The measures required for the withdrawal of the old paper notes (assignats) formed the subject of lengthy discussions in which Speranski took an active part. In 1839 the silver ruble (of the same weight as the one that circulated up to the revolution of 1917) was declared to be "the legal standard for all money circulating in the state," and its value fixed in relation to paper. One silver ruble was worth 3.5 paper rubles. Four years later the government offered to buy assignats at this rate of exchange and pay for them either in silver coin or new "credit notes." After the withdrawal of the assignats gold and silver coins exchanged freely with paper and business was stabilized.

(4) Ever since the time of Emperor Paul (sec. 139) the government had shown a desire to improve the condition of the serfs. Under Alexander I (sec. 142), a law on "free agriculturists" was passed, pointing the way towards emancipation of the peasants, but the landlords ignored this law and serfdom persisted. When Nicholas ascended the throne he realized the importance of solving the peasant problem. There was no question in his mind but that the peasants should be freed, but he feared that the sudden liberation of millions of serfs might prove dangerous socially and politically. For that reason Nicholas stood for a gradual emancipation measure and in order to prevent premature public discussion of the subject he put it into the hands of secret committees. The first of these was the secret "Committee of the Sixth of December, 1826."

Speranski, who was a member of this body, held that if the government should take the lead in this movement of reform the private landlords would follow. This view was generally accepted and the whole problem turned over to Count P. D. Kiselev. Kiselev was a very able statesman and an authority on the subject. Years before he had submitted to Alexander a project for the emancipation of the serfs.

On Kiselev's recommendation there was established a Ministry of State Properties (1837) which took over the care of the crown lands and peasants. These peasants were formed into separate rural communes (of which there were nearly 6000) and several such communes into a township, or "volost." The rural communes, as well as the townships, were given the right to elect "Heads" and "Elders" for the administration of township and village affairs, to have special magistrates for the courts of justice, and to administer their own local affairs. Thus was established, in accordance with Count Kiselev's plans, the self-government of the crown peasants. Subsequently it served as a model for the organization of the serfs after their emancipation. Kiselev did not stop here. He inaugurated a number of measures for the economic improvement of the peasants. They were instructed in better farming methods, furnished with grain in time of crop failures, given additional allotments of land, and their condition was improved in many other ways. Kiselev's work forms one of the brightest pages in Nicholas' reign. The Emperor was greatly pleased with his minister and jestingly referred to him as his "Chief of Staff for Peasant Affairs."

For the serfs on private estates much less was done than for the crown peasants. Nicholas had more than once created secret committees on which Speranski and Kiselev sat to devise measures for the improvement of the condition of the serf. But aside from a few measures of no great importance little could be done to loosen the grip of the landlords on their serfs. The most important measure relating to serfdom was the law of 1842 on the so-called "bound peasants" proposed by Kiselev. By this law the landlord could emancipate his serfs and give them land in hereditary usufruct on such terms as they might agree upon among themselves. After such a transaction the serf became a "bound" peasant, bound to render certain agreed services to the landlord. This law was solemnly debated in the State Council, and Nicholas delivered a long speech on the subject. "There is no doubt," he said, "that serfdom in its present state is an evil, but to touch it at this time would, of course, prove a still greater evil." Emancipation of the serfs was to him a matter for the future, something that ought to be brought about by degrees, and under no consideration should the absolute right of the landlord over his land be touched. It was in this sense that the law of 1842 was framed. But even under these conditions the landlords were loath to emancipate their serfs, and the law on the "bound peasants" found almost no practical application.

The general economic and social progress of Russian life had so deeply undermined serfdom that an early fall of this institution was to be expected. Not only was public opinion against it but it was economically unprofitable. In good years the estates of the landlords brought no profit and in seasons of crop failure they sunk deeply in debt. It has been estimated that at the close of Nicholas' reign more than one half of all the serfs were mortgaged (about seven million souls out of a total of eleven million male serfs). To these economic troubles of the landlords was added the fear of unrest and riots among the peasantry. Although the reign of Emperor Nicholas was spared a widespread uprising like that of Pugachev, yet local disturbances were quite common. The expectation of the end of serfdom had penetrated to the masses of the peasantry and caused unrest. Social and economic conditions were taking a trend which made the abolition of serfdom inevitable.

(5) Nicholas' educational policy was to encourage education but to regulate it and keep it from becoming the carrier of revolutionary ideas. Special military and technical schools and teachers' colleges were opened in different parts of the country to meet the practical needs of the state. In addition to these there were schools for more general training. Several colleges for women

(Women's Institutes) were opened. According to the ideas of Count S. S. Uvarov, Minister of Public Instruction, the intermediate schools (gymnasiums) were intended primarily for the children of the nobles and officials. In these schools classical courses were offered in order that "the newest Russian education might be firmly established upon the basis of the ancient civilization of that nation from which Russia received the sacred teachings of religion as well as the first beginnings of her own enlightenment." Children of merchants and common townsfolk had special schools and were not encouraged to attend the "gymnasiums." But by this time the thirst for knowledge among the common people had become so strong that notwithstanding these measures large numbers of the Raznochintsy (the new middle class) found their way into these schools.

This rush of the "Raznochintsy" to the gymnasiums and universities is an important characteristic of the period. Their coming changed the composition of educated Russian society (the Intelligentsia) which had until then been made up exclusively of the nobility.

The apprehensions felt by the government lest the schools become carriers of dangerous political influences resulted in a number of restrictive measures. The statutes of the universities framed by Count Uvarov in 1835 gave the universities some self-government and freedom of instruction, but after the outbreak of the revolutionary movements in 1848 the Russian universities were subjected to extraordinary restrictions and surveillance. The teaching of philosophy was abolished; young people were no longer sent abroad to prepare for professorships; and the number of students at each university was limited to three hundred. Military discipline was introduced into the universities and in the higher classes of the gymnasiums. The censorship was made much more strict and political discussions were prohibited either in print or on the platform. The slightest shadow of suspicion that a citizen had lost his "integrity of opinion" and had become unreliable in a political sense was sufficient to bring him into disfavor with the authorities and have him punished without trial.

152. FIRST WARS OF EMPEROR NICHOLAS. THE EASTERN QUESTION.—During the first years of Nicholas' reign Russia was at war with Persia (1826-1828) and with Turkey (1828-1829).

Relations with Persia were strained since the beginning of the nineteenth century owing to the incorporation of Georgia into the Russian Empire. This ancient Christian state had for many centuries asserted its independence against the Turks and the Persians. But domestic disturbances gradually weakened this country and made it possible for the Persians and Turks to gain domination. As far back as the sixteenth century the Georgians appealed to Christian Moscow for help against the Mohammedans, but Russia was not then in a position to do anything for them. The appeal was repeated at the end of the eighteenth century and Russia gave heed. Catherine's conquest reached as far as the Caucasus Mountains and she believed that if she could add Georgia to her empire she would be able to keep the warlike mountaineers in check and would acquire, in addition, a rich territory. In 1783 the Empress took Georgia under her protection and in 1801 Paul incorporated it into Russia. Soon afterwards Persia declared war on Russia on account of Georgia. The struggle lasted eight years (1805-1813) and ended in Russia's gaining a firm foothold in Georgia as well as on the western shore of the Caspian (Derbent, Baku).

In 1826 the Persian war broke out anew without any formal declaration of war on the part of Persia. Paskevich was sent to the Caucasus against the Persians. He defeated them at Elisavetpol, captured Erivan, crossed the Araxes River, took the city of Tabriz, and threatened the Persian capital, Teheran. The resistance of the enemy was broken and the Shah sued for peace. By the Treaty of Turkmanchay (1828) Persia ceded to Russia the territories on the left bank of the Arax, with Erivan, and paid a heavy contribution. This treaty put an end to Persian claims upon the Caucasus. Emperor Nicholas honored Paskevich for his achievements and bestowed on him the title of "Count of Erivan" and gave him a share of the Persian indemnity.

This war did not by any means put an end to fighting in the Caucasus. Some of the semi-barbarous mountain tribes, such as the Circassians, Chechentsy, and others were interfering with the Russian lines of communication with Transcaucasia and harassing the Russian settlements on the Kuban and Terek. Just when the Persian influence in the Caucasus was broken an independent anti-Russian movement raised its head among the Moslem mountaineers. This was the religious "Muridist" movement, led by the imams and sheiks, of whom the best known are Kazi-Mullah and Shamyl. They gathered about them large numbers of followers or "murids" and fought off the Russians for forty years. At times these warlike mountaineers took the offensive and attacked the invaders in their strongholds. In the long run the loose organization, the tribal feuds, and the poverty of the mountaineers proved unequal against Russian military discipline and resources. The Russians gained on them slowly and in the reign of Alexander II the tribes submitted to the authority of the Tsar.

The Turkish War (1828-1829) was the outcome of the Greek War of Independence which broke out in the time of Alexander I. Turkish atrocities, the glamour of the Greek name and the classical civilization of Hellas caused a widespread movement throughout Europe in favor of the Greeks. But the reactionary governments of Europe hesitated a long time to intercede for the rebellious Greeks against their legitimate sovereign, the Sultan of Turkey. This was pretty much the attitude of Nicholas when he became Emperor. Russia joined England and France in diplomatic steps to protest against the Turkish atrocities and to attempt to reconcile the Sultan with the Greeks. But when, in 1827, it had become manifest that diplomacy was unavailing and that further ill-treatment of the Greeks would be intolerable the three Powers agreed to put an end to this conflict. On October 20, 1827, the combined fleet of the Allies engaged the Turkish navy at Navarino and destroyed it. The Turkish Government held Russia largely responsible for this disaster and prepared to fight her.

The Russo-Turkish War began in 1828. A Russian army crossed the Danube and seized the Turkish fortress of Varna. This gave the Russians a base from which to supply the army and opened the way across the Balkans. For a time the army was detained at Shumla but when that fortress was taken it proceeded south. General Diebitsch crossed the Balkans and captured Adrianople. At the same time Paskevich took the fortresses of Kars, Akhaltsykh and Erzerum in Asiatic Turkey. Russian victories forced the Turk to sue for peace. This was finally concluded in 1829 at Adrianople and on the following terms: Russia acquired the left bank of the Lower Danube with the islands in its delta, and the eastern shore of the Black Sea (from the mouth of the Kuban to the port of St. Nicholas, and the city of Akhaltsykh with its surrounding territory.) The Sublime Porte granted commercial freedom to Russian subjects in Turkey, and threw the Bosporus and Dardanelles open to the ships of all friendly nations.

Another important provision of this peace treaty was that the Turkish dependencies of Moldavia, Wallachia and Serbia were granted complete internal autonomy and came under the protectorate of Russia. Under Russian pressure the Turks also recognized the independence of the Greek territories in the south of the Balkan Peninsula, and out of these the Kingdom of Greece was created in 1830. Under this treaty Russia secured the right to protect her co-religionists in Turkey, which meant intervention in Turkish domestic affairs. In 1833 a Russian force came to the help of the Sultan when he was attacked by the Pasha of Egypt. A Russian squadron landed troops on the coast of Asia Minor to protect the Bosporus from the invader. Out of gratitude for this Russian aid the Sultan concluded with Russia a separate treaty in which he undertook to close the Bosporus and Dardanelles to the war vessels of all foreign powers. This new treaty gave Russia a predominant influence in Turkey and the Tsar became the friend and protector of the "Sick Man of Europe."

European diplomacy tried in every way to nullify Russian successes and it managed to bring the new internal troubles of Turkey before a general European conference which met at London in 1840. This conference agreed to set up a joint protectorate of five powers (Russia, England, Austria, France and Prussia) over Turkey, and from that time on Russian influence in the Balkan Peninsula declined as rapidly as it had risen.

153. THE KINGDOM OF POLAND AND WESTERN RUSSIA.—It has been already noted that trouble had started in the Kingdom of Poland as soon as the "Constitutional Charter" granted by Alexander I (sec. 146) was inaugurated. The Polish patriots cherished the ambition to restore their country to the old boundaries before the partition of 1773. They resented Russian rule, particularly that of the Tsarevich Constantine, who resided at Warsaw and greatly influenced the administration. Some of the Poles demanded a republic while others advocated a reform of the existing constitution and an extension of the rights of the nation.

The Poles were organized in secret societies with branches in the army. The success of the French and Belgian revolutions of 1830 encouraged the Poles to rise and at the end of 1830 open insurrection broke out at Warsaw. Tsarevich Constantine was forced to evacuate the Polish capital with the troops he had with him. This was followed by the organization of a provisional government headed by a dictator. It endeavored to obtain from Emperor Nicholas a pledge of independence for Poland and the cession of Lithuania and Western Russia. When Nicholas refused to grant either of these demands the Polish Diet deposed the Romanov dynasty from the throne of Poland. This action was equivalent to a declaration of war.

In 1831 Emperor Nicholas ordered a large army commanded by Diebitsch to march into Poland. Diebitsch inflicted a serious defeat upon the Polish army at the village of Grochow near Warsaw. The war was drawn out for a considerable length of time, partly because of the terrible cholera which ravaged the whole empire and seriously retarded military operations. Both Tsarevich Constantine and General Diebitsch died from this plague. Count Paskevich who now took command managed the campaign in a vigorous, determined manner and brought the war to a successful end. The "Constitutional Charter" was revoked, the Diet abolished, the Polish army as a separate organization disbanded, the independent financial system terminated, and the institutions of higher learning closed. The Kingdom of Poland was divided into "Governments," such as existed in Russia proper and made part of the empire. From 1832 Poland was governed according to the "Organic Statute." At the head of the kingdom was placed a Viceroy (Count Paskevich, now given also the title of "Prince of Warsaw") assisted by a "Council" of the leading officials of the kingdom. Matters of greatest importance and questions of legislation were dealt with by the "State Council of the Kingdom of Poland" selected by the Tsar. The Russian element in Poland steadily increased, Russians were appointed to Polish offices, the Russian language was made compulsory in official transactions, and Russians were given land in Polish territory. The whole administration became increasingly Russian in character and Poland lost all vestiges of political independence.

A similar policy of Russification was pursued in Lithuania and West Russia. The Polish insurrection had spread also to these territories owing to the fact that the Polish magnates and gentry had preserved their old connections with Poland and were quite influential.

Prince Adam Czartoryski, as Superintendent of the Vilna School District, established Polish schools in his district and did what he could to Polonize Lithuania and White Russia. The University of Vilna, opened in 1803, became a hotbed of the Polish national agitation. One of the most prominent leaders of this Polish movement was Lelewel, Professor of History at the university.

When the rebellion broke out in Poland the Lithuanian provinces made an unsuccessful attempt to join it. After the suppression of the rebellion the University of Vilna was closed and various measures were adopted to do away with all Polish influence in this region. Great attention was now devoted to educating the young people in the Russian language and in Russian ideas. Grade schools were opened and a Russian university was established at Kiev in 1834. Vast tracts of land were confiscated from the rebellious Polish owners and given to Russians. Measures were taken to improve the condition of the Orthodox Russian peasants living on the lands of the Polish magnates. Steps were also taken to absorb the "Uniates" in the Orthodox Church.

The Union with the Catholic Church which was formed in southern and western Russia towards the end of the sixteenth century imposed a considerable hardship upon the Orthodox population. While Orthodoxy was not wiped out entirely a majority of the nobility and large numbers of the peasantry in West Russia joined this Union and came under the powerful influence of the Catholic clergy. Religious persecution continued in Poland up to the Partitions, and the Uniates suffered from it scarcely less than the Orthodox after the Partitions. The Uniate and Orthodox clergy began to seek an understanding with the view of reunion. The champion of this idea was Joseph Semashko, Uniate Bishop of Lithuania. After the suppression of the Polish rebellion he had the backing of the Emperor and the Holy Synod in this movement. In 1839 an assembly of the Uniate Bishops at Polotsk decided to apply to Emperor Nicholas for "permission to rejoin the ancestral Orthodox All-Russian Church." The Tsar granted the permission and the Synod solemnly executed the act of the reunion. The Catholic Union came to an end everywhere except in the diocese of Kholm where the population remained Uniate till the seventies of the nineteenth century.

Such were some of the consequences of the Polish movement of 1830-31. The Polish State ceased to exist, the Polish people suffered heavily, and Polish influence lost its force in West Russia.

154. SOCIAL MOVEMENTS IN THE TIME OF NICHOLAS THE FIRST.—We have seen (sec. 148) that two different intellectual currents, one a political and the other a philosophical, grew out of the wars of Alexander I. The former brought on the Decembrist revolt of 1825 and the latter stimulated the formation of circles devoted chiefly to the study of the German philosophy of Schelling and Hegel, in an endeavor to apply it to the interpretation of conditions existing in Russia. The Russian philosophers were divided into two groups, Slavophils and Westerners.

The Slavophils held that every nation had its own "individual" life, based upon a profound idealistic principle which they termed the "national spirit." This permeates the whole history and all aspects of national life. In order to understand clearly any nation one should first of all try to discover this national spirit. According to the Slavophils, the individuality of the Russian people found its expression in the peculiarities of the Russian Orthodox Church and in the Russian political and social institutions. Unlike the West, with its rationalism and personal freedom, ancient Russia lived by faith and community interest. In the West the state and society were organized by force and conquest; in Russia the state was built up through the voluntary invitation of a princely dynasty from abroad and antagonism, and struggle among the classes was unknown. Therein was Russia superior to the West. Possessed of the "inherent justice," of genuine Christianity, and having the advantage of a "mir" or communal social organization, Russia should serve as a worthy example to the West. But unfortunately the reforms of Peter the Great have led Russia astray. They have brought on needless imitations, have trained the educated classes in the alien spirit of the West, and have shaken the very foundations of society. Russia, to be her real self again, must direct Russian life into the old channels. Such was the theory of the Slavophils of the forties of the nineteenth century. Among its most noteworthy leaders were A. S. Khomiakov and the Kireevski brothers, and later I. T. Samarin and the Aksakov brothers.

The "Westerners" believed in the unity of human civilization, and held that Russia had become a civilized country only since the reforms of Peter the Great. Russia before his time, they said, had lived in a state of utter inertia without any historical forward movement, and the older generations had stagnated in the bliss of Asiatic ignorance. Under such conditions they could not possess any "individuality." By educating the Russians, Peter the Great made it possible for them to hold communion with more civilized peoples, and to advance in the path of culture. The aim of living Russians, according to the "Westerners" should be to seek complete affiliation with the West so as to form a single family of civilized humanity. The Westerners followed with keen interest the intellectual movement in Germany and the social ferment in France, and applauded the latest results of European learning as well as the latest developments in the political life of the most advanced countries of Europe. Among the outstanding representatives of the Westerners were V. G. Bielinski, T. N. Granovski and A. I. Herzen.

In spite of heated controversies between the Slavophils and Westerners they were substantially agreed in their criticism of Russian conditions. Both chafed under the open distrust which the government showed towards the public, and both suffered from the censor and police. They were particularly strong in their condemnation of the government for its indifference to the evils of serfdom. (The efforts of the secret committees and the Tsar's personal condemnation of serfdom [sec. 151] were not generally known.)

Under the then prevailing state of public life in Russia neither the Slavophils nor the Westerners were able to express their views freely in the press. The government prohibited all critical comments on the political and social order of the empire. In the eyes of Nicholas, Orthodoxy, Autocracy and Nationality were the foundations of Russian life and they were beyond criticism.

Notwithstanding the obstacles put in their way the ideas of the intellectuals spread rapidly. The educated classes were almost wholly against the government. This was very unfortunate. Men of education and ability were kept out of the government and men without talent and without initiative were at the head of affairs. At the close of his reign Nicholas had few capable ministers left. Stagnation, chaos, abuses of all kinds were rife in the government. From the distance the Intelligentsia condemned and criticized not merely the temporary shortcomings of Nicholas' reign but Russian civilization in general. As a result of this attitude there was a loss of that strong patriotic fervor for which Russia was so noted.

155. THE CRIMEAN WAR OF 1853-1855.—Russia's influence in the Balkans aroused Europe against her. While in western Europe the "policy of intervention" was rapidly coming into disfavor, Russia still adhered to it and interpreted it in her own way. It was not a mere accidental conflict of interests in the East but a fundamental difference in political principles which divided Russia from the West. The governments and peoples of western Europe had more than one occasion to observe the alacrity with which the Tsar intervened in foreign affairs. Russian military assistance to the Sultan against his rebellious Egyptians has been noted already (sec. 152). In 1849, a Russian army aided the Austrian monarchy in suppressing the Hungarian revolution. Emperor Nicholas could always be counted on the side against revolution. Though he restored the monarchy, Napoleon III was made to feel the displeasure of the Tsar. Nicholas openly condemned his coup d'état. Western Europe regarded the Tsar as the defender of political reaction, and the foe of democracy, and for these reasons it feared and disliked him and Russia.

Such was the general background against which the Eastern Question acquired its vast importance and acuteness. To counteract the Russian influence, British and French diplomacy (especially the British) succeeded in winning signal triumphs at Constantinople about the middle of the nineteenth century. The Turks were fearful of the Russians and readily accepted the protection of the British and French. Turkey would no longer do the bidding of Russia and bad feeling developed. A difference of opinion over the question of the holy places in Palestine led to serious trouble between them. The Sultan had granted certain privileges [4] to the Catholic clergy to the disadvantage of the Orthodox clergy. Emperor Nicholas inteceded for the Orthodox and demanded the restoration of their former privileges. The Sultan, backed by the French, refused to comply.

Nicholas sent an army to seize Moldavia and Wallachia and hold them "as security until Turkey satisfied the rightful demands of Russia." Turkey protested to the powers which formed the protectorate over her (sec. 152). Plenipotentiaries representing France, England, Austria and Prussia met at Vienna to discuss the whole question and to arrange a peaceful settlement. They failed in their efforts and war broke out between Russia and Turkey in the fall of 1853. Immediately afterwards English and French warships made their appearance in the Bosporus as if to threaten Russia.

In November, 1853, a Russian squadron destroyed the Turkish fleet in the Bay of Sinope (Asia Minor). The French and British squadrons proceeded from the Bosporus to the Black Sea to aid the Turks. This move led to an open rupture with France and England. It was also likely that Austria and Prussia would come out

---

[4] The keys to the church at Bethlehem had been taken away from the Greeks and handed over to the Catholics.

against Russia.   Nicholas was forced to maintain an army ready to meet attacks from all quarters.   Russia found herself alone, without friends, and without even moral support in the face of a most powerful coalition of the nations of Western Europe.   This was the result of her policy of "intervention" which had, from the time of the Vienna Congress, kept Europe in perpetual apprehension of a Russian invasion.

In 1854 the Russian army crossed the Danube and laid siege to the fortress of Silistria, but was compelled by the hostile attitude of Austria to withdraw to the left bank of the Danube.   Austria demanded that the Russians evacuate the principalities of Moldavia and Wallachia on the ground that they were autonomous and neutral countries (sec. 152).   With the Austrians jeopardizing their rear and flanks the Russians found it impossible to fight on the Danube and therefore withdrew.   Russia had to fight a defensive war but she was not always sure where the Allies intended to deliver their heaviest blow. They attacked her on the Black Sea, on the White Sea, on the Baltic Sea, and even in Kamchatka.   Russia was compelled to scatter her armies and thus weaken herself.

By the fall of 1854 it was clear that the Crimea would be the chief scene of war.   Sebastopol was the principal base for the Russian Black Sea fleet and the Allies hoped, by capturing this base and fleet, to destroy completely the Russian naval power in the Black Sea.   In September, 1854, more than 60,000 French, British and Turkish soldiers were landed.

156. THE CRIMEAN CAMPAIGN.—The Allies moved southward on Sebastopol and were met by 30,000 Russians on the Alma.   The Russians were defeated and the road to Sebastopol was opened.   Had the Allies been

aware that this city was only poorly defended in the north they might have captured it without delay. But they did not expect any rapid success and therefore intrenched themselves on the southwestern promontory of the Crimean Peninsula, and from this base they laid siege to Sebastopol.

The defense of the city was at first entrusted to the navy. The officers decided to sink their ships at the entrance to the Bay of Sebastopol in order to bar the passage from the open sea and to transfer naval guns to the shore batteries. A ring of earthworks was erected by the engineer Todtleben and by the time the enemy was ready to begin the storm the city was able to offer serious resistance. Unfortunately the Russians were not able to concentrate sufficient forces at Sebastopol to dislodge the enemy from his entrenchments. Troops were needed at the other theatres of war and on the frontiers of Austria and Prussia. It was difficult to send reënforcements and supplies for other reasons. Russia had only a very primitive land transport system and no sea communication at all with the besieged.

The siege lasted through many weary months, or, to be more exact, 350 days. Sebastopol was turned into a mass of ruins and the forts could barely hold out. Nevertheless the garrison kept up its spirits and fought with extraordinary devotion and bravery. Despairing of capturing Bastion Number Four the besiegers transferred their attacks to Malakhov Hill which formed part of the eastern line of fortifications. Todtleben had anticipated this move and had managed to strengthen this sector of the front so that the enemy found himself checked. By this time Sardinia joined the Allies but all of them together were unable to take the place. Emperor Nicholas, in recognition of the heroism and suffering of the defenders, ordered a month of service in the besieged fortress to be counted as a full year.

On February 18, 1855, Nicholas died and on the following day his heir, Alexander II, ascended the throne. This change of rulers did not affect the course of the war. Sebastopol still defied the enemy and every gain of the Allies was purchased at the price of heavy casualties. It was only in August, 1855, that they finally succeeded in pushing their trenches close to the breastworks of Malakhov Hill. On the 27th of August they launched their general assault upon the fortress and the French succeeded in capturing Malakhov Hill. At all other places the storm was beaten off. The loss of Malakhov Hill was serious, for the enemy could now easily penetrate and capture the other forts from the rear. Under the circumstances the Russians destroyed everything within the city proper and crossed the bridge over the bay to the north. Thus came to an end one of the most celebrated campaigns in the history of Russia.

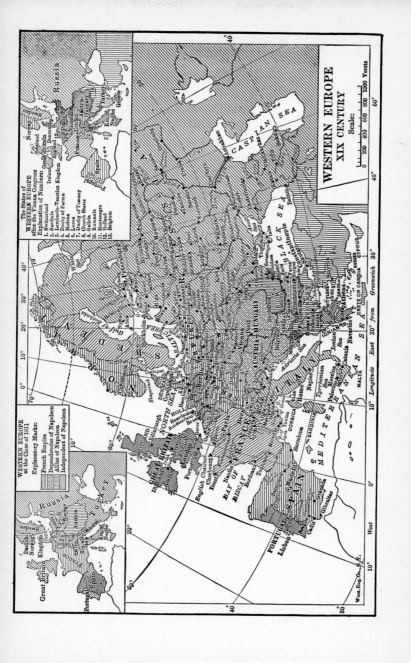

CHAPTER IX

THE EPOCH OF THE GREAT REFORMS

ALEXANDER THE SECOND, THE EMANCI-PATOR (1855-1881)

157. PERSONALITY AND EDUCATION OF ALEXANDER THE SECOND.—The sudden death of Emperor Nicholas marked the beginning of important changes in the Russian Empire. His successor was an entirely different man. While the father was of an austere and inflexible character, the son was of a gentle disposition and open to outside influence. The father had never received a proper education; the son had been carefully trained and prepared for the high function of tsar. Alexander came to the throne at the age of thirty-six (born 1818), a mature man experienced in affairs of state. The people were hopeful of much good from the new sovereign and in these hopes they were not to be disappointed.

Alexander's education had been well planned. Since early childhood he had had for tutor the humane and accomplished Captain Moerder. At the age of nine Alexander commenced to study under his "preceptor," the famous poet Zhukovski. The latter drew up a carefully planned curriculum for the tsarevich, which was approved by Emperor Nicholas. In 1837 he made a long journey through Russia and Western Siberia. When he reached the age of twenty-three he married Maria

Alexandrovna, Princess of Hesse-Darmstadt, whom he had met during an extended tour abroad.

After his marriage Alexander took an active part in the government. Nicholas put a great deal of responsibility on his son and entrusted him with important matters. For ten years the two worked side by side and helped one another. Nicholas was greatly attached to Alexander and shortly before his death he said to him, "By taking upon myself all that was hard and difficult I intended to leave to you a peaceful, well-organized, prosperous country . . . but Providence has decreed otherwise."

Providence did, indeed, decree otherwise. Alexander II ascended the throne at a time of grave difficulties. The exhausting and unsuccessful war had shaken the foundations of the empire. Great skill and efforts were needed to maintain the dignity of the state and to bring about an honorable and a satisfactory peace. To this problem all the attention of the new emperor was devoted.

158. THE END OF THE WAR.—After the fall of Sebastopol in the autumn of 1855 the Russians won a brilliant victory by capturing the fortress of Kars in Asia. Everywhere else military operations were at a standstill and towards winter there was absolute calm on all fronts. In the fall the Emperor visited the Crimea and personally thanked the army of Sebastopol for its heroism. This personal acquaintance with conditions in the South convinced him of the difficulty of continuing the fight and the victory of Kars enabled him to start peace negotiations on a more or less equal footing. His efforts were made easier by the fact that Napoleon was also anxious for peace. Thanks to the mediation of Austria and Prussia a peace congress was called to meet at Paris in

the beginning of 1856. The Treaty of Paris which was signed in March was a setback for Russian ambitions in the Balkans. Russia gave up her possessions on the Danube; she lost her right to keep a navy in the Black Sea, and the Bosporus and Dardanelles were closed to her warships just as they were to those of other nations. Lastly, Russia lost the exclusive right to exercise a protectorate over Turkey's Christian subjects. These were henceforth under the protection of all the great powers.

When the treaty had been signed Alexander issued a proclamation to his people in which he expressed a desire and hope for internal reforms. In concluding he said: "May Russia's domestic prosperity be consolidated and enhanced; may justice and mercy reign in her tribunals; may there be everywhere, with redoubled vigor, a striving for enlightenment and all useful activities." These words held out a promise, as it were, of internal reforms the need for which had been felt by the government and public. These reforms were not long in coming. In 1861 the serfs were emancipated; in 1864 there were reforms in provincial administration; in 1870 a decree was issued for city government; and in 1874 compulsory military service was introduced. In addition to these measures there were improvements in education, finance, censorship and the press. [The "Epoch of the Great Reforms" affected every class of Russian society.]

159. EMANCIPATION OF THE PEASANTS.—Serfdom was obviously out of date and it was impossible any longer to leave the peasants in a state of slavery. So long as the estates of the landlords were cultivated by serfs, it was impossible to expect the resources of the country to grow and develop further. The Crimean War had clearly demonstrated the great backwardness

and dangerous weakness of the Russian Empire and the need of reforms. Every one realized that these reforms ought to begin with the "amelioration of the condition of the peasant serfs."

Shortly after the conclusion of peace Alexander, in a conversation with the deputies of the nobility at Moscow, made the memorable remark that it were "better to abolish serfdom from above than wait till it abolishes itself from below." This remark had reference to the restlessness of the serfs who were waiting anxiously for emancipation. This speech of the Emperor brought the peasant problem into the open. There was of course no unanimity of opinion. Some defended the old order and the protection of the rights of the proprietors, others demanded the emancipation of the peasants on the best possible conditions for the latter.

A number of plans were submitted on the subject of emancipation. One of these recommended that the peasants should be liberated and given land at the same time. This plan was supported by the Tsar's brother, the Grand Duke Constantine, and Grand Duchess Helena Pavlovna, the widow of Grand Duke Michael Pavlovich. Thanks to their personal influence, men like Nicholas A. Miliutin, Prince V. A. Cherkasski, Iuri T. Samarin, and other such ardent champions of the peasant interests, were enlisted in the cause of peasant reform. Emancipation with land was advocated also by Count Jacob I. Rostovtsev, a favorite of the Emperor and his close collaborator in the administration of the military schools. In a series of written and oral reports Rostovtsev explained to the Tsar the technical details of the contemplated reform and convinced him of the necessity for granting land to the peasants to prevent them from be-

coming landless farm laborers. Thus it happened that
the Emperor himself came to favor emancipation with
land.

In the beginning of 1857 the "secret" committee organized by the Tsar took up the question of peasant reform. It proposed to emancipate the serfs by degrees so
as to avoid abrupt and radical changes. This was disapproved by the Emperor, who insisted upon a speedy and
final solution of the problem. When the committee received a statement from the nobility of the Lithuanian
governments of Vilna, Kovno and Grodno that they
would like to emancipate their serfs without land the
Emperor requested that this matter be discussed without
delay.

Opinion in the committee was divided. Some of its
members, led by Grand Duke Constantine, favored
emancipation with land and recommended that the government make a public announcement on this subject so
that the country might know its attitude. The Emperor
accepted this view and in November, 1857, he asked the
Governor-General of Vilna to notify the Lithuanian
nobles to organize "provincial committees" of the nobility
for the discussion of the terms on which the serfs were
to be set free. Alexander hoped that the nobles of the
other provinces would take the hint and ask permission
to set up similar committees. In this he was not disappointed. From all parts of the empire there came a
hearty response and committees were organized. To
bring unity into all the measures adopted in the interests
of the peasantry, the "secret" committee was transformed
into a "Main Committee" presided over by the Emperor
himself (1858).

In this manner began the serious discussion of the

peasant reform. The projects of the provincial committees were submitted for the approval of the Main Committee. This body was divided into sub-committees which
included officials, nobles and other interested parties.
Delegates of the nobility were twice called to the capital
to lend a hand in the work of the committees. They discussed with the members of the committees all the fundamental problems of the reform.

At the beginning of 1861 the Main Committee submitted a report on the whole question to the State Council. The Tsar himself opened the session of the State
Council and made it plain that the abolition of serfdom
was his "direct will." In compliance with the sovereign
will the State Council examined and approved the emancipation measure submitted by the Main Committee. On
the anniversary of his accession, February 19, 1861,
Alexander signed the celebrated manifesto abolishing
serfdom in Russia and ratified the "Statutes Concerning
the Peasants who have Passed from the Dependence of
Serfdom." The great work of the "Tsar-Emancipator"
was done. On the 5th of March his "Manifesto" was
proclaimed to the nation.

The basic principles of the peasant reform were the
following: the right of landlords to hold peasants in
servitude was abolished forever and the serfs were liberated without compensation to their masters. This was
not regarded by the government as a violation of the
rights of the landlords. In his address to the State Council Alexander pointed out that serfdom in Russia "was
established by the authority of the autocracy and the
autocracy may abolish it."

The land upon which the serfs had lived and labored
was recognized as the property of the landlords. The

peasants were set free with the understanding that the landlords would permit them to use their homesteads (small plot of land on which stood their house and garden) and other lands (the so-called "field portion"). But for the use of their homesteads and "field portions" the peasants were to pay the landlords either in money or labor. The law permitted the peasants to buy their homesteads and "field portions." When they did so they became peasant proprietors; when they failed to do so and merely worked on them they were in a state of dependence upon the landlords and known as "temporarily bound" peasants. The freed serfs combined in "village communities" and these in *volosts* (townships) for the purpose of dividing the land among the members and carrying out the other communal duties. In these villages and townships the peasants were granted self-government on the same model as had been provided for the benefit of the crown peasants under Count Kiselev (sec. 151).

One of the most difficult and vexing problems of the reform was to determine the proper size of the "field portions." In the north, where the land was poor, the landlord was eager to sell as much of it as he could but in the south, where it was fertile, he desired to keep all he could. In the face of such divergent local conditions it became necessary to determine the land allotments separately in each "belt" of the country (the northern, the black earth, and the steppe), and sometimes in each separate province and even district. Serfs who worked in the fields were allowed a "portion of land," but those serfs who were employed as domestic servants were liberated without land.

The purchase by the freed peasants of their homesteads and field portions would have been impossible had not the government come to their assistance through a special "buying out fund." Under the law of February 19 the landlords could obtain from the government a "buying out loan" as soon as their land deals with the peasants were settled and the field portions of the peasants clearly defined. Such loans were charged against the peasants, who were given forty-nine years in which to pay it.

The carrying out of the actual details of the reform, both in respect of size of land allotment and the obligations of the peasant to his former master, were left to the two parties concerned. Whatever agreements they made were to be recorded in a "Statutory Letter" within two years from the date of emancipation. It was foreseen that the landlords and peasants would not be able in all cases to terminate in a fair and friendly manner their old relationships, and therefore the institution of "peace arbitrators" was created. The arbitrators were nobles and it was their duty to see to it that each party had fair play and a fair deal. They confirmed the validity of "statutory letters"; they watched over the proceedings of the peasants in village and *volost*, and they reported to the general assembly of the peace arbitrators of the entire district. The general direction of the reform in each province was entrusted to "Provincial Boards on Peasant Affairs," presided over by the provincial governors and made up of the highest officials of the province and representatives of the local nobility.

In this manner the great work of the abolition of serfdom was accomplished. The emancipation of the peasants changed most radically all the foundations of Russia's political and social life. In the central and southern regions there came into being a new social class, the freed peasants (up to 22,000,000 people). Before the emancipation they were governed by the landlord but after it they had to be taken over by the state. [Catherine's old institutions which gave self-government to the nobility did not meet the needs of the new situation and it was necessary to create a new local administration and courts of justice.] In this way the emancipation of the peasantry brought other reforms and changes in its train.]

160. RURAL AND MUNICIPAL SELF-GOVERNMENT.— Under the old laws self-government was provided for certain classes only, but the new laws gave it to all classes.

All who owned land of a certain value, and village communities, were entitled to elect representatives to the "District Zemstvo Assembly." These assemblies were presided over by the leader or "Marshal" of the nobility of the district and met every year for a short period to manage the economic affairs of the district. The assembly chose from among its own members the "District Zemstvo Board," consisting of a president and two members. This board functioned as a permanent organ and had full charge of all Zemstvo affairs in the district. Once a year the deputies from the district Zemstvos met at the capital of the government (gubernia) and formed a "Provincial Zemstvo Assembly." The work of the Zemstvo institutions was under the supervision of the Governor of the province and of the Minister of the Interior. In case of misunderstanding the Zemstvo had the right of appeal to the Senate.

The Zemstvo had jurisdiction over schools, public health, food supply, roads, insurance and other similar institutions. It had authority to levy taxes, to impose certain duties for the needs of the Zemstvos, to accumulate funds, and to acquire property.

Prior to the reform the district was governed by the nobility acting on behalf of all the free inhabitants. In the new Zemstvo the nobles retained the dominant position but other classes were also admitted to a share in the local government. Instead of narrow class interests those of the community at large were considered. [Such a broad character did this self-government acquire that many people were inclined to regard it as a transition to a genuinely representative form of government.] This was more than the government intended and in order to keep the Zemstvos in their places they were held strictly to local affairs and discouraged from having anything to do with the Zemstvos of the other provinces.

Somewhat later than the establishment of the Zemstvos new forms of self-government were created for the municipalities. The "Municipal Statutes of 1870" left unaltered the old division of the city inhabitants into merchant guilds, craft guilds and other such corporate bodies (sec. 109, 128). The new law provided that all those city people who paid municipal taxes on their real estate, trades and industries should elect representatives to the "Municipal Council." This body met from time to time to plan for the welfare of the city just as the Zemstvo planned for the country. The councilmen elected from their number a permanent executive committee made up of a mayor and a municipal board. The work of the municipal councils and boards was supervised by the "Provincial Board of Municipal Affairs," presided over by the Governor of the province.

City life in Russia during the second half of the nineteenth century was favorably influenced not only by the new administrative system but also by the general changes that had taken place in the social order of the country.

Down to the time of emancipation of the serfs there had continued in the greater part of the country the old, patriarchal forms of landlords' economy based on serf-dom. The people on each estate made the things they needed and had little occasion to go to town to make purchases. As a result there were few commercial cities and the town population was not very enterprising. After the emancipation of the serfs, however, rural life began to develop more rapidly. Zemstvos with their various economic activities came into being; railways were built; and commercial and industrial enterprises sprang up. This economic progress of the country had a far-reaching effect upon the towns. They became more active, took on an entirely new appearance, and, thanks to municipal self-government, changed from mere administrative headquarters to commercial and economic centers.

161. JUDICIAL REFORMS.—Hand in hand with the Zemstvo reform went the judicial reform. In 1864 the new "Judicial Statutes" were published which changed the old forms of judicial organization and procedure.

There were to be no more class tribunals. From now on justice was to be "equal for all subjects." Minor cases were tried before the Zemstvo or Municipal Justice of the Peace Courts. The principal function of these courts was to persuade the litigants to settle their differences amicably, but if they refused and demanded a judgment it was to be rendered. Appeals could be taken from the Justice of the Peace to the Assembly of the Justices of the Peace, and from there to the Higher Courts at the capital of the province. In the last named courts the judges were appointed by the government. Criminal cases of more than average importance were brought before juries chosen by lot from among the local inhabitants. Appeals from the decisions of the Higher Court, if rendered without the aid of a jury, could be taken to the Court of Appeal, and if with the aid of a jury to the Senate. This body was the highest court of appeal in the Empire.

Under this system the administration of justice was separated from the other branches of government. Judges were appointed or chosen for life and made independent of outside control. Elected juries and justices of the peace participated in judicial affairs. Alexander II had a right to claim that he had given his country "prompt, fair, merciful justice, equal for all subjects."

In the new courts a more modern procedure was introduced. The former tribunals were strongly influenced by the administration and were not above bribery. Police investigation was inefficient and slow, and the accused were intimidated and ill-treated to extort confessions. Trials were conducted and verdicts rendered in the absence of the defendant. Legal formality was more important than evidence, and there was no proper provision for appeal.

An entirely different order was established by the "Judicial Statutes" of 1864. A special "Court Investigator," or investigating magistrate, was put on each case and he reported his findings to the court. This was followed by a public trial and the defendant was provided with an experienced lawyer. Both the prosecuting attorney and the defendant's counsel addressed the jury. The jurors deliberated secretly and rendered their verdict and the court gave the decision. The Judicial Statutes of 1864 enjoyed a well-deserved high reputation. They gave fair trials, they won the confidence of the people and fostered a respect for law. Hand in hand with the establishment of the new judicial institutions went the mitigation of the penal system. Certain forms of corporal punishment (rods, flogging, running the gantlet, bastinado, branding, and other such cruelties) were abolished.

162. COMPULSORY MILITARY SERVICE.—Under Peter the Great all the nobles had to serve in the army and the other classes furnished a certain number of soldiers. During the eighteenth century the nobles managed to have themselves exempted from military duty and that burden fell almost exclusively on the poorer classes, for the richer could hire substitutes. Military service became a heavy and hateful burden to the masses; it ruined the poorer families by taking away their bread-winners for twenty-five years.

Under the law of 1874 all men of the age of twenty-one were liable to military service. From the large number available the army selected by lot as many as it needed and the national militia took the remainder. Service in the army was reduced to fifteen years, six in active duty and nine in reserve. The reservists were summoned from time to time but for such a short period that it interfered little with their occupations. Men of education served less than six years in the ranks. [The new method of recruiting and the humane spirit behind it changed most profoundly the whole military organization of the empire. Harshness disappeared to a very great extent and military service came to be regarded as a sacred and honorable duty rather than as a mark of servitude.] In addition to military training the soldiers were taught reading and writing, and an effort was made to develop in them an intelligent attitude towards their duty and a clearer understanding of military matters. Compulsory military service answered two important demands of the time. In the first place it emphasized the equality of all classes before the law, and in the second place it helped to bring the Russian army in line with that of Western Europe.

163. FINANCES.—The cost of the Crimean War and the money needed to carry out the peasant and other reforms put a heavy burden on the state. An attempt was made to cover the annual deficit by borrowing, by lotteries and by issues of paper money. These questionable financial methods did more harm than good and compelled the government in 1863 to adopt a budget system. Whereas until then each ministry had acted independently in financial matters, from this time forth it had to submit its estimates to the Ministry of Finance. In this way a "Fiscal Unity" was secured. A Ministry of State Control planned and apportioned the budget. Although this reorganization did not succeed in balancing the income and the expenditure, it did bring about more economy and a more businesslike system. Among the measures adopted to increase the revenue were the raising of the tariff and the levying of excise taxes on alcoholic beverages, tobacco, salt and sugar. The importance of developing trade and industry was realized and, with that in mind, the building of railroads by private capital was encouraged. In this way about 20,000 miles of line were constructed. This was followed by a rapid increase in exports and imports, by a growing number of commercial and industrial enterprises and credit institutions of all kinds. Russia was gradually losing its patriarchal, agricultural character and becoming a modern industrial and commercial state.

164. THE CENSORSHIP AND THE PRESS.—Alexander II gradually removed the restrictions upon the press and education which had been imposed by his father. At first the censorship of the press was relaxed. It was transferred from the Ministry of Public Instruction to that of the Interior and put under a special Press Bureau. By the decree of 1865 publishers of books, magazines and newspapers were allowed great freedom but were held responsible. If they printed "pernicious" matter they were brought before the courts and "warned" once, twice, and the third time the publication was suspended. This freedom, coming as it did at a time when the public was overflowing with reform ideas, brought forth a considerable literature and much interesting discussion.

In these discussions one catches a deep note of disappointment. There were those who had hoped that local self-government would lead to national self-government, and there were others who saw before them a new heaven and a new earth. The sudden turn from the darkness to the light, from serfdom to freedom, from class privileges to social and legal equality, from censorship to a free press, blinded, as it were, some people. They could see nothing good in the past, they scoffed at the civilization of the present, and dreamed of a new society where all would be perfectly equal and each individual would have absolute freedom. In this way arose extreme "radical" currents in political and social questions, and a literature of "negation" sprang up.[1]

The representative periodicals of this literature in

[1] This radical group came to be called Nihilists. In this connection it is interesting to refer to Turgenev's novels, especially "Fathers and Children."

Russia were the *Sovremennik* and *Russkoe Slovo*, and *Kolokol* published in London.[2] The growth of this radical journalism was a source of great chagrin and uneasiness to the government. At the beginning of the sixties it thought it necessary to curb the freedom of the periodical press. After April 4, 1866, when a revolutionist, Karakozov, fired on Alexander II the censorship was made more stringent and the *Sovremennik* and *Russkoe Slovo* were suspended. By this time the Nihilist influence had grown to such magnitude that these measures failed to put an end to the intellectual ferment. In a certain section of society a revolutionary sentiment was growing in favor of a direct political and social revolution and little by little revolutionary circles were being formed in the seventies of the nineteenth century to bring this about.

During this time the Slavophils published two periodicals, *Molva* and *Russkaia Besieda*, but they were not widely read. In this period of modernism and liberalism the teachings of the Slavophils found little favor, even in government circles. Among the moderately progressive journals the *Russki Viestnik*, published by Katkov, enjoyed a lasting success. It became especially influential during the Polish troubles of 1862-1863, when Katkov, its editor, published a number of brilliant patriotic articles. Katkov, writing in the *Russki Viestnik* and the *Moskovskia Viedomosti*, aroused a strong national consciousness and became the spokesman of Russian nationalism. From that time on Katkov followed a

[2] *Sovremennik* was edited by Chernyshevski and Dobroliubov and dealt largely with political questions; the *Russkoe Slovo*, edited by Pisarev, was devoted to the propaganda of Nihilism; the *Kolokol*, edited by the exile A. I. Herzen, agitated in favor of the emancipation of the peasants and the freedom of the press in Russia.

conservative policy and gained vast influence with the government.

165. EDUCATION.—At the outset of his reign Alexander II annulled the restrictive measures that had been imposed upon the educational institutions during the latter years of Nicholas I. More students were admitted to the universities, more freedom of teaching was given to the teachers and more university self-government to the faculties. Each university had its council of professors which elected its officers and managed university affairs. Students, however, were denied the right to organize corporations, and this ruling stirred up discontent and student riots.

Under the influence of the public ferment and student riots, Count D. A. Tolstoy, Minister of Public Instruction, reorganized the secondary school system. At the beginning of Alexander's reign the "gymnasiums" were open to "all classes, without distinction of calling or creed." Gymnasiums were of two types: "Classical" and "Real Gymnasium." In the first mentioned, emphasis was laid on classical studies, and in the second on natural sciences. After studying the question Count Tolstoy came to the conclusion that "one of the important causes of that materialism, Nihilism, and fatal self-conceit which has so strongly affected our studying youth" was the study of the natural sciences. With that in mind he drew up in 1871 a new statute for the gymnasiums.

The classical gymnasium was made the only type of secondary school offering a general educational program and open to all classes of the population. Only graduates of such schools were admitted to the universities. In place of the "real gymnasiums" were established real schools, something like the modern manual training or mechanics arts schools. After this reform classical schools greatly outnumbered the real.[3]

Together with the reform of the secondary schools for boys measures were taken to promote the education of girls. Until the beginning of Alexander's reign there were only Institutes and private boarding schools, and these were almost exclusively for the daughters of the nobility. Gradually women's gymnasiums were established for non-resident pupils of all classes of the population. At the same time parochial schools were opened by the church authorities for the daughters of the priests. The next step was to offer courses in higher education for women. The first attempt of this kind was made by the Principal of the women's gymnasium of St. Petersburg, N. A. Vyshnegradski. At his suggestion, "women's pedagogical courses" were introduced (1863) into the women's gymnasiums for the training of women teachers. In 1878 a group of advanced women, aided by Professor K. N. Bestuzhev-Riumin, opened the Bestuzhev College at St. Petersburg. Six years before that a medical school for women was organized at the capital. Following the example of St. Petersburg other university towns likewise opened on private initiative women's colleges. In this manner did the question of higher education for women receive a successful solution.

Thanks to the Zemstvos thousands of primary schools were opened all over the land. In order to train elemen-

[3] Unfortunately, the study of the classics was superficial and did not go beyond declensions and conjugations. In the absence of a sufficient number of Russian instructors in Latin and Greek it was necessary to bring in qualified teachers from abroad (mostly Czechs) who knew neither the Russian language nor Russian ways, and their teaching was consequently ineffective. Generally speaking, Count Tolstoy's reform was never widely accepted by Russian society, and it even aroused open hostility.

tary teachers the Ministry of Public Instruction and the Zemstvos established "Teachers' Seminaries." It should be said, however, that all these efforts to popularize learning proved inadequate to raise appreciably the low educational level of the country.

166. RESULTS OF THE REFORMS.—The emancipation of the serfs produced a profound change in the whole social order of the Russian Empire and inevitably led to other reforms. The end of serfdom was also the end of the predominant position of the nobility. From that time on the power which the nobles had held exclusively was shared by peasants and inhabitants of the cities. As trade and industry developed a new rich and a new educated class came into being. While the people in the cities were growing more prosperous the landed nobles were drifting towards bankruptcy. They could not adjust themselves to free labor and to the new conditions. Many of them had to sell their lands to their former serfs and managers.

Thus it came about that the very first results of the great reforms during the sixties of the nineteenth century were a decline of the nobility and a democratization of Russian society.

Another effect of these reforms was the intellectual ferment, with its radical political aspect. Alexander's political and social legislation had not aimed to alter the existing form of government or to develop a representative system. But the public was so excited by the many stirring events that it could not easily return to normal life and demanded even greater changes, constitutional government and even revolution. In the seventies revolutionary circles were formed in various cities to spread their ideas among the masses and prepare the ground for revolution. This activity provoked governmental persecution. Great political trials took place and they brought to light the vast extent of this revolutionary propaganda. Neither banishment nor other severe measures proved effective in putting down the movement. On the contrary, it became more and more extreme and assumed terroristic form. At the close of the seventies attempts were made upon the life of government officials and of the emperor himself. Russia entered upon a period of grave internal troubles.

167. THE POLISH INSURRECTION OF 1863.—For a quarter of a century following the revolt of 1831 the Polish provinces remained quiet. The Polish patriots, however, could not reconcile themselves to the loss of political autonomy and waited for an opportunity to protest against the policy of Nicholas. This opportunity came with the accession of Alexander II.

Alexander issued an amnesty to the Poles who took part in the revolt of 1830 and allowed them to return to their native country. This act was enough to fill the Poles with new hope and courage. They watched Alexander's reforms in Russia and demanded like reforms in Poland.

After hearing the arguments of the Polish patriots, especially Marquis Wielopolski, the Emperor decided to grant self-government to Poland (1861). He created a State Council and numerous local self-government councils for the provinces and districts similar to those in Russia. The courts, schools, and church affairs were handed over to the local Polish "Commissions," or Ministries. Wielopolski himself was placed at the head of the Polish administration and Grand Duke Constantine Nikolaevich, an advocate of liberal treatment of Poland, was appointed Viceroy. All these measures did not satisfy the Polish patriots who demanded political independence and the restoration of the old boundaries of Poland. When these demands were refused they started to make trouble. They made an attempt upon the life of the Grand Duke, and inflicted personal violence on Wielopolski. At last, in January, 1863, the insurrection broke out. On a prearranged day bands of "rebels" at different places in Poland and Lithuania attacked the Russian garrisons and terrorized the inhabitants.

This revolt led to the abandonment of Wielopolski's liberal policies and to the adoption of harsher measures. Count Berg, the new Viceroy, was ordered to suppress the uprising in Poland and Michael Muraviev in Lithuania. Within a half year Muraviev put down the revolt in a vigorous and cruel manner and thereby gained the bitter hatred of the Poles and the gratitude of the Russians whom he protected from the lawless bands. In Poland proper the suppression was slower, but even here order was restored by the summer of 1864.

At the height of the insurrection, April, 1863, the ambassadors of England, France, and Austria addressed a note to Prince A. M. Gorchakov, Russian Minister of Foreign Affairs, in which they expressed a hope that peace would soon be restored in Poland. This constituted an intervention in the domestic affairs of Russia. In the summer of the same year this act was repeated by many European Powers; France and England went so far as to propose the holding of a European conference to settle the Polish question. There was danger that in case Russia should reject the proposed conference there would be formed a new European coalition against her. Notwithstanding this possibility Emperor Alexander instructed Prince Gorchakov to make a firm refusal and to protest against foreign intervention in Russian affairs. Gorchakov's note was made public and was generally approved in Russia. At the very first rumors of foreign intervention all classes of the population came out on the side of the government. The courageous answer of the Emperor and the enthusiastic and popular support he received made an impression at home and abroad and may in part explain why the European Powers did not push their intervention beyond this point.

Shortly after the restoration of order the administration of Poland was reorganized. The old, official designation of "Kingdom" was abolished, and a new one, the "Vistula Territory," was soon given to the "governments." A peasant reform was introduced following closely the lines of the "Statutes of February 19, 1861" (sec. 159). The peasants were set free and provided with land and they did not have to pay for it to their landlords as the peasants in Russia had to do. They were granted self-government in their rural communities or townships.

The object at which the government aimed in its peasant reform in Poland was to attach the lower classes of the population to itself. The other classes of Polish society were deprived of self-government. In the Polish provinces was established the ordinary Russian administration and Russian was made the official language. In the schools likewise Russian was made compulsory. Large armed forces were garrisoned in the Vistula Territory. The last remaining Uniates in the diocese of Kholm were, in 1875, absorbed into the Orthodox Church. Thus perished all those peculiar features of self-government which had till then separated Poland from the other parts of the Russian Empire. Such were the consequences of the Polish rebellion.

Muraviev set to work to uproot Polish influence in the provinces of West Russia and Lithuania so that "there should be not even the slightest fear that this territory would ever become Polish." His policy was to "consolidate and elevate the Russian nationality and Orthodoxy"; to "support the Russian clergy"; to admit only Russians to administrative posts; to colonize Russians on the land; and in every possible way remove from the territory the hostile Polish element. A series of measures carried out in this spirit sapped the strength of Polish influence and destroyed the visible signs of Polish sway in the western and southwestern provinces. His persecution of Polish landlords and clergy for their part in the insurrection, and his campaign against the Polish language in the schools and public institutions, earned Muraviev the reputation of a tyrant in those circles which felt his heavy hand. But the Russian leaders who aided Muraviev in upholding the Russian interests in this territory felt profound respect for his patriotism, ability and firmness in Russianizing this region.

168. EVENTS IN ASIA AND THE CAUCASUS.—During the reign of Alexander II Russia acquired considerable territory in Asia. In the Far East she regained the vast Amur Territory (Treaty of Aigun, 1858) which had been ceded to China in 1689 (sec. 99). By the Treaty of Pekin of 1860 Russia also obtained the Ussuri Territory. In this way both banks of the Amur to its mouth were opened to Russian colonization. At the same time Russia acquired from the Japanese, in return for the Kuril Islands, the southern half of the Island of Sakhalin. Alaska was sold to the United States.

In Central Asia (Turkestan and Turania) Russian rule was firmly established. At this period there existed in the plains and deserts of Central Asia three Moslem khanates: Kokand, Bokhara and Khiva. Dependent upon these khanates were the semi-nomad Turko-Mongolian tribes of the Kirghiz, Turkomans, Uzbeks, etc. From time to time these half wild people raided Russian territory and carried off Russian prisoners. In 1717 Peter the Great attempted to take Central Asia under his control by siding with one khan against another and mixing up in their feuds, but only disaster came out of this. It was found advisable thereafter to advance more slowly and to erect in the steppes and deserts a number of forts to protect the frontier districts settled by Russians. This creeping up proceeded from two directions: from Siberia and the Urals in the north, and from the Caspian in the west. In the eighteenth century the principal bases of support for this slow offensive movement were the cities of Orenburg and Semipalatinsk in the north, and Krasnovodsk on the Caspian in the west. By the middle of the nineteenth century the Kirghiz of Northern Turkestan were already subjugated, and the Russian troops had gained a firm foothold on the Syr-Daria (the fortress of Perovsk) and the left bank of the Ili (the city of Vierny). After this began the conquest of the khanates proper.

In the sixties of the nineteenth century the Russian army took the offensive against Kokand and captured its most important towns—Turkestan and Tashkent. With this territory gone, the Khan of Kokand was reduced to a state of absolute dependence upon Russia. In 1876 there was a revolt against the Russians in

Kokand. It was put down and the khanate occupied and renamed "Ferghana Territory."

Soon after the first clashes with Kokand war commenced also with Bokhara. In 1868 a large part of this khanate was directly annexed to Russia and the remainder left in control of the khan on condition that he abolish slavery and open his markets to Russian traders.

In 1873 came the turn of Khiva. After a most difficult march across the arid desert the Russian troops appeared before the city of Khiva and captured it. The khan surrendered but was permitted to retain part of his dominions under such conditions as the Russians imposed.

In this manner the age-long anarchy which prevailed in Central Asia was suppressed. It only remained now to pacify the semi-nomadic, marauding Turkomans, and this was accomplished within a very short time. Pushing on towards the frontiers of Persia, China and Afghanistan, the Russians gradually brought the unruly natives to submission. Especially severe was the blow which the Russians struck at the Turkoman tribe of the Tekke by capturing their stronghold, Geok-Tepe, in 1881. When the Russians reached Afghanistan and approached the frontiers of India Great Britain showed grave concern, for it regarded the Russian advance as a threat to British control in India and Afghanistan. The British consequently made strenuous diplomatic efforts to halt the Russian advance in Central Asia. At times these diplomatic negotiations reached a dangerous stage, but war was averted. This civilizing mission of the Russians in the plains of Central Asia forms one of the most famous pages in the reign of Alexander II.

Peace was firmly established in the Caucasus during

this reign. The Muridist movement (sec. 152), which reached its highest point when Shamyl started upon his career, declined rapidly when the religious frenzy which had given birth to it abated. For a time Shamyl's authority was strong enough to unite the mountain tribes of the Eastern Caucasus, but it was a rather loose and weak union. When, in 1857, the Russians launched a vigorous offensive against Shamyl many of his followers deserted and acknowledged Russian authority. Shamyl's heroic resistance was finally broken and he surrendered at Gunib and was taken to Russia (1859).

It still remained to pacify the Western Caucasus bordering upon the Black Sea. The so-called "Warlike" Circassians were surrounded with a cordon of Russian troops, and the inhabitants forced from their mountains down to the valleys and the plains of the seaboard. They were offered the choice of settling where the Russians permitted, or emigrating to Turkey. About 200,000 of these mountaineers preferred to go to Turkey, and the others submitted to the Russians. Thus the Caucasus was pacified (1864).

169. THE TURKISH WAR AND THE CONGRESS OF BERLIN.—With the Treaty of Paris the seriousness of the Eastern Question was by no means ended for Russia. The Russian Government still felt that it could not renounce its traditional policy of protecting the Orthodox in Turkey, especially in view of the fact that the other Powers who promised to do so did very little. The harshness of the Turkish rule in the territories inhabited by the Serbians and Bulgarians caused Russia to intervene once more. This was strongly resented by Turkey and provoked alarm and jealousy in England. English policy both in the Balkans and Central Asia was distinctly anti-

Russian. Whenever Russia tried to intervene in Turkish affairs she was sure to find England aligned against her.

The situation in the Balkans became grave in 1875 when the Christians in Bosnia and Herzegovina and later in Bulgaria revolted (1876) against Turkish rule. The cruelty with which the Turks attempted to suppress the rebellion provoked a storm of indignation and aroused against them the Principalities of Montenegro and Serbia. In spite of the efforts of the Powers to allay the excitement, Montenegro and Serbia came out against Turkey in 1876. Serbian troops invaded Turkish territory but were unable to make much headway and were compelled to withdraw across the Serbian boundary line and take up a defensive position. It would have gone hard with them had not Russia insisted that Turkey cease hostilities.

The sufferings of the Balkan Slavs under the Turkish yoke and the chivalrous struggle of the Montenegrins and Serbs for their oppressed kinsmen aroused very deep feelings in Russia. There was an unmistakable expression of sympathy for these champions of national freedom. Special "Slav Committees" were organized to collect all kinds of offerings for the rebels. In many parts of the empire volunteer companies were raised to fight on the side of the Serbs. Public opinion expressed itself more and more openly for a vigorous attitude towards Turkey to force her to grant self-government and amnesty to the revolted Slavs. Through the efforts of the Russian Government a European conference was called at Constantinople in the beginning of 1877. The conference demanded that the Turks put a stop to their atrocities and that they grant immediate reforms to the Slav provinces, but the Sultan was unwilling to make the necessary concessions. Alexander II thereupon declared war on

Turkey (April 12, 1877). The Principality of Rumania, which had been created in 1859 out of Moldavia and Wallachia, not only agreed to let the Russian troops pass through its territory but came out openly as an ally of Russia. By the middle of the summer of 1877 the Russians had crossed the Danube and were making their way southward through the Balkan Mountains. At the Shipka Pass their advance came to a temporary stop. The Turks had strongly fortified themselves near the city of Plevna and blocked the way. It was necessary to gather a large Russian force, and that took a long time, to dislodge the Turk.

A similar delay occurred on the Asiatic front. In the spring of 1877 the Russian troops launched an offensive against Batum and Kars but found very strong resistance. Operations had to be stopped until the arrival of reënforcements. It was only in the fall of the year that the Russians could once more take the offensive. They captured Kars on November 16 and from there they moved on to Erzerum and took up their winter quarters near that place.

Almost at the same time that Kars was taken Plevna fell into the hands of the Russians (November 28). Encouraged by this success, the Russians, notwithstanding the winter cold, crossed the Balkans into Rumelia and proceeded to conquer bit by bit the Southern Balkans. Turkish resistance was slowly broken, Philippopolis and Adrianople were captured and the road to Constantinople was open. The Sultan now sued for peace.

Peace negotiations were greatly hampered by British interference. The Russian advance towards the Bosporus gave the British an excuse to send a fleet to the Sea of Marmora, and the arrival of a Russian army in sight of Constantinople afforded them a pretext for moving the fleet still nearer the city. As an answer to this challenge Alexander II ordered the Russian Army Headquarters moved to the village of San Stefano on the shore of the Sea of Marmora and about eight miles from Constantinople. On February 19, 1879, a preliminary peace treaty was signed at San Stefano. By this treaty Turkey recognized the independence of Montenegro, Serbia, and Rumania, ceded certain territories to Montenegro and Serbia; consented to the formation of her Bulgarian and Macedonian territories into a separate Principality of Bulgaria, pledged herself to reforms in Bosnia and Herzegovina, and gave to Russia the mouth of the Danube, lost in 1856, and the cities of Batum and Kars with their surrounding territories.

England and Austria protested against this treaty and their attitude towards Russia became so hostile that it looked like another war. Thanks to German mediation, a conflict was averted and a congress called to meet at Berlin. When the Russian delegation, headed by Prince Gorchakov, reached the congress, they found the combined diplomacy of Europe arrayed against them. The Congress of Berlin tore up the Treaty of San Stefano and made one of its own, the Treaty of Berlin, in favor of Turkey. It reduced in size Serbia and Montenegro, it cut Bulgaria into two parts (Bulgaria and Eastern Rumelia) and put both under the suzerainty of the Sultan, and placed Bosnia and Herzegovina under the temporary rule of Austria-Hungary.

The Treaty of Berlin caused profound disappointment throughout Russia and deepened the distrust of England and Austria, as well as Germany. People in Russia found it hard to reconcile themselves to the fact that the European Powers had shorn Russia of some of the fruits of her victories and had greatly impaired the results of the war of liberation. Bismarck, who styled himself at the Congress of Berlin an "honest broker," was regarded by the Russians as nothing but an enemy and betrayer. This hostile attitude of the Russian people and Government led Bismarck to form a secret alliance with Austria, and later also with Italy (the "Triple Alliance") as a guarantee in case of war with Russia.

The Balkan nations had not obtained either from Russia or from the states of western Europe all they had expected from the war of 1877-1878. Although they acknowledged Alexander II as their "Liberator," they made no secret of their unfriendliness towards Russia. Estrangement and misunderstandings ensued btoween Russia and the Balkan States. Bulgaria, which owed so much to Russia, became one of her bitterest enemies.

Thus the war of liberation of the Balkan Slavs was a disappointment to Russia. Military success was not accompanied by proportionate political success, and when it was all over Russia found herself isolated, without friends and without allies.

170. DEATH OF EMPEROR ALEXANDER II.—The Turkish War diverted for a short time the attention of Russian society from domestic to international problems. When the war was ended the discontent at home manifested itself in a series of acts of violence. Attempts upon the life of the Emperor followed one another in rapid succession. He was fired on as he walked through the streets, his train was wrecked, and a mine was exploded even in the Winter Palace. No one was willing to believe that only a small revolutionary society was responsible for these acts. On the contrary people sus-

pected some large, mysterious organization to be back of them. This view was strengthened by the fact that there were, generally speaking, great numbers of dissatisfied people everywhere in Russia clamoring for the continuation of the great reforms. The government took extraordinary measures to fight against this spirit, and all those who seemed even remotely suspicious and unreliable in a political sense were subjected to close surveillance. This severity proved unavailing, however, for the revolutionary terror did not cease, and the public, while outwardly intimidated by official reprisals, was kept in a state of excitement and resentment.

Early in 1880 Alexander created a special "Supreme Administrative Commission," with Count Loris-Melikov at the head, to suppress the revolutionary organizations and at the same time to remove some of the causes of the unrest.

Loris-Melikov now proceeded to carry out his plan. For a time it seemed as if he were having success, and that there would be no further need for the "Supreme Administrative Commission." The Commission was dissolved and Loris-Melikov was appointed MINISTER of the Interior. He applied himself to the preparation of new reforms to meet the desires of the Liberals and planned to admit representatives of the Zemstvo to the State Council. But the revolutionary leaders were still at liberty and their mind was set on killing the Emperor. They watched his every move and studied his habits and his walks. On March 1, 1881, as Alexander was driving through a certain street in the capital, a bomb was thrown at him which demolished his carriage. As he stepped out another was hurled which so injured him that he died the same day.

Alexander II was followed on the throne by his son, Alexander III. Count Loris Melikov was retired and his reform program abandoned.

SUCCESSORS OF ALEXANDER THE SECOND

171. EMPEROR ALEXANDER III (1881-1894).—The chief aim of Alexander III was to strengthen the autocracy and the political order undermined by the revolutionary movement. This object was to be attained, first of all, by a firm suppression of every trace of "revolutionism," and, in the second place, by a revision and "improvement" of the laws and institutions created by the great reforms of Alexander II. The struggle against the subversive movement appeared to be successful and terrorism ceased. The legislation of Alexander III affected every phase of the political and social life and aimed to give the government more influence in the administration of justice to enhance the authority of the monarch. Thus the liberal institutions of the preceding reign were hedged in with a number of restrictions which gave to the reign of Alexander III a markedly conservative and even reactionary character.

The following important legislation of the reign of Alexander III deserves special mention:

1. A number of measures were adopted to improve the condition of the different social classes. The nobles were suffering from a severe economic crisis as a result of the emancipation of the serfs. They could not make their lands pay and they were, therefore, selling out and moving into the cities. The government tried to uphold this

rapidly declining class by various means. By manipulating the electoral system and by creating the office of Rural District Chief in place of the Justice of the Peace, the nobles were given control of the Zemstvos and the districts. The government also helped the nobles with money by opening the "Land Bank of the Nobility," which granted loans to the nobles, secured by their landed property, on very favorable terms.

The peasants were not forgotten. At many places the land parcels allotted to the peasants had proved inadequate. To help them acquire more the government opened a "Peasants' Land Bank." It also encouraged the landless to settle on the free lands of Siberia and Central Asia. The development of the factory system in Russia during the second half of the nineteenth century gave employment to many idle peasants and turned them into an industrial proletariat. Their condition was rather miserable and conflicts between them and their employers became common and at times serious. In the reign of Alexander III a beginning was made in labor legislation in order to protect the employees from undue exploitation by their employers.

2. In the domain of finances and public economy important measures were introduced under Alexander III, and with good results. Many causes were responsible for the unsatisfactory financial situation of the country after the war of 1877-1878 (sec. 163). The rate of exchange for paper currency was extremely low and always fluctuating. There was an annual deficit in the budget. Alexander III adopted a policy of economy and introduced order into the financial organization of the state. A high protective tariff was adopted, partly for revenue

and partly to encourage Russian industry. By these means a gold reserve was secured. With the aid of this reserve a monetary reform was planned and carried through later in the reign of Nicholas II. During 1895-1898 the gold ruble was made the standard and its rate was fixed at one and one half rubles paper. After a short time gold and paper money were put on a par and exchanged freely. At the same time there were put into circulation new five and ten ruble gold pieces.

To promote the economic progress of the borderlands and knit them closer with the governmental center, the Trans-Siberian Railway and the Trans-Caspian Railways were constructed.

3. The foreign policy of Alexander III was conspicuous for its firmness and stability. Faithfully watching over Russian national interests he steadfastly declined to intervene in the affairs of Western Europe and always worked for peace. Just as soon as the Bulgarians and Serbians made it clear that they resented the Russian protectorate Alexander let them go their own ways. After having been rudely shaken in his confidence in Germany at the Congress of Berlin, Alexander's friendship for the Hohenzollerns cooled. In the Triple Alliance which Germany had formed with Austria and Italy Alexander saw a constant menace to European peace, as well as to the interests of Russia and France. This is why he approached France and formed with her a defensive alliance to restore the balance of power in Europe. The constancy of Alexander III in maintaining general tranquillity, and the obvious sincerity of his pacific intentions, brought him the reputation of the "Peace Maker," a title which came to be attached per-

manently to his name. Throughout his reign Russia had but one armed conflict, and this a trifling one,—with the Afghans on the Kushk River (1885) when Russia annexed the Merv and Pendeh oases.

4. At home Alexander pursued a national policy. He sought to bring about a closer union between the alien border provinces and Russia, and to Russianize the non-Russians as quickly as possible. This policy of Russification met with strong opposition in the Baltic Provinces, Poland and Finland. Decisive measures were adopted in Finland. Under Alexander the Second the Finns had obtained a form of self-government that had turned Finland from an autonomous province of Russia into what seemed like an entirely independent state. The Finns had their own coinage, postal system, customs service, railroads, and even army. All these signs of independent political life made the Finns look upon their country as a separate State that was merely in a personal union with the crown of Russia. By the time Alexander III ascended the throne this idea had already caused a series of misunderstandings between the Russian Government and the Finnish Diet and Senate. Alexander was opposed to Finnish separatism and announced in 1890 that the Grand Duchy of Finland was "in the ownership and sovereign possession of the Russian Empire," and that it should be brought into closer relations with the rest of his empire. In accordance with this idea Russian control over the Finnish administration was increased and the autonomy of Finland limited.

Alexander III was noted for his great physical strength and excellent health. He lived a rather retired life and comparatively little was known about him. His death in October, 1894, came as a great shock to the world. He was then only fifty years of age. He was succeeded by his son, Nicholas II.[4]

172. EMPEROR NICHOLAS II (1894-1917).—Within a few months after his accession the young Emperor made it quite plain that he intended to follow in the footsteps of his father and to "preserve the principle of autocracy firmly and immutably." In foreign relations he likewise strove to follow the policy of peace. He went even farther and invited the powers to discuss the problem of "setting a limit to ceaseless armaments and to find a means of averting the calamities which threaten the whole world." The result of this appeal was the calling of the two "Peace Conferences" (1899 and 1907) at the Hague. These gatherings tried to find ways and means to solve international conflicts amicably and to place a limit on armaments. They did not altogether achieve these objects but they did succeed in bringing about agreements to make the laws and methods of warfare more humane. They were powerless to prevent armed conflicts and they could not stop the expansion of the so-called "militarism," with its enormous cost.

At the time of the first Hague Conference Russia was forced to intervene actively in the domestic troubles of China. In 1895, Russia prevented Japan from securing the Liao-tung Peninsula with the fortress of Port Arthur, and in 1898 Russia herself leased Port Arthur with its territory from the Chinese and built a branch line of the Trans-Siberian Railway to Port Arthur. This placed the Chinese province of Manchuria through which the rail-

[4] In November, 1894, Nicholas married Princess Alice of Hesse, who assumed the name of Alexandra Feodorovna. From this union were born four daughters and a son, Alexis (1904).

way ran in semi-dependence upon Russia. In 1902 Russia occupied Manchuria and certain parts of Korea for military and commercial purposes. Japan was alarmed at the Russian occupation of Port Arthur and other Chinese territories, and when diplomatic negotiations failed to settle the differences between Russia and Japan the two powers resorted to arms (January 26, 1904).

This war turned out disastrously for Russia. Japan was stronger than Russia thought. It was exceedingly difficult for Russia to fight so far away from home and with such poor railway communications. The Japanese landed a strong army on the mainland, surrounded Port Arthur by land and sea, blocked the Russian navy in Port Arthur, and forced the Russian army to fall back from Southern Manchuria to the north. At the close of 1904 Port Arthur capitulated to the Japanese, and in the beginning of 1905 the Russians lost the decisive battle of Mukden. In May of that year the Russian Baltic fleet, having gone all the way around Africa to the Pacific, was defeated and destroyed by the Japanese near the Island of Tsushima. Russia no longer believed it possible to win the war, and Japan was utterly exhausted by the hard struggle. Through the mediation of President Roosevelt of the United States peace negotiations were opened in that country at Portsmouth, New Hampshire, and a treaty of peace was signed in August, 1905. Under the terms of this treaty Russia lost Port Arthur to Japan, renounced all claims to influence in Korea and Southern Manchuria, and ceded to Japan the southern half of Sakhalin Island (sec. 168).

The Japanese War delivered a serious blow to Russia's prestige. It became quite evident that unless Russia strengthened her military forces she would lose her place as a world power. Germany and Austria took advantage of Russia's unpreparedness to disregard her wishes in Balkan affairs and to dominate Serbia.

In 1914, Austria presented to Serbia an ultimatum that affected the sovereignty of the Serbian Kingdom. Russia, contrary to German and Austrian calculations, interceded in behalf of her Slav kinsmen and mobilized her army. Germany and Austria declared war on Russia and on France, her ally. Thus began in August, 1914, that frightful war which spread practically all over the world. Russia was overwhelmed by one disaster after another. She lost millions of men and thousands of square miles of territory.

In the administration of his empire Nicholas thought it best to adhere to the conservative principles of his father, although the problems were different. When Alexander came to the throne the country was in a state of sedition, but when Nicholas assumed power quiet reigned. Nicholas' problems were largely economic and social. The crop failure and famine in 1891-1892 brought to light the fact that the general prosperity of the nation had greatly declined and that the measures by which the government had expected to improve conditions (sec. 171) had been unavailing. Even in the most fertile sections of the country the peasants were barely able to exist in time of plenty, but in time of crop failure suffered hunger and destitution. The industrial classes were still too much at the mercy of their employers, for the laws were not sufficiently strict to prevent undue exploitation.

The misery of the people which was so evident during the famine of 1891-1892 increased as time went on and stirred up a widespread agitation throughout the country. Thoughtful people realized that charity and doles would not solve the problem, that a change was indispensable in the general system of administration, and that the inefficient and corrupt bureaucracy must be done away with. Among the constructive measures of reform suggested was closer coöperation between the Central Government and the Zemstvos. Several Zemstvo assemblies took advantage of the change on the throne and during the very first days of Nicholas' reign offered coöperation. He declined the offer and persisted in governing the country with the aid of his bureaucracy and the clubs of the police.

The decidedly conservative policy of the government was so manifestly opposed to the crying needs of the nation and the sentiment of the Intelligentsia that it gave rise to a strong revolutionary opposition. During the last few years of the nineteenth century there were frequent political demonstrations among the university students, and strikes and riots among the factory workers. This growing public protest was silenced by harsh reprisals which affected not only those individuals who were actually involved but also the public at large, the Zemstvos, and the press. These attempts at suppression did not prevent the organization of secret societies or the preparations for more demonstrations of protest. The failure of the Japanese War brought the discontent to the point of explosion and caused revolutionary outbreaks. Political assassinations became frequent, resulting in the death of Grand Duke Sergius Alexandrovich, Minister Plehve and others. A huge procession of workingmen was organized in St. Petersburg on January 9, 1905, to march to the Winter Palace to lay a petition before the Emperor, but as they approached the palace they were fired upon and many were killed.

These revolutionary manifestations forced the government to make concessions. It declared itself ready to organize a popular representative body to advise in the work of legislation but this promise failed to quiet the unrest. In the summer of 1905 there were numerous peasant riots and a mutiny broke out in the navy. In October a general strike was called which interrupted all normal activity throughout the country. Under the pressure of these events the Emperor on the 17th of October granted the nation "unshakable foundations of civic liberty, freedom from arrest without cause, and freedom of conscience, speech, assembly, and association." The right to vote was conferred on the lower classes. A State Duma, or parliament, was created of elected representatives, to help in legislation, and no measure was legal without its approval.

The Manifesto of the 17th of October transformed the Russian Empire into a constitutional monarchy. In the spring of 1906 the first Duma met and eagerly went to work to bring about political and social reforms. Its activity and initiative did not please the Tsar and he dissolved it in the course of the summer. In February, 1907, the Second Duma assembled and as this body proved to be still more radical than the first it was dissolved June 3, 1907. On the same day a new electoral law was published which limited the suffrage so as to keep down the opposition. The Third Duma, which convened in the fall of 1907, was less fiery and worked in greater harmony with the Tsar. Its dealings with the government were facilitated by the fact that at the head of the Council of Ministers (1906-1911) was P. A. Stolypin, a man of ability and personal charm. It seemed as if Russia was about to enter upon a normal and tranquil political life along the lines and principles of the Manifesto of October 17.

These very hopes and desires frightened the bureaucratic and reactionary elements of the government. They did not wish to see any changes; they were opposed to the pledges of the October Manifesto and to the development of a democratic and representative system of government. Contrary to the obvious trend of the times these reactionary circles cherished hopes of maintaining autocracy and class privileges. It seemed as if even Stolypin fell under the influence of this standpat group. After his assassination in Kiev (Sept. 1, 1911) the government became openly reactionary and clashed with the Duma. The Fourth Duma (1912), although very moderate, condemned more than once the course followed by the ministers but was powerless to alter it. The government was obviously sliding back to the old order of things, and it looked as if the Duma would become a mere figurehead.

It was under these conditions that Russia entered the World War. The defects of the Russian military organization were felt, first of all, in the supply and hospital departments. It was necessary for the All-Russian Zemstvo and Municipal Union to come to the aid of the government, and through their help some system was developed. In 1915, the army ran out of ammunition and once more public organizations were called in.

The participation of the Zemstvo organizations in the defense of the nation enabled the general public to gain full knowledge of the inefficiency of the War Department. The Duma repeatedly urged the government to change the existing régime, to place in power men who had the full confidence of the country, and to remove the pernicious influence of irresponsible intriguers who had found access to the court by all kinds of dubious paths. At the session of the Duma on November 1, 1916, this protest found its fullest expression. Patriotic and loyal as the speeches of the popular representatives were, they were filled at the same time with the firm resolve to force the indispensable changes in the government and obtain a responsible ministry. The demands of the Duma were upheld by the State Council, the united nobility, and other public organizations. Nicholas II failed to grasp the significance of this general outcry and persisted in the belief that he would be able to rule contrary to the sentiment of the nation. It was then that the revolution broke out.

173. THE YEAR 1917.—The apparent occasion for the revolution was furnished by the disorganization of railway shipments of food and fuel to the capitals. Beginning with the 24th of February, 1917, demonstrations were held in the streets of St. Petersburg. In the course of the next few days the authorities attempted to disperse the crowds with the aid of the military, but on the 27th the soldiers themselves joined the civilians, and on the 28th the monarchy was overthrown.

When the disorders began the government attempted to dismiss the Duma. It refused to be dismissed and proceeded to choose from among its own members an Executive Committee headed by the President of the Duma, M. V. Rodzianko. At the same time the workers and soldiers formed a "Council (Soviet) of Workers' and Soldiers' Deputies." These revolutionary organs came to an agreement and established a Provisional Government with Prince G. E. Lvov as Prime Minister. This Ministry was at once recognized in Moscow and through-cut the rest of the country. The Emperor was at the front when these important events were taking place and by the time that he decided what to do the Revolution had established itself. On March 2, at Pskov, he abdicated in favor of his brother, Grand Duke Michael. When the honor was offered to the Grand Duke on the following day he declined the crown until "a Constituent Assembly should express itself on the form of government that Russia should have."

In this manner the dynasty came to an end. Nicholas Romanov and his family were placed under arrest and confined for a time to Tsarskoe Selo and later sent to Siberia. In the course of a week the most autocratic country in Europe became the most democratic republic in the world. But that in itself was not enough to save Russia from the misery into which she had fallen.

In the newly organized Provisional Government there was constant conflict between the moderate and radical members, and Prince Lvov had to give way to Kerenski. Pressure on the Provisional Government was brought to bear by the numerous Soviets that were organized all over the country and which were led by the radical wing of the Socialists. On the initiative of the Petrograd Soviet all the Soviets of the country formed in the spring of the year an All-Russian Soviet Congress. The influence of this Socialist organ upon the administration and the political life of the country grew steadily and impaired the singleness of governmental authority. The efforts of the Provisional Government to reconcile the antagonisms of the classes and to continue the war to a successful conclusion were paralyzed by the opposition of the Soviets. Civil war between the radical and conservative elements began to be talked of as early as April and the first skirmish occurred at the capital in July, 1917, when some of the Socialist groups attempted to seize power by armed force. Although the attempt failed it made the government hasten with its preparations for a Constituent Assembly.

Influenced by the July uprising, General Kornilov, Commander-in-Chief of the Russian Army (August) issued an ultimatum to Kerenski to place the direction of affairs under military control, to form a stronger government with the aid of the army, and thus restore among the masses the necessary discipline. The Provisional Government rejected the proposal, accused him of treason and had him arrested.

These uprisings on the right and left caused the Provisional Government not to wait for the opening of the Constituent Assembly, but to summon immediately a "Council of the Russian Republic" or "Preliminary Parliament" made up of representatives of various public organizations and political parties. At its sessions in October the antagonisms and differences of point of view between the Provisional Government and the Soviets became more and more apparent. Both sides saw a fight looming. But while the government displayed a total lack of action the leaders of the Soviets worked with extraordinary energy. During the night of October 25, after a fight in the streets of the capital, the Provisional Government was overthrown, Kerenski was driven from the city, the ministers were arrested, and the authority was taken over by Bolsheviks. A new government, The Russian Socialist Federated Soviet Republic,[1] was organized and it has been in power ever since.

[1] The present (1925) name of the government is the Union of Socialist Soviet Republics.

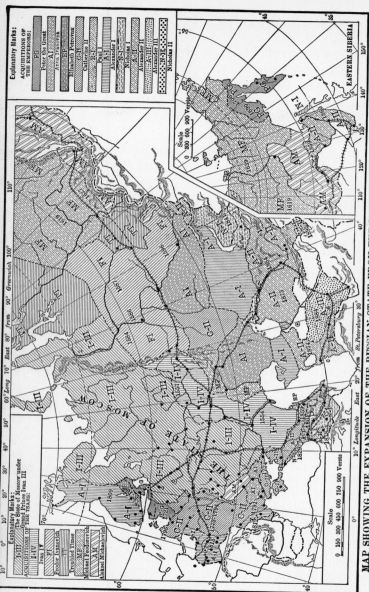

MAP SHOWING THE EXPANSION OF THE RUSSIAN STATE FROM THE XVI CENTURY UP TO OUR OWN TIME

CHRONOLOGICAL TABLE

860—First attack of Russians on Constantinople.
862—Invitation of the Varangian princes.
862-879—Prince Rurik at Novgorod.
907—Oleg's campaign against Constantinople.
912—Death of Oleg.
957—Voyage of Princess Olga to Constantinople.
972—Death of Prince Sviatoslav.
988-989—Christianity established as the religion of **Russia.**
1015—Death of Prince Vladimir.
1054—Death of Prince Iaroslav the Wise.
1113-1125—Vladimir Monomakh in Kiev.
1147—First reference to Moscow.
1157—Death of Prince Iuri Dolgoruki.
1175—Death of Prince Andrei Bogoliubski.
1176-1212—Prince Vsevolod III in Vladimir.
1187—Death of Prince Iaroslav Osmomysl of **Galicia.**
1199—Prince Roman of Volynia takes Galich.
1223—Battle of the Kalka with the Tartars.
1237-1238—Baty's invasion. Battle of the Sit **River.**
1240—Kiev taken by the Tartars.
1240—Prince Alexander Nevski defeats the Swedes.
1242—He defeats the Germans ("Ice Battle").
1263—His death.
1263—Death of Prince Mindovg of Lithuania.
1264—Death of Prince Daniel of Galicia.
1317-1341—Prince Gedimin in Lithuania.
1328-1341—Grand Prince Ivan Kalita.
1341-1359—Grand Princes Simeon the Proud and Ivan II, the **Red.**
1341-1377—Prince Olgerd in Lithuania.
1359-1389—Grand Prince Dmitri Donskoi.
1380—Battle of Kulikovo.
1386—Union of Lithuania with Poland.
1392-1430—Prince Vitovt in Lithuania.
1410—Battle of Grunewald and Tannenberg.
1413—Diet of Gorodlia.
1425—Death of Grand Prince Vasili I.
1439—Florentine Union.
1450—Grand Prince Vasili II, the Dark, defeats **Prince Dmitri Shemiaka.**
1462-1505—Grand Prince Ivan III.
1472—His marriage with Sophia Paleologus.
1478—Fall of Novgorod the Great.
1480—End of the Tartar yoke.
1485—Annexation of Tver to Moscow.
1505-1533—Grand Prince Vasili III.

1510—Fall of Pskov.
1514—Smolensk captured by Moscow.
1523—Annexation of last appanages to Moscow.
1530—Birth of Ivan the Terrible.
1533-1584—Grand Prince and Tsar Ivan IV, the Terrible.
1547—Assumption of title of "Tsar," and marriage of Ivan the Terrible.
1550-1551—The "Sudebnik" and "Stoglav" codes.
1552—Conquest of Kazan.
1556—Conquest of Astrakhan.
1558—Beginning of Livonian War.
1560—Death of Tsaritsa Anastasia.
1565—The "Oprichnina."
1569—The Union of Lublin and of the Polish "Commonwealth."
1582—Conquest of Siberia.
1582-1583—Ivan the Terrible concludes peace with Batory and Sweden.
1584-1598—Tsar Fedor Ivanovich.
1589—Establishment of Patriarchate at Moscow.
1591—Death of Tsarevich Dmitri at Uglich.
1596—The Church Union of Brest.
1598—End of Moscow dynasty and accession of Boris Godunov.
1605—Death of Tsar Boris and accession of the Pretender Dmitri.
1606-1610—Tsar Vasili Shuiski.
1610—Election of Prince Wladyslaw of Poland to the throne of Moscow.
1611—The army of Procopius Liapunov.
1611-1612—The army of Prince Pozharski and Minin.
1612—The freeing of Moscow.
1613—Michael Romanov is chosen Tsar.
1613-1645—Tsar Michael Romanov.
1617—The peace of Stolbovo with Sweden.
1618—The peace with Poland (Truce of Deulino).
1632-1634—War with Poland and the Peace of Polianovo.
1637-1642—The problem of Azov.
1645-1676—Tsar Aleksei.
1649—The "Sobor" Code of Laws.
1652-1658—The Patriarchate of Nikon and correction of church books.
1653-1654—Annexation of Little Russia.
1654-1667—Wars with Poland, and Truce of Andrusovo (1667).
1656-1659—The Swedish War.
1666-1667—Church congresses and deposition of Nikon.
1670-1671—Stenka Razin's rebellion.
1672—Birth of Peter the Great.
1676-1682—Tsar Fedor Alekseievich.
1682—Accession of Peter the Great and the revolt of the Streltsy.
1682-1689—Reign of Tsarevna Sophia.
1686—The "Eternal Peace" with Poland.
1695-1696—The Azov campaigns.
1697-1698—Peter's foreign voyages.
1700-1721—The Great Northern War.
1703—Foundation of St. Petersburg.
1709—Battle of Poltava.
1711—The campaign of the Pruth. Establishment of the Senate.
1714—Victory of Hangoudd.
1721—The Peace of Nystad. Establishment of the Holy Synod.

1721—Assumption of title of Emperor, by Peter the Great.
1722—The law on the succession. "The Legality of the Monarch's Will."
1725—Death of Peter the Great.
1725-1727—Empress Catherine I.
1727-1730—Emperor Peter II.
1730-1740—Empress Anna.
1740-1741—Emperor Ivan Antonovich III.
1741-1761—Empress Elizabeth.
1757-1761—Russia takes part in the Seven Years' War.
1761-1762—Emperor Peter III.
1762-1796—Empress Catherine II.
1767-1768—The Commission for framing a new code of laws.
1768-1774—First Turkish War and the Peace of Kuchuk-Kainardji.
1773-1775—The Pugachev rebellion.
1773—First Partition of Poland.
1775—"Institutions" for the administration of the "gubernias."
1783—Annexation of the Crimea.
1785—Charters granted to the various classes of the population.
1787-1791—Second Turkish War and the Peace of Iassy.
1788-1790—Swedish War.
1793-1795—Second and Third Partitions of Poland.
1796-1801—Emperor Paul.
1797—Statutes on the Imperial Family.
1799—Suvorov's campaigns in Italy and Switzerland.
1801—Annexation of Georgia.
1801-1825—Emperor Alexander I.
1802—Establishment of the Ministries.
1805—Battle of Austerlitz.
1807—Peace of Tilsit.
1809—Annexation of Finland.
1810—Establishment of State Council.
1812—Annexation of Bessarabia.
1812—The Patriotic (Napoleonic) War.
1813-1814—War for the liberation of Europe.
1815—The Congress of Vienna.
1825-1855—Emperor Nicholas I.
1826-1828—Persian War.
1827—Navarino.
1828-1829—The Turkish War and the Peace of Adrianople.
1830-1832—The Polish rebellion and the "Organic Statute."
1833—Code of Laws collected and published.
1839-1843—Financial reform.
1842—The law on the "Bound Peasants."
1849—Hungarian campaign.
1853-1855—Crimean War and the Peace of Paris.
1855-1881—Emperor Alexander II.
1858—Annexation of Amur Territory.
1860—Annexation of Ussury Territory.
1861—Emancipation of the serfs.
1863—Polish insurrection.
1864—Pacification of the Caucasus.
1864—Court reforms. Zemstvo institutions.
1868—Annexation of Bokhara.

1870—Laws on municipal self-government.
1873—Annexation of Khiva.
1876—Annexation of Kokand (Ferghana).
1877-1878—The Turkish War and the Congress of Berlin.
1881-1894—Emperor Alexander III.
1894-1917—Emperor Nicholas II.

GENEALOGICAL TABLES

GENEALOGICAL TABLE

I

DYNASTY OF ST. VLADIMIR.

St. Vladimir (972-1015).

Sviatopolk the Accursed (1015-1016). Iaroslav the Wise (1016-1054). Boris (+ 1015). Glieb (+ 1015).

Vladimir (1034-1052). Iziaslav (1076-1078). Sviatoslav (1073-1076). Vsevolod (1078-1093).

Rostislav (1052-1065). Sviatopolk (1093-1113). Oleg (1076-1115). Iaroslav (1097-1129). Vladimir Monomakh (1113-1125).

Vsevolod (1127-1146). Sviatoslav (1137-1165). Mstislav (1125-1132). Iuri Dolgoruki (1154-1157).

Igor (1169-1202). Vsevolod (1185-1196). Iziaslav (1146-1154). Andrei Bogoliubski (1169-1175). Vsevolod "The Big Nest" (1176-1212).

Mstislav (1167-1170).

Roman (1188-1205).

Daniel of Galicia (1205-1264).

Vasilko (1080-1124). Volodar (1098-1124).

Vladimirko (1124-1152).

Iaroslav (1152-1187) "Osmomysl".

GENEALOGICAL TABLE

II

DYNASTY OF VSEVOLOD "THE BIG NEST."

Vsevolod (1176-1212).

Constantine (1205-1217). Iuri (1212-1238). Iaroslav (1238-1246).

Alexander Nevski (1252-1263). Andrei (1246-1252). Daniel (1261-1303). Iaroslav of Tver (1247-1271). Vasili of Kostroma (1272-1276).

Andrei (1281-1304). Dimitri (1250-1294). Michael of Tver (1285-1319).

Iuri (1303-1325). Ivan I "Kalita" (1328-1341). Alexander (1326-1328).

Simeon (1341-1353). Ivan II (1353-1359). Michael (1368-1399).

Dmitri Donskoi (1359-1389).

Vasili I (1389-1425). Iuri (1389-1434).

Vasili II, the Blind (1425-1462). Vasili the Squint-Eyed (1434-1448). Dimitri Shemiaka (1446-1447).

Ivan III (1462-1505).

Vasili III (1505-1533).

Ivan IV, the Terrible (1533-1584).

Ivan (——+1581). Fedor (1584-1598). Dmitri (——+1591).

GENEALOGICAL TABLE

III

DYNASTY OF THE ROMANOVS.

Roman Iurievich Zakharin-Koshkin.

Nikita Romanovich (Boyar). Anastasia Romanovna (Consort of Ivan the Terrible).

Fedor Nikitich (Patriarch Philaret).

Tsar Michael Fedorovich (1613-1645).

Tsar Aleksei Mikhailovich (1645-1676).

Tsar Fedor (1676-1682). Tsar Ivan (1682-1689). Emperor Peter I, the Great (1682-1725) = Catherine I (1725-1727).

Catherine (Mecklenburg). Anna (Courland)
(1730-1740)

Anna Leopoldovna (Brunswick).

Ivan VI Antonovich (1740-1741).

Aleksei. Anna (Holstein). Elizabeth (1741-1761).

Peter II (1727-1730). Peter III (1761-1762) = Catherine II (1762-1796).

Paul I (1796-1801).

Alexander I (1801-1825). Constantine. Nicholas I (1825-1855). Michael.

Alexander II (1855-1881). Constantine. Nicholas. Michael.

Alexander III (1881-1894). Vladimir. Aleksei. Sergei. Paul.

Nicholas. Nicholas II (1894-1917) Michael.

Aleksei

BIBLIOGRAPHY

ALEXANDRA, Empress Consort of Nicholas II, *Letters of the Tsaritsa to the Tsar*, 1914-1916, with an introduction by Sir Bernard Pares, London, 1923.

ALEXINSKY, G., *Modern Russia*, N. Y., 1913. *Russia and the Great War*, London, 1915. *Russia and Europe*, London, 1917.

Antiquities, Russe, Copenhagen, 1850-2.

BADDELEY, J. F., *The Russian Conquest of the Caucasus*, London, 1908.

BAIN, R. N., *Slavonic Europe*, Camb. Univ. Press, 1894. *The Pupils of Peter the Great*, Westminster, 1899. *The Daughter of Peter the Great*, London, 1902. *Peter III, Emperor of Russia*, London, 1902. *The Last King of Poland*, London, 1909. *The First Romanovs*, London, 1905.

BARING, M., *The Russian People*, London, 1911. *A Year in Russia*, London, 1907.

BEAZLEY, FORBES, and BIRKETT, *Russia from the Varangians to the Bolsheviks*, Oxford, 1918.

BESTUSHEV-RIUMIN, K. N., *Geschichte Russlands*, Mitau, 1877.

BEVERIDGE, A., *The Russian Advance*, N. Y., 1903.

BIENSTOCK, J., *Histoire du Mouvement Revolutionnaire en Russie*, Paris, 1920.

BROWNING, O., *Peter the Great*, London, 1898.

BRUCKNER, A., *Geschichte Russlands*, Gotha, F. A. Perthes, 1896, 2 vols.

BUCHANAN, G., *My Mission to Russia*, Boston, 1923.

Cambridge Modern History, Cambridge Univ. Press.

CURTIN, J., *The Mongols in Russia*, Boston, 1908.

DAUDET, E., *Soixantes Années du Regne des Romanoffs*, Paris, 1919.

DILLON, E. J., *The Eclipse of Russia*, London, 1918.

DRAGE, G., *Russian Affairs*, N. Y., 1904.

EVERSLEY, LORD, *The Partitions of Poland*, London, 1915.

FLETCHER, G., *Of the Russe Commonwealth*, Hakluyt Society Publications.

FRANCIS, D. R., *Russia from the American Embassy*, N. Y., 1921.

GILLIARD, P., *Thirteen Years at the Russian Court*, London, 1921.

GAUTIER, TH., *Russia*, Philadelphia, 1905, 2 vols.

HEARD, A. F., *The Russian Church*, N. Y., 1887.

HERODOTUS. Book IV. Loeb Classical Library, Vol. II.

HERZEN, A. I., *Memoirs of Empress Catherine II*, N. Y., 1859.

HERZEN, A. I., *Le Monde Russe et la Revolution*, Paris, 1860.

HOETZSCH, O., *Russland*, Berlin, 1913.

IZVOLSKI, A. P., *The Memoirs of Alexander Izvolski*, London, 1920.

KARAMSIN, M., *Histoire de l'Empire Russe*, Paris, 1918, 2 vols.

KLIUCHEVSKI, V., *History of Russia*, London, 1913, 3 vols.

KONDAKOFF, N., *Antiquités de la Russie Méridionale*, Paris, 1891-93.

KORFF, S. A., *Autocracy and Revolution in Russia*, N. Y., 1923.

KORNILOV, A., *Modern Russian History*, N. Y., 1917, 2 vols.

KOVALEVSKI, M. M., *Russian Political Institutions*, Chicago, 1902.

KOVALEVSKI, M. M., *LaCrise Russe*, Paris, 1906.

KOSTOMAROW, N., *Russische Geschichte*, Leipzig, 1886.

KRAUSSE, A., *Russia in Asia*, N. Y., 1899.

KROPOTKIN, P., *Ideals and Realities in Russian Literature*, N. Y., 1916.

LEROY-BEAULIEU, A., *The Empire of the Tsars*, N. Y., 1896, 3 vols.

LORD, R. H., *The Second Partition of Poland*, Harvard University Press, 1915.

MASARYK, T. G., *The Spirit of Russia*, N. Y., 1919, 2 vols.

MAVOR, J., *The Economic History of Russia*, London, 1914, 2 vols.

MARCHAND, R., *Les Grandes Problemes de la Politique Intérieure Russe*, Paris, 1912.

MILIUKOV, P., *Essais sur l'Histoire de la Civilization Russe*, Paris, 1901. *Russia and Its Crisis*, Chicago, 1905. *Russian Realities*, Cambridge Univ. Press, 1917. *Le Mouvement Intellectuel Russe*, Paris, 1918.

MINNS, E. H., *Scythians and Greeks*, Cambridge University Press, 1913.

MORFILL, W., *The Story of Russia*, London, 1890, 1915. *A History of Russia*, London, 1902.

MOURAVIEFF, A. N., *A History of the Church of Russia*, Oxford, 1842.

NESTOR'S *Chronicle*, translated by Louis Paris, Paris, 1834-5; by Louis Leger, Paris, 1884.

The Chronicle of Novgorod, English translation by Mitchell, Forbes, Beazley, London, 1914.

PALEOLOGUE, M., *La Russie des Tsars pendant la Grande Guerre*, Paris, 1921-22, 3 vols.

PARES, B., *Russia and Reform*, London, 1907.

PERRIS, G. H., *Russia in Revolution*, London, 1905.

Procopius, Books V, VI, VII, Loeb Classical Library, Vols. III, IV.

RALSTON, W. R. S., *The Songs of the Russian People*, London, 1872. *Russian Folk Tales*, London, 1873. *Early Russian History*, London, 1874.

RAMBAUD, A., *La Russie Epique*, Paris, 1876. *The Expansion of Russia*, N. Y., 1904. *History of Russia*, N. Y., 1886, 3 vols.

ROCCA, F., *Les Zemskie Sobors*, Paris, 1898.

ROSEN, R. R., *Forty Years of Diplomacy*, N. Y., 1922, 2 vols.

ROSTOVTSEV, M. I., *Iranians and Greeks*, Clarendon Press, 1922. *Les Origines de la Russie Kievienne*, Paris, 1922.

ROUIRE, D., *La Rivalité Anglo-Russe au XIXe Siècle en Asie*, Paris, 1908.

SACK, A. J., *The Birth of the Russian Democracy*, N. Y., 1920.

SCHIEMANN, T., *Geschichte Russlands unter Kaiser Nikolaus I*, Berlin, 1904-19, 4 vols.

SCHUYLER, E., *Peter the Great*, N. Y., 1884, 2 vols.

SKRINE, F. H., *The Expansion of Russia*, Cambridge Univ. Press, 1903.

STANLEY, A. P., *The Eastern Church*, London, 1861.

THOMSEN, V., *The Relation Between Ancient Russia and Scandinavia*, London, 1877.

TURGENEFF, W., *La Russie et les Russes*, Paris, 1847.

VOGUE, E. M. DE, *The True Story of Mazeppa*, London, 1884.

WALLACE, D. M., *Russia*, London, 1912.

WALLING, W. E., *Russia's Message*, N. Y., 1908.

WALISZEVSKI, K., *L'Héritage de Pierre le Grande: règne des femmes*, Paris, 1900. *La Dernière des Romanov: Elizabeth I*, Paris, 1902. *La Crise Révolutionnaire*, Paris, 1908.

WALISZEVSKI, K., *A History of Russian Literature*, N. Y., 1900. *Romance of an Empress: Catherine II*, N. Y., 1894. *Peter the Great*, N. Y., 1898. *Ivan the Terrible*, Philadelphia, 1904. *Paul the First of Russia*, London, 1913.

WIENER, L., *An Interpretation of the Russian People*, N. Y., 1915.

WIENER, L., *Anthology of Russian Literature*, N. Y., 1902-3, 2 vols.

WILLIAMS, H. W., *Russia of the Russians*, N. Y., 1915.

WITTE, S., *The Memoirs of Count Witte*, N. Y., 1921.

WRIGHT, G. F., *Asiatic Russia*, N. Y., 1902-3, 2 vols.

ZILLIACUS, K., *The Russian Revolutionary Movement*, London, 1905.

INDEX